THE COMPLETE WORKS

OF

SAINT ALPHONSUS DE LIGUORI,

DOCTOR OF THE CHURCH,

Bishop of Saint Agatha, and Founder of the Congregation of the Most Holy Redeemer.

TRANSLATED FROM THE ITALIAN.

EDITED BY

REV. EUGENE GRIMM,

Priest of the Congregation of the Most Holy Redeemer.

———◆———

THE ASCETICAL WORKS.
Volume III.

THE GREAT MEANS OF SALVATION

AND

OF PERFECTION.

*(PRAYER. MENTAL PRAYER. THE EXERCISES OF A RETREAT.
CHOICE OF A STATE OF LIFE, AND THE VOCATION TO THE
RELIGIOUS STATE AND TO THE PRIESTHOOD.*

THE COMPLETE ASCETICAL WORKS

OF

ST. ALPHONSUS DE LIGUORI.

Each book is complete in itself, and any volume will be sold separately.

THE
GREAT MEANS OF SALVATION
AND
OF PERFECTION.

PRAYER—MENTAL PRAYER—THE EXER-
CISES OF A RETREAT — CHOICE OF A
STATE OF LIFE, AND THE VOCATION
TO THE RELIGIOUS STATE AND
TO THE PRIESTHOOD.

BY

St. ALPHONSUS DE LIGUORI
Doctor of the Church.

EDITED BY

REV. EUGENE GRIMM,
Priest of the Congregation of the Most Holy Redeemer.

REDEMPTORIST FATHERS
BROOKLYN
ST. LOUIS   TORONTO

Nihil obstat.

Arthur J. Scanlan, S.T.D.,
Censor Librorum.

Imprimatur.

† Patritius Cardinalis Hayes,
Archiepiscopus Neo-Eboracensis

Neo-Eboraci

Die 24 Mar., 1927

APPROBATION.

By virtue of the authority granted me by the Most Rev. Patrick Murray, Superior General of the Congregation of the Most Holy Redeemer, I hereby sanction the publication of the work entitled "THE GREAT MEANS OF SALVATION AND OF PERFECTION", which is Vol. III. of the complete edition in English of the works of Saint Alphonsus de Liguori.

JAMES BARRON, C.SS.R.,
Provincial

BROOKLYN, N. Y., March 2, 1927.

PRAYER,

**THE GREAT MEANS OF OBTAINING SALVATION AND ALL THE GRACES
WHICH WE DESIRE OF GOD.**

A Work of Ascetic Theology.

TO THE INCARNATE WORD,

Jesus Christ,

THE BELOVED OF THE ETERNAL FATHER,
THE BLESSED OF THE LORD,
THE AUTHOR OF LIFE,
THE KING OF GLORY,
THE SAVIOUR OF THE WORLD,
THE EXPECTED OF NATIONS,
THE DESIRE OF THE ETERNAL HILLS,
THE BREAD OF HEAVEN,
THE JUDGE OF ALL,
THE MEDIATOR BETWEEN GOD AND MAN.
THE MASTER OF VIRTUES,
THE LAMB WITHOUT SPOT,
THE MAN OF SORROWS,
THE ETERNAL PRIEST, AND VICTIM OF LOVE,
THE HOME OF SINNERS,
THE FOUNTAIN OF GRACES,
THE GOOD SHEPHERD,
THE LOVER OF SOULS,

ALPHONSUS THE SINNER

CONSECRATES THIS BOOK.

Dedication to Jesus and Mary.

———◆———

O INCARNATE WORD, Thou hast given Thy Blood and Thy Life to confer on our prayers that power by which, according to Thy promise, they obtain for us all that we ask. And we, O God, are so careless of our salvation, that we will not even ask Thee for the graces that we must have if we should be saved! In prayer Thou hast given us the key of all Thy divine treasures; and we, rather than pray, choose to remain in our misery. Alas! O Lord, enlighten us, and make us know the value of prayers, offered in Thy name and by Thy merits, in the eyes of Thy Eternal Father. I consecrate to Thee this my book; bless it, and grant that all those into whose hands it falls may have the will to pray always, and may exert themselves to stir up others also to avail themselves of this great means of salvation.

To thee also do I recommend my little work, O Mary, great Mother of God: patronize it, and obtain for all who read it the spirit of prayer, and of continual recourse in all their necessities to thy Son, and to thee, who art the Dispenser of graces, the Mother of mercy, and who never leavest unsatisfied him who recommends himself to thee, O mighty Virgin, but obtainest from God for thy servants whatever thou askest.

This book, which was published in 1759, is one of the most important works of Saint Alphonsus. He himself explains, in the *Introduction* and the *Conclusion*, what it has cost him, and the value that he sets upon it. In his preface to the "Preparation for Death," he speaks thus: "This book, though small, has cost me a great deal of labor. I regard it as of extreme utility to all sorts of persons; and I unhesitatingly assert that among all spiritual treatises, there is none, and there can be none, more necessary than that which treats on prayer as a means of obtaining eternal salvation."—ED.

CONTENTS.

PRAYER,

The great means of obtaining Salvation and all the graces which we desire of God.

A WORK OF ASCETIC THEOLOGY.

PART I.

PART II.

WHICH PROVES THAT THE GRACE OF PRAYER IS GIVEN TO ALL, AND WHICH TREATS OF THE ORDINARY MODE IN WHICH THIS GRACE OPERATES.

INTRODUCTION,

I HAVE published several spiritual works,—on visiting the Blessed Sacrament, on the Passion of Jesus Christ, on the Glories of Mary, and, besides, a work against the Materialists and Deists, with other devout little treatises. Lately I brought out a work on the Infancy of our Saviour, entitled *Novena for Christmas;* and another entitled *Preparation for Death*, besides the one on the Eternal Maxims, most useful for meditation and for sermons, to which are added nine discourses suitable during seasons of divine chastisements. But I do not think that I have written a more useful work than the present, in which I speak of prayer as a necessary and certain means of obtaining salvation, and all the graces that we require for that object. If it were in my power, I would distribute a copy of it to every Catholic in the world, in order to show him the absolute necessity of prayer for salvation.

I say this, because, on the one hand, I see that the absolute necessity of prayer is taught throughout the Holy Scriptures, and by all the holy Fathers; while, on the other hand, I see that Christians are very careless in their practice of this great means of salvation. And, sadder still, I see that preachers take very little care to speak of it to their flocks, and confessors to their penitents ; I see, moreover, that even the spiritual books now popular do not speak sufficiently of it; for there is not a thing preachers, and confessors, and spiritual books should insist upon with more warmth and energy than prayer; not but that they teach many excellent means of keeping ourselves in the grace of God, such as avoiding the occasions of sin, frequenting the sacraments, resisting temptations, hearing the Word of God, meditating on the eternal truths, and other means,—all of them, I admit, most useful; but, I say, what profit is there in sermons, meditations, and all the other means pointed out by masters of the spiritual life, if we forget to pray? since our Lord has declared that he will grant his graces to no one who does not pray. *Ask and ye shall receive.*[1] Without prayer, in the ordinary course of Providence, all the meditations that we make, all our resolutions, all our promises, will be useless. If we do not pray, we shall always be unfaithful to the inspirations of God, and to the promises we make to him. Because, in order actually to do good, to conquer temptations, to practise virtues, and to observe God's law, it is not enough to receive illumination from God, and to meditate and make resolutions, but we require, moreover, the actual assistance of God; and, as we shall soon see, he does not give this assistance except to those who pray, and pray with perseverance. The light we receive, and the considerations and good resolutions that we make, are of use to incite us to the act of prayer when we are in danger, and are tempted to transgress God's law; for then prayer will obtain for us God's help, and we shall be preserved from sin; but if in such moments we do not pray, we shall be lost.

My intention in prefacing my book with this sentiment is, that my readers may thank God for giving them an opportunity, by means of this little book, to receive the grace of reflecting more deeply on the importance of prayer; for all adults who are saved, are ordinarily saved

---

[1] " Petite, et accipietis."—*John*, xvi. 24.

by this single means of grace. And therefore I ask my readers to thank God; for surely it is a great mercy when he gives the light and the grace to pray. I hope, then, that you, my beloved brother, after reading this little work, will never from this day forward neglect to have continual recourse to God in prayer, whenever you are tempted to offend him. If ever in times past you have had your conscience burdened with many sins, know that the cause of this has been the neglect of prayer, and not asking God for help to resist the temptations that assailed you. I pray you, therefore, to read it again and again with the greatest attention; not because it is my production, but because it is a means that God offers you for the good of your eternal salvation, thereby giving you to understand that he wishes you to be saved. And after having read it yourself, induce as many of your friends and neighbors as you can to read it also. Now let us begin in the name of the Lord.

DEFINITION OF PRAYER.

The Apostle writes to Timothy: *I beseech, therefore, that first of all supplications, petitions, and thanksgivings be made.*[1] St. Thomas explains, that prayer is properly the lifting up of the soul to God.[2] *Petition* is that kind of prayer which begs for determinate objects; when the thing sought is indeterminate (as when we say, " Incline to my aid, O God !") it is called *supplication.* *Obsecration* is a solemn adjuration, or representation of the grounds on which we dare to ask a favor; as when we say, " By Thy cross and Passion, O Lord, deliver us !" Finally, *thanksgiving* is the returning of thanks for benefits received, whereby, says St. Thomas, we merit to receive greater

---

[1] "Obsecro igitur primum omnium fieri obsecrationes, orationes, postulationes, gratiarum actiones."—I *Tim.* ii. 1.

[2] 2. 2. q. 83, a. 17.

favors. Prayer, in a strict sense, says the holy Doctor, means recourse to God; but in its general signification it includes all the kinds just enumerated. It is in this latter sense that the word is used in this book.

PLAN OF THE WORK.

In order, then, to attach ourselves to this great means of salvation, we must first of all consider how necessary it is to us, and how powerful it is to obtain for us all the graces that we can desire from God, if we know how to ask for them as we ought. Hence, in the first part, we will speak first of the necessity and power of prayer; and next, of the conditions necessary to make it efficacious with God. Then, in the second part, we will show that the grace of prayer is given to all; and there we will treat of the manner in which grace ordinarily operates.

PART I.

The Necessity, Power, and Conditions of Prayer.

CHAPTER I.

THE NECESSITY OF PRAYER.

I.

Prayer is a Means Necessary to Salvation.

ONE of the errors of Pelagianism was the assertion that prayer is not necessary for salvation. Pelagius, the impious author of that heresy, said that man will only be damned for neglecting to know the truths necessary to be learned. How astonishing! St. Augustine said: "Pelagius discussed everything except how to pray," [1] though, as the saint held and taught, prayer is the only means of acquiring the science of the saints; according to the text of St. James: *If any man want wisdom, let him ask of God, who giveth to all abundantly, and upbraideth not.* [2] The Scriptures are clear enough in pointing out how necessary it is to pray, if we would be saved. *We ought always to pray, and not to faint.* [3] *Watch and pray, that ye enter not into temptation.* [4] *Ask, and it shall be given you.* [5]

---

[1] "Omnia potius disputat (Pelagius), quam ut oret."—*De Nat. et Grat.* c. 17.

[2] "Si quis autem vestrum indiget sapientia, postulet a Deo, qui dat omnibus affluenter, et non improperat."—*James*, i. 5.

[3] "Oportet semper orare."—*Luke*, xviii. 1.

[4] "Vigilate et orate, ut non intretis in tentationem."—*Matt.* xxvi. 41.

[5] "Petite et dabitur vobis."—*Matt.* vii. 7.

The words " we ought," "pray," "ask," according to the
general consent of theologians, impose the precept, and
denote the necessity of prayer. Wickliffe said, that
these texts are to be understood, not precisely of prayer,
but only of the necessity of good works, for in his system
prayer was only well-doing; but this was his error, and
was expressly condemned by the Church. Hence Lessius
wrote that it is heresy to deny that prayer is necessary
for salvation in adults; as it evidently appears from
Scripture that prayer is the means, without which we
cannot obtain the help necessary for salvation.[1]

The reason of this is evident. Without the assistance of
God's grace we can do no good thing: *Without Me, ye
can do nothing.*[2] St. Augustine remarks on this passage,
that our Lord did not say, " Without Me, ye can complete nothing," but "without Me, ye can do nothing;"[3]
giving us to understand, that without grace we cannot
even begin to do a good thing. Nay more, St. Paul
writes, that of ourselves we cannot even have the wish
to do good. *Not that we are sufficient to think anything of
ourselves, but our sufficiency is from God.*[4] If we cannot
even think a good thing, much less can we wish it. The
same thing is taught in many other passages of Scripture: *God worketh all in all. I will cause you to walk in My
commandments, and to keep My judgments, and do them.*[5] So
that, as St. Leo I. says, " Man does no good thing, except

---

[1] " Fide tenendum est, orationem adultis ad salutem esse necessariam, ut colligitur ex Scripturis; quia oratio est medium sine quo auxilium ad salutem necessarium obtineri nequit."—*De just. lib.* 2. c. 37,
d. 3.

[2] " Sine me nihil potestis facere."— *John*, xv. 5.

[3] "Non ait: Perficere; sed: Facere."—*Contra ep. pel.* l. 2. c. 8.

[4] " Non quod sufficientes simus cogitare aliquid a nobis, quasi ex
nobis; sed sufficientia nostra ex Deo est."—2 *Cor.* iii. 5.

[5] " Deus qui operatur omnia in omnibus."—1 *Cor.* xii. 6. " Faciam
ut in præceptis meis ambuletis, et judicia mea custodiatis et opere-
mini."—*Ezek.* xxxvi. 27.

that which God, by his grace, enables him to do,"[1] and hence the Council of Trent says: "If any one shall assert, that without the previous inspiration of the Holy Ghost, and his assistance, man can believe, hope, love, or repent, as he ought, in order to obtain the grace of justification, let him be anathema."[2]

The author of the *Opus Imperfectum* says, that God has given to some animals swiftness, to others claws, to others wings, for the preservation of their life; but he has so formed man, that God himself is his only strength.[3] So that man is completely unable to provide for his own safety, since God has willed that whatever he has, or can have, should come entirely from the assistance of his grace.

But this grace is not given in God's ordinary Providence, except to those who pray for it; according to the celebrated saying of Gennadius, "We believe that no one approaches to be saved, except at the invitation of God; that no one who is invited works out his salvation, except by the help of God; that no one merits this help, unless he prays."[4] From these two premises, on the one hand, that we can do nothing without the assistance of grace; and on the other, that this assistance is only given ordinarily by God to the man that prays, who does not see that the consequence follows, that prayer is absolutely necessary to us for salvation? And although the first

[1] "Nulla facit homo bona, quæ non Deus præstat ut faciat homo."— *Conc. Araus.* ii. *cap.* 20.

[2] "Si quis dixerit sine præveniente Spiritus Sancti inspiratione, atque ejus adjutorio, hominem credere, sperare, diligere, aut pœnitere posse, sicut oportet ut ei justificationis gratia conferatur, anathema sit."—*Sess.* 6, *Can.* 3.

[3] "Alios munivit cursu, alios unguibus, alios pennis; hominem autem sic disposuit, ut virtus illius ipse sit."—*Hom.* 18.

[4] "Nullum credimus ad salutem, nisi Deo invitante, venire; nullum invitatum salutem suam, nisi Deo auxiliante, operari; nullum, nisi orantem, auxilium promereri."—*De Eccl. Dogm.* c. 26.

graces that come to us without any co-operation on our part, such as the call to faith or to penance, are, as St. Augustine says, granted by God even to those who do not pray; yet the saint considers it certain that the other graces, and specially the grace of perseverance, are not granted except in answer to prayer : "God gives us some things, as the beginning of faith, even when we do not pray. Other things, such as perseverance, he has only provided for those who pray." [1]

Hence it is that the generality of theologians, following St. Basil, St. Chrysostom, Clement of Alexandria, St. Augustine, and other Fathers, teach that prayer is necessary to adults, not only because of the obligation of the precept (as they say), but because it is necessary as a means of salvation. That is to say, in the ordinary course of Providence, it is impossible that a Christian should be saved without recommending himself to God, and asking for the graces necessary to salvation. St. Thomas teaches the same: "After baptism, continual prayer is necessary to man, in order that he may enter heaven; for though by baptism our sins are remitted, there still remain concupiscence to assail us from within, and the world and the devil to assail us from without." [2] The reason then which makes us certain of the necessity of prayer is shortly this, in order to be saved we must contend and conquer : *He that striveth for the mastery is not crowned except he strive lawfully.* [3] But without the divine assistance we cannot resist the might of so many and so powerful

[1] "Constat Deum alia dare etiam non orantibus, sicut initium fidei; alia non nisi orantibus præparasse, sicut usque in finem perseverantiam."—*De dono pers.* c. 16.

[2] "Post baptismum autem, necessaria est homini jugis oratio, ad hoc quod cœlum introeat; licet enim per baptismum remittantur peccata, remanet tamen fomes peccati nos impugnans interius, et mundus et dæmones qui impugnant exterius."—*P.* 3, *q.* 39, *a.* 5.

[3] "Qui certat in agone, non coronatur, nisi legitime certaverit."—*2 Tim.* ii. 5.

enemies : now this assistance is only granted to prayer; therefore without prayer there is no salvation.

Moreover, that prayer is the only ordinary means of receiving the divine gifts is more distinctly proved by St. Thomas in another place, where he says, that whatever graces God has from all eternity determined to give us, he will only give them if we pray for them. St. Gregory says the same thing: " Man by prayer merits to receive that which God had from all eternity determined to give him." [1] Not, says St. Thomas, that prayer is necessary in order that God may know our necessities, but in order that we may know the necessity of having recourse to God to obtain the help necessary for our salvation, and may thus acknowledge him to be the author of all our good. [2] As, therefore, it is God's law that we should provide ourselves with bread by sowing corn, and with wine by planting vines; so has he ordained that we should receive the graces necessary to salvation by means of prayer: *Ask, and it shall be given you; seek, and ye shall find.* [3]

We, in a word, are merely beggars, who have nothing but what God bestows on us as alms: *But I am a beggar and poor.* [4] The Lord, says St. Augustine, desires and wills to pour forth his graces upon us, but will not give them except to him who prays. "God wishes to give, but only gives to him who asks." [5] This is declared in the words, *Seek, and it shall be given to you.* Whence it follows, says St. Teresa, that he who seeks not, does not receive. As moisture is necessary for the life of plants, to

[1] " Homines postulando merentur accipere quod eis Deus ante sæcula disposuit donare."—*Dial. l.* 1, *c.* 8.

[2] " Sed ut nos consideremus in his ad divinum auxilium esse recurrendum, . . . et recognoscamus eum esse bonorum nostrorum auctorem."—*Loco cit. ad i. et* 2.

[3] "Petite, et dabitur vobis; quærite et invenietis."—*Matt.* vii. 7.

[4] " Ego autem mendicus sum et pauper."—*Ps.* xxxix. 18.

[5] " Deus dare vult, sed non dat nisi petenti."—*In Ps.* 102.

prevent them from drying up, so, says St. Chrysostom, is prayer necessary for our salvation. Or, as he says in another place, prayer vivifies the soul, as the soul vivifies the body : "As the body without the soul cannot live, so the soul without prayer is dead and emits an offensive odor."[1] He uses these words, because the man who omits to recommend himself to God, at once begins to be defiled with sins. Prayer is also called the food of the soul, because the body cannot be supported without food; nor can the soul, says St. Augustine, be kept alive without prayer: "As the flesh is nourished by food, so is man supported by prayers."[2] All these comparisons used by the holy Fathers are intended by them to teach the absolute necessity of prayer for the salvation of every one.

II.

Without Prayer it is Impossible to Resist Temptations and to Keep the Commandments.

Moreover, prayer is the most necessary weapon of defence against our enemies; he who does not avail himself of it, says St. Thomas, is lost. He does not doubt that the reason of Adam's fall was, because he did not recommend himself to God when he was tempted: "He sinned because he had not recourse to the divine assistance."[3] St. Gelasius says the same of the rebel angels: "Receiving the grace of God in vain, they could not persevere, because they did not pray."[4] St. Charles Borromeo, in

[1] "Sicut corpus sine anima non potest vivere, sic anima sine oratione mortua est et graviter olens."—*De or. D. l.* 1.

[2] "Sicut escis alitur caro, ita orationibus homo interior nutritur."— *De sal. Doc. c.* 28.

[3] "(Peccavit) quia ad divinum auxilium recursum non habuit."— *P.* 1, *q.* 94, *a.* 4.

[4] "Dei gratiam in vacuum recipientes, non orando constare nequiverunt."—*Tr. adv. pelag. hær.*

a pastoral letter, observes, that among all the means of salvation recommended by Jesus Christ in the Gospel, the first place is given to prayer; and he has determined that this should distinguish his Church from all false religions, when he calls her "the house of prayer:" *My house is a house of prayer.*[1] St. Charles concludes that prayer is "the beginning and progress, and the completion of all virtues."[2] So that in darkness, distress, and danger, we have no other hope than to raise our eyes to God, and with fervent prayers to beseech his mercy to save us: *As we know not,* said king Josaphat, *what to do, we can only turn our eyes to Thee.*[3] This also was David's practice, who could find no other means of safety from his enemies, than continual prayer to God to deliver him from their snares: *My eyes are ever towards the Lord; for He shall pluck my feet out of the snare.*[4] So he did nothing but pray: *Look Thou upon me, and have mercy on me; for I am alone and poor. I cried unto Thee, O Lord; save me that I may keep Thy commandments.*[5] Lord, turn Thine eyes to me, have pity on me, and save me; for I can do nothing, and beside Thee there is none that can help me.

And, indeed how could we ever resist our enemies and observe God's precepts, especially since Adam's sin, which has rendered us so weak and infirm, unless we had prayer as a means whereby we can obtain from God sufficient light and strength to enable us to observe them? It was a blasphemy of Luther's to say, that after the sin

---

[1] "Domus mea, Domus orationis vocabitur."—*Matt.* xxi. 13.

[2] "Principium, progressus, et complementum est omnium virtutum."—*Litt. past. de or. in comm.*

[3] "Sed cum ignoremus quid agere debeamus, hoc solum habemus residui, ut oculos nostros dirigamus ad te."—2 *Par.* xx. 12.

[4] "Oculi mei semper ad Dominum, quoniam ipse evellet de laqueo pedes meos."—*Ps.* xxiv. 16.

[5] "Respice in me et miserere mei; quia unicus et pauper sum ego."—*Ibid.* 15. "Clamavi ad te, salvum me fac, ut custodiam mandata tua."—*Ps.* cxviii. 146.

of Adam the observance of God's law has become absolutely impossible to man.   Jansenius also said that there
are some precepts which are impossible even to the just,
with the power which they actually have, and so far his
proposition bears a good sense; but it was justly condemned by the Church for the addition he made to it,
when he said that they have not the grace to make the
precepts possible.[1]   It is true, says St. Augustine, that
man, in consequence of his weakness, is unable to fulfil
some of God's commands with his present strength and
the ordinary grace given to all men; but he can easily,
by prayer, obtain such further aid as he requires for his
salvation : " God commands not impossibilities, but by
commanding he suggests to you to do what you can, to
ask for what is beyond your strength; and he helps you,
that you may be able." [2]   This is a celebrated text,
which was afterwards adopted and made a doctrine of
faith by the Council of Trent.[3]   The holy Doctor immediately adds, " Let us see whence ?" (i. e., how man is
enabled to do that which he cannot).   " By medicine he
can do that which his natural weakness renders impossible to him." [4]   That is, by prayer we may obtain a
remedy for our weakness; for when we pray, God gives
us strength to do that which we cannot do of ourselves.

We cannot believe, continues St. Augustine, that God
would have imposed on us the observance of a law, and
then made the law impossible.   When, therefore, God
shows us that of ourselves we are unable to observe all
his commands it is simply to admonish us to do the
easier things by means of the ordinary grace which he

---

[1] Deest quoque gratia, qua possibilia fiant.

[2] Deus impossibilia non jubet; sed jubendo monet, et facere quod
possis, et petere quod non possis; et adjuvat ut possis.

[3] *Sess.* 6, *c.* 11.

[4] " Videamus unde possit, unde non possit . . . medicina poterit,
quod vitio non potest."—*De Natura et gr.* c. 43.

senius), that we ought not to say that the precept of chastity, or any other, is impossible to us ; for though we cannot observe it by our own strength, we can by God's assistance. " We must say, that what we can do with the divine assistance is not altogether impossible to us." [1] Nor let it be said that it appears an injustice to order a cripple to walk straight. No, says St. Augustine, it is not an injustice, provided always means are given him to find the remedy for his lameness ; for after this, if he continues to go crooked, the fault is his own. "It is most wisely commanded that man should walk uprightly, so that when he sees that he cannot do so of himself, he may seek a remedy to heal the lameness of sin." [2] Finally, the same holy Doctor says, that he will never know how to live well who does not know how to pray well. "He knows how to live aright who knows how to pray aright;" [3] and, on the other hand, St. Francis of Assisi says, that without prayer you can never hope to find good fruit in a soul.

Wrongly, therefore, do those sinners excuse themselves who say that they have no strength to resist temptation. But if you have not this strength, why do you not ask for it ? is the reproof which St. James gives them: *You have it not, because you ask it not.* [4] There is no doubt that we are too weak to resist the attacks of our enemies. But, on the other hand, it is certain that God is faithful, as the Apostle says, and will not permit us to be tempted beyond our strength: *God is faithful, who will not suffer you to be tempted above that which you are able; but will make*

---

[1] " Dicendum quod illud quod possumus cum auxilio divino, non est nobis omnino impossibile."—1. 2. q. 109, a. 4.

[2] " Consultissime homini præcipi, ut rectis passibus ambulet, ut, cum se non posse perspexerit, medicinam requirat ad sanandam peccati claudicationem."—*De Perf. Just. hom.* c. 3.

[3] " Novit recte vivere, qui recte novit orare."—*Serm.* 55, *E. B. app.*

[4] " Non habetis, propter quod non postulatis."—*James,* iv. 2.

also with the temptation issue, that ye may be able to bear it.[1]
"He will provide an issue for it," says Primasius, "by
the protection of his grace, that you may be able to with-
stand the temptation."[2] We are weak, but God is strong;
when we ask him for aid, he communicates his strength
to us; and we shall be able to do all things, as the Apostle reasonably assured himself: *I can do all things in Him
who strengtheneth me.*[3] He, therefore, who falls has no excuse (says St. Chrysostom), because he has neglected to
pray; for if he had prayed, he would not have been overcome by his enemies. "Nor can any one be excused
who, by ceasing to pray, has shown that he did not wish
to overcome his enemy."[4]

III.

Invocation of the Saints.

I. IS IT GOOD AND USEFUL TO HAVE RECOURSE TO THE
INTERCESSION OF THE SAINTS?

Here a question arises, whether it is necessary to have
recourse also to the intercession of the saints to obtain
the grace of God.

That it is a lawful and useful thing to invoke the
saints, as intercessors, to obtain for us, by the merits of
Jesus Christ, that which we, by our demerits, are not
worthy to receive, is a doctrine of the Church, declared
by the Council of Trent. "It is good and useful to invoke them by supplication, and to fly to their aid and as-

---

[1] "Fidelis autem Deus est, qui non patietur vos tentari supra id
quod potestis, sed faciet etiam cum tentatione proventum ut possitis
sustinere."—I *Cor.* x. 13.

[2] Illud faciet provenire (gratiæ præsidio), quo possitis (tentationem) sustinere.

[3] "Omnia possum in eo qui me confortat."—*Phil.* iv. 13.

[4] "Nec quisquam poterit excusari, qui hostem vincere noluit, dum
ab orando cessavit."—*Serm. de Moyse.*

sistance to obtain benefits from God through his Son Jesus Christ."[1]

Such invocation was condemned by the impious Calvin, but most illogically.   For if it is lawful and profitable to invoke living saints to aid us, and to beseech them to assist us in prayers, as the Prophet Baruch did: *And pray ye for us to the Lord our God*[2] and St. Paul: *Brethren, pray for us;*[3] and as God himself commanded the friends of Job to recommend themselves to his prayers, that by the merits of Job he might look favorably on them: *Go to my servant Job, ... and my servant Job shall pray for you; his face I will accept;*[4] if, then, it is lawful to recommend ourselves to the living, how can it be unlawful to invoke the saints who in heaven enjoy God face to face? This is not derogatory to the honor due to God, but it is doubling it; for it is honoring the king not only in his person but in his servants. Therefore, says St. Thomas, it is good to have recourse to many saints, "because by the prayers of many we can sometimes obtain that which we cannot by the prayers of one."[5] And if any one object, But why have recourse to the saints to pray for us, when they are already praying for all who are worthy of it? The same Doctor answers, that no one can be said to be worthy that the saints should pray for him ; but that "he becomes worthy by having recourse to the saint with devotion."[6]

[1] "Bonum atque utile est suppliciter eos invocare, et ob beneficia impetranda a Deo per Filium ejus Jesum Christum ad eorum orationes, opem, auxiliumque, confugere."—*Sess.* 25, *De inv. Sanct.*

[2] "Et pro nobis ipsis orate ad Dominum Deum nostrum."—*Bar.* i. 13.

[3] "Fratres, orate pro nobis."—1 *Thess.* v. 25.

[4] "Ite ad servum meum Job; . . . Job autem servus meus orabit pro vobis; faciem ejus suscipiam."—*Job*, xlii. 8.

[5] Quia plurium orationibus quandoque impetratur, quod unius oratione non impetraretur.

[6] "Ex hoc fit dignus quod ad ipsum (sanctum) cum devotione recurrit."—*In* 4, *Sent. dist.* 45, q. 3, a. 2

2. IS IT GOOD TO INVOKE ALSO THE SOULS IN PURGATORY ?

Again, it is disputed whether there is any use in re-commending one's self to the souls in purgatory.   Some say that the souls in that state cannot pray for us; and these rely on the authority of St. Thomas, who says that those souls, while they are being purified by pain, are in-ferior to us, and therefore " are not in a state to pray for us, but rather require our prayers." [1]   But many other Doctors, as Bellarmine,[2] Sylvius,[3] Cardinal Gotti,[4] Les-sius,[5] Medina and others, affirm with great probability, that we should piously believe that God manifests our prayer to those holy souls, in order that they may pray for us; and that so the charitable interchange of mutual prayer may be kept up between them and us.   Nor do St. Thomas's words present much difficulty; for, as Syl-vius and Gotti say, it is one thing not to be in a state to pray, another not to be able to pray.   It is true that those souls are not in a state to pray, because, as St. Thomas says, while suffering they are inferior to us, and rather require our prayers; nevertheless, in this state they are well able to pray, as they are friends of God.   If a father keeps a son whom he tenderly loves in confinement for some fault ; if the son then is not in a state to pray for himself, is that any reason why he cannot pray for others ? and may he not expect to obtain what he asks, knowing, as he does, his father's affection for him ?   So the souls in purgatory, being beloved by God, and confirmed in grace, have absolutely no impediment to prevent them

---

[1] " Non sunt in statu orandi, sed magis ut oretur pro eis."—2. 2. q. 83, a. 11.

[2] *De Purg.* l. 2, c. 15.

[3] *In Suppl.* q. 71, a. 6.

[4] *De St. an. p. vit.* q. 4, d. 2.

[5] *De Just.* l. 2, c. 37, d. 5.

from praying for us. Still the Church does not invoke them, or implore their intercession, because ordinarily they have no cognisance of our prayers. But we may piously believe that God makes our prayers known to them ; and then they, full of charity as they are, most assuredly do not omit to pray for us. St. Catharine of Bologna, whenever she desired any favor, had recourse to the souls in purgatory, and was immediately heard. She even testified that by the intercession of the souls in purgatory she had obtained many graces which she had not been able to obtain by the intercession of the saints.

3. IT IS OUR DUTY TO PRAY FOR THE SOULS IN PURGATORY.

But here let me make a digression in favor of those holy souls. If we desire the aid of their prayers, it is but fair that we should mind to aid them with our prayers and good works. I said it is fair, but I should have said it is a Christian duty; for charity obliges us to succor our neighbor when he requires our aid, and we can help him without grievous inconvenience. Now it is certain that amongst our neighbors are to be reckoned the souls in purgatory, who, although no longer living in this world, yet have not left the communion of saints. " The souls of the pious dead," says St. Augustine, " are not separated from the Church,"[1] and St. Thomas says more to our purpose, that the charity which is due to the dead who died in the grace of God is only an extension of the same charity which we owe to our neighbor while living: "Charity, which is the bond which unites the members of the Church, extends not only to the living, but also to the dead who die in charity."[2] There-

---

[1] "Piorum animæ mortuorum non separantur ab Ecclesia."—*De Civitate Dei*, l. 20, c. 9.

[2] "Charitas quæ est vinculum uniens membra Ecclesiæ, non solum ad vivos se extendit, sed etiam ad mortuos qui in charitate decedunt." —*In* 4. *Sent. d.* 45. *q.* 2. *s.* 2.

fore, we ought to succor, according to our ability, those holy souls as our neighbors; and as their necessities are greater than those of our other neighbors, for this reason our duty to succor them seems also to be greater.

But now, what are the necessities of those holy prisoners? It is certain that their pains are immense. The fire that tortures them, says St. Augustine, is more excruciating than any pain that man can endure in this life: " That fire will be more painful than anything that man can suffer in this life." [1] St. Thomas thinks the same, and supposes it to be identical with the fire of hell: " The damned are tormented and the elect purified in the same fire." [2] And this only relates to the pains of sense. But the pain of loss (that is, the privation of the sight of God), which those holy souls suffer, is much greater; because not only their natural affection, but also the supernatural love of God, wherewith they burn, draws them with such violence to be united with their Sovereign Good, that when they see the barrier which their sins have put in the way, they feel a pain so acute, that if they were capable of death, they could not live a moment. So that, as St. Chrysostom says, this pain of the deprivation of God tortures them incomparably more than the pain of sense: " The flames of a thousand hells together could not inflict such torments as the pain of loss by itself." [3] So that those holy souls would rather suffer every other possible torture than be deprived for a single instant of the union with God for which they long. So St. Thomas says, that the pain of purgatory exceeds anything that can be endured in this

[1] " Gravior erit ille ignis, quam quidquid potest homo pati in hac vita."—*In Ps.* 37.

[2] " Sub eodem igne, peccator crematur, et electus purgatur."—*In* 4. *Sent. d.* 21. *q.* I. *a.* I.

[3] Mille inferni ignes simul uniti non darent tantam pœnam, quanta est sola pœna damni.

life: " The pain of purgatory must exceed all pain of this life."[1] And Dionysius the Carthusian relates, that a dead person, who had been raised to life by the intercession of St. Jerome, told St. Cyril of Jerusalem that all the torments of this earth are refreshing and delightful when compared with the very least pain of purgatory: "If all the torments of the world were compared with the least that can be had in purgatory they would appear comfortable."[2] And he adds, that if a man had once tried those torments, he would rather suffer all the earthly sorrows that man can endure till the Day of Judgment, than suffer for one day the least pain of purgatory. Hence St. Cyril wrote to St. Augustine: "That as far as regards the infliction of suffering, these pains are the same as those of hell—their only difference being that they are not eternal."[3] Hence we see that the pains of these holy souls are excessive, while, on the other hand, they cannot help themselves; because as Job says: *they are in chains, and are bound with the cords of poverty.*[4] They are destined to reign with Christ; but they are withheld from taking possession of their kingdom till the time of their purgation is accomplished. And they cannot help themselves (at least not sufficiently, even according to those theologians who assert that they can by their prayers gain some relief,) to throw off their chains, until they have entirely satisfied the justice of God. This is precisely what a Cistercian monk said to the sacristan of his monastery: "Help me, I beseech you, with your prayers; for of myself I can obtain nothing."

---

[1] "Oportet quod pœna purgatorii, quantum ad pœnam damni excedat omnem pœnam istius vitæ."—*Loco cit.*

[2] "Si omnia tormenta mundi minori, quæ in purgatorio habetur, pœnæ comparentur, solatia erunt."—*De Quat. Nov. a.* 53.

[3] *Int. Op. Aug. Ep.* 19. *E. B. app.*

[4] "Si fuerint in catenis, et vinciantur funibus paupertatis."—*Job*, xxxvi. 8.

And this is consistent with the saying of St. Bonaventure: "Destitution prevents solvency."[1] That is, those souls are so poor, that they have no means of making satisfaction.

On the other hand, since it is certain, and even of faith, that by our suffrages, and chiefly by our prayers, as particularly recommended and practised by the Church, we can relieve those holy souls, I do not know how to excuse that man from sin who neglects to give them some assistance, at least by his prayers. If a sense of duty will not persuade us to succor them, let us think of the pleasure it will give Jesus Christ to see us endeavoring to deliver his beloved spouses from prison, in order that he may have them with him in paradise. Let us think of the store of merit which we can lay up by practising this great act of charity; let us think, too, that those souls are not ungrateful, and will never forget the great benefit we do them in relieving them of their pains, and in obtaining for them, by our prayers, anticipation of their entrance into glory; so that when they are there they will never neglect to pray for us. And if God promises mercy to him who practises mercy towards his neighbor—*Blessed are the merciful, for they shall obtain mercy*[2]—he may reasonably expect to be saved who remembers to assist those souls so afflicted, and yet so dear to God. Jonathan, after having saved the Hebrews from ruin by a victory over their enemies, was condemned to death by his father Saul for having tasted some honey against his express commands; but the people came before the king, and said, *Shall Jonathan then die, who hath wrought this great salvation in Israel?*[3] So may we expect, that if any of us ever obtains, by his

---

[1] "Mendicitas impedit solutionem."—*Serm. de mort.*

[2] "Beati misericordes, quoniam ipsi misericordiam consequentur." *Matt.* v. 7.

[3] "Ergone Jonathas morietur, qui fecit salutem hanc magnam in Israel?"—1 *Kings*, xiv. 45.

prayers, the liberation of a soul from purgatory, that soul will say to God: "Lord, suffer not him who has delivered me from my torments to be lost." And if Saul spared Jonathan's life at the request of his people, God will not refuse the salvation of a Christian to the prayers of a soul which is his own spouse. Moreover, St. Augustine says that God will cause those who in this life have most succored those holy souls, when they come to purgatory themselves, to be most succored by others. I may here observe that, in practice, one of the best suffrages is to hear Mass for them, and during the Holy Sacrifice to recommend them to God by the merits and Passion of Jesus Christ. The following form may be used: "Eternal Father, I offer Thee this Sacrifice of the Body and Blood of Jesus Christ, with all the pains which he suffered in his life and death; and by his Passion I recommend to Thee the souls in Purgatory, and especially that of," etc. And it is a very charitable act to recommend, at the same time, the souls of all those who are at the point of death.

4. IS IT NECESSARY TO INVOKE THE SAINTS?

Whatever doubt there may be whether or not the souls in purgatory can pray for us, and therefore whether or not it is of any use to recommend ourselves to their prayers, there can be no doubt whatever with regard to the saints. For it is certain that it is most useful to have recourse to the intercession of the saints canonized by the Church, who are already enjoying the vision of God. To suppose that the Church can err in canonizing, is a sin, or is heresy, according to St. Bonaventure, Bellarmine, and others; or at least next door to heresy, according to Suarez, Azorius, Gotti, etc.; because the Sovereign Pontiff, according to St. Thomas, is guided by the infallible influence of the Holy Ghost in an especial way when canonizing the saints.[1]

But to return to the question just proposed: are we obliged to have recourse to the intercession of the saints? I do not wish to meddle with the decision of this question; but I cannot omit the exposition of a doctrine of St. Thomas. In several places above quoted, and especially in his book of Sentences, he expressly lays it down as certain that every one is bound to pray; because (as he asserts) in no other way can the graces necessary for salvation be obtained from God, except by prayer: "Every man is bound to pray, from the fact that he is bound to procure spiritual good for himself, which can only be got from God; so it can only be obtained by asking it of God."[2] Then, in another place of the same book, he proposes the exact question, "Whether we are bound to pray to the saints to intercede for us?"[3] And he answers as follows—in order to catch his real meaning, we will quote the entire passage: "According to Dionysius, the order which God has instituted for his creatures requires that things which are remote may be brought to God by means of things which are nearer to him. Hence, as the saints in heaven are nearest of all to him, the order of his law requires that we who 'remaining in the body are absent from the Lord,' should be brought to him by means of the saints; and this is effected by the divine goodness pouring forth his gifts through them. And as the path of our return to God should correspond to the path of the good things which proceed from him to us, it

---

[1] *Quodl.* 9. *a.* 16. *ad* 1.

[2] "Ad orationem quilibet tenetur, ex hoc ipso quod tenetur ad bona spiritualia sibi procuranda, quæ nonnisi divinitus dantur; unde alio modo procurari non possunt, nisi ut a Deo petantur."—*In* 4, *Sent. d.* 15. *q.* 4. *a.* 1.

[3] "Utrum debeamus Sanctos orare ad interpellandum pro nobis." *Dist.* 45, *q.* 3, *a.* 2.

follows that, as the benefits of God come down to us by means of the suffrages of the saints, we ought to be brought to God by the same way, so that a second time we may receive his benefits by the mediation of the saints. Hence it is that we make them our intercessors with God, and as it were our mediators, when we ask them to pray for us." Note well the words—"The order of God's law requires;" and especially note the last words —"As the benefits of God come down to us by means of the suffrages of the saints, in the same way we must be brought back to God so that a second time we may receive his benefits by the mediation of the saints." [1] So that, according to St. Thomas, the order of the divine law requires that we mortals should be saved by means of the saints, in that we receive by their intercession the help necessary for our salvation. He then puts the objection, that it appears superfluous to have recourse to the saints, since God is infinitely more merciful than they, and more ready to hear us. This he answers by saying: "God has so ordered, not on account of any want of mercy on his part, but to keep the right order which he has universally established, of working by means of second causes. It is not for want of his mercy, but to preserve the aforesaid order in the creation. [2]

In conformity with this doctrine of St. Thomas, the Continuator of Tourneley and Sylvius writes, that although God only is to be prayed to as the Author of grace, yet we are bound to have recourse also to the intercession of the saints, so as to observe the order which God has established with regard to our salvation, which is, that the inferior should be saved by imploring the aid of the

---

[1] Hoc divinæ legis ordo requirit . . . sicut mediantibus Sanctorum suffragiis Dei beneficia in nos deveniunt, ita oportet nos in Deum reduci, ut iterato beneficia ejus sumamus mediantibus Sanctis.

[2] Non est propter defectum misericordiæ ipsius, sed ut ordo prædictus conservetur in rebus.

superior. " By the law of nature we are bound to observe
the order which God has appointed; but God has appointed that the inferior should obtain salvation by imploring the assistance of his superior." [1]

IV.

The Intercession of the Blessed Virgin.

And if this is true of the saints, much more is it true
of the intercession of the Mother of God, whose prayers
are certainly of more value in his sight than those of all
the rest of the inhabitants of heaven together. For St.
Thomas says, that the saints, in proportion to the merits
by which they have obtained grace for themselves, are
able also to save others; but that Jesus Christ, and so
also his Mother, have merited so much grace, that
they can save all men. " It is a great thing in any saint
that he should have grace enough for the salvation of
many beside himself; but if he had enough for the salvation of all men, this would be the greatest of all; and
this is the case with Christ, and with the Blessed
Virgin," [2] And St. Bernard speaks thus to Mary :
" Through thee we have access to thy Son, O discoverer
of grace and Mother of salvation, that through thee he
may receive us, who through thee was given to us." [3]
These words signify, that as we only have access to the
Father by means of the Son, who is the Mediator of

[1] " Quia lege naturali tenemur eum ordinem observare, quem Deus
instituit; at constituit Deus ut inferiores ad salutem perveniant,
implorato superiorum subsidio."—*De Relig. p.* 2, *c.* 2, *a.* 5.

[2] " Magnum est enim in quolibet sancto, quando habet tantum de
gratia quod sufficit ad salutem multorum; sed, quando haberet tantum quod sufficeret ad salutem omnium, hoc esset maximum, et hoc
est in Christo et in Beata Virgine."—*Expos. in Sal. Ang.*

[3] " Per te accessum habeamus ad Filium, o Inventrix gratiæ,
Mater salutis, ut per te nos suscipiat, qui per te datus est nobis !"—
In Adv. Dom. s. 2,

justice, so we only have access to the Son by means of the Mother, who is mediator of grace, and who obtains for us, by her intercession, the gifts which Jesus Christ has merited for us. And therefore, St. Bernard says, in another place, that Mary has received a twofold fulness of grace. The first was the Incarnation of the Word, who was made Man in her most holy womb; the second is that fulness of grace which we receive from God by means of her prayers. Hence the saint adds: " God has placed the fulness of all good in Mary, that if we have any hope, any grace, any salvation, we may know that it overflows from her who ' ascendeth abounding with delights.' " [1] She is a garden of delights, whose odors spread abroad and abound; that is, the gifts of graces. So that whatever good we have from God, we receive all by the intercession of Mary. And why so? Because, says St. Bernard, it is God's will: " Such is his will, who would have us receive everything through Mary." [2] But the more precise reason is deduced from the expression of St. Augustine, that Mary is justly called our Mother, because she co-operated by her charity in the birth of the faithful to the life of grace, by which we become members of Jesus Christ, our head: " But clearly she is the mother of his members (which we are); because she co-operated by her charity in the birth of the faithful in the Church, and they are members of that Head." [3] Therefore, as Mary co-operated by her charity in the spiritual birth of the faithful, so also God willed that she

---

[1] " Totius boni plenitudinem posuit (Deus) in Maria, ut proinde, si quid spei in nobis est, si quid gratiæ, si quid salutis, ab ea noverimus redundare, quæ ascendit deliciis affluens: hortus deliciarum, ut undique fluant et effluant aromata ejus, charismata scilicet gratiarum." —*De Aquæd.*

[2] " Sic est voluntas ejus, qui totum nos habere voluit per Mariam."

[3] " Sed plane Mater membrorum ejus, quod nos sumus; quia co-operata est charitate, ut fideles in Ecclesia nascerentur, qui illius capitis membra sunt."—*De S. Virginit. c.* 6.

should co-operate by her intercession to make them enjoy the life of grace in this world, and the life of glory
in the next; and therefore the Church makes us call her
and salute her, without any circumlocution, by the names,
" our life, our sweetness, and our hope." [1]

Hence St. Bernard exhorts us to have continual recourse to the Mother of God; because her prayers are certain to be heard by her Son: " Go to Mary, I say, without
hesitation; the Son will hear the Mother." And then he
says: " My children, she is the ladder of sinners, she is
my chief confidence, she is the whole ground of my
hope." [2] He calls her " ladder," because, as you cannot
mount the third step except you first put your foot on the
second, nor can you arrive at the second except by the
first, so you cannot come to God except by means of
Jesus Christ, nor can you come to Christ except by means
of his Mother. Then he calls her " his greatest security,
and the whole ground of his hope;" because, as he
affirms, God wills that all the graces which he gives us
should pass through the hands of Mary. And he concludes by saying, that we ought to ask all the graces
which we desire through Mary; because she obtains whatever she seeks, and her prayers cannot be rejected. " Let
us seek grace, and let us seek it through Mary; because
what she seeks she finds, and she cannot be disap-
pointed." [3] The following saints teach the same as St.
Bernard: St. Ephrem, " We have no other confidence
than from thee, O purest Virgin !" [4] St. Ildephonsus,
" All the good things that the divine Majesty has de-

---

[1] " Vita, Dulcedo, et Spes nostra ! salve."

[2] " Ad Mariam recurre; non dubius dixerim, exaudiet utique
Matrem Filius.—Filioli, hæc peccatorum scala, hæc mea maxima
fiducia est, hæc tota ratio spei meæ."—*De Aquæd.*

[3] " Quæramus gratiam, et per Mariam quæramus; quia, quod
quærit, invenit, et frustrari non potest."

[4] " Nobis non est alia quam a te fiducia, o Virgo sincerissima !"—
De Laud. B. M. V.

termined to give them, he has determined to commit to
thy hands; for to thee are intrusted the treasures and the
wardrobes of grace." [1] St Germanus, " If thou desertest
us, what will become of us, O life of Christians?" [2] St.
Peter Damian, "In thy hands are all the treasures of the
mercies of God." [3] St. Antoninus, "Who seeks without
her aid, attempts to fly without wings." [4] St. Bernardine of Sienna, "Thou art the dispenser of all graces; our
salvation is in thy hands." [5] In another place, he not
only says that all graces are transmitted to us by means
of Mary, but he also asserts that the Blessed Virgin,
from the time she became Mother of God, acquired a
certain jurisdiction over all the graces that are given to
us. "Through the Virgin the vital graces are transfused
from Christ, the Head, into his mystical body." [6] From
the time when the Virgin Mother conceived in her
womb the Word of God, she obtained a certain jurisdiction (if I may so speak) over every temporal procession
of the Holy Ghost; so that no creature could obtain any
grace from God, except by the dispensation of his sweet
Mother." [7] And he concludes, "Therefore all gifts, vir-

[1] "Omnia bona quæ illic summa Majestas decrevit facere, tuis
manibus voluit commendare; commissi quippe sunt tibi thesauri . . .
et ornamenta gratiarum."—*De Cor. Virg. c.* 15.

[2] "Si nos deserueris, quid de nobis fiet, O Vita christianorum !"—
De zona Deip.

[3] "In manibus tuis sunt thesauri miserationum Domini."—*De
Nativ. s.* 1.

[4] "Qui petit sine ipsa duce, sine alis tentat volare."—*P.* 4, *tit.* 15,
c. 22.

[5] "Tu dispensatrix omnium gratiarum ; salus nostra in manu tua
est."

[6] "Per Virginem a Capite Christo vitales gratiæ in ejus corpus mys-
ticum transfunduntur."

[7] "A tempore quo Virgo Mater concepit in utero Verbum Dei,
quamdam, ut sic dicam, jurisdictionem obtinuit in omni Spiritu
Sancti processione temporali; ita quod nulla creatura a Deo obtinuit
gratiam, nisi secundum ipsius piæ Matris dispensationem."

tues, and graces are dispensed through her hands to
whom she wills, and as she wills."[1]   St. Bonaventure
says the same: " Since the whole divine nature was in
the womb of the Virgin, I do not fear to teach that she
has a certain jurisdiction over all the streams of grace;
as her womb was, as it were, an ocean of the divine
nature, whence all the streams of grace must emanate."[2]
On the authority of these saints, many theologians have
piously and reasonably defended the opinion, that there
is no grace given to us except by means of the intercession of Mary; so Mendoza, Vega, Paciucchelli, Segneri,
Poiré, Crasset, and others, as also the learned Alexander
Natalis who says: "It is God's will that we should look
to him for all good things, to be procured by the most
powerful intercession of the Blessed Virgin, when we invoke her, as it is fit."[3]   And he quotes in confirmation
the passage of St. Bernard: "Such is his will, who has
determined that we should receive all through Mary."[4]
Contenson says the same, in a comment on the words
addressed by Jesus on the cross to St. John, "Behold thy
Mother:" As though he had said, "No one shall be partaker of my blood except by the intercession of my
Mother.[5]   My wounds are fountains of grace; but their
streams shall flow to no one, except through the canal of
Mary.   O my disciple John, I will love you as you love

[1] " Ideo omnia dona, virtutes et gratiæ, quibus vult, per ipsius manus
dispensantur."—*S. d. Nat. M. V. c.* 8.

[2] "Cum tota natura divina intra Virginis uterum extiterit, non
timeo dicere quod in omnes gratiarum effluxus quandam jurisdictionem habuerit hæc Virgo, de cujus utero, quasi de quodam divinitatis
oceano, flumina emanant omnium gratiarum."

[3] "Deus vult ut omnia bona ab ipso expectemus, potentissima
Virginis Matris intercessione, cum eam, ut par est, invocamus, impetranda."—*Ep.* 50, *in calce Theol.*

[4] " Sic est voluntas ejus, qui totum nos habere voluit per Mariam."—
De Aquæd.

[5] " Ecce Mater tua."—*John.* xix. 27.

her !"[1] For the rest, it is certain, that if God is pleased when we have recourse to the saints, he will be much more pleased when we avail ourselves of the intercession of Mary, that she, by her merits, may compensate for our unworthiness, according to the words of St. Anselm: " That the dignity of the intercessor may supply for our poverty. So that, to invoke the Virgin, is not to distrust God's mercy, but to fear our own unworthiness."[2] St. Thomas, speaking of her dignity, calls it, as it were, infinite: "From the fact that she is the Mother of God, she has a certain infinite dignity."[3] So that it may be said with reason, that the prayers of Mary have more power with God than those of all heaven together.

CONCLUSION OF THE CHAPTER.

Let us conclude this first point by giving the gist of all that has been said hitherto. He who prays is certainly saved. He who prays not is certainly damned. All the blessed (except infants) have been saved by prayer. All the damned have been lost through not praying; if they had prayed, they would not have been lost. And this is, and will be, their greatest torment in hell, to think how easily they might have been saved, only by asking God for his grace; but that now it is too late,—the time of prayer is over.

[1] " Quasi diceret: Nullus sanguinis illius particeps erit, nisi intercessione Matris meæ. Vulnera gratiarum fontes sunt; sed ad nullos derivabuntur rivi, nisi per Marianum canalem. Joannes discipule, tantum a me amaberis, quantum eam amaveris."—*Theol. ment. et cord. t.* 2, *l.* 10, *d.* 4, *c.* 1.

[2] " Ut dignitas intercessoris suppleat inopiam nostram. Unde, Virginem interpellare non est de divina misericordia diffidere, sed de propria indignitate timere."—*De incarn. q.* 37, *a.* 4, *d.* 23, *s.* 3.

[3] " Ex hoc quod est Mater Dei, habet quandam dignitatem infinitam."—*P.* 1, *q.* 25, *a.* 6. *ad* 4.

CHAPTER II.

THE POWER OF PRAYER.

I.

Excellence of Prayer and its Power with God.

OUR prayers are so dear to God, that he has appointed the angels to present them to him as soon as they come forth from our mouths. "The angels," says St. Hilary, "preside over the prayers of the faithful, and offer them daily to God."[1]   This is that smoke of the incense, which are the prayers of saints, which St. John saw ascending to God from the hands of the angels;[2] and which he saw in another place represented by golden phials full of sweet odors, very acceptable to God.   But in order to understand better the value of prayers in God's sight, it is sufficient to read both in the Old and New Testaments the innumerable promises which God makes to the man that prays. *Cry to Me, and I will hear thee.*[3]   *Call upon Me, and I will deliver thee.*[4]   *Ask, and it shall be given you; seek, and you shall find; knock, and it shall be opened unto you. He shall give good things to them that ask Him.*[5]   *Every one that asketh receiveth, and he that seeketh findeth.*[6]   *Whatso-*

---

[1] "Angeli præsunt fidelium orationibus, et eas quotidie Deo offerunt."—*In Matt. Can.* 18.

[2] *Apoc.* viii. 3.

[3] "Invoca me in die tribulationis; eruam te."—*Ps.* xlix. 15.

[4] "Clama ad me, et exaudiam te."—*Jer.* xxxiii. 3.

[5] "Petite, et dabitur vobis; quærite, et invenietis; pulsate, et aperietur vobis . . . Pater vester, qui in cœlis est, dabit bona petentibus se."—*Matt.* vii. 7.

[6] "Omnis qui petit, accipit."—*Luke,* xi. 10.

ever they shall ask, it shall be done for them by My Father.[1]
*All things whatsoever you ask when you pray, believe that you
shall receive them, and they shall come unto you.*[2] *If you ask
Me anything in My name, that will I do.*[3] *You shall ask
whatever you will, and it shall be done unto you. Amen, amen,
I say unto you, if you ask the Father anything in My name,
He will give it you.*[4] There are a thousand similar texts;
but it would take too long to quote them.

God wills us to be saved; but for our greater good, he
wills us to be saved as conquerors. While, therefore, we
remain here, we have to live in a continual warfare; and
if we should be saved, we have to fight and conquer.
"No one can be crowned without victory," says St.
Chrysostom.[5] We are very feeble, and our enemies are
many and mighty; how shall we be able to stand against
them, or to defeat them? Let us take courage, and say
with the Apostle, *I can do all things in Him who strengtheneth
me.*[6] By prayer we can do all things; for by this means
God will give us that strength which we want. Theo-
doret says, that prayer is omnipotent; it is but one, yet
it can do all things: "Though prayer is one, it can do all
things."[7] And St. Bonaventure asserts that by prayer
we obtain every good, and escape every evil: "By it is
obtained the gain of every good, and liberation from every
evil."[8] St. Laurence Justinian says, that by means of

---

[1] "Quodcumque volueritis, petetis, et fiet vobis."—*John*, xv. 7.

[2] "De omni re, quamcumque petierint, fiet illis a Patre meo."—
Matt. xviii. 19.

[3] "Omnia quæcumque orantes petitis, credite quia accipietis, et
evenient vobis."—*Mark* xi. 24.

[4] "Si quid petieritis me in nomine meo, hoc faciam.—Amen, amen,
dico vobis: si quid petieritis Patrem in nomine meo, dabit vobis."—
John, xiv. 14.—xvi. 23.

[5] "Nullus sine victoria poterit coronari."—*De Mart.* s. 1.

[6] "Omnia possum in eo qui me confortat."—*Phil.* iv. 13.

[7] "Oratio, cum sit una, omnia potest."—*Ap. Rodrig.* p. 1, tr. 5, c. 14.

[8] "Per ipsam impetratur obtentio omnis boni et amotio omnis
mali."—*In Luc.* 11.

prayer we build for ourselves a strong tower, where we shall be secure from all the snares and assaults of our enemies: " By the exercise of prayer man is able to erect a citadel for himself." [1] " The powers of hell are mighty," says St. Bernard; " but prayer is stronger than all the devils." [2] Yes; for by prayer the soul obtains God's help, which is stronger than any created power. Thus David encouraged himself in his alarms: *Praising I will call upon the Lord, and I shall be saved from my enemies.* [3] For, as St. Chrysostom says, " prayer is a strong weapon, a defence, a port, and a treasure." [4] It is a weapon sufficient to overcome every assault of the devil; it is a defence to preserve us in every danger; it is a port where we may be safe in every tempest; and it is at the same time a treasure which provides us with every good.

II.

Power of Prayer against Temptation.

God knows the great good which it does us to be obliged to pray, and therefore permits us (as we have already shown in the previous chapter) to be assaulted by our enemies, in order that we may ask him for the help which he offers and promises to us. But as he is pleased when we run to him in our dangers, so is he displeased when he sees us neglectful of prayer. "As the king," says St. Bonaventure, " would think it faithlessness in an officer, when his post was attacked, not to ask him for reinforcements, he would be reputed a traitor if he

---

[1] "Per orationis exercitium, secum habitare arcemque erigere valet homo."—*De Cast. Conn.* c. 22.

[2] "Oratio dæmoniis omnibus malis prævalet."—*De Modo bene viv.* s. 49.

[3] "Invocabo Dominum, et ab inimicis salvus ero."—*Ps.* xvii. 4.

[4] "Magna armatura precatio, tutela, portus, et thesaurus."—*Hom. in Ps.* 145.

did not request help from the king;"[1] so God thinks himself betrayed by the man who, when he finds himself surrounded by temptations, does not run to him for assistance. For he desires to help us; and only waits to be asked, and then gives abundant succor. This is strikingly shown by Isaias, when, on God's part, he told the king Achaz to ask some sign to assure himself of God's readiness to help him: *Ask thee a sign of the Lord Thy God.*[2] The faithless king answered: *I will not ask, and I will not tempt the Lord;*[3] for he trusted in his own power to overcome his enemies without God's aid. And for this the Prophet reproved him: *Hear, therefore, O house of David; is it a small thing for you to be grievous to men, that you are grievous to my God also?*[4] because that man is grievous and offensive to God who will not ask him for the graces which he offers.

Come to Me, all you that labor and are burdened, and I will refresh you.[5] "My poor children," says our Saviour, "though you find yourselves assailed by enemis, and oppressed with the weight of your sins, do not lose heart but have recourse to me in prayer, and I will give you strength to resist, and I will give you a remedy for all your disasters." In another place he says, by the mouth of Isaias, *Come and accuse Me, saith the Lord; if your sins be as scarlet, they shall be made white as snow.*[6] O men, come to me; though your consciences are horribly defiled, yet come; I even give you leave to reproach me

---

[1] "Reputaretur infidelis, nisi expectaret a rege auxilium."—*Diæta sal.* t. 2. c. 5.

[2] "Pete tibi signum a Domino Deo tuo."—*Is.* vii. 11.

[3] "Non petam, et non tentabo Dominum."

[4] "Audite ergo, Domus David: Numquid parum vobis est molestos esse hominibus, quia molesti estis et Deo meo?"

[5] "Venite ad me omnes, qui laborati et onerati estis, et ego reficiam vos."—*Matt.* xi. 28.

[6] "Venite, et arguite me, dicit Dominus: si fuerint peccata vestra ut coccinum, quasi nix dealbabuntur."—*Is.* i. 18.

(so to speak), if after you have had recourse to me, I do not give you grace to become white as snow.

What is prayer? It is, as St. Chrysostom says, "the anchor of those tossed on the sea, the treasure of the poor, the cure of diseases, the safeguard of health."[1] It is a secure anchor for him who is in peril of shipwreck; it is a treasury of immense wealth for him who is poor; it is a most efficacious medicine for him who is sick; and it is a certain preservative for him who would keep himself well. What does prayer effect? Let us hear St. Laurence Justinian: "It pleases God, it gets what it asks, it overcomes enemies, it changes men."[2] It appeases the wrath of God, who pardons all who pray with humility. It obtains every grace that is asked for; it vanquishes all the strength of the tempter, and it changes men from blind into seeing, from weak into strong, from sinners into saints. Let him who wants light ask it of God, and it shall be given. As soon as I had recourse to God, says Solomon, he granted me wisdom: *I called upon God, and the Spirit of wisdom came to me.*[3] Let him who wants fortitude ask it of God, and it shall be given. As soon as I opened my mouth to pray, says David, I received help from God: *I opened my mouth, and drew in the Spirit.*[4] And how in the world did the martyrs obtain strength to resist tyrants, except by prayer, which gave them force to overcome dangers and death?

"He who uses this great weapon," says St. Chrysostom, "knows not death, leaves the earth, enters heaven, lives with God."[5] He falls not into sin; he loses affec-

[1] "Oratio est fluctuantibus anchora, pauperum thesaurus, morborum curatio, custodia sanitatis."—*Hom. de Consubst. cont. Anom.*

[2] "Placat Deum, postulata reportat, adversarios superat, immutat homines."—*De Perf.* c. 12.

[3] "Invocavi, et venit in me spiritus sapientiæ."—*Wis.* vii. 7.

[4] "Os meum aperui, et attraxi spiritum."—*Ps.* cxviii. 131.

[5] "Nescit mortem, relinquit terras, cœlos intrat, convivit Deo."—*Serm.* 45.

tion for the earth; he makes his abode in heaven; and
begins, even in this life, to enjoy the conversation of God.
How then can you disquiet such a man by saying: "How
do you know that you are written in the book of life?"
How do you know whether God will give you efficacious
grace and the gift of perseverance? *Be nothing solicitous,*
says St. Paul, *but in everything by prayer and supplication,
with thanksgiving, let your petitions be known unto God.*[1] What
is the use, says the Apostle, of agitating yourselves with
these miseries and fears? Drive from you all these cares,
which are of no use but to lessen your confidence, and to
make you more tepid and slothful in walking along the
way of salvation. Pray and seek always, and make your
prayers sound in God's ears, and thank him for having
promised to give you the gifts which you desire whenever you ask for them, namely efficacious grace, perseverance, salvation, and everything that you desire. The
Lord has given us our post in the battle against powerful foes; but he is faithful in his promises, and will never
allow us to be assaulted more violently than we can
resist: *God is faithful, who will not suffer you to be tempted
above that which ye are able.*[2] He is faithful, since he instantly succors the man who invokes him. The learned
Cardinal Gotti writes, that God has bound himself not
only to give us grace precisely balancing the temptation
that assails us, but that he is obliged, when we are
tempted, and have recourse to him, to afford us, by
means of that grace which is kept ready for and offered
to all, sufficient strength for us actually to resist the
temptation. "God is bound, when we are tempted, and
fly to his protection, to give us by the grace prepared

---

[1] "Nihil solliciti sitis; sed in omni oratione et obsecratione, cum
gratiarum actione, petitiones vestræ innotescant apud Deum."—
Phil. iv. 6.

[2] "Fidelis autem Deus est, qui non patietur vos tentari supra id
quod potestis."—1 *Cor.* x. 13.

and offered to all such strength as will not only put us in the way of being able to resist, but will also make us resist; 'for we can do all things in him who strengthens us' by his grace, if we humbly ask for it."[1] We can do all things with God's help, which is granted to every one who humbly seeks it; so that we have no excuse when we allow ourselves to be overcome by a temptation. We are conquered solely by our own fault, because we would not pray. By prayer all the snares and power of the devil are easily overcome. "By prayer all hurtful things are chased away," says St. Augustine.[2]

III.

God is always ready to hear us.

St. Bernardine of Sienna says that prayer is a faithful ambassador, well known to the King of Heaven, and having access to his private chamber, and able by his importunity to induce the merciful heart of the King to grant every aid to us his wretched creatures, groaning in the midst of our conflicts and miseries in this valley of tears. "Prayer is a most faithful messenger, known to the King, who is used to enter his chamber, and by his importunity to influence the merciful mind of the King, and to obtain us assistance in our toils."[3] Isaias also assures us, that as soon as the Lord hears our prayers, he is moved with compassion towards us; and

---

[1] "Respondeo . . . , cum tentamur, nobis ad Deum confugientibus, per gratiam a Deo paratam et oblatam, vires adfuturas, qua et possimus resistere et actu resistamus ; omnia enim possumus in eo qui nos confortat per gratiam, si humiliter petamus."—*De Grat. q.* 2. *d.* 5, § 3.

[2] "Per orationes cuncta noxia effugantur."—*De Sal. Doc. c.* 28.

[3] "Est oratio nuncius fidelissimus, notus Regi, qui cubiculum Regis adire, et sua importunitate pium Regis animum flectere, et laborantibus opem impetrare solitus est."—*T.* 4. *s. in Dom.* 5. *p. Pasc.*

does not leave us to cry long to him, but instantly re-plies, and grants us what we ask: *Weeping, thou shalt not weep; He will surely have pity upon thee: the voice of thy cry as soon as He shall hear, He will answer thee.*[1] In another place he complains of us by the mouth of Jeremias: *Am I become a wilderness to Israel, or a lateward springing land? Why then have My people said, we are revolted, and will come to Thee no more!*[2] Why do you say that you will no more have recourse to me? Has my mercy become to you a barren land, which can yield you no fruits of grace? or a cold soil, which yields its fruit too late! So has our loving Lord assured us that he never neglects to hear us, and to hear us instantly when we pray; and so does he reproach those who neglect to pray through distrust of being heard.

If God were to allow us to present our petitions to him once a month, even this would be a great favor. The kings of the earth give audiences a few times in the year, but God gives a continual audience. St. Chrysostom writes, that God is always waiting to hear our prayers, and that a case never occurred when he neglected to hear a petition offered to him properly : " God is always prepared for the voice of his servants, nor did he ever, when called upon as he ought to be, neglect to hear." [3] And in another place he says, that when we pray to God, before we have finished recounting to him our supplications, he has already heard us: " It is always obtained, even while we are yet praying." [4] We even

---

[1] " Plorans nequaquam plorabis. miserans miserebitur tui; ad vocem clamoris tui, statim ut audierit. respondebit tibi."—*Is.* xxx. 19.

[2] "Numquid solitudo factus sum Israeli, aut terra serotina? quare ergo dixit populus meus: Recessimus, non veniemus ultra ad te?"—*Jer.* ii. 31.

[3] "Deus paratus continue ad vocem servorum suorum est, nec unquam, ut oportet vocatus, non obaudivit."—*In Matt. hom.* 55.

[4] " Semper obtinetur, etiam dum adhuc oramus."

have the promise of God to do this: *As they are yet speaking I will hear.*[1] The Lord, says David, stands near to every one who prays, to console, to hear, and to save him: *The Lord is nigh to all them that call upon Him; to all that call upon Him in truth* (that is, as they ought to call). *He will do the will of them that fear Him; and He will hear their prayer and will save them.*[2] This it was in which Moses gloried, when he said: *There is not another nation so great, that has gods so nigh them, as our God is present to all our petitions.*[3] The gods of the Gentiles were deaf to those who invoked them, for they were wretched fabrications, which could do nothing. But our God, who is Almighty, is not deaf to our prayers, but always stands near the man who prays, ready to grant him all the graces which he asks: *In what day soever I shall call upon Thee, behold I shall know that Thou art my God.*[4] Lord, says the Psalmist, hereby do I know that Thou, my God, art all goodness and mercy, in that, whenever I have recourse to Thee, Thou dost instantly help me.

IV.

We should not limit ourselves to asking for little things. To pray is better than to meditate.

We are so poor that we have nothing; but if we pray we are no longer poor. If we are poor, God is rich; and God, as the Apostle says, is all liberality to him that

---

[1] "Adhuc illis loquentibus, ego audiam."—*Is.* lxv. 24.

[2] "Prope est Dominus omnibus invocantibus eum, omnibus invocantibus eum in veritate; voluntatem timentium se faciet, et deprecationem eorum exaudiet, et salvos faciet eos."—*Ps.* cxliv. 18.

[3] "Nec est alia natio tam grandis, quæ habeat deos appropinquantes sibi, sicut Deus noster adest cunctis obsecrationibus nostris." —*Deut.* iv. 7.

[4] "In quacumque die invocavero te, ecce cognovi quoniam Deus meus es."—*Ps.* lv. 10.

calls for his aid: *Rich unto all who call upon Him.*[1] Since, therefore (as St. Augustine exhorts us), we have to do with a Lord of infinite power and infinite riches, let us not go to him for little and valueless things, but let us ask some great thing of him: "You seek from the Almighty,—seek something great."[2] If a man went to a king to ask some trumpery coin, like a farthing, methinks that man would but insult his king. On the other hand, we honor God, we honor his mercy, and his liberality, when, though we see how miserable we are, and how unworthy of any kindness, we yet ask for great graces, trusting in the goodness of God, and in his faithfulness to his promises of granting to the man who prays whatever grace he asks: *Whatsoever you will, ask, and it shall be done unto you.*[3] St. Mary Magdalene of Pazzi said, "that God feels himself so honored and is so delighted when we ask for his grace, that he is, in a certain sense, grateful to us; because when we do this we seem to open to him a way to do us a kindness, and to satisfy his nature, which is to do good to all." And let us be sure that, when we seek God's grace, he always gives us more than we ask: *If any of you want wisdom, let him ask of God, who giveth to all abundantly, and upbraideth not.*[4] Thus speaks St. James, to show us that God is not like men, parsimonious of his goods; men, though rich and liberal, when they give alms, are always somewhat close-handed, and generally give less than is asked of them, because their wealth, however great it be, is always finite; so that the more they give the less they have. But God, when he is asked, gives his good things "abundantly," that is, with a generous hand, always giving

[1] "Dives in omnes qui invocant illum."—*Rom.* x. 12.

[2] "Ab Omnipotente petitis ; aliquid magnum petite."—*In Ps.* 62.

[3] "Quodcumque volueritis, petetis et fiet vobis."—*John*, xv. 7.

[4] "Si quis autem vestrum indiget sapientia, postulet a Deo, qui dat omnibus affluenter, et non improperat."—*James*, i. 5.

more than is asked, because his wealth is infinite, and the more he gives the more he has to give: *For Thou, O Lord, art sweet and mild ; and plenteous in mercy to all that call upon Thee.*[1] Thou, O my God, said David, art but too liberal and kind to him that invokes Thee; the mercies which thou pourest upon him are super-abundant, above all he asks.

On this point, then, we have to fix all our attention, namely, to pray with confidence, feeling sure that by prayer all the treasures of heaven are thrown open to us. "Let us attend to this," says St. Chrysostom, "and we shall open heaven to ourselves."[2] Prayer is a treasure; he who prays most receives most. St. Bonaventure says that every time a man has recourse to God by fervent prayer, he gains good things that are of more value than the whole world: "Any day a man gains more by devout prayer than the whole world is worth."[3] Some devout souls spend a great deal of time in reading and in meditating, but pay but little attention to prayer. There is no doubt that spiritual reading, and meditation on the eternal truths, are very useful things; "but," says St. Augustine, "it is of much more use to pray." By reading and meditating we learn our duty; but by prayer we obtain the grace to do it. "It is better to pray than to read: by reading we know what we ought to do; by prayer we receive what we ask."[4] What is the use of knowing our duty, and then not doing it, but to make us more guilty in God's sight? Read and meditate as we like, we shall never satisfy our obligations, unless we ask of God the grace to fulfil them.

[1] " Quoniam tu, Domine, suavis et mitis et multæ misericordiæ omnibus invocantibus te."—*Ps.* lxxxv. 5.

[2] " Hoc studeamus, et aperiemus nobis cœlum."—*In Act. hom.* 36.

[3] " In quacunque die, lucratur homo oratione devota plus quam valeat totus mundus."—*De Perf. vitæ, c.* 5.

[4] " Melius est orare quam legere : in lectione cognoscimus quæ facere debemus, in oratione accipimus quæ postulamus."

And, therefore, as St. Isidore observes, the devil is never more busy to distract us with the thoughts of worldly cares than when he perceives us praying and asking God for grace: " Then mostly does the devil insinuate thoughts, when he sees a man praying." [1] And why? Because the enemy sees that at no other time do we gain so many treasures of heavenly goods as when we pray. This is the chief fruit of mental prayer, to ask God for the graces which we need for perseverance and for eternal salvation; and chiefly for this reason it is that mental prayer is morally necessary for the soul, to enable it to preserve itself in the grace of God. For if a person does not remember in the time of meditation to ask for the help necessary for perseverance, he will not do so at any other time; for without meditation he will not think of asking for it, and will not even think of the necessity for asking it. On the other hand, he who makes his meditation every day will easily see the needs of his soul, its dangers, and the necessity of his prayer; and so he will pray, and will obtain the graces which will enable him to persevere and save his soul. Father Segneri said of himself, that when he began to meditate, he aimed rather at exciting affections than at making prayers. But when he came to know the necessity and the immense utility of prayer, he more and more applied himself, in his long mental prayer, to making petitions.

As a young swallow, so will I cry, said the devout king Hezekias.[2] The young of the swallow does nothing but cry to its mother for help and for food; so should we all do, if we would preserve our life of grace. We should be always crying to God for aid to avoid the death of sin, and to advance in his holy love. Father Rodriguez relates, that the ancient Fathers, who were our first in-

---

[1] " Tunc magis diabolus cogitationes curarum sæcularium ingerit, quando orantem aspexerit."—*Sent.* l. 3, c. 7.

[2] " Sicut pullus hirundinis, sic clamabo."—*Is.* xxxviii. 14.

structors in the spiritual life, held a conference to determine which was the exercise most useful and most necessary for eternal salvation; and that they determined it was to repeat over and over again the short prayer of David, *Incline unto my aid, O God!* [1] "This," says Cassian, "is what every one ought to do who wishes to be saved: he ought to be always saying, My God, help me! my God, help me!" We ought to do this the first thing when we awake in the morning; and then to continue doing it in all our needs, and when attending to our business, whether spiritual or temporal; and most especially when we find ourselves troubled by any temptation or passion. St. Bonaventure says, that at times we obtain a grace by a short prayer sooner than by many other good works: "Sometimes a man can sooner obtain by a short prayer what he would be a long time obtaining by pious works." [2] St. Ambrose says, that he who prays, while he is praying obtains what he asks, because the very act of prayer is the same as receiving: "He who asks of God, while he asks receives; for to ask is to receive." [3] Hence St. Chrysostom wrote, that "there is nothing more powerful than a man who prays," [4] because such a one is made partaker of the power of God. To arrive at perfection, says St. Bernard, we must meditate and pray: by meditation we see what we want; by prayer we receive what we want. "Let us mount by meditation and prayer: the one teaches what is deficient, the other obtains that there should be nothing deficient." [5]

[1] "Deus, in adjutorium meum intende."—*Ps.* lxix. 2.

[2] "Quandoque citius brevi oratione aliquis obtinet, quod piis operibus vix obtineret."—*De Prof. rel.* l. 2, c. 65.

[3] "Qui petit a Deo, dum petit, accipit; ipsum namque petere est accipere."

[4] "Nihil potentius homine probo orante."—*In Matt. hom.* 58.

[5] "Ascendamus meditatione et oratione; illa docet quid desit, hæc ne desit obtinet."—*De S. And.* s. 1.

CONCLUSION OF THE CHAPTER.

In conclusion, to save one's soul without prayer is most difficult, and even (as we have seen) impossible, according to the ordinary course of God's Providence. But by praying our salvation is made secure, and very easy. It is not necessary in order to save our souls to go among the heathen, and give up our life. It is not necessary to retire into the desert, and eat nothing but herbs. What does it cost us to say, My God, help me! Lord, assist me! have mercy on me! Is there anything more easy than this? and this little will suffice to save us, if we will be diligent in doing it. St. Laurence Justinian specially exhorts us to oblige ourselves to say a prayer at least when we begin any action: " We must endeavor to offer a prayer at least in the beginning of every work." [1] Cassian attests that the principal advice of the ancient Fathers was to have recourse to God with short but frequent prayers. Let no one, says St. Bernard, think lightly of prayer, because God values it, and then gives us either what we ask, or what is still more useful to us: " Let no one undervalue his prayer, for God does not undervalue it . . . . he will give either what we ask, or what he knows to be better." [2] And let us understand, that if we do not pray, we have no excuse, because the grace of prayer is given to every one. It is in our power to pray whenever we will, as David says of himself: *With me is prayer to the God of my life; I will say to God, Thou art my support.* [3] On this point I shall speak at length in

---

[1] " Innitendum est ut in primordio saltem cujusque operis dirigatur oratio."—*Lign. vitæ de or.* c. 6.

[2] " Nemo parvipendat orationem suam quia Deus non parvipendit eam . . . aut dabit quod petimus, aut quod noverit esse utilius."—*De Quad.* s. 5.

[3] " Apud me oratio Deo vitæ meæ; dicam Deo: susceptor meus es."—*Ps.* xli. 9.

the second part, where I will make it quite clear that God gives to all the grace of prayer, in order that thereby they may obtain every help, and even more than they need, for keeping the divine law, and for persevering till death. At present, I will only say, that if we are not saved, the whole fault will be ours; and we shall have our own failure to answer for, because we did not pray.

CHAPTER III.

THE CONDITIONS OF PRAYER.

I.

Which are the Requisite Conditions.

OBJECT OF PRAYER.

Amen, amen, I say to you, if you ask the Father anything in My name, He will give it you.[1] Jesus Christ then has promised, that whatever we ask his Father in his name, his Father will give us. But always with the understanding that we ask under the proper conditions. Many seek, says St. James, and obtain not, because they seek improperly: *Ye ask and receive not, because ye ask amiss.*[2] So St. Basil, following out the argument of the Apostle, says, " You sometimes ask and receive not, because you have asked badly; either without faith, or you have requested things not fit for you, or you have not persevered;"[3] " faithlessly," that is, with little faith, or little confidence; "lightly," with little desire of the grace you ask; "things not fit for you," when you seek good things that will not be conducive to your salvation; or you have left off praying, without perseverance. Hence St. Thomas reduces to four the conditions required in prayer, in order that it may produce its effect:

---

[1] " Amen, amen dico vobis: si quid petieritis Patrem in nomine meo, dabit vobis."—*John*, xvi. 23.

[2] " Petitis, et non accipitis, eo quod male petatis."—*James*, iv. 3.

[3] " Ideo, quandoque petis, et non accipis, quia perperam postulasti, vel infideliter, vel leviter, vel non conferentia tibi, vel destitisti."—*Const. Mon.* c. I.

these are, that a man asks (1) *for himself;* (2) *things neces-sary for salvation;* (3) *piously;* and (4) *with perseverance.*[1]

CAN WE PRAY EFFICACIOUSLY FOR OTHERS?

The first condition then of prayer is, that you make it *for yourself;* because St. Thomas holds, that one man cannot *ex condigno* (*i. e.* in the fitness of things) obtain for another eternal life; nor, consequently, even those graces which are requisite for his salvation. Since, as he says, the promise is made not to others, but only to those that pray: "He shall give to you." Nevertheless, there are many theologians, Cornelius à Lapide, Sylvester, Tolet, Habert, and others, who hold the opposite doctrine, on the authority of St. Basil, who teaches that prayer, by virtue of God's promise, is infallibly efficacious, even for those for whom we pray, provided they put no positive impediment in the way. And they support their doc-trine by Scripture: *Pray one for another, that you may be saved; for the continual prayer of the just man availeth much.*[2] *Pray for them that persecute and calumniate you.*[3] And bet-ter still, on the text of St. John: *He that knoweth his brother to sin a sin which is not to death, let him ask, and life shall be given to him who sinneth not unto death. There is a sin unto death; for that I say not that any man ask.*[4] St. Am-brose, St. Augustine, the Ven. Bede, and others,[5] explain the words "who sinneth not unto death" to mean, pro-vided the sinner is not one who intends to remain ob-stinate till death; since for such a one a very extraordin-

---

[1] "Pro se, necessaria ad salutem, pie, et perseveranter."—2. 2. q. 83, a. 15.

[2] "Et orate pro invicem, ut salvemini: multum enim valet depre-catio justi assidua."—*James,* v. 16.

[3] "Orate pro persequentibus et calumniantibus vos."—*Luke,* vi. 28.

[4] "Qui scit fratrem suum peccare peccatum non ad mortem, petat, et dabitur ei vita peccanti non ad mortem."—1 *John,* v. 16.

[5] *Apud Calm. in loc. cit.*

ary grace would be required. But for other sinners, who are not guilty of such malice, the Apostle promises their conversion to him who prays for them: *Let him ask, and life shall be given him for him that sinneth.*

WE OUGHT TO PRAY FOR SINNERS.

Besides, it is quite certain that the prayers of others are of great use to sinners, and are very pleasing to God; and God complains of his servants who do not recommend sinners to him, as he once complained to St. Mary Magdalene of Pazzi, to whom he said one day: " See, my daughter, how the Christians are in the devil's hands; if my elect did not deliver them by their prayers they would be devoured." But God especially requires this of priests and religious. The same saint used to say to her nuns: " My sisters, God has not separated us from the world, that we should only do good for ourselves, but also that we should appease him in behalf of sinners; " and God one day said to her, " I have given to you my chosen spouses the City of Refuge (i.e., the Passion of Jesus Christ), that you may have a place where you may obtain help for my creatures. Therefore have recourse to it, and thence stretch forth a helping hand to my creatures who are perishing, and lay down your lives for them." For this reason the saint, inflamed with holy zeal, used to offer God the blood of the Redeemer fifty times a day in behalf of sinners, and was quite wasted away for the desire she had for their conversion. Oh, she used to say, what pain is it, O Lord, to see how one could help Thy creatures by giving one's life for them, and not be able to do so! For the rest, in every exercise she recommended sinners to God; and it is written in her life, that she scarcely passed an hour in the day without praying for them. Frequently, too, she arose in the middle of the night, and went to the Blessed Sacrament to pray for them; and yet for all this, when she was once found bathed in tears, on being asked the cause, she answered, " Because I seem to myself to do nothing for the salvation of sinners." She went so far as to offer to endure even the pains of hell for their conversion, pro-vided that in that place she might still love God; and often God gratified her by inflicting on her grievous pains and infirmities for the salvation of sinners. She prayed especially for priests, seeing that their good life was the occasion of salvation to others, while their bad life was the cause of ruin to many; and therefore she prayed God to visit their faults upon her, saying, " Lord, make me die and return to life again as many times as is neces-sary to satisfy Thy justice for them!" And it is related in her life, that the saint, by her prayers, did indeed re-lease many souls from the hands of Lucifer.

I wished to speak rather particularly of the zeal of this saint; but, indeed, no souls that really love God neglect to pray for poor sinners. For how is it possible for a person who loves God, and knows what love he has for our souls, and what Jesus Christ has done and suffered for their salvation, and how our Saviour desires us to pray for sinners,—how is it possible, I say, that he should be able to look with indifference on the numbers of poor souls who are living without God, and are slaves of hell, without being moved to importune God with frequent prayers to give light and strength to these wretched be-ings, so that they may come out from the miserable state of living death in which they are slumbering? True it is that God has not promised to grant our requests, when those for whom we pray put a positive impediment in the way of their conversion; but still, God of his goodness has often deigned, at the prayer of his servants, to bring back the most blinded and obstinate sinners to a state of salvation, by means of extraordinary graces. Therefore let us never omit, when we say or hear Mass, when we receive Holy Communion, when we make our meditation or our visit to the Blessed Sacrament, to recommend poor sinners to God. And a learned author says, that he who prays for others will find that his prayers for himself are heard much sooner. But this is a digression. Let us now return to the examination of the other conditions that St. Thomas lays down as necessary to the efficacy of prayer.

WE MUST ASK FOR GRACES NECESSARY TO SALVATION.

The second condition assigned by the saint is, that we ask those favors which are necessary to salvation ; because the promise annexed to prayer was not made with reference to temporal favors, which are not necessary for the salvation of the soul. St. Augustine, explaining the words of the Gospel, "whatever ye shall ask in my name," says, that "nothing which is asked in a way detrimental to salvation is asked in the name of the Saviour."[1] Sometimes, says the same Father, we seek some temporal favors, and God does not hear us ; but he does not hear us because he loves us, and wishes to be merciful to us. "A man may pray faithfully for the necessities of this life, and God may mercifully refuse to hear him ; because the physician knows better than the patient what is good for the sick man."[2] The physician who loves his patient will not allow him to have those things that he sees would do him harm. Oh, how many, if they had been sick or poor, would have escaped those sins which they commit in health and in affluence! And, therefore, when men ask God for health or riches, he of-

---

[1] "Non petitur in nomine Salvatoris, quidquid petitur contra rationem salutis."—*In Jo. tr.* 102.

[2] "Fideliter supplicans Deo pro necessitatibus hujus vitæ, et misericorditer auditur, et misericorditer non auditur; quid enim infirmo sit utile, magis novit medicus quam ægrotus."—*Ap. s. Prosp. Sent.* 212.

ten denies them because he loves them, knowing that
these things would be to them an occasion of losing his
grace, or at any rate of growing tepid in the spiritual
life. Not that we mean to say that it is any defect to
pray to God for the necessaries of this present life, so
far as they are not inconsistent with our eternal salvation, as the Wise man said: *Give me only the necessaries of
life.*[1] Nor is it a defect, says St. Thomas,[2] to have anxiety about such goods, if it is not inordinate. The defect
consists in desiring and seeking these temporal goods,
and in having an inordinate anxiety about them, as
if they were our highest good. Therefore, when we ask
of God these temporal favors, we ought always to ask
them with resignation, and with the condition, if they
will be useful to our souls; and when we see that God
does not grant them, let us be certain that he then denies them to us for the love he bears us, and because he
sees that they would be injurious to the salvation of our
souls.

It often happens that we pray God to deliver us from
some dangerous temptation, and yet that God does not
hear us, but permits the temptation to continue troubling
us. In such a case, let us understand that God permits
even this for our greater good. It is not temptation or
bad thoughts that separate us from God, but our consent to the evil. When a soul in temptation recommends
itself to God, and by his aid resists, oh, how it then advances in perfection, and unites itself more closely to
God! and this is the reason why God does not hear it.
St. Paul prayed instantly to be delivered from the temptation of impurity: *There was given me a sting of my flesh
an angel of Satan to buffet me; for which thing thrice I be-*

[1] " Tribue tantum victui meo necessaria."—*Prov.* xxx. 8.
[2] 2. 2. q. 83, a. 6.

sought the Lord, that it might depart from me.[1] But God answered him, that it was enough to have his grace: *My grace is sufficient for thee.*[2] So that even in temptations we ought to pray with resignation, saying, Lord, deliver me from this trouble, if it is expedient to deliver me; and if not, at least give me help to resist. And here comes in what St. Bernard says, that when we beg any grace of God, he gives us either that which we ask, or some other thing more useful to us. He often leaves us to be buffeted by the waves, in order to try our faithfulness, and for our greater profit. It seems then that he is deaf to our prayers. But no; let us be sure that God then really hears us, and secretly aids us, and strengthens us by his grace to resist all the assaults of our enemies. See how he himself assures us of this by the mouth of the Psalmist: *Thou calledst upon me in affliction, and I delivered thee: I heard thee in the secret place of tempest; I proved thee at the waters of contradiction.*[3]

OTHER CONDITIONS OF PRAYER.

The other conditions assigned by St. Thomas to prayer are, that it is to be made piously and perseveringly; by piously, he means with humility and confidence—by perseveringly, continuing to pray until death. We must now speak distinctly of each of these three conditions, which are the most necessary for prayer, namely of humility, confidence, and perseverance.

[1] "Datus est mihi stimulus carnis meæ, angelus satanæ, qui me colaphizet; propter quod ter Dominum rogavi ut discederet a me."—2 *Cor.* xii. 7.

[2] "Sufficit tibi gratia mea."

[3] "In tribulatione invocasti me, et liberavi te; exaudivi te in abscondito tempestatis; probavi te apud aquam contradictionis."—*Ps.* lxxx. 8.

II.

The Humility with which we should Pray.

The Lord does indeed regard the prayers of his servants, but only of his servants who are humble. *He hath
had regard to the prayer of the humble.*[1] Others he does not
regard, but rejects them: *God resisteth the proud, and giveth
grace to the humble.*[2] He does not hear the prayers of the
proud who trust in their own strength; but for that reason leaves them to their own feebleness; and in this state
deprived of God's aid, they must certainly perish. David
had to bewail this case: *Before I was humbled I offended.*[3]
I sinned because I was not humble. The same thing
happened to St. Peter, who, though he was warned by
our Lord that all the disciples would abandon Him on
that night—*All you shall be scandalised in Me this night*[4]—
nevertheless, instead of acknowledging his own weakness, and begging our Lord's aid against his unfaithful-
ness, was too confident in his own strength, and said,
that though all should abandon him he would never
leave him: *Although all shall be scandalised in Thee, I will
never be scandalised.*[5] And although our Saviour again
foretold to him, in a special manner, that in that very
night, before the cock-crow, he should deny him three
times; yet, trusting in his own courage, he boasted, saying, *Yea, though I should die with Thee, I will not deny
Thee.*[6] But what came of it? Scarcely had the unhappy
man entered the house of the high priest, when he was
accused of being a disciple of Jesus Christ, and three

---

[1] " Respexit in orationem humilium."—*Ps.* ci. 18.

[2] " Deus superbis resistit."—*James* iv. 6.

[3] " Priusquam humiliarer, ego deliqui."—*Ps.* cxviii. 67.

[4] " Omnes vos scandalum patiemini in me in ista nocte."—*Matt.*
xxvi. 31.

[5] " Etsi omnes scandalizati fuerint in te, ego nunquam scandali-
zabor."

[6] " Etiamsi oportuerit me mori tecum, non te negabo."

times did he deny with an oath that he had ever known him: *And again he denied with an oath, that I know not the Man.*[1] If Peter had humbled himself, and had asked our Lord for the grace of constancy, he would not have denied him.

We ought all to feel that we are standing on the edge of a precipice, suspended over the abyss of all sins, and supported only by the thread of God's grace. If this thread fails us, we shall certainly fall into the gulf, and shall commit the most horrible wickedness. *Unless the Lord had been my helper, my soul had almost dwelt in hell.*[2] If God had not succored me, I should have fallen into a thousand sins, and now I should be in hell. So said the Psalmist, and so ought each of us to say. This is what St. Francis of Assisi meant, when he said that he was the worst sinner in the world. But, my Father, said his companion, what you say is not true; there are many in the world who are certainly worse than you are. Yes, what I say is but too true, answered St. Francis; because if God did not keep his hand over me, I should commit every possible sin.

It is of **faith**, that without the aid of grace we cannot do any **good** work, nor even think a good thought. "Without grace men do no good whatever, either in thought or in deed," says St. Augustine.[3] As the eye cannot see without light, so, say the holy Father, man can do no good without grace. The Apostle had said the same thing before him: *Not that we are sufficient to think anything of ourselves, as of ourselves; but our sufficiency is of God.*[4] And David had said it before St. Paul: *Un-*

---

[1] "Et iterum negavit cum juramento: Quia non novi hominem."

[2] "Nisi quia Dominus adjuvit me, paulo minus habitasset in inferno anima mea."—*Ps.* xciii. 17.

[3] "Sine gratia, nullum prorsus, sive cogitando, sive agendo, faciunt homines bonum."—*De Corr. et Gr.* c. 2.

[4] "Non quod sufficientes simus cogitare aliquid a nobis, quasi **ex** nobis; sed sufficientia nostra ex Deo est."—2 *Cor.* iii. 5.

less the Lord build the house, they labor in vain that build it.[1]
In vain does man weary himself to become a saint, unless
God lends a helping hand: *Unless the Lord keep the city, he
watcheth in vain that keepeth it.*[2]   If God did not preserve
the soul from sins, in vain will it try to preserve itself by
its own strength: and therefore did the holy prophet protest, *I will not trust in my bow.*[3]   I will not hope in my
arms; but only in God, who alone can save me.

Hence, whoever finds that he has done any good, and
does not find that he has fallen into greater sins than
those which are commonly committed, let him say with
St. Paul, *By the grace of God I am what I am ;*[4] and for
the same reason, he ought never to cease to be afraid of
falling on every occasion of sin: *Wherefore, he that thinketh
himself to stand, let him take heed lest he fall.*[5]   St. Paul
wishes to warn us that he who feels secure of not falling,
is in great danger of falling; and he assigns the reason
in another place, where he says, *If any man think himself
to be something, whereas he is nothing, he deceiveth himself.*[6]
So that St. Augustine wrote wisely, "the presumption of
stability renders many unstable; no one will be so firm
as he who feels himself infirm."[7]   If a man says he has
no fear, it is a sign that he trusts in himself, and in his
good resolutions; but such a man, with his mischievous
confidence, deceives himself, because, through trust in
his own strength, he neglects to fear; and through not

---

[1] "Nisi Dominus ædificaverit domum, in vanum laboraverunt qui
ædificant eam."—*Ps.* cxxvi. 1.

[2] "Nisi Dominus custodierit civitatem, frustra vigilat qui custodit
eam."—*Ibid.*

[3] "Non enim in arcu meo sperabo."—*Ps.* xliii. 7.

[4] "Gratia autem Dei sum id quod sum."—1 *Cor.* xv. 10.

[5] "Itaque, qui se existimat stare, videat ne cadat."—1 *Cor.* x. 12.

[6] "Nam, si quis existimat se aliquid esse, cum nihil sit, ipse se
seducit."—*Gal.* vi. 3.

[7] "Multos impedit a firmitate præsumptio firmitatis; nemo erit a
Deo firmus, nisi qui se a seipso sentit infirmum."—*Serm.* 76 *E. B.*

fearing he neglects to recommend himself to God, and then he will certainly fall. And so, for like reasons, we should all abstain from noticing with any vain-glory the sins of other people; but rather we should then esteem ourselves as worse in ourselves than they are, and should say, Lord, if thou hadst not helped me, I should have done worse. Otherwise, to punish us for our pride, God will permit us to fall into worse and more shameful sins. For this cause St. Paul instructs us to labor for our salvation; but how? always in fear and trembling: *With fear and trembling work out your salvation.*[1] Yes; for he who has a great fear of falling, distrusts his own strength, and therefore places his confidence in God, and will have recourse to him in dangers; and God will aid him, and so he will vanquish his temptations, and will be saved. St. Philip Neri, walking one day through Rome, kept saying, "I am in despair!" A certain religious rebuked him, and the saint thereupon said, "My father, I am in despair for myself; but I trust in God." So must we do, if we would be saved; we must always live in despair of doing anything by our own strength; and in so doing we shall imitate St. Philip, who used to say to God the first moment he woke in the morning, "Lord, keep Thy hands over Philip this day; for if not, Philip will betray Thee."

This, then, we may conclude with St. Augustine, is all the grand science of a Christian,—to know that he is nothing, and can do nothing. "This is the whole of the great science, to know that man is nothing."[2] For then he will never neglect to furnish himself, by prayer to God, with that strength which he has not of himself, and which he needs in order to resist temptation, and to do good; and so, with the help of God, who never refuses anything to the man who prays to him in humility, he

[1] "Cum metu et tremore vestram salutem operamini."—*Phil.* ii. 12.
[2] "Hæc est tota scientia magna, scire quia homo nihil est."—*In Ps.* lxx. s. 1.

will be able to do all things: *The prayer of him that hum-
bleth himself shall pierce the clouds, and he will not depart
until the Most High behold.*[1] The prayer of an humble
soul penetrates the heavens, and presents itself before
the throne of God; and departs not without God's looking on it and hearing it. And though the soul be guilty
of any amount of sin, God never despises a heart that
humbles itself: *A contrite and humble heart, O God, Thou
wilt not despise ;*[2] *God resisteth the proud, but giveth grace to
the humble.*[3] As the Lord is severe with the proud, and
resists their prayers, so is he kind and liberal to the
humble. This is precisely what Jesus Christ said one
day to St. Catharine of Sienna: "Know, my daughter,
that a soul that perseveres in humble prayer gains every
virtue."[4]

It will be of use to introduce here the advice which the
learned and pious Palafox, Bishop of Osma, gives to
spiritual persons who desire to become saints. It occurs
in a note to the 18th letter of St. Teresa, which she
wrote to her confessor, to give him an account of all the
grades of supernatural prayer with which God had favored her. On this the bishop writes, that these supernatural graces which God designed to grant to St.
Teresa, as he has also done to other saints, are not
necessary in order to arrive at sanctity, since many souls
have become saints without them; and, on the other
hand, many have arrived at sanctity, and yet have, after
all, been damned. Therefore he says it is superfluous,
and even presumptuous, to desire and to ask for these

---

[1] "Oratio humiliantis se nubes penetrabit, . . . et non discedet
donec Altissimus aspiciat."—*Ecclus.* xxxv. 21.

[2] "Cor contritum et humiliatum, Deus, non despicies."—*Ps.* l. 19.

[3] "Deus superbis resistit, humilibus autem dat gratiam."—*James*
iv. 6.

[4] "Scito, filia, quod anima perseverans in humili oratione adipisci-
tur omnem virtutem."—*Ap. Blos. in Concl.* p. 2, c. 3.

supernatural gifts, when the true and only way to become a saint is, to exercise ourselves in virtue and in the love of God; and this is done by means of prayer, and by corresponding to the inspirations and assistance of God, who wishes nothing so much as to see us saints. *For this is the will of God, your sanctification.*[1]

Hence Bishop Palafox, speaking of the grades of supernatural prayer mentioned in St. Teresa's letter, namely, the prayer of quiet, the sleep or suspension of the faculties, the prayer of union, ecstasy or rapture, flight and impulse of the spirit, and the wound of love, says, very wisely, that as regards the *prayer of quiet*, what we ought to ask of God is that he would free us from attachment to worldly goods, and the desire of them, which give no peace, but bring disquiet and affliction to the soul: *Vanity of vanities*, as Solomon well called them, *and vexation of spirit.*[2] The heart of man will never find true peace, if it does not empty itself of all that is not God, so as to leave itself all free for his love, that he alone may possess the whole of it. But this the soul cannot do of itself; it must obtain it of God by repeated prayers. As regards *the sleep and suspension of the faculties*, we ought to ask God for grace to keep them asleep for all that is temporal, and only awake them to consider God's goodness, and to set our hearts upon his love and eternal happiness. As regards the *union of the faculties*, let us pray him to give us grace not to think, nor to seek, nor to wish anything but what God wills; since all sanctity and the perfection of love consists in uniting our will to the will of God. As regards *ecstasy and rapture*, let us pray God to draw us away from the inordinate love of ourselves and of creatures, and to draw us entirely to himself. As regards *the flight of the spirit*, let us pray him to give us grace to live altogether detached

---

[1] " Hæc est enim voluntas Dei, sanctificatio vestra."—1 *Thess.* iv. 3.
[2] "Universa vanitas et afflictio spiritus."—*Eccles.* i. 14.

from this world, and to do as the swallows, that do not settle on the ground even to feed, but take their food flying;—so should we use our temporal goods for all that is necessary for the support of life, but always flying, without settling on the ground to look for earthly pleasures. As regards *impulse of spirit*, let us pray him to give us courage and strength to do violence to ourselves, whenever it is necessary, for resisting the assaults of our enemies, for conquering our passions, and for accepting sufferings even in the midst of desolation and dryness of spirit. Finally, as regards *the wound of love*, as a wound by its pain perpetually renews the remembrance of what we suffer, so ought we to pray God to wound our hearts with his holy love in such a way that we shall always be reminded of his goodness and the love which he has borne us; and thus we should live in continual love of him, and should be always pleasing him with our works and our affections. But none of these graces can be obtained without prayer; and with prayer, provided it be humble, confident, and persevering, everything is obtained.

III.

The Confidence with which we ought to pray.

EXCELLENCE AND NECESSITY OF THIS VIRTUE.

The principal instruction that St. James gives us, if we wish by prayer to obtain grace from God, is, that we pray with a confidence that feels sure of being heard, and without hesitating: *Let him ask in faith, nothing wavering.*[1] St. Thomas teaches that as prayer receives its power of meriting from charity, so, on the other hand, it receives from faith and confidence its power of being efficacious to obtain: " Prayer has its power of meriting from charity, but its efficacity of obtaining from faith

---

[1] " Postulet autem in fide, nihil hæsitans."—*James.* i. 6.

and confidence." [1] St. Bernard teaches the same, saying that it is our confidence alone which obtains for us the divine mercies: "Hope alone obtains a place of mercy with Thee, O Lord." [2] God is much pleased with our confidence in his mercy, because we then honor and exalt that infinite goodness which it was his object in creating us to manifest to the world: *Let all those, O my God,* says the royal prophet, *who hope in Thee be glad, for they shall be eternally happy, and Thou shalt dwell in them.* [3] God protects and saves all those who confide in him: *He is the Protector of all that hope in Him.* [4] *Thou who savest them that trust in Thee.* [5] Oh, the great promises that are recorded in the Scriptures to all those who hope in God! He who hopes in God will not fall into sin: *None of them that trust in Him shall offend.* [6] Yes, says David, because God has his eyes turned to all those who confide in his goodness to deliver them by his aid from the death of sin. *Behold, the eyes of the Lord are on them that fear Him, and on them that hope for His mercy to deliver their souls from death.* [7] And in another place God himself says: *Because he hoped in me I will deliver him ; I will protect him ; I will deliver him and I will glorify him.* [8] Mark the word " be-

---

[1] "Quantum ad efficaciam merendi, oratio innititur principaliter charitati ; quantum ad efficaciam impetrandi, innititur principaliter fidei."—2. 2. q. 83, a. 15.

[2] "Sola spes apud te (Domine) miserationis obtinet locum."—*De Annunt.* s. 3.

[3] "Lætentur omnes qui sperant in te ; in æternum exsultabunt, et habitabis in eis."—*Ps.* v. 12.

[4] "Protector est omnium sperantium in se."—*Ps.* xvii. 31.

[5] "Qui salvos facis sperantes in te."—*Ps.* xvi. 7.

[6] "Non delinquent omnes qui sperant in eo."—*Ps.* xxxiii. 23.

[7] "Ecce oculi Domini super metuentes eum, et in eis qui sperant super misericordia ejus, ut eruat a morte animas eorum."—*Ps.* xxxii. 18.

[8] "Quoniam in me speravit, liberabo eum, protegam eum, ... eripiam eum, et glorificabo eum."—*Ps.* xc. 14.

cause." *Because* he confided in Me, I will protect, I will deliver him from his enemies, and from the danger of falling; and finally I will give him eternal glory. Isaias says of those who place their hope in God: *They that hope in the Lord shall renew their strength; they shall take wings as the eagles; they shall run and not be weary: they shall walk and not faint.*[1] They shall cease to be weak as they are now, and shall gain in God a great strength; they shall not faint; they shall not even feel weary in walking the way of salvation, but they shall run and fly as eagles; *in silence and in hope shall your strength be.*[2] All our strength, the prophet tells us, consists in placing all our confidence in God, and in being silent; that is, in reposing in the arms of his mercy, without trusting to our own efforts, or to human means.

And when did it ever happen that a man had confidence in God and was lost? *No one hath hoped in the Lord and hath been confounded.*[3] It was this confidence that assured David that he should not perish: *In Thee, O Lord, have I trusted; I shall not be confounded forever.*[4] Perhaps, then, says St. Augustine, God could be a deceiver, who offers to support us in dangers if we lean upon him, and would then withdraw himself if we had recourse to him? "God is not a deceiver, that he should offer to support us, and then when we lean upon him should slip away from us."[5] David calls the man happy who trusts in God: *Blessed is the man that trusteth in*

---

[1] "Qui autem sperant in Domino, mutabunt fortitudinem, assument pennas sicut aquilæ, current et non laborabunt, ambulabunt et non deficient."—*Is.* xl. 31.

[2] "In silentio et in spe erit fortitudo vestra."—*Is.* xxx. 15.

[3] "Nullus speravit in Domino, et confusus est."—*Ecclus.* ii. 11.

[4] "In te, Domine, speravi; non confundar in æternum."—*Ps.* xxx. 2.

[5] "Non est illusor Deus, ut se ad supportandum nos offerat, et nobis innitentibus ei se subtrahat."—*S. Thomas. Erud. Princ.* l. 2. c. 5.

Thee.[1] And why? because, says he, he who trusts in God will always find himself surrounded by God's mercy. *Mercy shall encompass him that hopeth in the Lord.*[2] So that he shall be surrounded and guarded by God on every side in such a way that he shall be prevented from losing his soul.

It is for this cause that the Apostle recommends us so earnestly to preserve our confidence in God; for (he tells us) it will certainly obtain from him a great remuneration: *Do not therefore lose your confidence, which hath a great reward.*[3] As is our confidence, so shall be the graces we receive from God: if our confidence is great, great too will be the graces: "Great faith merits great things."[4] St. Bernard writes that the divine mercy is an inexhaustible fountain, and that he who brings to it the largest vessel of confidence shall take from it the largest measure of gifts: "Neither, O Lord, dost Thou put the oil of thy mercy into any other vessel than that of confidence."[5] The Prophet had long before expressed the same thought: *Let thy mercy, O Lord, be upon us* (*i.e.*, in proportion) *as we have hoped in Thee.*[6] This was well exemplified in the centurion to whom our Saviour said, in praise of his confidence, *Go, and as thou hast believed, so be it done unto thee.*[7] And our Lord revealed to St. Gertrude that he who prays with confidence does him in a manner such violence that he cannot

---

[1] "Beatus homo qui sperat in te."—*Ps.* lxxxiii. 13.

[2] "Sperantem autem in Domino misericordia circumdabit."—*Ps.* xxxi. 10.

[3] "Nolite itaque amittere confidentiam vestram, quæ magnam habet remunerationem."—*Hebr.* x. 35.

[4] "Magna fides, magna meretur."—*In Cant.* s. 32.

[5] "Nec oleum misericordiæ nisi in vasa fiduciæ (Domine) ponis."—*De Annunt.* s. 3.

[6] "Fiat misericordia tua, Domine, super nos, quemadmodum speravimus in te."—*Ps.* xxxii. 22.

[7] "Vade, et sicut credidisti, fiat tibi."—*Matt.* viii. 12.

but hear him in everything he asks: " Prayer," says St. John Climacus, " does a pious violence to God." It does him a violence, but a violence which he likes, and which pleases him.

Let us go, therefore, according to the admonition of St. Paul, *with confidence to the throne of grace, that we may obtain mercy, and find grace in seasonable aid.*" [1] The throne of grace is Jesus Christ, who is now sitting on the right hand of the Father; not on the throne of justice, but of grace, to obtain pardon for us if we fall into sin, and help to enable us to persevere if we are enjoying his friendship. To this throne we must always have recourse with confidence; that is to say, with that trust which springs from faith in the goodness and truth of God, who has promised to hear him who prays to him with confidence, but with a confidence that is both sure and stable. On the other hand, says St. James, let not the man who prays with hesitation think that he will receive anything: " *For he who wavereth is like a wave of the sea, which is moved and carried about by the wind. Therefore let not that man think to receive anything of the Lord.*[2] He will receive nothing, because the diffidence which agitates him is unjust towards God, and will hinder his mercy from listening to his prayers: " Thou hast not asked rightly, because thou hast asked doubtingly," says St. Basil; " thou hast not received grace, because thou hast asked it without confidence."[3] David says that our confidence in God ought to be as firm as a mountain, which is not moved by each gust of wind. *They who trust in the Lord are as Mount*

---

[1] " Adeamus ergo cum fiducia ad thronum gratiæ, ut misericordiam consequamur, et gratiam inveniamus in auxilio opportuno."—*Hebr.* iv. 16.

[2] " Qui enim dubitat, similis est fluctui maris, qui a vento movetur et circumfertur; non ergo æstimet homo ille quod accipiat aliquid a Domino."—*James,* i. 6.

[3] " Non recte petisti, quia dubitabundus petisti."—*Const. mon.* c. 2.

Sion ; he shall not be moved forever.[1] And it is this that our Lord recommends to us, if we wish to obtain the graces which we ask: *Whatsoever you ask when you pray, believe that you shall receive, and they shall come unto you.*[2] Whatever grace you require, be sure of having it, and so you shall obtain it.

FOUNDATION OF OUR CONFIDENCE.

But on what, a man will say, am I, a miserable sinner, to found this certain confidence of obtaining what I ask? On what? On the promise made by Jesus Christ: *Ask, and you shall receive.*[3] "Who will fear to be deceived, when the truth promises?" says St. Augustine.[4] How can we doubt that we shall be heard, when God, who is truth itself, promises to give us that which we ask of him in prayer? "We should not be exhorted to ask," says the same Father, "unless he meant to give."[5] Certainly God would not have exhorted us to ask him for favors, if he had not determined to grant them; but this is the very thing to which he exhorts us so strongly, and which is repeated so often in the Scriptures—pray, ask, seek, and you shall obtain what you desire: *Whatever you will, seek and it shall be done to you.*[6] And in order that we may pray to him with due confidence, our Saviour has taught us, in the "Our Father," that when we have recourse to him for the graces necessary to salvation (all of which are included in the petitions of the Lord's Prayer) we should call him, not Lord, but Father—" Our

---

[1] "Qui confidunt in Domino, sicut mons Sion."—*Ps.* cxxiv. 1.

[2] "Quæcumque orantes petitis, credite quia accipietis, et evenient vobis."—*Mark*, xi. 24.

[3] "Petite, et accipietis."—*John*, xvi. 24.

[4] "Quis falli timeat, cum promittit Veritas?"—*Conf.* l. 12, c. 1.

[5] "Non nos tantum hortaretur ut peteremus, nisi dare vellet."—*Serm.* 105, *E. B.*

[6] "Quodcumque volueritis, petetis, et fiet vobis."—*John*, xv. 7.

Father"—because it is his will that we should ask God for grace with the same confidence with which a son, when in want or sick, asks food or medicine from his own father. If a son is dying of hunger, he has only to make his case known to his father, and his father will forthwith provide him with food; and if he has received a bite from a venomous serpent, he has only to show his father the wound, and the father will immediately apply whatever remedy he has.

Trusting, therefore, in God's promises, let us always pray with confidence; not vacillating, but stable and firm, as the Apostle says: *Let us hold fast the confession of our hope without wavering; for He is faithful that hath promised.*[1] As it is perfectly certain that God is faithful in his promises, so ought our faith also to be perfectly certain that he will hear us when we pray. And although sometimes, when we are in a state of aridity, or disturbed by some fault we have committed, we perhaps do not feel while praying that sensible confidence which we would wish to experience, yet, for all this, let us force ourselves to pray, and to pray without ceasing; for God will not neglect to hear us. Nay, rather he will hear us more readily; because we shall then pray with more distrust of ourselves; and confiding only in the goodness and faithfulness of God, who has promised to hear the man who prays to him. Oh, how God is pleased in the time of our tribulations, of our fears, and of our temptations, to see us hope against hope; that is, in spite of the feeling of diffidence which we then experience because of our desolation! This is that for which the Apostle praises the patriarch Abraham, *who against hope, believed in hope.*[2]

St. John says that he who reposes a sure trust in God

[1] "Teneamus spei nostræ confessionem indeclinabilem; fidelis enim est qui repromisit."—*Hebr.* x. 23.

[2] "Qui contra spem in spem credidit."—*Rom.* iv. 18.

certainly will become a saint: *And every one that hath this hope in Him sanctifieth himself, as he also is holy.*[1] For God gives abundant graces to them that trust in him. By this confidence the host of martyrs, of virgins, even of children, in spite of the dread of the torments which their persecutors prepared for them, overcame both their tortures and their persecutors. Sometimes, I say, we pray, but it seems to us that God will not hear us. Alas! let us not then neglect to persevere in prayer and in hope; let us then say, with Job, *Although He should kill me, I will trust in Him.*[2] O my God! though Thou hast driven me from Thy presence, I will not cease to pray, and to hope in Thy mercy. Let us do so, and we shall obtain what we want from God. So did the Canaanitish woman, and she obtained all that she wished from Jesus Christ. This woman had a daughter possessed by a devil, and prayed our Saviour to deliver her: *Have mercy on me, my daughter is grievously tormented by a devil.*[3] Our Lord answered her, that he was not sent for the Gentiles, of whom she was one, but for the Jews. She, however, did not lose heart, but renewed her prayer with confidence: Lord, Thou canst console me! Thou must console me: *Lord, help me!*[4] Jesus answered, But as to the bread of the children, it is not good to give it to the dogs: *It is not good to take the children's bread, and to cast it to the dogs.*[5] But, my Lord, she answered, even the dogs are allowed to have the fragments of bread which fall from the table: *Yea, Lord; for the whelps eat of the crumbs that fall from the tables of their masters.*[6] Then our Saviour, seeing the

[1] " Et omnis qui habet hanc spem in eo, sanctificat se, sicut et ille sanctus est."—1 *John,* iii. 3.

[2] "Etiam si occiderit me, in ipso sperabo."—*Job,* xiii. 15.

[3] " Miserere mei, Domine, Fili David: filia mea male a dæmonio vexatur."—*Matt.* xv. 22.

[4] " Domine, adjuva me."

[5] " Non est bonum sumere panem filiorum, et mittere canibus."

[6] " Et catelli edunt de micis."

great confidence of this woman, praised her, and did what she asked, saying: *O woman, great is thy faith; be it done to thee as thou wilt.*[1] For who, says Ecclesiasticus, has ever called on God for aid, and has been neglected and left unaided by him? *Or who hath called upon Him, and He hath despised him?*[2]

St. Augustine says that prayer is a key which opens heaven to us; the same moment in which our prayer ascends to God, the grace which we ask for descends to us: "The prayer of the just is the key of heaven; the petition ascends, and the mercy of God descends."[3] The royal prophet writes that our supplications and God's mercy are united together: *Blessed is God, who has not turned away my prayer, nor His mercy for me.*[4] And hence the same St. Augustine says that when we are praying to God, we ought to be certain that God is hearing us: "When you see that your prayer is not removed from you, be sure that his mercy is not removed from you."[5] And for myself, I speak the truth, I never feel greater consolation, nor a greater confidence of my salvation, than when I am praying to God, and recommending myself to him. And I think that the same thing happens to all other believers; for the other signs of our salvation are uncertain and unstable; but that God hears the man who prays to him with confidence is an infallible truth, as it is infallible that God cannot fail in his promises.

When we find ourselves weak, and unable to overcome any passion, or any great difficulty, so as to fulfil that

[1] "O mulier! magna est fides tua; fiat tibi sicut vis."

[2] "Quis invocavit eum, et despexit illum?"—*Ecclus.* ii. 12.

[3] "Oratio justi clavis est cœli: ascendit precatio, et descendit Dei miseratio."—*Serm.* 47, *E. B. app.*

[4] "Benedictus Deus, qui non amovit orationem meam et misericordiam suam a me."—*Ps.* lxv. 20.

[5] "Cum videris non a te amotam deprecationem tuam, securus esto quia non est a te amota misericordia ejus."—*In Ps.* lxv.

which God requires of us, let us take courage and say, with the Apostle, *I can do all things in Him, who strengtheneth me.*[1] Let us not say, as some do, I cannot; I distrust myself. With our own strength certainly we can do nothing; but with God's help we can do everything. If God said to any one, Take this mountain on your back, and carry it, for I am helping you, would not the man be a mistrustful fool if he answered, I will not take it; for I have not strength to carry it? And thus, when we know how miserable and weak we are, and when we find ourselves most encompassed with temptations, let us not lose heart; but let us lift up our eyes to God, and say, with David, *The Lord is my helper; and I will despise my enemies.*[2] With the help of my Lord, I shall overcome and laugh to scorn all the assaults of my foes. And when we find ourselves in danger of offending God, or in any other critical position, and are too confused to know what is best to be done, let us recommend ourselves to God, saying, *The Lord is my light and my salvation; whom shall I fear?*[3] And let us be sure that God will then certainly give us light, and will save us from every evil.

THE PRAYER OF SINNERS.

But I am a sinner, you will say; and in the Scriptures I read, *God heareth not sinners.*[4] St. Thomas answers (with St. Augustine) that this was said by the blind man, who, when he spoke, had not as yet been enlightened: "That is the word of a blind man not yet perfectly enlightened, and therefore it is not authoritative."[5]

---

[1] "Omnia possum in eo qui me confortat."—*Phil.* iv. 13.

[2] "Dominus mihi adjutor, et ego despiciam inimicos meos."—*Ps.* cxvii. 7.

[3] "Dominus illuminatio mea et salus mea, quem timebo?"—*Ps.* xxvi. 1.

[4] "Peccatores Deus non audit."—*John,* ix. 31.

[5] "Illud verbum est cœci nondum perfecte illuminati, et ideo non est ratum."—2. 2. q. 83, a. 16.

Though, adds St. Thomas, it is true of the petition which the sinner makes, "so far forth as he is a sinner;" that is, when he asks from a desire of continuing to sin; as, for instance, if he were to ask assistance to enable him to take revenge on his enemy, or to execute any other bad intention. The same holds good for the sinner who prays God to save him, but has no desire to quit the state of sin. There are some unhappy persons who love the chains with which the devil keeps them bound like slaves. The prayers of such men are not heard by God; because they are rash, presumptuous, and abominable. For what greater presumption can there be than for a man to ask favors of a prince whom he not only has often offended, but whom he intends to offend still more? And this is the meaning of the Holy Spirit, when he says that the prayer of him who turns away his ears so as not to hear what God commands is detestable and odious to God: *He who turneth away his ears from learning the law, his prayer shall be an abomination.*[1] To these people God says, It is of no use your praying to me, for I will turn My eyes from you, and will not hear you: *When you stretch forth your hands, I will turn away my eyes from you; and when you multiply prayer, I will not hear.*[2] Such, precisely, was the prayer of the impious King Antiochus, who prayed to God, and made great promises, but insincerely, and with a heart obstinate in sin; the sole object of his prayer being to escape the punishment that impended over him; therefore God did not hear his prayer, but caused him to die devoured by worms: *Then this wicked man prayed to the Lord, of whom he was not to obtain mercy.*[3]

[1] " Qui declinat aures suas ne audiat legem, oratio ejus erit execrabilis."—*Prov.* xxviii. 9.

[2] " Cum extenderitis manus vestras, avertam oculos meos a vobis; et cum multiplicaveritis orationem, non exaudiam."—*Is.* i. 15.

[3] "Orabat hic scelestus Dominum, a quo misericordiam non esset consecuturus."—2 *Mach.* ix. 13.

But others, who sin through frailty, or by the violence of some great passion, and who groan under the yoke of the enemy, and desire to break these chains of death, and to escape from their miserable slavery, and therefore ask the assistance of God; the prayer of these, if it is persevering, will certainly be heard by him, who says that every one that asks receives; and he who seeks grace finds it: *For every one that asketh receiveth, and he that seeketh findeth.*[1] "Every one, whether he be a just man or a sinner," says the author of the *Opus Imperfectum.*[2] And in St. Luke, our Lord, when speaking of the man who gave all the loaves he had to his friend, not so much on account of his friendship as because of the other's importunity, says, *If he shall continue knocking, I say to you, although he will not rise and give him because he is his friend, yet because of his importunity he will rise and give him as many as he needeth.*[3] *And so I say unto you, Ask, and it shall be given you.*[4] So that persevering prayer obtains mercy from God, even for those who are not his friends. That which is not obtained through friendship, says St. Chrysostom, is obtained by prayer: "That which was not effected by friendship was effected by prayer." He even says that prayer is valued more by God than friendship: "Friendship is not of such avail with God as prayer; that which is not effected by friendship is effected by prayer.[5] And St. Basil doubts not that even sinners obtain what they ask if they persevere in pray-

---

[1] "Omnis enim qui petit, accipit, et qui quærit, invenit."—*Matt.* vii. 8.

[2] "Omnis, sive justus, sive peccator sit."—*Hom.* 18.

[3] "Dico vobis, et si non dabit illi surgens eo quod amicus ejus sit, propter improbitatem tamen ejus surget, et dabit illi quotquot habet necessarios."—*Luke*, xi. 8.

[4] "Et ego dico vobis: Petite, et dabitur vobis."

[5] "Non tam valet amicitia apud Deum, quam oratio; et quod amicitia non perfecit, perfectum est ab oratione."—*Hom. Non esse desp.*

ing: "Sinners obtain what they seek, if they seek perseveringly."[1] St. Gregory says the same: "The sinner
also shall cry, and his prayer shall reach to God."[2] So
St. Jerome,[3] who says that even the sinner can call God
his Father, if he prays to him to receive him anew as a
son; after the example of the Prodigal Son, who called
him Father, *Father, I have sinned*,[4] even though he had
not as yet been pardoned. If God did not hear sinners,
says St. Augustine, in vain would the Publican have
asked for forgiveness: "If God does not hear sinners, in
vain would that Publican have said, God be merciful to
me a sinner."[5] But the Gospel assures us that the Publican did by his prayer obtain forgiveness: *This man went
down to his house justified.*[6]

But further still, St. Thomas examines this point more
minutely, and does not hesitate to affirm that even the
sinner is heard if he prays; for though his prayer is not
meritorious, yet it has the power of impetration,—that is,
of obtaining what we ask; because impetration is not
founded on God's justice, but on his goodness. "Merit,"
he says, "depends on justice; impetration, on grace."[7]
Thus did Daniel pray, *Incline, O my God, Thine ear and
hear. . . . For not in our justifications do we present our
prayers before Thy face, but in the multitude of Thy mercies.*[8]

---

[1] "Peccatores impetrant quod petunt, si perseveranter petunt."—
Const. Mon. c. 1.

[2] "Clamet et peccator, ut ad Deum sua perveniat oratio."—*In Ps.*
vi. *pœn.*

[3] *Ep. ad Dam. de Fil. prod.*

[4] "Pater, peccavi."—*Luke*, xv. 21.

[5] "Si enim peccatores Deus non exaudiret, frustra ille Publicanus
diceret: Deus, propitius esto mihi peccatori."—*In Jo. tr.* 44.

[6] "Descendit hic justificatus in domum suam."—*Luke*, xviii. 14.

[7] "Meritum innititur justitiæ, sed impetratio innititur gratiæ."—2.
2. q. 83, a. 16.

[8] "Inclina, Deus meus, aurem tuam, et audi . . .; neque enim in
justificationibus nostris prosternimus preces ante faciem tuam, sed in
miserationibus tuis multis."—*Dan.* ix. 18.

Therefore, when we pray, says St. Thomas, it is not necessary to be friends of God, in order to obtain the grace we ask; for prayer itself renders us his friends: "Prayer itself makes us of the family of God."[1] Moreover, St. Bernard uses a beautiful explanation of this, saying that the prayer of a sinner to escape from sin arises from the desire to return to the grace of God. Now this desire is a gift, which is certainly given by no other than God himself; to what end, therefore, says St. Bernard, would God give to a sinner this holy desire, unless he meant to hear him ? "For what would he give the desire, unless he willed to hear?"[2] And, indeed, in the Holy Scriptures themselves there are multitudes of instances of sinners who have been delivered from sin by prayer. Thus was King Achab[3] delivered; thus King Manasses;[4] thus King Nabuchodonosor;[5] and thus the good thief.[6] Oh, the wonderful! oh, the mighty power of prayer ! Two sinners are dying on Calvary by the side of Jesus Christ: one, because he prays, "Remember me," is saved; the other, because he prays not, is damned.

And, in fine, St. Chrysostom says, "No man has with sorrow asked favors from him, without obtaining what he wished."[7] No sinner has ever with penitence prayed to God, without having his desires granted. But why should we cite more authorities, and give more reasons, to demonstrate this point, when our Lord himself says, *Come to Me, all you that labor and are burdened, and I will refresh you.*[8] The "burdened," according to Saints

[1] "Ipsa oratio familiares nos Deo facit."—*Comp. Theol.* p. 2, c. 2.

[2] "Desiderium ad quid daret, nisi vellet exaudire?"

[3] 3 *Kings*, xxi. 27.

[4] 2 *Par.* xxxiii. 12.

[5] *Dan.* iv. 31.

[6] *Luke*, xxiii. 42.

[7] "Nullus ab eo beneficia dolenter postulavit, qui non impetravit quod voluit."—*Hom. de Moys.*

[8] "Venite ad me omnes, qui laboratis et onerati estis, et ego reficiam vos."—*Matt.* xi. 28.

Augustine, Jerome, and others, are sinners in general, who groan under the load of their sins; and who, if they have recourse to God, will surely, according to his promise, be refreshed and saved by his grace. Ah, we cannot desire to be pardoned so much as he longs to pardon us. "Thou dost not," says St. Chrysostom, "so much desire thy sins to be forgiven, as he desires to forgive thy sins."[1] There is no grace, he goes on to say, that is not obtained by prayer, though it be the prayer of the most abandoned sinner, provided only it be persevering: "There is nothing which prayer cannot obtain, though a man be guilty of a thousand sins, provided it be fervent and unremitting."[2] And let us mark well the words of St. James: *If any man wanteth wisdom, let him ask of God, who giveth to all abundantly, and upbraideth not.*[3] All those, therefore, who pray to God, are infallibly heard by him, and receive grace in abundance: *He giveth to all abundantly.* But you should particularly remark the words which follow, *and upbraideth not.* This means that God does not do as men, who, when a person who has formerly done them an injury comes to ask a favor, immediately upbraid him with his offence. God does not do so to the man who prays, even though he were the greatest sinner in the world, when he asks for some grace conducive to his eternal salvation. Then he does not upbraid him with the offences he has committed; but, as though he had never displeased him, he instantly receives him, he consoles him, he hears him, and enriches him with an abundance of his gifts. To crown all, our Saviour, in order to encourage us to

---

[1] "Non adeo cupis dimitti peccata tua, sicut ille cupit peccata dimittere."—*In Act. hom.* 36.

[2] "Nihil est quod non obtineat oratio, etiamsi mille peccatis obnoxius sis, sed vehemens, sed assidua."

[3] "Si quis autem vestrum indiget sapientia, postulet a Deo, qui dat omnibus affluenter, et non improperat."—*James,* i. 5.

pray, says, *Amen, amen, I say to you, if you ask the Father anything in My name, He will give it you.*[1] As though he had said, Courage, O sinners; do not despair: do not let your sins turn you away from having recourse to My Father, and from hoping to be saved by him, if you desire it. You have not now any merits to obtain the graces which you ask for, for you only deserve to be punished; still do this: go to My Father in My name, through My merits ask the favors which you want, and I promise and swear to you ("Amen, amen, I say to you," which, according to St. Augustine, is a species of oath) that whatever you ask, My Father will grant. O God, what greater comfort can a sinner have after his fall than to know for certain that all that he asks from God in the name of Jesus Christ will be given to him!

I say "all;" but I mean only that which has reference to his eternal salvation; for with respect to temporal goods, we have already shown that God, even when asked, sometimes does not give them; because he sees that they would injure our soul. But so far as relates to spiritual goods, his promise to hear us is not conditional, but absolute; and therefore St. Augustine tells us, that those things which God promises absolutely, we should demand with absolute certainty of receiving: "Those things which God promises, seek with certainty."[2] And how, says the saint, can God ever deny us anything, when we ask him for it with confidence? how much more does he desire to dispense to us his graces, than we to receive them! "He is more willing to be munificent of his benefits to thee than thou art desirous to receive them."[3]

St. Chrysostom says that the only time when God is

---

[1] "Amen, amen dico vobis: si quid petieritis Patrem in nomine meo, dabit vobis."—*John*, xvi. 23.

[2] "Quæ Deus promittit, securi petite."—*Serm.* 354. *E. B.*

[3] "Plus vult ille dare, quam nos accipere."—*Serm.* 105. *E. B*

angry with us is when we neglect to ask him for his gifts: "He is only angry when we do not pray."[1] And how can it ever happen that God will not hear a soul who asks him for favors all according to his pleasure? When the soul says to him, Lord, I ask Thee not for goods of this world,—riches, pleasures, honors; I ask Thee only for Thy grace: deliver me from sin, grant me a good death, give me Paradise, give me Thy holy love (which is that grace which St. Francis de Sales says we should seek more than all others), give me resignation to Thy will; how is it possible that God should not hear! What petitions wilt Thou, O my God, ever hear (says St. Augustine), if Thou dost not hear those which are made after Thy own heart? "What prayers dost Thou hear, if Thou hearest not these?"[2] But, above all, our confidence ought to revive, when we pray to God for spiritual graces, as Jesus Christ says: *If you, being evil, know how to give good gifts to your children, how much more will your Father from heaven give the good Spirit to them that ask Him!*[3] If you, who are so attached to your own interests, so full of self-love, cannot refuse your children that which they ask, how much more will your heavenly Father, who loves you better than any earthly father, grant you his spiritual goods when you pray for them!

IV.

The Perseverance Required in Prayer.

Our prayers, then, must be humble and confident; but this is not enough to obtain final perseverance, and thereby eternal life. Individual prayers will obtain the indi-

[1] "Nonnisi quando non postulamus, irascitur."—*In Matt. hom.* 23.

[2] "Quas preces exaudis, si has non exaudis?"—*De Civ. Dei,* l. 22, c. 8.

[3] "Si ergo vos, cum sitis mali, nostis bona data dare filiis vestris; quanto magis Pater vester de cœlo dabit spiritum bonum petentibus se!"—*Luke,* xi. 15.

vidual graces which they ask of God ; but unless they are persevering, they will not obtain final perseverance : which, as it is the accumulation of many graces, requires many prayers, that are not to cease till death. The grace of salvation is not a single grace, but a chain of graces, all of which are at last linked with the grace of final perseverance. Now, to this chain of graces there ought to correspond another chain (as it were) of our prayers; if we, by neglecting to pray, break the chain of our prayers, the chain of graces will be broken too ; and as it is by this that we have to obtain salvation, we shall not be saved.

It is true that we cannot merit final perseverance, as the Council of Trent teaches: " It cannot be had from any other source but from him who is able to confirm the man who is standing, that he may stand with perseverance." [1] Nevertheless, says St. Augustine, this great gift of perseverance can in a manner be merited by our prayers; that is, can be obtained by praying: " This gift, therefore, can be suppliantly merited; that is, can be obtained by supplication." [2] And F. Suarez adds, that the man who prays, infallibly obtains it. But to obtain it, and to save ourselves, says St. Thomas, a persevering and continual prayer is necessary : " After baptism continual prayer is necessary to a man in order that he may enter heaven." [3] And before this, our Saviour himself had said it over and over again : *We ought always to pray, and not to faint.*[4] *Watch ye therefore, praying at all times, that you may be accounted worthy to escape all these things that are*

[1] " Aliunde haberi non potest, nisi ab eo qui potens est, eum qui stat, statuere ut perseveranter stet."—*Sess.* 6, c. 13.

[2] " Hoc Dei donum suppliciter emereri potest."—*De Dono pers.* c. 6.

[3] " Post baptismum autem, necessaria est homini jugis oratio, ad hoc quod cœlum introeat."—*P.* 3. q. 39. a. 5.

[4] " Oportet semper orare, et non deficere."—*Luke,* xviii. 1.

to come, and to stand before the Son of man.[1] The same had
been previously said in the Old Testament : *Let nothing
hinder thee from praying always.*[2] *Bless God at all times,
and desire Him to direct thy ways.*[3] Hence the Apostle in-
culcated on his disciples never to neglect prayer : *Pray
without intermission.*[4] *Be instant in prayer, watching in it
with thanksgiving.*[5] *I will therefore that men pray in every
place.*[6] God does indeed wish to give us perseverance,
says St. Nilus, but he will only give it to him who prays
for it perseveringly : "He willeth to confer benefits on
him who perseveres in prayer."[7] Many sinners by the
help of God's grace come to be converted, and to receive
pardon. But then, because they neglect to ask for perseverance, they fall again, and lose all.

Nor is it enough, says Bellarmine, to ask the grace of
perseverance once, or a few times ; we ought always to
ask it, every day till our death, if we wish to obtain it :
"It must be asked day by day, that it may be obtained
day by day."[8] He who asks it one day, obtains it for
that one day ; but if he does not ask it the next day, the
next day he will fall.

And this is the lesson which our Lord wished to teach
us in the parable of the man who would not give his
loaves to his friend who asked him for them until he had
become importunate in his demand : *Although he will not*

---

[1] " Vigilate itaque omni tempore orantes, ut digni habeamini fugere
ista omnia quæ futura sunt, et stare ante Filium hominis."—*Luke.* xxi.
36.

[2] " Non impediaris orare semper."—*Ecclus.* xviii. 22.

[3] "Omni tempore benedic Deum, et pete ab eo ut vias tuas diri-
gat."—*Job*, iv. 20.

[4] "Sine intermissione orate."—1 *Thess.* v. 17.

[5] "Orationi instate, vigilantes in ea."—*Col.* iv. 2.

[6] "Volo ergo viros orare in omni loco."—1 *Tim.* ii. 8.

[7] "Vult beneficio afficere in oratione perseverantem."—*De Orat.* c.
32.

[8] "Quotidie petenda est. ut quotidie obtineatur."

rise and give because he is his friend, yet because of his impor-
tunity, he will rise and give him as many as he needeth.[1] Now
if this man, solely to deliver himself from the troublesome importunity of his friend, gave him even against
his own will the loaves for which he asked, "how much
more," says St. Augustine, "will the good God give, who
both commands us to ask, and is angry if we ask not!"[2]
How much more will God, who, as he is infinite goodness, has a commensurate desire to communicate to us
his good things,—how much more will he give his graces
when we ask him for them! And the more, as he himself tells us to ask for them, and as he is displeased when
we do not demand them. God, then, does indeed wish to
give us eternal life, and therein all graces; but he wishes
also that we should never omit to ask him for them, even
to the extent of being troublesome. Cornelius à Lapide
says on the text just quoted, "God wishes us to be persevering in prayer to the extent of importunity."[3] Men
of the world cannot bear the importunate; but God not
only bears with them, but wishes us to be importunate in
praying to him for graces, and especially for perseverance. St. Gregory says that God wishes us to do him
violence by our prayers; for such violence does not annoy,
but pleases him: "God wills to be called upon, he wills
to be forced, he wills to be conquered by importunity.
. . . Happy violence, by which God is not offended, but
appeased!"[4]

[1] "Si non dabit ille surgens eo quod amicus ejus sit, propter improbitatem tamen ejus surget, et dabit illi quotquot habet necessarios."—*Luke*, xi. 8.

[2] "Quanto magis dabit (Deus) bonus, qui nos hortatur ut petamus,
cui displicet, si non petamus!"—*Serm.* 61, *E. B.*

[3] "Vult Deus nos in oratione esse perseverantes usque ad impor-
tunitatem."—*In Luc.* xi. 8.

[4] "Vult Deus rogari, vult cogi, vult quadam importunitate vinci.
. . . Bona violentia, qua Deus non offenditur. sed placatur."—*In Ps.
pœnit.* vi.

7

So that to obtain perseverance we must always recommend ourselves to God morning and night, at meditation, at Mass, at Communion, and always; especially in time of temptation, when we must keep repeating, Lord, help me; Lord, assist me; keep Thy hand upon me; leave me not; have pity upon me ! Is there anything easier than to say, Lord, help me, assist me! The Psalmist says, *With me is prayer to the God of my life.*[1] On which the gloss is as follows: " A man may say, I cannot fast, I cannot give alms; but if he is told to pray, he cannot say this.[2] Because there is nothing easier than to pray. But we must never cease praying; we must (so to speak) continually do violence to God, that he may assist us always—a violence which is delightful and dear to him." " This violence is grateful to God," says Tertullian;[3] and St. Jerome says that the more persevering and importunate our prayers are, so much the more are they acceptable to God: " Prayer, as long as it is importunate, is more acceptable."[4]

Blessed is the man that heareth me, and that watcheth daily at my gates.[5] Happy is that man, says God, who listens to Me, and watches continually with holy prayers at the gates of My mercy And Isaias says, *Blessed are all they that wait for Him.*[6] Blessed are they who till the end wait (in prayer) for their salvation from God. Therefore in the Gospel Jesus Christ exhorts us to pray; but how ? *Ask, and ye shall receive; seek, and ye shall find;*

---

[1] " Apud me oratio Deo vitæ meæ."—*Ps.* xli. 9.

[2] " Dicet quis: Non possum jejunare, dare eleemosynas;—si dicitur ei: Ora; non potest hoc dicere."

[3] " Hæc vis Deo grata est."—*Apolog.* c. 39.

[4] " Oratio, quamvis importuna, plus amica est."—*Hom. in Matt.*

[5] " Beatus homo qui audit me, et qui vigilat ad fores meas quotidie."—*Prov.* viii. 34.

[6] " Petite, et dabitur vobis: quærite, et invenietis; pulsate, et aperietur vobis."—*Luke,* xi. 9.

knock, and it shall be opened to you.[1] Would it not have been enough to have said, "ask?" why add "seek" and "knock?" No, it was not superfluous to add them; for thereby our Saviour wished us to understand that we ought to do as the poor who go begging. If they do not receive the alms they ask (I speak of licensed beggars), they do not cease asking; they return to ask again; and if the master of the house does not show himself any more, they set to work to knock at the door, till they become very importunate and troublesome. That is what God wishes us to do: to pray, and to pray again, and never leave off praying, that he would assist us and succor us, that he would enlighten us and strengthen us, and never allow us to forfeit his grace. The learned Lessius says[2] that the man cannot be excused from mortal sin who does not pray when he is in sin, or in danger of death; or, again, if he neglects to pray for any notable time, as (he says) for one or two months. But this does not include the time of temptations; because whoever finds himself assailed by any grievous temptation, without doubt sins mortally if he does not have recourse to God in prayer, to ask for assistance to resist it; seeing that otherwise he places himself in a proximate, nay, in a certain, occasion of sin.

WHY GOD DELAYS GRANTING US FINAL PERSEVERANCE.— CONCLUSION.

But, some one will say, since God can give and wishes to give me the grace of perseverance, why does he not give it me all at once, when I ask him?

The holy Fathers assign many reasons:

1. God does not grant it at once, but delays it, first, that he may better prove our confidence.

---

[1] " Beati omnes qui exspectant eum."—*Is.* xxx. 18.
[2] *De Just. et Jure*, l. 2, c. 37, d. 3.

2. And, further, says St. Augustine, that we may long for it more vehemently. Great gifts, he says, should be greatly desired; for good things soon obtained are not held in the same estimation as those which have been long looked for: "God wills not to give quickly, that you may learn to have great desire for great things; things long desired are pleasanter to obtain, but things soon given are cheapened."[1]

3. Again, the Lord does so that we may not forget him; if we were already secure of persevering and of being saved, and if we had not continual need of God's help to preserve us in his grace and to save us, we should soon forget God. Want makes the poor keep resorting to the houses of the rich; so God, to draw us to himself, as St. Chrysostom says, and to see us often at his feet, in order that he may thus be able to do us greater good, delays giving us the complete grace of salvation till the hour of our death: "It is not because he rejects our prayers that he delays, but by this contrivance he wishes to make us careful, and to draw us to himself."[2] Again, he does so in order that we, by persevering in prayer, may unite ourselves closer to him with the sweet bonds of love: "Prayer," says the same St. Chrysostom, "which is accustomed to converse with God, is no slight bond of love to him."[3] This continual recurrence to God in prayer, and this confident expectation of the graces which we desire from him, oh, what a great spur and chain is it of love to inflame us, and to bind us more closely to God!

[1] "Non vult (Deus) cito dare, ut discas magna magne desiderare: diu desiderata dulcius obtinentur; cito autem data vilescunt."—*Serm.* 61, *E. B.*

[2] "Neque renuens nostras preces differt; sed hac arte, sedulos nos efficiens, ad semetipsum attrahere vult."—*In Gen. hom.* 30.

[3] "Oratio non parvum vinculum est dilectionis in Deum, quæ cum eo colloqui assuefacit."—*In Ps.* iv.

But, till what time have we to pray? Always, says the same saint, till we receive favorable sentence of eternal life; that is to say, till our death: "Do not leave off till you receive." [1] And he goes on to say that the man who resolves, I will never leave off praying till I am saved, will most certainly be saved: "If you say, I will not give in till I have received, you will assuredly receive." [2] The Apostle writes that many run for the prize, but that he only receives it who runs till he wins: *Know you not that they who run in the race, all run indeed, but one receiveth the prize? So run that you may obtain.* [3] It is not, then, enough for salvation simply to pray; but we must pray always, that we may come to receive the crown which God promises, but promises only to those who are constant in prayer till the end.

So that if we wish to be saved, we must do as David did, who always kept his eyes turned to God, to implore his aid against being overcome by his enemies: *My eyes are ever towards the Lord, for He shall pluck my feet out of the snare.* [4] As the devil does not cease continually spreading snares to swallow us up, as St. Peter writes: *Your adversary the devil, as a roaring lion, goeth about, seeking whom he may devour;* [5] so ought we ever to stand with our arms in our hands to defend ourselves from such a foe, and to say, with the royal prophet, *I will pursue after my enemies; and I will not turn again till they are consumed.* [6]

---

[1] "Non desistas, donec accipias."—*In Matt. hom.* 24.

[2] "Si dixeris: Nisi accepero, non recedam;—prorsus accipies."

[3] "Nescitis quod, ii qui in stadio currunt, omnes quidem currunt, sed unus accipit bravium? Sic currite ut comprehendatis."—1 *Cor.* ix. 24.

[4] "Oculi mei semper ad Dominum, quia ipse evellet de laqueo pedes meos."—*Ps.* xxiv. 15.

[5] "Adversarius vester diabolus, tamquam leo rugiens, circuit quæ-rens quem devoret."—1 *Pet.* v. 8.

[6] "Persequar inimicos meos, . . . et non convertar, donec deficiant."—*Ps.* xvii. 38.

I will never cease fighting till I see my enemies conquered. But how can we obtain this victory, so important for us, and so difficult? "By most persevering prayers,"[1] says St. Augustine,—only by prayers, and those most persevering; and till when? As long as the fight shall last. "As the battle is never over," says St. Bonaventure, "so let us never give over asking for mercy."[2] As we must be always in the combat, so should we be always asking God for aid not to be overcome. Woe, says the Wise Man, to him who in this battle leaves off praying: *Woe to them that have lost patience.*[3] We may be saved, the Apostle tells us, but on this condition, *if we retain a firm confidence and the glory of hope until the end;*[4] if we are constant in praying with confidence until death.

Let us, then, take courage from the mercy of God, and his promises, and say with the same Apostle, *Who then shall separate us from the love of Christ? Shall tribulation, or distress, or danger, or persecution, or the sword?*[5] Who shall succeed in estranging us from the love of Jesus Christ? Tribulation, perhaps, or the danger of losing the goods of this world? The persecutions of devils or men? The torments inflicted by tyrants? *In all these we overcome* (it is St. Paul who encourages us), *because of Him that hath loved us.*[6] No, he says, no tribulation, no misery, danger, persecution, or torture, shall ever be able to separate us from the love of Jesus Christ; because with God's

---

[1] "Perseverantissimis precibus."

[2] "Sicut nunquam deficit pugna, sic nunquam cessemus petere misericordiam."—*De uno Conf.* s. 5.

[3] "Væ his qui perdiderunt sustinentiam."—*Ecclus.* ii. 16.

[4] "Si fiduciam et gloriam spei, usque ad finem, firmam retineamus."—*Heb.* iii. 6.

[5] "Quis ergo nos separabit a charitate Christi? tribulatio, an angustia,—an periculum, an persecutio, an gladius?"—*Rom.* viii. 35, 37.

[6] "Sed in his omnibus superamus, propter eum qui dilexit nos."—*Ibid.*

help we shall overcome all, if we fight for love of him who gave his life for us.

F. Hippolitus Durazzo, the day when he resolved to relinquish his dignity of prelate at Rome, and to give himself entirely to God by entering the Society of Jesus (which he afterwards did), was so afraid of being faithless by reason of his weakness that he said to God, "Forsake me not, Lord, now that I have given myself wholly to Thee; for pity's sake, do not forsake me!" But he heard the whisper of God in his heart, "Do not thou forsake Me; rather," said God, "do I say to thee, Forsake Me not." And so at last the servant of God, trusting in his goodness and help, concluded, "Then, O my God, Thou wilt not leave me,[1] and I will not leave Thee."[2]

Finally, if we wish not to be forsaken by God, we ought never to forsake praying to him not to leave us. If we do thus, he will certainly always assist us, and will never allow us to perish, and to be separated from his love. And to this end let us not only take care always to ask for final perseverance, and the graces necessary to obtain it, but let us, at the same time, always by anticipation ask God for grace to go on praying; for this is precisely that great gift which he promised to his elect by the mouth of the prophet: *And I will pour out upon the house of David, and upon the inhabitants of Jerusalem, the spirit of grace and prayers.*[3] Oh, what a great grace is the spirit of prayer; that is, the grace which God confers on a soul to enable it to pray always! Let us, then, never neglect to beg God to give us this grace, and this spirit of continual prayer; because if we pray always, we shall certainly obtain from God perseverance and every other gift which we desire, since his promise of hearing who-

---

[1] "Non me deseras."

[2] "Tu non me deseras."

[3] "Et effundam super domum David et super habitatores Jerusa-lem spiritum gratiæ et precum."—*Zach.* xii. 10.

ever prays to him cannot fail. *For we are saved by hope.*[1]
With this hope of always praying, we may reckon ourselves saved. "Confidence will give us a broad entrance
into this city."[2] This hope, said Venerable Bede, will
give us a safe passage into the city of Paradise.

[1] "Spe enim salvi facti sumus."—*Rom.* viii. 24.
[2] "Hujus nobis urbis fiducia latum præbebit ingressum."—*In solemn. omn. SS. hom.* 2.

PART II.

Which proves that the Grace of Prayer is given to all, and which treats of the Ordinary Mode in which this Grace operates.

INTRODUCTION.

Taking, then, for granted that prayer is necessary for the attainment of eternal life, as we have proved in Part I., chap. i., we should consequently, also, take for granted that every one has sufficient aid from God to enable him actually to pray, without need of any further special grace; and that by prayer he may obtain all other graces necessary to enable him to persevere in keeping the commandments, and so gain eternal life; so that no one who is lost can ever excuse himself by saying that it was through want of the aid necessary for his salvation. For as God, in the natural order, has ordained that man should be born naked, and in want of several things necessary for life, but then has given him hands and intelligence to clothe himself and provide for his other needs; so, in the supernatural order, man is born unable to obtain salvation by his own strength; but God in his goodness grants to every one the grace of prayer, by which he is able to obtain all other graces which he needs in order to keep the commandments and to be saved.

But before I explain this point, I must prove two preliminary propositions. First, that God wills all men to be saved; and therefore that Jesus Christ has died for all. Secondly, that God, on his part, gives to all men the graces necessary for salvation; whereby every one may be saved if he corresponds to them.

CHAPTER I.

GOD WISHES ALL MEN TO BE SAVED, AND THEREFORE CHRIST DIED TO SAVE ALL MEN.

I.

God wishes All Men to be saved.

GOD loves all things that he has created: *For Thou lovest all things that are, and hatest none of the things that Thou hast made.*[1] Now love cannot be idle: "All love has a force of its own, and cannot be idle,"[2] says St. Augustine. Hence love necessarily implies benevolence, so that the person who loves cannot help doing good to the person beloved whenever there is an opportunity: "Love persuades a man to do those things which he believes to be good for him whom he loves,"[3] says Aristotle. If, then, God loves all men, he must in consequence will that all should obtain eternal salvation, which is the one and sovereign good of man, seeing that it is the one end for which he was created: *You have your fruit unto sanctification; but your end eternal life.*[4]

This doctrine, that God wishes all men to be saved, and that Jesus Christ died for the salvation of all, is now a certain doctrine taught by the Catholic Church, as theologians in common teach, namely, Petavius, Gonet,

---

[1] " Diligis enim omnia quæ sunt, et nihil odisti eorum quæ fecisti." — *Wis.* xi. 25.

[2] " Habet omnis amor vim suam, nec potest vacare."—*In Ps.* cxxi.

[3] " Amor, quæ bona illi esse credit quem amat, ea studet efficere." —*Rhetor.* l. 2, c. 4.

[4] " Habetis fructum vestrum in sanctificationem, finem vero vitam æternam."—*Rom.* vi. 22.

Gotti, and others, besides Tourneley, who adds, that it is a doctrine all but of faith.[1]

I. DECISION OF THE CHURCH.

With reason, therefore, were the predestinarians condemned, who, among their errors, taught (as may be seen in Noris, Petavius, and more especially in Tourneley) that God does not will all men to be saved; as Hincmar, Archbishop of Rheims, testifies of them in his first letter, where he says, "The ancient predestinarians asserted that God does not will all men to be saved, but only those who are saved."[2] These persons were condemned, first in the Council of Arles, A.D. 475, which pronounced "anathema to him that said that Christ did not die for all men, and that he does not will all to be saved."[3] They were next condemned in the Council of Lyons, A.D. 490, where Lucidus was forced to retract and confess, "I condemn the man who says that Christ did not suffer death for the salvation of all men."[4] So also in the ninth century, Gotheschalcus, who renewed the same error, was condemned by the Council of Quercy, A.D. 853, in the third article of which it was decided "God wills all men, without exception, to be saved, although all men be not saved;" and in the fourth article: "There is no man for whom Christ did not suffer, although all men be not redeemed by the mystery of his Passion."[5] The same error was finally condemned in

[1] Proxima fidei.

[2] "Veteres prædestinatiani dixerunt, quoniam non vult Deus omnes salvos fieri, sed tantum eos qui salvantur."

[3] "Anathema illi qui dixerit quod Christus non pro omnibus mortuus sit, nec omnes homines salvos esse velit."—*Anath.* 6.

[4] "Damno eum qui dicit quod Christus mortem non pro omnium salute susceperit."

[5] "Deus omnes homines sine exceptione vult salvos fieri, licet non omnes salventur.—Nullus est pro quo (Christus) passus non fuerit, licet non omnes passionis ejus mysterio redimantur."—*Art.* 3, 4.

the 12th and 13th Propositions of Quesnel. In the
former it was said: "When God wills to save a soul, the
will of God is undoubtedly effectual;" in the latter: "All
whom God wills to save through Christ are infallibly
saved."[1] These propositions were justly condemned,
precisely because they meant that God does not will all
men to be saved; since from the proposition that those
whom God wills to be saved are infallibly saved, it logi-
cally follows that God does not will even all the faithful
to be saved, let alone all men.

This was also clearly expressed by the Council of
Trent, in which it was said that Jesus Christ died, "that
all might receive the adoption of sons," and in chapter
iii.: "But though he died for all, yet all do not receive
the benefits of his death."[2] The Council then takes for
granted that the Redeemer died not only for the elect,
but also for those who, through their own fault, do not
receive the benefit of Redemption. Nor is it of any use
to affirm that the Council only meant to say that Jesus
Christ has given to the world a ransom sufficient to save
all men; for in this sense we might say that he died also
for the devils. Moreover, the Council of Trent intended
here to reprove the errors of those innovators, who, not
denying that the blood of Christ was sufficient to save
all, yet asserted that in fact it was not shed and given
for all; this is the error which the Council intended to
condemn when it said that our Saviour died for all.
Further, in chapter vi. it says that sinners are put in a
fit state to receive justification by hope in God through
the merits of Jesus Christ: "They are raised to hope,

[1] " Quando Deus vult salvare animam, effectus indubitabilis sequitur voluntatem Dei.—Omnes quos vult Deus salvare per Christum,
salvantur infallibiliter."

[2] " Ut omnes adoptionem filiorum reciperent.—Verum, etsi ille pro
omnibus mortuus est, non omnes tamen mortis ejus beneficium reci-
piunt."—*Sess.* 6. c. 2–3.

trusting that God will be merciful to them through Christ." [1] Now, if Jesus Christ had not applied to all the merits of his Passion, then, since no one (without a special revelation) could be certain of being among the number of those to whom the Redeemer had willed to apply the fruit of his merits, no sinner could entertain such hope, not having the certain and secure foundation which is necessary for hope; namely, that God wills all men to be saved, and will pardon all sinners prepared for it by the merits of Jesus Christ. And this, besides being the error formerly condemned in Baius, who said that Christ had only died for the elect, is also condemned in the fifth proposition of Jansenius: "It is Semi-Pelagianism to say that Christ died or shed his blood for all men." [2] And Innocent X., in his Constitution of A.D. 1653, expressly declared that to say Christ died for the salvation of the elect only is an impious and heretical proposition.

2. THE CELEBRATED TEXT OF ST. PAUL.

On the other hand, both the Scriptures and all the Fathers assure us that God sincerely and really wishes the salvation of all men and the conversion of all sinners, as long as they are in this world. For this we have, first of all, the express text of St. Paul: *Who will have all men to be saved, ana to come to the knowledge of the truth.* [3] The sentence of the Apostle is absolute and indicative—*God wills all men to be saved.* These words in their natural sense declare that God truly wills all men to be saved; and it is a certain rule, received in common by all, that

[1] "In spem eriguntur, fidentes Deum sibi propter Christum propitium fore."—*Sess.* 6, c. 6.

[2] "Semipelagianum est dicere Christum pro omnibus omnino hominibus mortuum esse, aut sanguinem suum fudisse."

[3] "Omnes homines vult salvos fieri, et ad agnitionem veritatis venire."—1 *Tim.* ii. 4.

the words in Scripture are not to be distorted to an un-
natural sense, except in the sole case when the literal
meaning is repugnant to faith or morals. St. Bonaventure writes precisely to our purpose when he says, " We
must hold that when the Apostle says, God wills all men
to be saved, it is necessary to grant that he does will it." [1]

It is true that St. Augustine and St. Thomas mention
different interpretations which have been given to this
text; but both these Doctors understand it to mean a
real will of God to save all, without exception.

And concerning St. Augustine, we shall see just now
that this was his true opinion; so that St. Prosper protests against attributing to him the supposition that God
did not sincerely wish the salvation of all men, and of
each individual, as an aspersion on the holy Doctor.
Hence the same St. Prosper, who was a most faithful
disciple of his, says, " It is most sincerely to be believed
and confessed that God wills all men to be saved; since
the Apostle (whose very words these are) is particular
in commanding that prayers should be made to God for
all." [2]

The argument of the saint is clear, founded on St.
Paul's words in the above-cited passage—*I beseech therefore, first of all, that prayers should be made for all men;* [3]
and then he adds, *For this is good and acceptable before God
our Saviour, who wills all men to be saved.* [4] So the Apostle

[1] " Dicendum quod, cum Apostolus dicat quod Deus ' Omnes homines vult salvos fieri,' necesse habemus concedere quod Deus velit."
—*In* 1 *Sent.* d. 46, a. 1, q. 1.

[2] "Sincerissime credendum atque profitendum est Deum velle ut
omnes homines salvi fiant; siquidem Apostolus, cujus ista sententia
est, sollicitissime præcipit ut Deo pro omnibus supplicetur."—*Resp.
ad* 2 *obj. Vincent.*"

[3] " Obsecro igitur primum omnium fieri obsecrationes . . . pro omnibus hominibus."

[4] " Hoc enim bonum est et accceptum coram Salvatore nostro Deo,
qui omnes homines vult salvos fieri."

wishes us to pray for all, exactly in the same sense that God wishes the salvation of all. St. Chrysostom uses the same argument: "If he wills all to be saved, surely we ought to pray for all. If he desires all to be saved, do you also be of one mind with him." [1] And if in some passages in his controversy with the Semi-Pelagians, St. Augustine seems to have held a different interpretation of this text, saying that God does not will the salvation of each individual, but only of some, Petavius well observes that here the holy Father speaks only incidentally, not with direct intention; or, at any rate, that he speaks of the grace of that absolute and victorious will (*voluntas absoluta et victrix*) with which God absolutely wills the salvation of some persons, and of which the saint elsewhere says, "The will of the Almighty is always invincible." [2]

Let us hear how St. Thomas uses another method of reconciling the opinion of St. Augustine with that of St. John Damascene, who holds that antecedently God wills all and each individual to be saved: "God's first intention is to will all men to be saved, that as good he may make us partakers of his goodness; but after we have sinned, he wills to punish us as just." [3] On the other hand, St. Augustine (as we have seen) seems in a few passages to think differently. But St. Thomas reconciles these opinions, and says that St. Damascene spoke of the antecedent will of God, by which he really wills all men to be saved, while St. Augustine spoke of the consequent will. He then goes on to explain the mean-

---

[1] "Si omnes ille vult salvos fieri, merito pro omnibus oportet orare; si omnes ipse salvos fieri cupit, illius et tu concorda voluntati."—*In I Tim. hom.* 7.

[2] "Omnipotentis voluntas semper invicta est."—*Enchir.* c. 102.

[3] "Deus praecedenter vult omnes salvari. Efficit nos bonitatis suae participes, ut bonus; peccantes autem punire vult, ut justus."—*De Fid. orth.* l. 2, c. 29.

ing of antecedent and consequent will: "Antecedent will is that by which God wills all to be saved; but when all the circumstances of this or that individual are considered, it is found to be good that all men should be saved; for it is good that he who prepares himself, and consents to it, should be saved; but not he who is unwilling and resists, etc. And this is called the consequent will, because it presupposes a foreknowledge of a man's deeds, not as a cause of the act of will, but as a reason for the thing willed and determined."[1]

So that St. Thomas was also of opinion that God truly wills all men and each individual to be saved. This opinion he reasserts in several other places. On the text—*Him that cometh to Me I will not cast out,*"[2] he quotes St. Chrysostom, who makes our Lord say, "If then I was incarnate for the salvation of men, how can I cast them out?" And this is what He means when He says, "Therefore I cast them not out, because I came down from heaven to do My Father's will, who wills all men to be saved."[3] And again, "God, by his most liberal will, gives (grace) to every one that prepares himself,"—*who wills all men to be saved;* and therefore the grace of God is wanting to no man, but as far as He is concerned He communicates it to every one."[4] Again, he declares the

[1] "Voluntas antecedens est qua (Deus) omnes homines salvos fieri vult. Consideratis autem omnibus circumstantiis personæ, sic non invenitur de omnibus bonum esse quod salventur; bonum est enim eum, qui se præparat et consentit, salvari, non vero nolentem et resistentem. Et hæc est voluntas consequens, eo quod præsupponit præscientiam operum, non tamquam causam voluntatis, sed quasi rationem voliti."

[2] "Eum qui venit ad me, non ejiciam foras."—*John.* vi. 37.

[3] "Secundum Chrysostomum: Si ergo pro salute hominum incarnatus sum, quomodo debeo eos ejicere? et hoc est quod dicit: Ideo non ejicio, quia descendi de cœlo ut faciam voluntatem Patris, qua vult omnes salvos fieri."—*In Joan.* vi. *lect.* 4.

[4] "Deus voluntate sua liberalissima dat (gratiam) omni præparanti se, 'Qui omnes homines vult salvos fieri;' et ideo gratia Dei nulli deest, sed omnibus, quantum in se est, se communicat."—*In Heb.* xii. *lect.* 3.

same thing more expressly in his explanation of the text of St. Paul—*God wills all men to be saved.* "In God," he says, "the salvation of all men, considered in itself, belongs to that class of things which he wishes, and this is his antecedent will; but when the good of justice is taken into consideration, and the rightness of punishing sin, in this sense he does not will the salvation of all, and this is his consequent will."[1] Here we may see how consistent St. Thomas was in his explanation of antecedent and consequent will; for he here repeats what he had said in the passage quoted a little before. In this place he only adds the comparison of a merchant, who antecedently wills to save all his merchandise; but if a tempest comes on, he willingly throws it overboard, in order to preserve his own life. In like manner, he says, God, considering the iniquity of some persons, wills them to be punished in satisfaction of his justice, and consequently does not will them to be saved; but antecedently, and considered in itself, he wills with a true desire the salvation of all men. So that, as he says in the former passage, God's will to save all men is on his part absolute; it is only conditional on the part of the object willed, that is, if man will correspond to what the right order demands, in order to be saved. "Nor yet," he says, "is there imperfection on the part of God's will, but on the part of the thing willed; because it is not accepted with all the circumstances which are required, in order to be saved in the proper manner."[2] And he again and more distinctly declares what he means by ante-

[1] "In Deo salus omnium hominum secundum se considerata habet rationem ut sit volibilis, et sic ejus voluntas est antecedens; sed, si consideretur bonum justitiæ, et quod peccata puniantur, sic non vult; et hæc est voluntas consequens."—*In* 1 *Tim.* ii. *Lect.* 1.

[2] "Nec tamen est imperfectio ex parte voluntatis divinæ, sed ex parte voliti, quod non accipitur cum omnibus circumstantiis quæ exiguntur ad rectum ordinem in salutem."—*In* 1 *Sent. d.* 46, *q.* 1, *a.* 1.

cedent and consequent will: "A judge antecedently wishes every man to live, but he consequently wishes a murderer to be hanged; so God antecedently wills every man to be saved, but he consequently wills some to be damned; in consequence, that is, of the exigencies of his justice."[1]

I have no intention here of blaming the opinion that men are predestined to glory previously to the prevision of their merits; I only say that I cannot understand how those who think that God, without any regard to their merits, has elected some to eternal life, and excluded others, can therefore persuade themselves that he wills all to be saved; unless, indeed, they mean that this will of God is not true and sincere, but rather a hypothetical or metaphorical will. I cannot understand, I say, how it can be maintained that God wills all men to be saved, and to partake of his glory, when the greater part of them have been already excluded from this glory antecedently to any demerit on their part. Petavius says, in defence of his contrary opinion, What was the use of God's giving to all men the desire of eternal happiness, when he had excluded the majority of them from it antecedently to any demerits of theirs? What was the use of Jesus Christ's coming to save all men by his death, when so many poor creatures had been already deprived by God of all benefit therefrom? What was the use of giving them so many means of salvation, when they had been already excluded from the attainment of the end? Therefore, adds Petavius (and this is a most weighty reflection), if this ever was the case, we must say that God, who loves all things that he has created, yet in creating mankind did not love them all, but rather utterly detested the greater part of

[1] " Justus judex antecedenter vult omnem hominem vivere, sed consequenter vult homicidam suspendi; similiter Deus antecedenter vult omnem hominem salvari, sed consequenter vult quosdam damnari, secundum exigentiam suæ justitiæ."—*P.* 1. *q.* 19, *a.* 6.

them, in excluding them from the glory for which he had created them. It is certain that the happiness of a creature consists in the attainment of the end for which it was created. On the other hand, it is certain that God creates all men for eternal life. If, therefore, God, having created some men for eternal life, had thereupon, without regard to their sins, excluded them from it, he would in creating them have utterly hated them without cause, and would have done them the greatest injury they could possibly suffer in excluding them from the attainment of their end, that is, of the glory for which they had been created—"For," says Petavius in a passage which we abridge, "God cannot feel indifferent between love and hatred towards his creatures, especially towards men, whom he either loves to eternal life, or hates to damnation; but it is the greatest evil of man to be alienated from God and to be reprobate; wherefore, if God wills the everlasting destruction of any man's soul, he does not love him, but hates him with the greatest hatred possible, in that kind which transcends the natural order."[1] And by this eternal ruin or "everlasting destruction," he does not mean the positive damnation which God destines for certain individuals, but simply the exclusion from glory; since in fact, as Tertullian says, of what use would it ever be to us that God had not created us for hell, if in creating us he had separated us from the number of his elect? since the separation from the elect necessarily implies the loss of salvation, and therefore damnation; since there is no mean between them. "For what," says Tertullian, "will be the end of

---

[1] "Non enim medio quodam modo amorem inter et odium circa creaturas potest affici Deus, maxime erga homines, quos vel amat ad vitam perpetuam vel odit ad damnationem. Est autem summum hominis malum alienari a Deo ac reprobari. Quare, si cui Deus sempiternum vult exitium animæ, hunc non amat, sed odit odio illo quod esse maximum potest in eo genere quod naturalem ordinem excedit."

the separated ?   Will it not be the loss of salvation ?"[1]
Whence Petavius concludes—"Wherefore, if God loves
every man with a love which is antecedent to their merits,
he does not hate his soul, and therefore he does not desire the greatest evil to him."[2]   If, therefore, God loves
all men, as is certain, we ought to hold that he wills all
to be saved, and that he has never hated any one to such
a degree, that he has willed to do him the greatest evils,
by excluding him from glory previously to the prevision
of his demerits.

I say notwithstanding, and repeat again and again,
that I cannot understand it; for this matter of predestination is so profound a mystery, that it made the Apostle
exclaim: *Oh, the depth of the riches of the wisdom and the
knowledge of God !   How incomprehensible are His judgments, and how unsearchable His ways !   For who hath known
the mind of the Lord ?*[3]   We ought to submit ourselves to
the will of God, who has chosen to leave this mystery in
obscurity to his Church, that we all might humble ourselves under the deep judgments of his divine Providence.   And the more, because divine grace, by which
alone men can gain eternal life, is dispensed more or less
abundantly by God entirely gratuitously, and without
any regard to our merits.   So that to save ourselves it
will always be necessary for us to throw ourselves into
the arms of the divine mercy, in order that he may
assist us with his grace to obtain salvation, trusting
always in his infallible promises to hear and save the man
who prays to him.

[1] "Quis erit enim exitus segregatorum ? nonne amissio salutis ?"—
Adv. Marc. l. 4.

[2] "Quamobrem, si omnes Deus amat homines eo affectu, qui
merita illorum antecedit, non eorum odit animas, ac proinde non
summum vult illis malum."— *De Deo. l.* 10, *c.* 3, *n.* 5.

[3] "O altitudo divitiarum sapientiæ et scientiæ Dei ! quam incom-
prehensibilia sunt judicia ejus, et investigabiles viæ ejus !   Quis enim
cognovit sensum Domini ?"—*Rom.* xi. 44.

3. OTHER TEXTS OF SCRIPTURE.

But let us return to our point, that God sincerely wills all men to be saved. There are other texts which prove the same thing, as when God says: *As I live, saith the Lord, I desire not the death of the wicked, but that the wicked man turn from his way and live.*[1] He not only says that he wills not the death, but that he wills the life of a sinner; and he swears, as Tertullian observes, in order that he may be more readily believed in this: "When moreover he swears, saying, as I live, he desires to be believed."[2]

Further, David says: *For wrath is in His indignation, and life in His will.*[3] If he chastises us, he does it because our sins provoke him to indignation; but as to his will, he wills not our death, but our life: *Life in His will.* St. Basil says about this text, that God wills all to be made partakers of life.[4] David says elsewhere: *Our God is the God of salvation; and of the Lord of the Lord are the issues from death.*[5] On this Bellarmine says: "This is proper to him, this is his nature, our God is a saving God, and his are the issues from death—that is, liberation from it;"[6] so that it is God's proper nature to save all, and to deliver all from eternal death.

Again, our Lord says: *Come to Me, all ye that labor and*

[1] "Vivo ego, dicit Dominus Deus: nolo mortem impii, sed ut convertatur impius a via sua, et vivat."—*Ezek.* xxxiii. 11.

[2] "Jurans etiam, ʻ Vivo !ʼ dicens, cupit credi sibi."—*De Pœnit.*

[3] "Quoniam ira in indignatione ejus, et vita in voluntate ejus."—*Ps.* xxix. 6.

[4] "Quid ergo dicit? nimirum quod vult Deus omnes vitæ fieri participes."

[5] "Deus noster, Deus salvos faciendi; et Domini Domini exitus mortis."—*Ps.* lxvii. 21.

[6] "Hoc est illi proprium, hæc est ejus natura, Deus noster est Deus salvans. et Dei nostri sunt exitus mortis, id est, liberatio a morte."

are burdened, and I will refresh you.[1]   If he calls all to salvation, then he truly wills all to be saved.   Again, St. Peter says: *He willeth not that any should perish, but that all should return to penance.*[2]   He does not will the damnation of any one, but he wills that all should do penance, and so should be saved.

Again, our Lord says: *I stand at the gate and knock; if any one will open, I will enter.*[3]   *Why will you die, O house of Israel? return and live.*[4]   *What is there that I ought to do more to My vineyard, that I have not done to it?*[5]   *How often would I have gathered together thy children, as the hen gathereth her chickens under her wings, and thou wouldst not!*[6]   How could our Lord have said that he stands knocking at the heart of us sinners?   How exhort us so strongly to return to his arms?   How reproach us by asking what more he could have done for our salvation?   How say that he has willed to receive us as children, if he had not a true will to save all men?   Again, St. Luke relates that our Lord, looking over Jerusalem from a distance, and contemplating the destruction of its people because of their sin: *Seeing the city, He wept over it.*[7]   Why did he weep then, says Theophylact (after St. Chrysostom), seeing the ruin of the Jews, unless it was because he really desired their salvation?   Now then, after so many attes-

---

[1] " Venite ad me omnes, qui laboratis et onerati estis, et ego reficiam vos."—*Matt.* xi. 28.

[2] " Nolens aliquos perire, sed omnes ad pœnitentiam reverti."—2 *Pet.* iii. 9.

[3] " Ecce sto ad ostium et pulso; si quis audierit vocem meam, et aperuerit mihi januam, intrabo ad illum et cœnabo cum illo, et ipse mecum."—*Apoc.* iii. 20.

[4] " Et quare moriemini, Domus Israel?   Quia nolo mortem morientis, dicit Dominus Deus, revertimini et vivite."—*Ezek.* xviii. 31.

[5] " Quid debui ultra facere vineæ meæ, et non feci ei?"—*Is.* v. 4.

[6] " Quoties volui congregare filios tuos, quemadmodum gallina congregat pullos suos sub alas, et noluisti!"—*Matt.* xxiii. 37.

[7] " Videns civitatem, flevit super illam."—*Luke*, xix. 41.

tations of our Lord, in which he makes known to us that
he wills to see all men saved, how can it ever be said that
God does not will the salvation of all? "But if these texts
of Scripture," says Petavius, "in which God has testified his will in such clear and often-repeated expressions,
nay even with tears and with an oath, may be abused
and distorted to the very opposite sense,—namely, that
God determined to send all mankind (except a few) to
perdition, and never had a will to save them, what dogma
of faith is so clear as to be safe from similar injury and
cavil?"[1] This great writer says, that to deny that God
really wills the salvation of all men is an insult and cavil
against the plainest doctrines of the faith. And Cardinal
Sfondrati adds: "Those who think otherwise, seem to
me to make God a mere stage-god; like those people
who pretend to be kings in a play, when indeed they are
anything but kings."[2]

4. GENERAL CONSENT OF THE FATHERS.

Moreover, this truth, that God wills all men to be
saved, is confirmed by the general consent of the Fathers.
There can be no doubt that all the Greek Fathers have
been uniform in saying that God wills all and each individual to be saved. So St. Justin, St. Basil, St. Gregory,
St. Cyril, St. Methodius, and St. Chrysostom, all adduced
by Petavius. But let us see what the Latin Fathers
say.

[1] " Quod si ista Scripturæ loca, quibus hanc suam voluntatem et affectum tam illustribus ac tam sæpe repetitis sententiis, imo lacrymis
ac jurejurando, testatus est Deus, calumniari licet et in contrarium
detorquere sensum, ut, præter paucos, genus hominum omne perdere
statuerit, nec eorum servandorum voluntatem habuerit, quid est adeo
dissertum in fidei decretis, quod simili ab injuria et cavillatione tutum
esse possit?"—*De Deo. lib.* 10, c. 15, n. 5.

[2] " Plane qui aliter sentiunt, nescio an ex Deo vero deum scenicum
faciant, quales sunt qui reges in theatro se fingunt, cum tamen nihil
minus quam reges sint."—*Nodus præd.* p. 1, § 1.

St. Jerome: (God) " wills to save all; but since no man is saved without his own will, he wills us to will what is good, that when we have willed, he may also will to fulfil his designs in us;" [1] and in another place, " God therefore willed to save those who desire (to be saved); and he invited them to salvation, that their will might have its reward; but they would not believe in him." [2]

St. Hilary: " God would that all men were saved, and not those alone who are to belong to the number of the elect, but all absolutely, so as to make no exception." [3]

St. Paulinus: " Christ says to all, *Come to Me*, etc.; for he, the Creator of all men, so far as he is concerned, wills every man to be saved." [4]

St. Ambrose: " Even with respect to the wicked he had to manifest his will (to save them), and therefore he could not pass over his betrayer, that all might see that in the election even of the traitor he exhibits (his desire) of saving all . . . and, so far as God is concerned, he shows to all that he was willing to deliver all." [5]

The author of the work known as the *Commentaries of St. Ambrose* (supposed by Petavius to be Hilary the Deacon) in speaking of the text of St. Paul (*Who wills*

[1] " Vult (Deus) salvari omnes; sed quia nullus absque propria voluntate salvatur, vult nos bonum velle, ut, cum voluerimus, velit in nobis et ipse suum implere consilium."—*In Eph.* i.

[2] " Voluit itaque Deus salvare cupientes, et provocavit ad salutem, ut voluntas haberet præmium; sed illi credere noluerunt."—*In Is.* lxiii.

[3] " Ut omnes homines Deus salvos fieri velit, et non eos tantum qui ad sanctorum numerum pertinebunt, sed omnes omnino, ut nullus habeatur exceptus."—*Ep. ad Aug.*

[4] " Omnibus dicit Christus: ' Venite ad me, etc.;' omnem enim, quantum in ipso est, hominem salvum fieri vult qui fecit omnes."—*Ep.* 24. *ad Sever.*

[5] " Etiam circa impios ostendere suam debuit voluntatem; et ideo nec proditurum debuit præterire, ut adverterent omnes quod in electione etiam proditoris sui servandorum omnium insigne prætendit . . . Et quod in Deo fuit, ostendit omnibus quod omnes voluit liberare."—*De Parad.* c. 8.

all men,[1] etc.), asks this question: "But since God wills that all should be saved, as he is Almighty, why are there so many who are not saved?" And he answers: "He wills them to be saved, if they also are willing; for he who gave the law excluded no one from salvation . . . . this medicine is of no use to the unwilling."[2] He says that God has excluded no one from glory, and that he gives grace to all to be saved, but on condition that they are willing to correspond to it; because his grace is of no use to the man who rejects it. St. Chrysostom in like manner asks, "Why then are not all men saved, if God wills all to be saved?" and he answers, "Because every man's will does not coincide with his will, and he forces no man."[3] St. Augustine: "God wills all men to be saved, but not so as to destroy their free will."[4] He says the same thing in several other places, which we shall shortly have to produce.

II.

Jesus Christ Died to Save All Men.

That Jesus Christ, therefore, died for all and each of mankind, is clear, not only from the Scriptures, but from the writings of the Fathers. Great certainly was the ruin which the sin of Adam occasioned to the whole human race ; but Jesus Christ, by the grace of Redemption, repaired all the evils which Adam introduced. Hence the Council of Trent has declared that baptism

---

[1] "Qui omnes homines vult salvos fieri."

[2] "Vult illos salvari, si et ipsi velint; nam utique qui legem dedit, nullum excipit a salute . . Hæc medicina non profuit invitis."

[3] "Cur igitur non omnes salvi fiunt, si vult Deus omnes salvos esse ? Quoniam non omnium voluntas illius voluntatem sequitur; porro ipse neminem cogit."—*De Mut. nom. hom.* 3, *E. B.*

[4] "Vult Deus omnes homines salvos fieri, non sic tamen ut eis adimat liberum arbitrium."—*De Spir. et Litt.* c. 33.

renders the soul pure and immaculate ; and that the sin which remains in it is not for its harm, but to enable it to gain a higher crown, if it resists so as not to consent to it : "For in the regenerate God hates nothing . . . they are made innocent, immaculate, pure, and beloved of God. . . . But this holy synod confesses and feels that concupiscence or the fuel (of sin) remains in baptized persons ; but as it was left for our probation, it cannot injure those who do not consent to it ; nay rather, he who contends lawfully (against it) shall be crowned."[1] Thus, as St. Leo says, "we have gained greater things by the grace of Christ than we had lost through the envy of the devil."[2] The gain which we have made by the redemption of Jesus Christ is greater than the loss which we suffered by the sin of Adam. The Apostle plainly declared this when he said, *Not as the offence, so also the gift. For where the offence abounded, there did grace more abound.*[3] Our Lord says the same : *I am come that they may have life, and have it more abundantly.*[4] David and Isaias had predicted it : *With Him is plentiful redemption.—She hath received of the hand of the Lord double for all her sins.*[5] About which words the interpreter says: "God has so forgiven iniquities through Christ, that men have re-

[1] "In renatis enim nihil odit Deus . . . : innocentes, immaculati, puri, innoxii ac Deo dilecti effecti sunt, etc. Manere autem in baptizatis concupiscentiam vel fomitem, hæc sancta Synodus fatetur et sentit: quæ cum ad agonem relicta sit, nocere non consentientibus . . . non valet; quinimo, qui legitime certaverit, coronabitur."—*Sess.* 5, *De pecc. or. n.* 5.

[2] "Ampliora adepti (sumus) per Christi gratiam, quam per diaboli amiseramus invidiam."—*De Asc.* s. 1.

[3] "Non sicut delictum, ita et donum. . . Ubi autem abundavit delictum, superabundavit gratia."—*Rom.* v. 15, 20.

[4] "Ego veni ut vitam habeant, et abundantius habeant."—*John,* x. 10.

[5] "Et copiosa apud eum redemptio."—*Ps.* cxxix. 7.—"Suscepit (Jerusalem) de manu Domini duplicia pro omnibus peccatis suis."—*Isa.* xl. 2.

ceived double—that is, very much greater good, instead of the punishment of sin which they deserved." [1]

Now that our Saviour, as I said, died for all, and that he offered the work of his redemption to the Eternal Father for the salvation of each one, the holy Scriptures assure us of the following :

I. THE TESTIMONY OF HOLY SCRIPTURE.

The Son of Man came to save that which was lost.[2] *Who gave Himself a redemption for all.*[3] *Christ died for all, that they also who live may not now live to themselves, but to Him who died for them.*[4] *For hereunto we labor and are reviled, because we hope in the living God, who is the Saviour of all men, especially of the faithful.*[5] *And he is the propitiation for our sins; and not for ours only, but also for those of the whole world.*[6] *For the charity of Christ presseth us, judging this that, if one died for all, then all were dead.*[7] And to speak only of this last text, I ask, how could the Apostle ever have concluded that all were dead, because Christ died for all, unless he had been certain that Christ had really died for all ? And the more, because St. Paul uses

[1] " Deus ita dimisit Ecclesiæ iniquitates per Christum, ut duplicia, id est, multiplicia bona susceperit pro pœnis peccatorum quas merebatur."

[2] " Venit Filius hominis salvare quod perierat."—*Matt.* xviii. 11.

[3] " Qui dedit redemptionem semetipsum pro omnibus."—1 *Tim.* ii. 6.

[4] " Pro omnibus mortuus est Christus, ut et qui vivunt, non jam sibi vivant, sed ei qui pro ipsis mortuus est."—2 *Cor.* v. 15.

[5] " In hoc enim laboramus et maledicimur, quia speramus in Deum vivum, qui est Salvator omnium hominum, maxime fidelium."—1 *Tim* iv. 10.

[6] " Et ipse est propitiatio pro peccatis nostris; non pro nostris autem tantum, sed etiam pro totius mundi."—1 *John,* ii. 2.

[7] " Charitas enim Christi urget nos: æstimantes hoc, quoniam si unus pro omnibus mortuus est, ergo omnes mortui sunt."—2 *Cor.* v. 14.

this truth as an argument for the love which it should kindle in us towards our Saviour. But by far the best passage to exhibit the desire and wish which God has to save all men, is another text of St. Paul: *He that spared not His own son, but delivered Him for us all.*[1] The force of this passage is increased by what follows: *How hath He not also with Him given us all things.*[2] If God has given us all things, how can we henceforth fear that he has denied us the election to glory, always on condition that we correspond (to his grace)? And if he has given us his Son, says Cardinal Sfondrati, how will he deny us the grace to be saved? " Here he clearly instructs us" (he is speaking of St. Paul) " that God assures us that he will not refuse us the less after he has given the greater; that he will not deny us grace to save ourselves, after giving his Son that we might be saved."[3] And in truth, how could St. Paul have said that God, in giving us his Son, has given us all things, if the Apostle had believed that God had excluded many from the glory which is the one good and the one end for which they were created? Has then God given "all things" to these "many," and yet denied them the best thing—namely, eternal happiness, without which (as there is no middle way) they cannot but be eternally miserable? Unless we would say another thing still more unseemly, as another learned author well observes—namely, that God gives to all the grace to attain glory, but then refuses to allow many to enter on its enjoyment; that he gives the means, and refuses the end.

[1] "Qui etiam proprio Filio suo non pepercit, sed pro nobis omnibus tradidit illum."—*Rom.* viii. 32.

[2] "Quomodo non etiam cum illo omnia nobis donavit?"—*Rom.* viii. 32.

[3] "Quid enim potuit negare, quibus Filium dedit? Absurdissimum est dicere Deum, qui dedit quod majus, noluisse dare quod est minus, hoc est, omnia ad salutem consequendam necessaria."—*Nod. præd.* p. I, § 2, n. 1.

2. THE TEACHING OF THE HOLY FATHERS.

For the rest, all the holy Fathers agree in saying that Jesus Christ died to obtain eternal salvation for all men.

St. Jerome: "Christ died for all; he was the only one who could be offered for all, because all were dead in sins."[1]

St. Ambrose: "Christ came to cure our wounds; but since all do not search for the remedy . . , therefore he cures those who are willing; he does not force the unwilling."[2] In another place: "He has provided for all men the means of cure, that whoever perishes may lay the blame of his death on himself, because he would not be cured when he had a remedy; and that, on the other hand, the mercy of Christ to all may be openly proclaimed, who wills that all men should be saved."[3] And more clearly still in another place: "Jesus did not write his will for the benefit of one, or of few, but of all; we are all inscribed therein as his heirs; the legacy is in common, and belongs by right to all; the universal heritage, belonging wholly to each."[4] Mark the words, "We are all inscribed as heirs; the Redeemer has written us all down as heirs of heaven."[5]

[1] "Pro omnibus mortuus est Christus; solus inventus est qui, pro omnibus qui erant in peccatis mortui, offerretur."—*In 2 Cor.* v.

[2] "Venit ut vulnera nostra curaret; sed, quia non omnes medicinam expetunt . . . ideo volentes curat, non adstringit invitos."—*In Ps.* lxxii.

[3] "Omnibus opem sanitatis detulit, ut quicumque perierit, mortis suæ causas sibi adscribat, qui curari noluit, cum remedium haberet. Christi autem manifesta in omnes prædicetur misericordia, 'Qui omnes vult salvos fieri.'"—*De Abel.* l. 2, c. 3.

[4] "Non ad unum quidem, non ad paucos, sed ad omnes testamentum suum scripsit Jesus; omnes scripti heredes sumus; testamentum commune est et jus omnium; hereditas universorum et soliditas singulorum."—*In Ps.* cxviii. s. 14.

[5] "Omnes scripti heredes sumus."

St. Leo: "As Christ found no one free from guilt, so he came to deliver all."[1]

St. Augustine, on the words of St. John, *For God did not send His Son to judge the world, but that the world might be saved through Him,*[2] says: "So, as far as it lies with the physician, he came to heal the sick man."[3] Mark the words, "as far as it lies with the physician." For God, as far as he is concerned, effectually wills the salvation of all, but (as St. Augustine goes on to say) cannot heal the man who will not be healed: "He heals universally, but he heals not the unwilling.[4] For what can be happier for thee, than, as thou hast thy life in thy hands, so to have thy health depend on thy will?"[5] When he says "He heals," he speaks of sinners who are sick, and unable to get well by their own strength; when he says "universally" (*omnino*), he declares that nothing is wanting on God's part for sinners to be healed and saved. Then when he says, "as thou hast thy life in thy hands, so thy health depends on thy will," he shows that God for his part really wills us all to be saved; otherwise, it would not be in our power to obtain health and eternal life. In another place, "He who redeemed us at such a cost, wills not that we perish; for he does not purchase in order to destroy, but he redeems in order to give life."[6] He has redeemed us all, in order to save us all. And

---

[1] "Sicut Christus nullum a reatu liberum reperit, ita liberandis omnibus venit."—*In Nat. Dom.* s. 1

[2] "Non enim misit Deus Filium suum in mundum, ut judicet mundum, sed ut salvetur mundus per ipsum."—*John*, iii. 17.

[3] "Ergo, quantum in medico est, sanare venit ægrotum."—*In Jo. tr.* 12.

[4] "Sanat omnino ille quemlibet languidum, sed non sanat invitum."—*In Ps.* cii.

[5] "Quid autem te beatius, quam ut, tamquam in manu tua vitam, sic habeas in voluntate sanitatem tuam?"

[6] "Qui nos tanto pretio redemit, non vult perire quos emit; non emit quos perdat, sed emit quos vivificet."—*Serm.* 22, *E. B.*

hence he encourages all to hope for eternal bliss in that celebrated sentence: "Let human frailty raise itself; let it not say, I shall never be happy. . . . It is a greater thing that Christ has done, than that which he has promised. What has he done? He has died for thee. What has he promised? That thou shalt live with him."[1]

Some have pretended to say that Jesus Christ offered his blood for all, in order to obtain grace for them, but not salvation. But Petrocorensis will not hear of this opinion, of which he says: "O disputatious frivolity! How could the wisdom of God will the means of salvation, without willing its end."[2] St. Augustine, moreover, speaking against the Jews, says: "Ye acknowledge the side which ye pierced, that it was opened both by you and for you."[3] If Jesus Christ had not really given his blood for all, the Jews might have answered St. Augustine, that it was quite true they had opened the side of our Saviour, but not that it was opened for them.

In like manner, St. Thomas has no doubt that Jesus Christ died for all; whence he deduces that he wills all to be saved: "Christ Jesus is mediator between God and men; not between God and some men, but between him and all men; and this would not be, unless he willed all to be saved."[4] This is confirmed, as we have already said, by the condemnation of the fifth proposition of Jansenius, who said, "It is semi-Pelagianism to assert

[1] "Erigat se humana fragilitas; non dicat: Non ero (beatus). . . . Plus est quod (Christus) fecit, quam quod promisit; quid fecit? mortuus est pro te; quid promisit? ut vivas cum illo."—*In Ps.* cxlviii.

[2] "O contentiosam nugacitatem! Quomodo Dei sapientia medium voluit et non finem salutis?"—*Lib.* iii. c. 3, q. 4.

[3] "Agnoscitis latus quod pupugistis, quoniam et per vos et propter vos apertum est?"—*De Symb. ad cat.* l. 2, c. 8.

[4] "Christus Jesus est Mediator Dei et hominum, non quorumdam, sed inter Deum et omnes homines; et hoc non fuisset, nisi vellet omnes salvare."—*In* 1 *Tim.* ii. *lect.* 1.

that Christ died or shed his blood for all men."[1] The
sense of this, according to the context of the other condemned propositions, and according to the principles of
Jansenius, is as follows: Jesus Christ did not die to merit
for all men the graces sufficient for salvation, but only for
the predestined; or, in Jansenius's own expressed words.
"It is in no way consonant to the principles of Augustine, to think that Christ our Lord died or shed his blood
for the eternal salvation either of unbelievers, who die in
their unbelief, or of the just, who do not persevere."[2]
Therefore the contrary and Catholic belief is as follows:
It is not semi-Pelagianism, but it is right to say that
Jesus Christ died to merit not only for the predestinate,
but for all, even for the reprobate, grace sufficient to obtain eternal salvation in the ordinary course of Providence.

Further, that God truly, on his part, wills all men to
be saved, and that Jesus Christ died for the salvation of
all, is certified to us by the fact that God imposes on us
all the precept of hope. The reason is clear. St. Paul
calls Christian hope the anchor of the soul, secure and
firm: *Who have fled for refuge to hold fast the hope set before
us which we have as an anchor of the soul, sure and firm.*[3]
Now in what could we fix this sure and firm anchor of
our hope, except in the truth that God wills all to be
saved? "With what confidence," says Petrocorensis,
"will men be able to hope for God's mercy, if it is not
certain that God wills the salvation of all of them?
With what confidence will they offer the death of Christ

[1] "Semipelagianum est dicere Christum pro omnibus mortuum esse
et sanguinem fudisse."

[2] "Nullo modo principiis ejus (Augustini) consentaneum est, ut
Christus Dominus, vel pro infidelium in infidelitate morientium, vel
pro justorum non perseverantium æterna salute, mortuus esse et
sanguinem fudisse sentiatur."—*De Grat. Chr.* c. 20.

[3] "Confugimus ad tenendam propositam spem, quam sicut anchoram habemus animæ tutam ac firmam."—*Heb.* vi. 18.

to God, in order to obtain pardon, if it is uncertain whether he was offered up for them?"[1] And Cardinal Sfondrati says, that if God had elected some to eternal life, and excluded others, we should have a greater motive to despair than to hope; seeing that, in fact, the elect are much fewer than the damned: "No one could have a firm hope, since he would have more grounds of despair than of hope; for the reprobate are much more numerous than the elect."[2] And if Jesus Christ had not died for the salvation of all, how could we have a sure ground to hope for salvation through the merits of Jesus Christ, without a special revelation? But St. Augustine had no doubt when he said, "All my hope, and the certainty of my faith, is in the precious blood of Christ, which was shed for us and for our salvation."[3] Thus the saint placed all his hope in the blood of Jesus Christ; because the faith assured him that Christ died for all. But we shall have a better opportunity of examining this question of hope in chapter iii., where we shall establish the principal point—namely, that the grace of prayer is given to all.

III.

Children who Die without Baptism.

Here it only remains for us to answer the objection which is drawn from children being lost when they die

---

[1] "Qua fiducia divinam misericordiam sperare poterunt scelerati homines, si certum non sit quod Deus salutem eorum velit? Qua fiducia Christi mortem Deo offerre poterunt, ut indulgentiam consequantur, si incertum est an pro ipsis oblata sit?"—*Lib.* 3, *c.* 3, *q.* 4.

[2] "Nemo firmiter sperare posset, dum ei plura desperandi quam sperandi fundamenta suppetunt; nam plures sunt relicti quam electi."—*Nod. præd. p.* 1. § 1.

[3] "Omnis namque spes et totius fidei certitudo mihi est in pretioso sanguine Christi, qui effusus est propter nos et propter nostram salutem."—*Medit. c.* 14.

before baptism, and before they come to the use of reason. If God wills all to be saved, it is objected, how is
it that these children perish without any fault of their
own, since God gives them no assistance to attain eternal salvation? There are two answers to this objection,
the latter more correct than the former. I will state
them briefly.

First, it is answered that God, by antecedent will,
wishes all to be saved, and therefore has granted universal means for the salvation of all; but these means at
times fail of their effect, either by reason of the unwillingness of some persons to avail themselves of them, or
because others are unable to make use of them, on account of secondary causes (such as the death of children),
whose course God is not bound to change, after having
disposed the whole according to the just judgment of
his general Providence; all this is collected from what
St. Thomas says. Jesus Christ offered his merits for all
men, and instituted baptism for all; but the application
of this means of salvation, so far as relates to children
who die before the use of reason, is not prevented by
the direct will of God, but by a merely permissive will;
because as he is the general provider of all things, he is
not bound to disturb the general order, to provide for
the particular order.

The second answer is, that to perish is not the same
as not to be blessed: since eternal happiness is a gift entirely gratuitous; and therefore the want of it is not a
punishment. The opinion, therefore, of St. Thomas is
very just, that children who die in infancy have neither
the pain of sense nor the pain of loss; not the pain of
sense, he says, "because pain of sense corresponds to
conversion to creatures; and in original sin there is not
conversion to creatures" (as the fault is not our own),
"and therefore pain of sense is not due to original

sin;" because original sin does not imply an act.[1] Ob-
jectors oppose to this the teaching of St. Augustine,
who in some places shows that his opinion was that children are condemned even to the pain of sense. But in
another place he declares that he was very much confused about this point. These are his words: "When I
come to the punishment of infants, I find myself (believe
me) in great straits; nor can I at all find anything to
say."[2] And in another place he writes, that it may be
said that such children receive neither reward nor punishment: "Nor need we fear that it is impossible there
should be a middle sentence between reward and punishment; since their life was midway between sin and
good works."[3] This was directly affirmed by St. Gregory Nazianzen: "Children will be sentenced by the
just judge neither to the glory of heaven nor to punishment."[4] St. Gregory of Nyssa was of the same opinion: "The premature death of children shows that they
who have thus ceased to live will not be in pain and un-
happiness."[5]

And as far as relates to the pain of loss, although
these children are excluded from glory, nevertheless St.
Thomas,[6] who had reflected most deeply on this point,

---

[1] "Pœna sensus respondet conversioni ad creaturam, et in peccato
originali non est conversio ad creaturam; et ideo peccato originali non
debetur pœna sensus."—*De Mal. q.* 5, *a.* 2.

[2] "Cum ad pœnas ventum est parvulorum, magnis, mihi crede,
coarctor angustiis, ne quid respondeam prorsus invenio."—*Epist.*
166, *E. B.*

[3] "Non enim metuendum est ne vita esse potuerit media quædam
inter recte factum atque peccatum, et sententia judicis media esse non
possit inter præmium et supplicium."—*De Lib. Arb. l.* 3, *c.* 23.

[4] "Parvuli nec cœlesti gloria nec suppliciis a Justo Judice afficien-
tur."—*Serm. in S. Lav.*

[5] "Immatura mors infantium demonstrat neque in doloribus et
mœstitia futuros eos qui sic vivere desierunt."—*De Infant. etc.*

[6] *In* 2 *Sent. d.* 33, *q.* 2, *a.* 2.

teaches that no one feels pain for the want of that good
of which he is not capable; so that as no man grieves
that he cannot fly, or no private person that he is not
emperor, so these children feel no pain at being deprived
of the glory of which they were never capable; since
they could never pretend to it either by the principles of
nature, or by their own merits. St. Thomas adds, in
another place,[1] a further reason, which is, that the supernatural knowledge of glory comes only by means of actual faith, which transcends all natural knowledge; so
that children can never feel pain for the privation of that
glory, of which they never had a supernatural knowledge. He further says, in the former passage, that such
children will not only not grieve for the loss of eternal
happiness, but will, moreover, have pleasure in their
natural gifts; and will even in some way enjoy God, so
far as is implied in natural knowledge, and in natural
love: "Rather will they rejoice in this, that they will
participate much in the divine goodness, and in natural
perfections."[2] And he immediately adds, that although
they will be separated from God, as regards the union
of glory, nevertheless "they will be united with him by
participation of natural gifts; and so will even be able
to rejoice in him with a natural knowledge and love."[3]

[1] *De Mal. q.* 5, *a.* 3.

[2] "Imo magis gaudebunt de hoc quod participabunt multum de
divina bonitate et perfectionibus naturalibus."

[3] "Deo conjunguntur per participationem naturalium bonorum, et
ita etiam de ipso gaudere poterunt naturali cognitione et dilectione."
—*In* 2. *Sent. d.* 33, *q.* 2, *a.* 2.

CHAPTER II.

GOD COMMONLY GIVES TO ALL THE JUST THE GRACE NECESSARY FOR THE OBSERVANCE OF THE COMMANDMENTS, AND TO ALL SINNERS THE GRACE NECESSARY FOR CONVERSION.

I.

Proofs.

IF then God wills all to be saved, it follows that he gives to all that grace and those aids which are necessary for the attainment of salvation, otherwise it could never be said that he has a true will to save all. "The effect of the antecedent will," says St. Thomas, "by which God wills the salvation of all men, is that order of nature the purpose of which is our salvation, and likewise those things which conduce to that end, and which are offered to all in common, whether by nature or by grace." [1] It is certain, in contradiction to the blasphemies of Luther and Calvin, that God does not impose a law that is impossible to be observed. On the other hand, it is certain, that without the assistance of grace the observance of the law is impossible; as Innocent I. declared against the Pelagians when he said, "It is certain, that as we overcome by the aid of God, so without his aid we must be overcome." [2] Pope Celestine declared

[1] "Antecedentis voluntatis, qua Deus vult omnium salutem, effectus est ipse ordo naturæ in finem salutis, et promoventia in finem omnibus communiter proposita, tam naturalia quam gratuita."—*In* 1 *Sent. d.* 46. *q.* 1. *a.* 1.

[2] "Necesse est ut, quo (Deo) auxiliante vincimus, eo non adjuvante vincamur."—*Rescr. ad Conc. Carthag.*

the same thing.   Therefore, if God gives to all men a
possible law, it follows that he also gives to all men the
grace necessary to observe it, whether immediately, or
mediately, by means of prayer, as the Council of Trent
has most clearly defined: "God does not command impossibilities; but by commanding he admonishes you
both to do what you can, and to ask for that which is
beyond your power, and by his help enables you to do
it." [1]   Otherwise, if God refused us both the proximate
and remote grace to enable us to fulfil the law, either
the law would have been given in vain, or sin would be
necessary, and if necessary would be no longer sin, as
we shall shortly prove at some length.

I. TEACHING OF THE FATHERS OF THE GREEK CHURCH.

And this is the general opinion of the Greek Fathers:
St. Cyril of Alexandria says: "But if a man endowed
as others, and equally with them, with the gifts of divine
grace, has fallen by his own free will, how shall Christ
be said not to have saved even him, since he delivered
the man and gave him the necessary aid to avoid
sin." [2]   How, says the saint, can that sinner, who has received the assistance of grace equally with those who
remained faithful, and has of his own accord chosen to
sin, how can he blame Jesus Christ, who has, as far as
he is concerned, delivered him by means of the assistance
granted to him ?   St. John Chrysostom asks: "How is it
that some are vessels of wrath, others vessels of mercy?"

[1] "Deus impossiblia non jubet, sed jubendo monet, et facere quod
possis et petere quod non possis; et adjuvat ut possis."—*Sess.* 6,
cap. 11.

[2] "Quod si (quis), perinde atque alii, et ex æquo cum ipsis divinæ
gratiæ opibus præditus, propria voluntate delapsus est, quomodo
non eum servasse dicitur Christus, qui, quantum ad cavendi peccati
auxilia concessa pertinet, hominem liberavit?"—*In Jo. l.* 11. *c.* 21.

And he answers, "Because of each person's free will; for, since God is very good, he manifests equal kindness to all." [1]   Then, speaking of Pharaoh, whose heart is said in Scripture to have been hardened, he adds, "If Pharaoh was not saved, it must all be attributed to his will, since no less was given to him than to those who were saved." [2]   And in another place, speaking of the petition of the mother of Zebedee's sons, on the words, "*It is not mine to give, etc.,*" [3] he observes: "By this Christ wished to show that it was not simply his to give, but that it also belonged to the combatants to take; for if it depended only on himself, all men would be saved." [4]

St. Isidore of Pelusium: "For God wills seriously, and in all ways, to assist those who are wallowing in vice, that he may deprive them of all excuse." [5]

St. Cyril of Jerusalem: "God has opened the gate of eternal life, so that, as far as he is concerned, all may gain it without anything to hinder them." [6]

But the doctrine of these Greek Fathers does not suit Jansenius, who has the temerity to say that they have spoken most imperfectly on grace: "None have spoken in grace more imperfectly than the Greeks." [7]   In matters

[1] "Ex libera sua utique voluntate; nam Deus, cum sit valde bonus, in utrisque parem benignitatem ostendit."

[2] "Si salutem Pharao non est adeptus, totum id illius voluntati tribuendum est, cum nihil minus, quam qui salutem assecuti sunt, concessum illi fuerit."—*In Rom. hom.* 16.

[3] "Non est meum dare vobis, etc."—*Matt.* xx. 23.

[4] "Hoc illum (Christum) significare voluisse, non suum esse tantummodo dare, sed et certantium esse capere; nam, si istud ex se uno penderet, omnes utique salvi essent homines."—*Hom. in loco cit. cont. Anom.*

[5] "Etenim serio et modis omnibus (Deus) vult eos adjuvare qui in vitio volutantur, ut omnem eis excusationem eripiat."—*Lib.* 2. *ep.* 270.

[6] "Multas æternæ vitæ januas (Dominus) aperuit, ut omnes, quantum in ipso est, absque impedimento illa potiri possint."—*Catech.* 18.

[7] "Nulli imperfectius de gratia quam Græci locuti sunt."

of grace, then, are we not to follow the teaching of the Greek Fathers, who were the first masters and columns of the Church? Perhaps the doctrine of the Greeks, especially in this important matter, was different from that of the Latin Church? On the contrary, it is certain that the true doctrine of faith came from the Greek to the Latin Church; so that, as St. Augustine wrote against Julian, who opposed to him the authority of the Greek Fathers, there can be no doubt that the faith of the Latins is the same as that of the Greeks. Whom, then, are we to follow? Shall we follow Jansenius, whose errors have already been condemned as heretical by the Church; who had the audacity to say that even the just have not the grace requisite to enable them to keep certain precepts; and that man merits and demerits, even though he acts through necessity, provided he is not forced by violence; these and all his other errors springing from his most false system of *the delectation relatively victorious*, of which we shall speak at length when we confute him in chapter iii.

2. TEACHING OF THE FATHERS OF THE LATIN CHURCH.

But since the Greek Fathers do not satisfy Jansenius, let us see what the Latins say on this subject. But they in no wise differ from the Greeks.

St. Jerome says, "Man can do no good work without God, who, in giving free will, did not refuse his grace to aid every single work."[1] Mark the words "did not refuse his grace for every single work." St. Ambrose: "He would never come and knock at the door, unless he wished to enter; it is our fault that he does not always enter."[2] St. Leo: "Justly does he insist on the com-

[1] "Nihil boni operis (homo) agere potest absque eo, qui ita concessit liberum arbitrium, ut suam per singula opera gratiam non negaret."—*Ep. ad Cyprian. presb.*

[2] "Qui enim venit et januam pulsat, vult semper intrare; sed in nobis est quod non semper ingreditur."—*In Ps.* cxviii. s. 12.

mand, since he furnishes beforehand aid to keep it."[1] St. Hilary: "Now the grace of justification has abounded through one gift to all men."[2]   Innocent I.: "He gives to man daily remedies; and unless we put confidence in them and depend upon them, we shall never be able to overcome human errors."[3]

St. Augustine: "It is not imputed to you as a sin if you are ignorant against your will, but if you neglect to learn that of which you are ignorant. Nor is it imputed as a sin that you do not bind up your wounded limbs, but (mark this) that you despise him who is willing to cure you. These are your own sins; for no man is deprived of the knowledge of how to seek with benefit to himself."   In another place: "Therefore if the soul is ignorant what it is to do, it proceeds from this, that it has not yet learned; but it will receive this knowledge if it has made a good use of what it has already received; for it has received in this that it can piously and diligently seek, if it will;" (mark the words) "it has received power to seek piously and diligently."[4] So that every one receives at least the remote grace to seek; and if he makes good use of this, he will receive the proximate grace to perform that which at first he could not do. St. Augustine founds all this on the principle, that no man sins in

---

[1] "Juste instat præcepto, qui præcurrit auxilio."—*De Pass.* s. 16.

[2] "Nunc per unum in omnes donum vitæ justificationis gratia abundavit."—*In Ps.* lix.

[3] "Quotidiana præstat (homini) remedia, quibus nisi freti nitamur, nullatenus humanos vincere poterimus errores."—*Rescr. ad Conc. Carthag.*

[4] "Non tibi deputatur ad culpam quod invitus ignoras, sed quod negligis quærere quod ignoras; neque illud quod vulnerata membra non colligis, sed quod volentem sanare contemnis. Ista tua propria peccata sunt: nulli enim homini ablatum est scire utiliter quærere.— Quod ergo ignorat (anima) quid sibi agendum sit, ex eo est quod nondum accepit; sed hoc quoque accipiet, si hoc quod accepit bene usa fuerit: accepit autem ut pie ac diligenter quærat, si volet."—*De Lib. Arb.* l. 3, c. 19, 22.

doing that which he cannot help; therefore, if a man
sins in anything, he sins in that he might have avoided
it by the grace of God, which is wanting to no man:
"Who sins in that which cannot in any way be helped?
but a man does sin, therefore it might have been
helped."[1] "But only by his aid, who cannot be deceived."[2] An evident reason, by which it becomes quite
clear (as we shall have to show further on, when we
speak of the sin of the obstinate), that if the grace
necessary to observe the commandments were wanting,
there would be no sin.

St. Thomas teaches the same in several places. In
one place, in explaining the text, *Who wills all men to be
saved*,[3] he says, "and therefore grace is wanting to no
man, but (as far as God is concerned) is communicated
to all; as the sun is present even to the blind."[4] So that
as the sun sheds its light upon all, and only those are
deprived of it who voluntarily blind themselves to its
rays, so God communicates to all men grace to observe
the law; and men are lost simply because they will
not avail themselves of it. In another place: "It belongs
to divine Providence to provide all men with what is
necessary to salvation, if only there be no impediment on
man's part."[5] If, then, God gives all men the graces
necessary for salvation, and if actual grace is necessary
to overcome temptations, and to observe the commandments, we must necessarily conclude that he gives all
men either immediately or mediately actual grace to do

[1] " Quis peccat in eo quod nullo modo caveri potest? peccatur autem; caveri igitur potest."—*De Lib. Arb.* l. 3, c. 18.

[2] " Sed opitulante illo qui non potest falli."—*De Nat. et Gr.* c. 67.

[3] " Qui omnes homines vult salvos fieri."—1 *Tim.* ii. 4.

[4] " Et ideo gratia nulli deest, sed omnibus, quantum in se est, se
communicat, sicut nec sol deest oculis cœcis."—*In Heb.* 12, *lect.* 3.

[5] " Hoc ad divinam Providentiam pertinet, ut cuilibet provideat de
necessariis ad salutem, dummodo ex parte ejus (hominis) non impediatur."—*De Ver.* q. 14, a. 11.

good; and when mediately, no further grace is necessary to enable them to put in practice the means (such
as prayer) of obtaining actual proximate grace. In another place, on the words of St. John's Gospel, *No man
cometh to Me*, etc.,[1] he says, "If the heart of man be not
lifted up, it is from no defect on the part of Him who
draws it, who as far as He is concerned, never fails; but
from an impediment caused by him who is being
drawn." [2]

Scotus says the same: "God wills to save all men, so
far as rests with him, and with his antecedent will, by
which he has given them the ordinary gifts necessary to
salvation." [3] The Council of Cologne in 1536: "Although no one is converted except he is drawn by the
Father, yet let no one pretend to excuse himself on the
plea of not being drawn. He stands at the gate, and
knocks by the internal and the external Word." [4]

3. TESTIMONY OF HOLY SCRIPTURE.

Nor did the Fathers speak without warrant of the
Holy Scriptures; for God in several places most clearly
assures us that he does not neglect to assist us with his
grace, if we are willing to avail ourselves of it either for
perseverance, if we are in a state of justification, or for
conversion, if we are in sin.

I stand at the gate and knock; if any man shall hear My

[1] "Nemo potest venire ad me, nisi Pater, qui misit me, traxerit
eum."

[2] "Si non elevatur (cor humanum), non est defectus ex parte tra-
hentis, qui, quantum in se est, nulli deficit; sed est propter impedimentum ejus qui trahitur."—*In Jo.* 6, *lect.* 5.

[3] "Vult (Deus) omnes homines salvare, quantum est ex parte sui et
voluntate sua antecedente, pro quanto dedit eis dona communia sufficientia ad salutem."—*In* 1 *Sent.* d. 46, q. un.

[4] "Quanquam nemo convertatur nisi tractus per Patrem, attamen
nemo excusationem prætexat quod non trahatur; ille semper stat ante
ostium pulsans per internum et externum verbum."—P. 7, c. 32.

voice and open to Me the gate, I will come in to him.[1] Bellarmine reasons well on this text, that our Lord who knows
that man cannot open without his grace, would knock in
vain at the door of his heart, unless he had first conferred on him the grace to open when he will. This is
exactly what St. Thomas teaches in explaining the text;
he says that God gives every one the grace necessary for
salvation, that he may correspond to it if he will: "God
by his most liberal will gives grace to every one that
prepares himself: *Behold I stand at the door and knock.*[2]
And therefore the grace of God is wanting to no one,
but communicates itself to all men, as far as it is concerned."[3] In another place he says, "It is the business
of God's Providence to provide every one with what is
necessary to salvation." So that as St. Ambrose says:
The Lord knocks at the gate, because he truly wishes to
enter; if he does not enter, or if after entering he does
not remain in our souls, it is because we prevent him
from entering, or drive him out when he has entered:
"Because he comes and knocks at the door, he always
wishes to enter; but it is through us that he does not
always go in, nor always remain."[4]

*What is there that I ought to do more to My vineyard that
I have not done to it? Was it that I expected that it should
bring forth grapes, and it hath brought forth wild grapes?*[5]
Bellarmine says on these words, "If he had not given the

---

[1] " Ecce sto ad ostium, et pulso; si quis . . . aperuerit mihi januam,
intrabo."—*Apoc.* iii. 20.

[2] "Deus voluntate sua liberalissima dat eam (gratiam) omni præparanti se."—*In Heb.* 12, *lect.* 3.

[3] "Et ideo gratia Dei nulli deest, etc. Hoc ad divinam Providentiam pertinet, etc."—Page 138.

[4] "Qui enim venit et januam pulsat, vult semper intrare; sed in nobis
est quod non semper ingreditur, non semper manet."—*In Ps.* cxviii.
s. 12.

[5] "Quid est quod debui ultra facere vineæ meæ, et non feci ei? an
quod exspectavi ut faceret uvas, et fecit labruscas?"—*Is.* v. 4.

power to bring forth grapes, how could God say, *I expected?* [1] And if God had not given to all men the grace necessary for salvation, he could not have said to the Jews, *What is there that I ought to have done more?* for they could have answered, that if they had not yielded fruit, it was for lack of necessary assistance. Bellarmine says the same on the words of our Lord: *How often would I have gathered together thy children, and thou wouldst not?* [2] "How did he wish to be sought for by the unwilling unless he helps them that they may be able to be willing?" [3]

We have received Thy mercy, O God, in the midst of Thy temple. [4] On this St. Bernard observes: "Mercy is in the midst of the temple, not in any hole and corner, because there is no acceptance of persons with God; [5] it is placed in public, it is offered to all, and no one is without it, except he who refuses it." [6]

Or despisest thou the riches of His goodness? Knowest thou not that the benignity of God leadeth thee to penance? [7] You see that it is through his own malice that the sinner is not converted, because he despises the riches of the divine goodness which calls him, and never ceases to

[1] "Si non dedisset facultatem ad faciendas uvas, quorsum diceret Dominus: 'Exspectavi?'"

[2] "Quoties volui congregare filios tuos . . . . et noluisti?"—*Matt.* xxiii. 37.

[3] "Quomodo voluit, ita ut queratur de nolentibus, si eos non juvit ut possent velle?"

[4] "Suscepimus, Deus, misericordiam tuam in medio templi tui."—*Ps.* xlvii. 10.

[5] "In medio enim templi misericordia est, non in angulo aut diversorio, quia 'Non est acceptio personarum apud Deum' (*Rom.* ii. 11)."

[6] "In communi posita est, offertur omnibus, et nemo illius expers, nisi qui renuit."—*In Purif. B. V.* s. 1.

[7] "An divitias bonitatis ejus . . . . contemnis? ignoras quoniam benignitas Dei ad pœnitentiam te adducit?"—*Rom.* ii. 4.

move him to conversion by his grace. God hates sin; but at the same time never ceases to love the sinful soul while it remains on earth, and always gives it the assistance it requires for salvation: *But Thou sparest all, because they are Thine, O Lord, who lovest souls.*[1] Hence we see, says Bellarmine, that God does not refuse grace to resist temptations to any sinner, however obstinate and blinded he may be: "Assistance to avoid new sin is always at hand for all men, either immediately or mediately (*i.e.*, by means of prayer), so that they may ask further aid from God, by the help of which they will avoid sin."[2] Here we may quote what God says by Ezechiel: *As I live, saith the Lord God, I desire not the death of the wicked, but that the wicked turn from his way and live.*[3] St. Peter says the same: *He beareth patiently for your sakes, not willing that any should perish, but that all should return to penance.*[4] If, therefore, God wishes that all should actually be converted, it must necessarily be held that he gives to all the grace which they need for actual conversion.

II.

Obstinate or Hardened Sinners, and the Abandonment of Them by God.

I know well that there are theologians who maintain that God refuses to certain obstinate sinners even suf-

[1] "Parcis autem omnibus, quoniam tua sunt, Domine, qui amas animas."— *Wisd.* xi. 27.

[2] "Auxilium ad novum peccatum vitandum semper omnibus adest, vel immediate vel mediate, quo possint a Deo majora præsidia impetrare, quibus adjuti peccata vitabunt."—*De Gr. et Lib. Arb.* l. 2, c. 7.

[3] "Vivo ego, dicit Dominus Deus: nolo mortem impii, sed ut convertatur impius a via sua, et vivat."—*Ezech.* xxxiii. 11.

[4] "Patienter agit propter vos, nolens aliquos perire, sed omnes ad pœnitentiam reverti."—2 *Peter*, iii. 9.

ficient grace. And, among others, they avail themselves of a position of St. Thomas, who says: "But although they who are in sin cannot through their own power avoid putting or interposing an obstacle to grace, unless they are prevented by grace, as we have shown; nevertheless, this also is imputed to them as a sin, because this defect is left in them from previous sin—as a drunken man is not excused from murder committed in that drunkenness which was incurred by his own fault. Besides, although he who is in sin has not this in his own power that he altogether avoid sin, yet he has power at this present moment to avoid this or that sin, as has been said; so that whatever he commits, he commits voluntarily; and therefore it is properly imputed to him as sin." [1] From this they gather that St. Thomas intends to say that sinners can indeed avoid particular sins, but not all sins; because in punishment for sins previously committed they are deprived of all actual grace.

But we answer that here St. Thomas is not speaking of actual, but of habitual or sanctifying, grace, without which the sinner cannot keep himself long from falling into new sins, as he teaches in several places. [2] And that he means the same in the passage just quoted is clear from the context, which we must here transcribe, in order to understand the true meaning of the saint.

[1] "Quamvis autem illi qui in peccato sunt, vitare non possint, per propriam potestatem, quin impedimentum gratiæ præstent vel ponant, ut ostensum est, nisi auxilio gratiæ præveniantur; nihilominus tamen hoc eis imputatur ad culpam, quia hic defectus ex culpa præcedente in eis relinquitur: sicut ebrius ab homicidio non excusatur, quod per ebrietatem committit quam sua culpa incurrit. Præterea, licet ille qui est in peccato, non habeat hoc in propria potestate, quod omnino vitet peccatum, habet tamen potestatem nunc vitare hoc vel illud peccatum, ut dictum est; unde, quodcumque committit, voluntarie committit, et ita non immerito sibi imputatur ad culpam."—*Contra Gent.* l. 3, c. 160.

[2] "Quod homo, in peccato existens, sine gratia peccatum vitare non potest."

In the first place, the title of chapter clx., where the quotation occurs, is as follows: "That man, when he is in sin, cannot avoid sin without grace." The very title shows that St. Thomas intended no more than he has said in the other places which we have referred to.

Moreover, in the course of the chapter he says: "For when the mind of man has declined from the state of uprightness, it is manifest that it has fallen from its relation, 'order' (*ordo*), to its true end. . . . Whensoever, therefore, anything shall have occurred to the mind conducive to the inordinate end, but improper for the true end, it will be chosen, unless the mind be brought back to its due relation, so as to prefer its true end to all others; and this is the effect of grace. But while anything repugnant to our last end is the object of our choice, it puts a hindrance in the way of the grace which conducts us to that end; whence it is manifest that, after sinning, man cannot altogether abstain from sin, before he is brought back by grace to the due order. And hence the opinion of the Pelagians is shown to be absurd, that man, being in sin, can without grace avoid (fresh) sin."[1] And then he goes on with the sentence quoted above: "But although they,"[2] etc., of which our opponents make use.

So that, in the first place, the intention of St. Thomas is

---

[1] "Cum enim mens hominis a statu rectitudinis declinaverit, manifestum est quod recessit ab ordine debiti finis. . . . . Quandocumque igitur occurrerit aliquid conveniens inordinato fini, repugnans fini debito, eligetur, nisi reducatur ad debitum ordinem, ut finem debitum omnibus præferat, quod est gratiæ effectus; dum autem eligitur aliquid quod repugnat ultimo fini, impedimentum præstat gratiæ, quæ dirigit in finem. Unde manifestum est quod, post peccatum, non potest homo abstinere ab omni peccato, antequam per gratiam ad debitum ordinem reducatur. . . . Unde apparet stulta Pelagianorum opinio, qui dicebant hominem, in peccato existentem, sine gratia posse vitare peccata."

[2] Quamvis autem illi, etc.

not to prove that some sinners are deprived of all actual grace, and therefore, being unable to avoid all sin, they do commit sin, and are worthy of punishment; but his intention is to prove against the Pelagians that a man who remains without sanctifying grace cannot abstain from sinning. And we see that he is here certainly speaking of sanctifying grace, for this is that which alone brings the soul back to the right order. It is of this same sanctifying grace that he intends to speak, when he says immediately after, " Except he be prevented by the assistance of grace;" [1] by which he means that if the sinner is not prevented—that is, is not previously informed (*informato*)—by grace, and brought back to the right order of holding God to be his last end, he cannot avoid committing fresh sins. And this is the meaning of the Thomists—for instance, of Ferrariensis (Silvestre) and Father Gonet—in their comments on this passage. But, without having recourse to other authors, it is quite clear from what St. Thomas himself says in his *Summa*, where he discusses the same point, and brings forward the identical reasons in the same words as in the 160th chapter of his book *Contra Gentes;* and there he expressly says that he is only speaking of habitual or sanctifying grace.

And it is impossible that the holy Doctor could have meant otherwise, since he elsewhere teaches that, on the one hand, God's grace is never wanting to any one, as he says in his commentary on St. John: " But lest you might suppose that this effect was consequent on the removal of the true light, the Evangelist, to obviate this opposition, adds, that was the true light which enlightens every man. For the Word enlightens, so far as he is concerned, because on his part he is wanting to no one, but wishes all men to be saved. But if any one is not enlightened, this

---

[1] " Nisi auxilio gratiæ præveniantur."

is the fault of the man who turns himself away from the light that would enlighten him."[1] And, on the other hand, he teaches that there is no sinner so lost and abandoned by grace as not to be able to lay aside his obstinacy, and to unite himself to the will of God, which he certainly cannot do without the assistance of grace: "During this life there is no man who cannot lay aside obstinacy of mind, and so conform to the divine will."[2] In another place he says, "So long as the use of free will remains to a man in this life . . . he can prepare himself for grace by being sorry for his sins."[3] But no one can make an act of sorrow for sin without grace. In another place he says, "No man in this life can be so obstinate in evil but that it is possible for him to co-operate to his own deliverance."[4] "To co-operate" necessarily implies grace to co-operate with.

In another place he observes, on the text of St. Paul, *He wills all to be saved.*[5] "Therefore the grace of God is wanting to no man; but, as far as it is concerned, it communicates itself to all."[6] Again, on the same words,

[1] "Ne credas effectum ipsum esse ex remotione veræ lucis: hoc excludens, Evangelista subdit: 'Erat lux vera quæ illuminat omnem hominem.' Illuminat scilicet Verbum, quantum de se est, quia ex parte sua nulli deest, immo, 'Omnes homines vult salvos fieri.' Quod si aliquis non illuminatur, ex parte hominis est avertentis se a lumine illuminante."—*In Jo.* i. *lect.* 5.

[2] "In statu viæ, nullus est qui mentis obstinationem non possit deponere, et sic divinæ voluntati conformari."—*In* I *Sent.* d. 48, q. 1, a. 3.

[3] "Quamdiu manet homini usus liberi arbitrii in hac vita, . . . potest se præparare ad gratiam, de peccatis dolendo."—*In* 4 *Sent.* d. 20, q. 1, a. 1.

[4] "Aliquis homo in statu viæ non potest esse ita obstinatus in malo, quin ad suam liberationem cooperari possit."—*De Ver.* q. 24, a. 11.

[5] "Omnes homines vult (Deus) salvos fieri."

[6] "Ideo gratia Dei nulli deest, sed omnibus, quantum in se est, se communicat."

"God, so far as he is concerned, is prepared to give grace to all men. . . . Those, therefore, only are deprived of grace who permit a hindrance to grace to exist in themselves; and, therefore, they cannot be excused if they sin." [1] And when St. Thomas says, "God is prepared to give grace to all," [2] he does not mean actual grace, but only sanctifying grace.

Cardinal Gotti justly contradicts those who say that God keeps ready at hand the aids necessary for salvation, but in matter of fact does **not** give them to all. Of what use would it be to a sick man (says this learned author) if the physician only kept the remedies ready, and then would not apply them? Then he concludes (quite to the point of our argument) that we must necessarily say, "God not only offers, but also confers on every individual, even on infidels and hardened sinners, help sufficient to observe the commandments, whether it be proximate or remote." [3]

For the rest, St. Thomas says that it is only the sins of the devils and the damned that cannot be wiped out by penance; but, on the other hand, "to say that there is any sin in this life of which a man cannot repent is erroneous . . . because this doctrine would derogate from the power of grace." [4] If grace were wanting to any one, certainly he could not repent. Moreover, as we have already seen, St. Thomas expressly teaches in several places, and especially in his comment on Heb.

---

[1] "Deus, quantum in se est, paratus est omnibus gratiam dare. . . . Illi (ergo) soli gratia privantur, qui in seipsis gratiæ impedimentum præstant."—*Contra Gent.* l. 3, c. 159.

[2] "Paratus est omnibus gratiam dare."

[3] "Deum, nedum offerre, sed etiam conferre singulis hominibus, et infidelibus et induratis, auxilia sufficientia, vel proxima, vel saltem remota, ad observanda præcepta."—*De Div. Vol.* q. 2, d. 3, § 2.

[4] "Dicere quod aliquod peccatum sit in hac vita de quo quis pœnitere non possit, erroneum est: . . . quia per hoc derogaretur virtuti gratiæ."—P. 3, q. 86 a. 1.

xii., that God, as far as he is concerned, refuses to no
man the grace necessary for conversion: "The grace of
God is wanting to no man; but, as far as it is concerned,
communicates itself to all."[1] So that the learned author
of the Theology for the use of the seminary of Peterkau
says, "It is a calumny to impute to St. Thomas that he
taught that any sinners were totally deserted by God."[2]

Bellarmine makes a sound distinction on this point,
and says that for avoiding fresh sins every sinner has at
all times sufficient assistance, at least mediately: "The
necessary and sufficient assistance for the avoidance of
sin is given by God's goodness to all men at all times,
either immediately or mediately. . . . We say *or mediately*
because it is certain that some men have not that help
by which they can immediately avoid sin, but yet have the
help which enables them to obtain from God greater
safeguards, by the assistance of which they will avoid
sins."[3] But for the grace of conversion, he says that
this is not given at all times to the sinner; but that
no one will be ever so far left to himself "as to be
surely and absolutely deprived of God's help through
all this life, so as to have cause to despair of salvation."[4]

And so say the theologians who follow St. Thomas—
thus Soto: "I am absolutely certain, and I believe that

---

[1] Gratia Dei nulli deest, sed omnibus, quantum in se est, se communicat.

[2] "Non nisi calumniose Sancto Thomæ imputari potest, quod peccatores aliquos a Deo totaliter deseri docuerit."—*Lib.* 3, c. 3, q. 4.

[3] "Auxilium sufficiens ac necessarium ad vitanda peccata omnibus
hominibus et omni tempore, vel immediate, vel mediate, a divina
benignitate præstatur. . . . Dicimus, 'Vel mediate;' quoniam certum est aliquos non habere auxilium quo possint immediate vitare
peccatum, tamen habere auxilium quo possint a Deo majora præsidia
impetrare, quibus adjuti peccata vitabunt."—*De Gr. et Lib. Arb.* l. 2,
c. 7.

[4] "Ut certo et absolute per omnem vitam destituatur auxilio Dei,
ut de salute desperare possit."—*Ibid.* c. 6.

all the holy Doctors who are worthy of the name were always most positive, that no one was ever deserted by God in this mortal life."[1] And the reason is evident; for if the sinner was quite abandoned by grace, either his sins afterwards committed could no longer be imputed to him, or he would be under an obligation to do that which he had no power to fulfil; but it is a positive rule of St. Augustine that there is never a sin in that which cannot be avoided: "No one sins in that which can by no means be avoided."[2] And this is agreeable to the teaching of the Apostle: *But God is faithful, who will not suffer you to be tempted above that which you are able; but will also make with the temptation issue, that you may be able to bear it.*[3] The word "issue" means the divine assistance, which God always gives to the tempted to enable them to resist, as St. Cyprian explains it: "He will make with the temptation a way of escape."[4] And Primasius more clearly: "He will so order the issue that we shall be able to endure; that is, in temptation he will strengthen you with the help of his grace, so that ye may be able to bear it."[5] St. Augustine and St. Thomas go so far as to say that God would be unjust and cruel if he obliged any one to a command which he could not keep. St. Augustine says, "It is the deepest injustice to reckon any one guilty of sin for not doing that which he could

---

[1] "Certo certior sum, quin vero et certissimos credo semper fuisse sanctos doctores qui fuerint hoc nomine digni, neminem unquam a Deo fuisse derelictum in hac mortali vita."—*De Nat. et Gr.* l. 1, c. 18.

[2] "Quis peccat in eo quod nullo modo caveri potest?"—*De Lib. Arb.* l. 3, c. 18.

[3] "Fidelis autem Deus est, qui non patietur vos tentari supra id quod potestis, sed faciet etiam cum tentatione proventum, ut possitis sustinere."—1 *Cor.* x. 13.

[4] "Faciet cum tentatione evadendi facultatem."—*Testim.* l. 3, n. 91.

[5] "Illud faciet provenire (gratiæ præsidio), quo possitis (tentationem) sustinere."

not do. [1] And St. Thomas: "God is not more cruel than man; but it is reckoned cruelty in a man to oblige a person by law to do that which he cannot fulfil; therefore we must by no means imagine this of God." [2] "It is, however, different," he says, "when it is through his own neglect that he has not the grace to be able to keep the commandments," [3] which properly means, when man neglects to avail himself of the remote grace of prayer, in order to obtain the proximate grace to enable him to keep the law, as the Council of Trent teaches: "God does not command impossibilities; but by commanding admonishes you to do what you can, and to ask for that which is beyond your power; and by his help enables you to do it." [4]

St. Augustine repeats his decision in many other places that there is no sin in what cannot be avoided. In one he says, "Whether there be iniquity or whether there be justice, if it was not in the man's power, there can be no just reward, no just punishment." [5] Elsewhere he says, "Finally, if no power is given them to abstain from their works, we cannot hold that they sin." [6] Again, "The devil, indeed, suggests; but with the help of God it is in our power to choose or to refuse his suggestions. And so, when by God's help it is in your power, why do you

[1] "Peccati reum tenere quemquam, quia non fecit quod facere non potuit, summæ iniquitatis est."—*De Duab. An.* c. 12.

[2] "Deus non est magis crudelis quam homo; sed homini imputatur in crudelitatem, si obliget aliquem per præceptum ad id quod implere non possit; ergo hoc de Deo nullo modo est æstimandum."—*In 2 Sent.* d. 28, q. 1, a. 3.

[3] "Quando ex ejus negligentia est quod gratiam non habet, per quam potest servare mandata."—*De Ver.* q. 24, a. 14.

[4] "Deus impossibilia non jubet; sed jubendo monet, et facere quod possis, et petere quod non possis; et adjuvat ut possis."—*Sess.* 6, cap. 11.

[5] "Sive autem iniquitas sive justitia, si in potestate non esset, nullum præmium, nulla pœna justa esset."—*Cont. Faust.* l. 22, c. 78.

[6] "Si denique his abstinendi ab opere suo potestas nulla conceditur, peccatum eorum tenere non possumus."—*De Duab. An.* c. 12.

not rather determine to obey God than him?"[1] Again, "No one, therefore, is answerable for what he has not received."[2] Again, "No one is worthy of blame for not doing that which he cannot do."[3]

Other Fathers have taught the same doctrine. So St. Jerome, "We are not forced by necessity to be either virtuous or vicious; for where there is necessity, there is neither condemnation nor crown."[4] Tertullian: "For a law would not be given to him who had it not in his power to observe it duly."[5] Marcus the Hermit: "Hidden grace assists us; but it depends on us to do or not to do good according to our strength."[6] So also St. Irenæus, St. Cyril of Alexandria, St. Chrysostom, and others.

Nor is there any difficulty in what St. Thomas says, that grace is denied to some persons, in punishment of original sin: "To whomsoever the assistance of grace is given, it is given through simple mercy; but from those to whom it is not given, it is withheld justly in punishment of previous sin, or at least of original sin, as Augustine says."[7] For, as Cardinal Gotti well observes, St. Augus-

---

[1] "Dat quidem ille (dæmon) consilium; sed, Deo auxiliante, nostrum est eligere vel repudiare quod suggerit; et ideo, cum per Dei adjutorium in potestate tua sit, quare non magis Deo quam ipsi obtemperare deliberas?"—*Serm.* 253, *E. B. App.*

[2] "Ex eo igitur quod non accepit, nullus reus est."—*De Lib. Arb.* l. 3, c. 16.

[3] "Nemo vituperatione dignus, qui id non facit quod facere non potest."—*De Duab. An.* c. 11.

[4] "Nec ad virtutes nec ad vitia necessitate trahimur; alioquin, ubi necessitas est, nec damnatio nec corona est."—*Cont. Jov.* l. 2.

[5] "Non enim poneretur lex ei qui non haberet obsequium debitum legi in sua potestate."—*Cont. Marcion.* l. 2.

[6] "Occulta nobis opitulatur gratia; verum in nobis situm est agere vel non agere bonum pro potestate."—*De Just. ex op.* c. 56.

[7] "Auxilium (gratiæ) quibuscumque datur, misericorditer datur; quibus autem non datur, ex justitia non datur, in pœnam præcedentis, aut saltem originalis peccati; ut Augustinus dicit."—2. 2. q. 2, a. 5.—*August. De Corr. et Grat* c. 11.

tine and St. Thomas are speaking of actual proximate grace to satisfy the precepts of faith and charity, of which, indeed, St. Thomas is speaking in this place; but, for all this, they do not intend to deny that God gives every man interior grace, by means of which he may at any rate obtain by prayer the grace of faith and of salvation; since, as we have already seen, these holy Doctors do not doubt that God grants to every man at least remote grace to satisfy the precepts. Here we may add the authority of St. Prosper, who says, "All men enjoy some measure of heavenly teaching; and though the measure of grace be small, it is sufficient to be a remedy for some, and to be a testimony for all."[1]

Nor could it be understood otherwise; for if it were true that any had sinned for want of even remote sufficient grace, withheld through original sin being imputed to them as a fault, it would follow that the liberty of will, which by a figure of speech we are said to have had in the sin of Adam, would be sufficient to make us actual sinners. But this cannot be said, as it is expressly condemned in the first proposition of Michael Baius, who said, "That liberty which caused sin to be voluntary and free in its cause—namely, in original sin, and in the liberty of Adam when sinning—is sufficient to (cause) formal sin (in us), and to make us deserve punishment."[2] Against this proposition we may make use of what Bellarmine said,[3] that to commit a personal sin distinct from the sin of Adam a new exertion of free will is requisite, and a free will distinct from that of Adam, otherwise

[1] "Adhibita semper est universis hominibus quædam supernæ mensura doctrinæ, quæ, etsi parcioris gratiæ fuit, sufficit tamen quibusdam ad remedium, omnibus ad testimonium."—*De Voc. Gent.* l. 2, c. 15.

[2] "Ad peccatum formale et ad demerendum, sufficit illa libertas qua voluntarium ac liberum fuit in causa sua, peccato originali et libertate Adami peccantis."

[3] *De Gr. et Lib. Arb.* l. 2. c. 7.

there is no distinct sin; according to the doctrine of St. Thomas, who teaches, "For a personal sin, absolute personal liberty is requisite."[1] Further, with respect to the baptized, the Council of Trent has declared that in them there remains nothing to condemn: "God hates nothing in the regenerate; for there is no condemnation to them who are truly buried with Christ by baptism unto death."[2] And it is added that concupiscence is not left in us as a punishment, "but for our trial; and it cannot harm those who do not consent to it."[3] On the contrary, the concupiscence left in us would do exceedingly great harm to man, if, on account of it, God denied him even the remote grace necessary to obtain salvation.

From all this, several theologians conclude that to say that God refuses to any one sufficient help to enable him to keep the commandments would be contrary to the faith, because in that case God would oblige us to impossibilities. So says F. Nuñez: "God never refused aid sufficient to keep the commandments, otherwise they could not be in any way fulfilled; and thus we should have the heresy of Luther back again, that God has obliged men to impossibilities."[4] And in another place, "It is of faith, so that the opposite doctrine is a manifest heresy, that every man, while he is alive, can do penance for his sins."[5] And Father Ledesma, "It is a

[1] "Ad peccatum personale requirit potentia absoluta personalis."

[2] "In renatis nihil odit Deus, quia nihil est damnationis iis qui vere consepulti sunt cum Christo per baptisma in mortem."

[3] "Quæ, cum ad agonem relicta sit, nocere non consentientibus . . . non valet."—*Sess.* 5. *De Pecc. or.* n. 5.

[4] "Deus nunquam denegat auxilium sufficiens ad implenda præcepta; alias nullo pacto possent impleri; et sic rediret Lutheri hæresis, quod Deus obligavit hominem ad impossibile."—*In* 1. 2. q. 109, a. 8.

[5] "Fides est, ita ut oppositum sit hæresis manifesta, quod omnis homo, dum est in via, potest pœnitentiam agere de peccatis."—*In P.* 3, q. 86, a. 1, d. 1.

certain truth of faith, that that is not sin which is not in the free power of man." [1]

Giovenino says that the sinner becomes guilty through the exercise of free will, in choosing voluntarily this or that sin; though at the time he is necessitated to sin, because he is without actual grace sufficient to deliver him from all sin. But this doctrine, that a man when fallen sins, not having liberty to do otherwise than to choose what sin he will commit, and is necessitated to commit some sin, justly offends Monseigneur de Saléon, Archbishop of Vienne, who, in his book *Jansenismus Redivivus*, writes as follows: "Who will endure to hear that a man once fallen, being deprived of grace, can enjoy no other liberty than that of choosing one sin rather than another, being necessitated to sin in some way." [2] So that a criminal condemned to death, who has no other liberty allowed him than to choose whether he will die by the sword, by poison, or by fire, may be said, when he has made his choice, to die a voluntary and free death. And how can sin be imputed to a man who *must* sin in some way or another? The 67th of the condemned Propositions of Baius is as follows: "Man sins damnably even in that which he does through necessity." [3] How can there be liberty, where there is necessity to sin? Jansenius answers, that the liberty of will, which by a figure of speech we are said to have had in Adam's sin, is sufficient to make us sinners. But this too was condemned in Baius' first proposition, "That liberty," etc., as we have seen above.

[1] "Certum est secundum fidem, quod non est peccatum illud quod non est in hominis libera potestate."—*De Aux.* q. un. a. 18.

[2] "Quis patienter audire potest hominem lapsum, absente gratia gradibus superiori, non alia gaudere libertate præter eam, qua necessitatus ad peccandum in genere, potest unum præ alio eligere peccatum."—P. 2, a. 6.

[3] "Homo peccat etiam damnabiliter in eo quod necessario facit."

Our opponents go on to say that though the sinner abandoned by grace cannot avoid all mortal sins collectively, yet he can avoid each sin distributively, or individually, "by a simple suspension or negation of activity," [1] as they say. But this cannot be admitted, for several reasons. First, because when a vehement temptation is assailing us, which it requires much strength to resist, it cannot morally be overcome (as all theologians agree) except by the assistance of grace, or else by yielding to another, but opposite, vicious passion; so that a sinner deprived of grace would be irremediably necessitated to sin in one or the other way; which it is horrible to affirm, as we have already shown. Secondly, when we are urged by a great concupiscence to sin in a particular way, there is not always—nay, it seldom happens that there is—another improper motive urging us to the contrary course, of sufficient force to hinder us from committing the first sin; so that, when this second motive is absent or weak, then it would be necessary for the sinner to commit that particular sin to which he feels inclined. Thirdly, this abstaining from sin "by a simple negation of activity," [2] as they say, can hardly be imagined in sins against the negative precepts; but, as Tourneley and Gotti well observe, is altogether impossible in cases where a positive precept obliges us to do some supernatural act; as, for instance, to make an act of faith, hope, love, and contrition: for as these acts are supernatural, they necessarily require the supernatural assistance of God to enable us to perform them. So that, at any rate in this case, if grace were wanting, man would be necessitated to sin, by not satisfying the positive precept, although he was unable to avoid the sin. But to assert this is, as F. Bannez observes, contrary to

[1] "Per simplicem suspensionem seu negationem actus."
[2] "Simplex negatio actus."

faith: "A man cannot sin without having first actually received an inspiration of divine grace. We assert this conclusion to be certainly of faith; because no one sins in not doing that which he cannot do, as it is certain *de fide;* but a man to whom nothing more is given than the bare faculties of human nature has no power to act above nature, and therefore does not sin in omitting to perform a supernatural act."[1]

Nor will it do to say that if the sinner is deprived of grace, he is deprived of it by his own fault; and therefore, though he is deprived of grace, yet he sins. For Cardinal Gotti well replies to this, that God can justly punish the sinner for his previous faults, but not for his future transgressions of precepts which he is no longer able to fulfil. If a servant, he says, were sent to a place, and if he, through his own fault, fell into a pit, his master might punish him for his carelessness in falling, and even for his subsequent disobedience, if means (such as a rope or ladder) were given him to get out of the pit, and he would not avail himself of them; but supposing that his master did not help him to get out, he would be a tyrant if he ordered him to proceed and punished him for not proceeding. Hence he concludes, "When, therefore, a man has by sin fallen into the ditch, and become unable to proceed on his way to eternal life, though God may punish him for this fault, and also if he refuses the offer of grace to enable him to proceed; yet if God chose to leave him to his own weakness, he cannot without

---

[1] "Quotiescumque aliquis peccat, necesse est ut ille de facto receperit aliquam divinam inspirationem. . . . Hæc conclusio asseritur a nobis certa secundum fidem; quia nemo peccat propter quod non facit quod facere non potest, ut certum est secundum fidem; sed homo, cui nihil aliud datum est quam quod ad naturam humanam pertinet, non habet unde possit operari supra naturam; ergo non peccat non operando aliquid supernaturale."—*In* P. 1, q. 23, a. 3, *concl.* 3.

injustice oblige him to proceed on the way, nor punish him if he does not proceed." [1]

Moreover, our opponents adduce many texts of Scripture where this abandonment is apparently expressed: *Blind the heart of this people . . . lest they see with their eyes . . . and be converted, and I heal them.*[2] *We would have cured Babylon, but she is not healed; let us forsake her.*[3] *Add thou iniquity upon their iniquity, and let them not come into Thy justice.*[4] *For this cause God delivered them up to shameful affections. He hath mercy on whom He will; and whom He will He hardeneth;*[5] and others similar. But it is usually and easily answered to all these in general, that in the Holy Scriptures God is often said to do what he only permits; so that if we would not blaspheme with Calvin, and say that God positively destines and determines some persons to sin, we must say that God permits some sinners, in penalty of their faults, to be on the one hand assailed by vehement temptations (which is the evil from which we pray God to deliver us when we say, *Lead us not into temptation*);[6] and, on the other hand, that they remain morally abandoned in their sin; so that their conversion, and the resistance they should make to temptation, although neither impossible nor desperate,

---

[1] "Cum ergo homo, peccando in foveam lapsus, impotens factus sit prosequendi iter ad æternam salutem, esto ipsum possit ob talem culpam punire; et similiter, si gratiam, qua fiat potens, oblatam respuat; sed si Deus ipsum in sua impotentia relinquere velit, non poterit nisi injuste obligare ut viam percurrat, et, nisi percurrat, punire."—*De Div. Vol.* q. 2, d. 3, § 3.

[2] "Excæca cor populi hujus . . . , ne forte videat . . . et convertatur, et sanem eum."—*Is.* vi. 10.

[3] "Curavimus Babylonem, et non est sanata; derelinquamus eam."—*Jer.* li. 9.

[4] "Appone iniquitatem super iniquitatem eorum, et non intrent in justitiam tuam."—*Ps.* lxviii. 28.

[5] "Propterea tradidit illos Deus in passiones ignomiæ.—Ergo cujus vult miseretur, et quem vult indurat."—*Rom.* i. 26; ix. 18.

[6] "Et ne nos inducas in tentationem."

is yet, through their faults and their bad habits, very difficult; since, in their laxity of life, they have only very rare and weak desires and motions to resist their bad habits, and to regain the way of salvation. And this is the imperfect obstinacy of the hardened sinner which St. Thomas describes: "He is hardened who cannot easily co-operate in his escape from sin; and this is imperfect obstinacy, because a man may be obstinate in this life, if he has a will so fixed upon sin, that no motions towards good arise, except very weak ones."[1] On one side, the mind is obscured, the will is hardened against God's inspirations, and attached to the pleasures of sense, so as to despise and feel disgust for spiritual blessings; the sensual passions and appetites reign in the soul through the bad habits that have been acquired; on the other side, the illuminations and the callings of God are, by its own fault, rendered scarcely efficacious to move the soul, which has so despised them, and made so bad a use of them, that it even feels a certain aversion towards them, because it does not want to be disturbed in its sensual gratifications. All these things constitute moral abandonment; and when a sinner has once fallen into it, it is only with the utmost difficulty that he can escape from his miserable state, and bring himself to live a well-regulated life.

In order to escape, and pass at once from such disorder to a state of salvation, a great and extraordinary grace would be requisite; but God seldom confers such a grace on these obstinate sinners. Sometimes he gives it, says St. Thomas, and chooses them for vessels of mercy, as the Apostle calls them, in order to make known his

---

[1] "(Obstinatum esse eum) qui non de facili possit cooperari ad hoc quod exeat de peccato; et hæc est obstinatio imperfecta, qua aliquis potest esse obstinatus in statu viæ, dum scilicet habet ita firmatam voluntatem in peccato, quod non surgunt motus ad bonum nisi debiles."—*De Ver.* q. 24, a. 11.

goodness; but to the rest he justly refuses it, and leaves them in their unhappy state, in order to show forth his justice and power: "Sometimes," says the Angel of the Schools, "out of the abundance of his goodness he prevents with his assistance even those who put a hindrance in the way of his grace, and converts them, etc. And as he does not enlighten all the blind, nor cure all the sick, so neither does he assist all who place an impediment to his grace, so as to convert them. . . . This is what the Apostle means when he says that God, *to show forth His anger, and to make His power known, endured with much patience the vessels of wrath, fitted for destruction, that He might show the riches of His glory upon the vessels of mercy, which He hath prepared unto glory.*" [1] Then he adds, "But since out of the number of those who are involved in the same sins, there are some to whom God gives the grace of conversion, while others he only endures, or allows to go on in the course of things, we are not to inquire the reason why he converts some and not others. For the Apostle says, *Has not the potter power over the clay, to make of the same mass one vessel to honor, and another to dishonor?*" [2]

We do not then deny (to bring this point to a conclu-

---

[1] "Interdum ex abundantia bonitatis suæ, etiam eos qui impedimentum gratiæ præstant, auxilio suo prævenit, avertens eos a malo et convertens ad bonum. Et sicut non omnes cæcos illuminat, nec omnes languidos sanat, ita non omnes qui gratiam impediunt, auxilio suo prævenit ut convertantur. . . . Hinc est quod Apostolus dicit: ' Deus volens ostendere iram et notam facere potentiam suam, sustinuit in multa patientia vasa iræ apta in interitum, ut ostenderet divitias gloriæ suæ in vasa misericordiæ, quæ præparavit in gloriam.'" —*Rom.* ix. 22.

[2] " Cum autem Deus, hominum qui in eisdem peccatis detinentur, hos quidem præveniens convertat, illos autem sustineat sive permittat secundum ordinem rerum procedere, non est ratio inquirenda, quare hos convertat, et non illos. Hinc est quod Apostolus dicit: 'An non habet potestatem figulus luti, ex eadem massa facere aliud quidem vas in honorem, aliud vero in contumeliam?'"—*Ibid.* 21, *Cont. Gent.* l. 3, c. 161.

sion) that there is such a thing as the moral abandonment of some obstinate sinners, so that their conversion
is morally impossible; that is to say, very difficult.   And
this concession is abundantly sufficient for the laudable
object which our opponents have in defending their opinion, which is to restrain evil-doers, and to induce them
to consider, before they come to fall into such a deplor-
able state.   But then it is cruelty (as Petrocorensis well
says) to take from them all hope, and entirely to shut
against them the way of salvation, by the doctrine that
they have fallen into so complete an abandonment as to
be deprived of all actual grace to enable them to avoid
fresh sins, and to be converted; at any rate, mediately
by means of prayer (which is not refused to any man
while he lives, as we shall prove in the last chapter),
whereby they can afterwards obtain abundant help for
placing themselves in a state of salvation: since the fear
of total abandonment would not only lead them to despair, but also to give themselves more completely to
their vices, in the belief that they are altogether destitute
of grace; so that they have no hope left of escaping
eternal damnation.   We do not then deny (to bring this

[1] "Interdum ex abundantia bonitatis suæ, etiam eos qui impedimentum gratiæ præstant, auxilio suo prævenit, avertens eos a malo et
convertens ad bonum. Et sicut non omnes cæcos illuminat, nec
omnes languidos sanat, ita non omnes qui gratiam impediunt auxilio
suo prævenit ut convertantur. . . . Hinc est quod Apostolus dicit:
'Deus volens ostendere iram et notam facere potentiam suam, sustinuit in multa patientia vasa iræ apta in interitum, ut ostenderet
divitias gloriæ suæ in vasa misericordiæ, quæ præparavit in gloriam.'"
—*Rom.* ix. 22.

[2] "Cum autem liceat, bonitatem qui in eisdem peccatis detinentur,
hos quidem præveniens convertat, illos autem sustineat sive permittat
secundum ordinem rerum procedere, non est ratio inquirenda, quare
hos convertat, et non illos. Hinc est quod Apostolus dicit: An non
habet potestatem figulus luti, ex eadem massa facere aliud quidem vas
in honorem, aliud vero in contumeliam?"—*Mat.* xii. *Cont. Gent.* l. 3.
c. 161.

CHAPTER III.

EXPOSITION AND CONFUTATION OF JANSENIUS' SYS-
TEM OF "DELECTATION RELATIVELY VICTORIOUS."*

I.

The System of Jansenius.

1. In the following chapter we will, as we promised,
demonstrate that the grace of prayer is given to all men.
But this doctrine does not please Jansenius; he goes so
far as to call it an hallucination: "It is an hallucination
to think that the grace of prayer is always present to a
man."[1] According to his system, he considers that without *the delectation relatively victorious* we cannot pray; but
this delight is not granted to all men, therefore (he adds)
all men have not sufficient grace and power to fulfil the

[1] "Hallucinatio est, qua putant semper adesse homini gratiam ut
petat."—*De Gr. Chr.* l. 3, c. 13.

---

* Jansenius *De grat. Christi*, lib. iii. c. 13, circa finem, p. 139,
"Delectatio relativè victrix." It is the distinct doctrine of the Jansenists that as a material atom within the influence of two opposite
attractions, by inevitable necessity obeys that which is *most powerful*,
so is it with the human will. At each waking moment, they say, a
man is attracted either by heavenly or earthly delight, or by both.
If the first, he necessarily loves God; if the second, he necessarily
sins; if the third, he necessarily obeys the "delectatio relativè victrix," that one of the two delights which is intrinsically the most in-
tense. The liberty requisite for merit or demerit, according to Jansenius' well-known proposition, consists not in any real *power of
choice*, or *freedom from necessity*, but wholly in exemption from *external
violence.*—ED.

commandments; for many are without even the remote grace to enable them to pray as they ought, or indeed to pray at all. "Since, therefore," he continues, "most men either do not ask for grace to enable them to fulfil the law, or do not ask for it as is necessary; and since God does not give all men the grace either to pray fervently, or even to pray at all, it is most evident that many of the faithful are without that sufficient grace, and, consequently, without that perpetual power of fulfilling the one precept (of the moment) which some theologians proclaim." [1] Before, then, we prove our own position, we must confute his pernicious system, from which all his errors are derived; and we must show that not we, but that he is laboring under an hallucination.

All know the five propositions of Jansenius which were condemned by the Church as heretical.* Now, as Tourneley proves, all these propositions follow if you once grant his system of preponderating delectation, on which Jansenius founds all his doctrine. [2] F. Ignatius Graveson says the same: "From this pernicious principle Jansenius and his followers derived these erroneous conclusions (the five propositions), which are most inti-

---

[1] "Cum ergo plurimi, vel non petant gratiam illam qua possint præcepta facere, vel non ita petant ut necessarium est, nec omnibus gratiam vel ferventer petendi vel omnino petendi Deus largiatur, apertissimum est fidelibus multis deesse illam sufficientem gratiam, et consequenter illam perpetuam, quam quidam prædicant, faciendi præcepti potestatem."

[2] *De Gr. Chr.* q. 3, *De Jans. ep.* 3.

---

* For the benefit of the reader we here subjoin the five propositions:

1. Some commandments of God are impossible to just men who wish to fulfil them, and who, for this purpose, make efforts according to the strength that they at present possess; and the grace that would render them possible is wanting to them.

2. In the state of fallen nature one never resists interior grace.

3. To merit or demerit in the state of fallen nature, there is not required in man freedom from interior necessity (*libertas a necessitate*),

mately connected and form one system with that principle."[1] So F. Berti, who says that "from the principle of the two invincible delectations, as from a root, almost all the other Jansenist errors have sprung, and especially the five condemned propositions."[2] And Father Fortunato da Brescia, in his lately published book, called *A Confutation of the System of Cornelius Jansenius,* proves to demonstration that, admitting this system, you must necessarily admit the five condemned propositions.

Let us, therefore, distinctly exhibit this system of Jansenius. He says that the will of man, since the fall of Adam, is unable to do otherwise than to follow either the pleasure of grace (which he calls the celestial delectation), or that of concupiscence (which he calls earthly delectation), according as one prevails over the others. So that if the heavenly delectation is greater, then it necessarily overcomes the other; if the earthly delectation preponderates, then the will necessarily yields to it.

And here we must remark that Jansenius does not hereby intend deliberate or consequent delectation, for thus he would be in accord with all Catholic Doctors;

[1] " Ex hoc infesto principio Jansenius ejusque discipuli has erroneas deducunt consecutiones, quæ cum illo principio arctissimo vinculo colligatæ cohærent."--*Ep. cl.* 1, *ep.* 1.

[2] " Ex principio duarum delectationum invincibilium tanquam ex radice fluere alios fere omnes Jansenii errores, ac præsertim quinque damnatas propositiones."—*Aug. syst. vind.* d. 4, c. 1, § 8.

---

but it is sufficient to have freedom from exterior compulsion (*libertas a coactione*).

4. The Semi-Pelagians admitted the necessity of an interior *preventing* grace for every act, even for the beginning of faith; they were heretics in that they maintained that the will of man can submit to this grace, or resist it.

5. It is a Semi-Pelagian error to say that Jesus Christ died or shed his blood for all men without exception.

These five propositions were condemned by Innocent X. in 1653.

ED.

since, when the pleasure we take in a thing is deliberate, and embraced not from necessity but from free choice of the will, then certainly it is necessary that the will should act according to the delectation. But Jansenius intends indeliberate delectation, and in this sense he understands the celebrated saying of St. Augustine: "It is necessary that our act should follow the greater pleasure."[1] Now, as we shall presently show, this sentence must necessarily be understood of deliberate and consequent delectation; but Jansenius falsely interprets (and on this false interpretation founds his whole doctrine) that it means indeliberate delectation, antecedent to any act of the will. So that, in his system, there is no such thing as sufficient grace; since it is either of too little weight, and necessarily insufficient, or else it preponderates over the concupiscence, and is then necessarily efficacious, since he makes the whole efficacy of grace consist in the relative preponderance of the indeliberate delectation: "There will be no such thing as sufficient grace" (these are his words); "but it will be either efficient, or so inefficient that no act can follow from it."[2]

When this system is once laid down, all the five condemned propositions follow as necessary conclusions from it. Let us omit the others, and speak here exclusively of the first and third, as being most to our purpose.

REFUTATION OF THE FIRST PROPOSITION.

The first is, "Some commands of God are impossible to just men, who wish to fulfil them and endeavor to do so according to the strength they at present possess. Moreover, grace is wanting to them, whereby these pre-

---

[1] "Quod amplius delectat, secundum id operemur necesse est."— *In Gal.* n. 49.

[2] "Non erit sufficiens gratia, sed vel efficax, vel ita inefficax ex qua operatio nequidem possit sequi."—*De Gr. Chr.* l. 4, c. 10.

cepts may become possible." [1] Some precepts (says he) become impossible even to the just, who have the will and strive to observe them, in proportion as they want the grace which should prevail over concupiscence: " Unless the heavenly delectation is greater than the earthly, it cannot but happen that we are overcome by the infirmity of our will." [2] And again: " While carnal delectation is in vigor, it is impossible that the thought of virtue should prevail." [3] Although, said Jansenius, grace regarded absolutely in itself, and apart from act and circumstance, may be abundantly sufficient to move the will to virtue; nevertheless, relatively considered,— that is, when the carnal delectation is greater than the heavenly (for when the carnal preponderates over grace, it is always accompanied by the act of will),—then grace is completely insufficient to draw to itself the consent of the will. And, as Father Graveson well observes, the absolute power to keep the commandments, which many would have by virtue of grace, whenever it is derived from a grace which is less than the concupiscence, is actually no longer power, but a true impotence; since the will is then entirely unable to act rightly, as the less weight cannot outweigh the greater.

How, then, can a man be blamed for not fulfilling the precept, when he is without grace even sufficient to enable him to do so? The objection is strong, and is most manifestly just; so much so, that Jansenius himself cannot help putting it: " How is it that they are not excused who are without this assistance, since without it they

---

[1] " Aliqua Dei præcepta hominibus justis, volentibus et conantibus, secundum præsentes quas habent vires, sunt impossibilia; deest quoque illis gratia qua possibilia fiant."—*Ibid,* l. 3, c. 13.

[2] " Nisi major fuerit cœlestis delectatio quam terrena, fieri non potest quin propriæ voluntatis infirmitate vincamur."

[3] " Vigente enim delectatione carnali, impossibile est ut virtutis consideratio prævaleat."—*De Gr. Chr.* l. 4, c. 6–9.

would not be able to fulfil the precept?"[1] Let us see
how he answers this question. The difficulty is great,
therefore he attempts to disembarrass himself of it in
several ways.

1. He answers that inability excuses when a man
wishes to fulfil the precept, but cannot; but not when he
does not wish to fulfil it. But we answer that when the
will, according to his principles, is necessarily obliged
to yield to the indeliberate pleasure of the concupiscence,
because of its outweighing grace, it is then physically impossible for a man to wish to fulfil the precept; since,
supposing the preponderance of the carnal pleasure,
grace has no longer sufficient active strength to overcome it. And of this principle Jansenius has no doubt,
for he says that the stronger delectation intrinsically
determines, and insuperably moves the will to accept it,
so that the will is then completely deprived of relative
power to resist. "Whence it follows," says Father
Graveson, "that this necessity, according to the doctrine
of Jansenius and his disciples, is not a moral but an
antecedent and invincible necessity, which cannot be admitted without open heresy."[2] Jansenius says, moreover, that except the delectation of grace preponderates,
it is as impossible for a man to fulfil the precept as it is
"for one without wings to fly, for the blind to see, for
the deaf to hear, or for a man with broken limbs to
walk straight."[3] It would be the same for a man who
had eyes but was deprived of light; because it is no
more physically impossible for a blind man without eyes

[1] "Quomodo non sint excusati qui illo adjutorio carent, quando-
quidem sine illo præceptum implere non possint?"—*Ibid.* l. 3, c. 15.

[2] "Quo fit ut hæc necessitas, in doctrina Jansenii ejusque disci-
pulorum, non sit necessitas moralis, sed antecedens et invincibilis;
quæ citra apertam hæresim admitti non potest."—*Ep. cl.* 2, *ep.* 3.

[3] "Sine qua non magis potest homo bene operari, quam volare sine
alis,—quam homini cæco ut videat, vel surdo ut audeat, vel tibiis
fracto ut recte gradiatur."—*De Gr.* l. 3, c. 15; l. 2, c. 1.

to see than it is for one who has eyes but is without light; for physical impossibility is simply that which exceeds the natural powers. So that any one can see how baseless is this first reply of Jansenius.

2. Let us examine the second, which is still more so. He says that all the commandments are possible to man, just so far as God can give him grace to make him keep them: "All men are said to be able to believe, to be able to love God . . . for this power is nothing else than a passive flexibility of capacity, through which they are able to receive faith and charity."[1] So that, according to Jansenius, man's sin in breaking the commandments is in proportion to his capacity of receiving grace to fulfil them. But by this rule we might say that the blind can see, and the deaf hear, because God can make them see and hear; but, for all that, it is physically impossible for the blind to see, or the deaf to hear, unless God gives them the power. So that to say that it is sufficient reason to call a precept possible, if it is possible to man in case God gives him the power, is either nonsense or fraud, intended to hide the truth; for, I ask, what help can a man have from that grace which he might have, but has not at the time? It is the same as saying, a man might observe all the precepts if he could observe them; but at present he cannot. When the sick man, says St. Augustine, needs care to cure him, he cannot get well without care, however he may wish it: "Nor yet can he become well when he will, but when he is healed by the use of proper care."[2]

3. Jansenius' third answer is, that liberty of will consists entirely in knowing the delightful object and in

[1] "Omnes homines dicuntur posse credere, posse diligere Deum; . . . hæc enim potestas non est aliud nisi flexibilis capacitas per quam possunt suscipere fidem et charitatem."—L. 3, c. 15.

[2] "Nec tamen, cum vult, potest, sed cum fuerit, adhibita curatione, sanatus."—*De Perf. just.* c. 3, rat. 5.

taking pleasure in it: "Wherefore" (these are his words), "after surveying the arguments of Augustine, on which the whole doctrine of free will depends, we think that it is nothing but knowledge and delectation, or a pleasurable complacency in the object which has the power over the free will to make it accept or reject. . . . Concerning knowledge we are not very particular, for scarcely any one doubts that it is necessary to an act of will." [1] So that, according to Jansenius, the liberty of man consists, on the one hand, in his complacency in the delectation; on the other hand, in his knowledge of the object, or, in other words, in that judgment indifferent (equally applicable either to good or evil) whereby he knows the good and evil of the action; as, for instance, in murder, he knows the evil of the sin and the pleasure of the revenge. Hence he says, in another place, that the wicked sin in proportion as they know by means of the law the malice of sin: "The first effect of the law is confessed to be, to give the knowledge of sin;" [2] and quotes the text of St. Paul: *I did not know sin but by the law.* [3] In this he followed Calvin, who said: "The object of the law is to render man inexcusable; and this would not be a bad definition of it—it is the knowledge of the conscience distinguishing between right and wrong, for the purpose of taking away the pretext of ignorance." [4] But

[1] "Quapropter, lustratis fundamentis Augustini, quibus tota doctrina de arbitrii libertate nititur, nihil aliud existimamus quam cognitionem ac delectationem seu delectabilem objecti complacentiam esse id quod tantam potestatem in liberum arbitrium habet, ut eam faciat velle vel nolle. . . . De cognitione hic non multum solliciti sumus; illam enim ad volendum esse necessarium vix quisquam dubitat."—L. 7, c. 3.

[2] "Profertur primus effectus legis dare cognitionem peccati."—L. 1, c. 7.

[3] "Peccatum non cognovi nisi per legem."—*Rom.* vii. 7.

[4] "Finis ergo legis est ut reddatur homo inexcusabilis; nec male hoc modo definietur quod sit conscientiæ agnitio inter justum et injustum discernentis, ad tollendum ignorantiæ prætextum."—*Inst.* l. 2, c. 2.

we may answer that the indifferent judgment, or the knowledge of good and evil which belongs only to the intellect, can never constitute the freedom of choice which belongs altogether to the will; for liberty consists simply in the free choice of the will to do or not to do a thing.

4. Jansenius gives a fourth reply; but this is more incongruous and untenable than any of the former. He says that for sin it is not requisite to have the liberty of indifference, so that a man should be free from all necessity of sinning; but that it is enough to have a liberty of exercise or of choice, so as to be able to abstain from the particular sin to which our concupiscence tempts us, but only by committing another. " So that" (these are his words) " a man may act, and abstain from this particular sin, at least by committing another;"[1] whereby he places man in such a dilemma that in order to avoid one sin he must necessarily commit another; and he says that such a liberty is sufficient to make a man guilty, though he may be necessitated to sin in one way or another. Thus he explains himself more clearly in another place: " The will of fallen man by no means ceases to be free in committing sin, although it be bound by a certain general necessity of sinning; for it will be free in its exercise (as they say), necessitated in the kind of thing it is to choose."[2] In answer to this we might repeat all that we said in Chap. II. § 2, p. 154, against Giovenino, who says that all sinners, though deprived of sufficient grace, yet sin by this liberty of exercise. But what kind of liberty is this, that a man, whether he be good or bad,

---

[1] " Qua quis potest facere (peccatum), et ab eo, saltem aliud perpetrando, abstinere."—*De St. nat. laps.* l. 4, c. 21.

[2] " Arbitrium lapsorum hominum nullo modo in peccando desinit esse liberum, quamvis generali quadam peccandi necessitate vinciatur; erit enim liberum quoad exercitium, ut loquuntur, necessitatum, quoad specificationem."—*Ibid.* c. 19.

could be called guilty, though he is necessitated to sin in one way or another? St. Thomas says that it is heresy to maintain that the will merits or demerits when it acts through necessity, although not compelled by violence to act: "Some have asserted that the will of man is necessarily moved to choose a thing, . . . but they still did not assert that the will is forced. . . . But this opinion is heretical, for it destroys the rule of merit or demerit in human actions; for there seems to be nothing meritorious or otherwise in a man acting from necessity in a way that he cannot help." [1] Moreover, when a man is necessitated to commit one or the other sin, according to the general consent of all theologians, if he chooses the less sin, even though he voluntarily chooses it, he does not sin; because he is without the liberty which is required before an action can be imputed to him as sin. So that, in our case, when, by reason of a concupiscence that outweighs grace, a man has chosen the less of two sins, he does not sin.

But, putting aside all these reflections, the direct answer is, that, supposing Jansenius' principle of the pleasure relatively preponderating to be true, this liberty of exercise to abstain from one sin by committing another becomes quite impossible. His principle, as we have already explained, is, that when the carnal pleasure outweighs the heavenly, then the will is necessitated to consent to that individual pleasure to which it is physically drawn. And therefore he somewhere says that the superior pleasure destroys the indifference of the will; for as a weight inclines the index of a balance, which

---

[1] " Quidam posuerunt quod voluntas hominis ex necessitate movetur ad aliquid eligendum; nec tamen ponebant quod voluntas cogeretur. . . . Hæc autem opinio est hæretica; tollit enim rationem meriti et demeriti in humanis actibus: non enim videtur meritorium vel demeritorium, quod aliquis sic ex necessitate agit quod vitare non possit."—*De Mal.* q. 6, *a. un.*

before stood in equilibrium, so does the pleasure move the will to consent to that concupiscence to which it tempts it: "Since (the carnal delight) by the persuasion of its motion is the cause that the man, who before the motion was indifferent whether he acted or not, should be by the very motion of the concupiscence impelled to one side or the other, like a balance into which a weight is put." [1] He says the same in another place, where he tries to refute those who will have it that the superior pleasure moves morally; and says that it does not draw and determine the will to accept the object proposed to it morally, but physically: "Since that is called moral predetermination, which is only in the object when it, as it were, counsels, orders, or beseeches; but this (delectation) has its seat in the very power of the will, which it sets in motion by the intensity of the pleasure it gives, and by setting it in motion determines it; since it makes the will determine its own object, and therefore it may be said to predetermine the will." [2] So that, according to Jansenius, the pleasure predetermines the will to embrace the object to which it moves it, before the will determines itself. And that this is the true meaning of Jansenius the learned Diroys has no doubt, who on this account says that Jansenius does not differ from the astrologers, who make the will of man subject to the influence of the planets; "so that the will is determined in the choice of its object by any im-

---

[1] "Cum hoc efficiat (delectatio carnalis) blanditiis motus sui, ut, qui ad agendum et non agendum ante motum esset indifferens, ipso motu libidinis in alteram partem, instar æquilibrii cui pondus additur, impellatur."—*De Gr.* l. 7, c. 14.

[2] "Siquidem moralis prædeterminatio illa dicitur quæ tantum se habet ex parte objecti, quemadmodum facit ille qui consulit, præcipit, rogat; sed hæc (delectatio) se habet in ipsa potentia voluntatis, quam propriæ suæ suavitatis magnitudine ad volendum applicat, et applicando determinat, utpote causans in ea hoc ipsum ut se determinet, ideoque prædeterminat."—L. 8, c. 3.

pression which may happen to precede its determination."[1] The Archbishop of Vienne says the same in his book *Baianism and Jansenism Revived:* "The Jansenists contend that by a pleasure superior in degree the will is invincibly determined in its operation, without any respect to the future determination of the will itself."[2]

Granting this system, how is the liberty of exercise possible? since, according to Jansenius, the preponderating pleasure by itself predetermines the will to accept it; so that, as in the balance the less weight necessarily gives way to the larger, so does the will necessarily yield to the preponderating pleasure. So that, for instance, if any one is drawn by this pleasure to take another man's property, it is true that he may be led to abstain from thieving by love for his own reputation; but in cases where this love either does not exist, or is not greater than the pleasure of stealing, the love of reputation certainly cannot conquer, and then evidently all liberty of exercise ceases.

REFUTATION OF THE THIRD PROPOSITION.

But let us now pass on to the third proposition of Jansenius: "To merit and demerit in a state of fallen nature, man does not require freedom from necessity, but freedom from compulsion."[3] He says then that, in order to merit or to sin, the liberty of indifference, which excludes necessity, is not wanted, but it is enough if the will is not repugnant. And he goes so far as to assert

[1] "Voluntas determinatur ad electionem sui finis aliqua impressione quæ illius determinationem antecedat."

[2] "Jansenistæ contendunt delectatione gradibus superiori voluntatem invincibiliter determinari ad operandum, absque ullo respectu ad futuram ipsius voluntatis determinationem."—*Bajan. et Jans. red. app.* 2.

[3] "Ad merendum et demerendum, in statu naturæ lapsæ, non requiritur in homine libertas a necessitate, sed sufficit libertas a coactione."

that it is a paradox to say that the act of will is free, so far forth as the will is at liberty to accept or refuse the object. This proposition, also condemned as heretical, follows similarly from his system; for, supposing that the will, when moved by a preponderating pleasure, must necessarily obey it, it necessarily follows (as Jansenius shows) that it is sufficient for merit or demerit that a man should be willing to consent to the pleasure, although he cannot do otherwise than be willing, and is even physically necessitated to be so. F. Serry well maintains that it is a monstrous doctrine to say "that merit can coexist with the necessity of acting."[1] And it was before this called heretical by St. Thomas, whose words, already quoted, I shall be pardoned for repeating here: "Some have asserted that the will of man is necessarily moved to choose a thing; but they still did not assert that the will is forced. But this opinion is heretical, for it destroys the rule of merit and demerit in human actions; for there seems to be nothing meritorious or otherwise in a man acting from neccessity in any way that he cannot help."[2]

And with reason it is called heresy, for it is contrary to Holy Scripture: *God is faithful, who will not suffer you to be tempted above that you are able; but will also make with the temptation issue, that you may be able to bear it.*[3] But Jansenius says that at times man is so completely deprived of grace that he cannot resist temptations, and is necessitated to succumb to them.

Moses said to the people: *This commandment that I command thee this day is not above thee.*[4] Again, *Blessed is he that*

[1] "Stare meritum posse cum agendi necessitate."
[2] Page 170.
[3] "Fidelis autem Deus est, qui non patietur vos tentari supra id quod potestis, sed faciet etiam cum tentatione proventum, ut possitis sustinere."—1 *Cor.* x. 13.
[4] "Mandatum hoc, quod ego præcipio tibi hodie, non supra te est."—*Deut.* xxx. 11.

could have transgressed, and hath not transgressed; and could do evil things, and hath not done them.[1] Therefore it is not sufficient for merit that a man should act willingly, but it is necessary that he also act freely; that is, that he should be able to neglect the commandments, and should not be necessitated to fulfil them; and, *vice versa* in sin, that he should have the grace to abstain, and that it should be his own fault if he does not abstain.

Nor is the reply of the impious Theodore Beza valid here; he says that the necessity does not depend on nature, but on original sin, by which man voluntarily deprived himself of liberty, and is therefore justly punished for sinning, though he be necessitated to sin; for it may be answered that if a servant had by his own fault broken his leg, his master would be unjust if, after having forgiven the fault, he commanded him to run, and punished him for not running. "To hold a man guilty of sin," says St. Augustine, "because he has not done what he could not do, is abominable iniquity and folly."[2]

Moreover, supposing that man could merit or demerit when acting by necessity, without any balance of power to do otherwise, I do not know how it could be reconciled with Holy Scripture, which says: *You have your choice; choose this day that which pleaseth you, whom you would rather serve, whether . . . the gods of the Amorites, etc.; . . . but as for me and my house, we will serve the Lord.*[3] A choice cannot be given where men act from necessity, and without liberty; so that this text clearly proves that man is free from necessity. "A full power of choosing either side," says Petavius on this passage, "is clearly shown;

[1] "Qui potuit transgredi, et non est transgressus; facere mala, et non fecit."—*Ecclus.* xxxi. 10.

[2] "Peccati reum tenere quemquam, quia non fecit quod facere non potuit, summæ iniquitatis esse et insaniæ."—*De Duab. an.* c. 12.

[3] "Optio vobis datur: eligite hodie quod placet, cui servire potissimum debeatis, utrum . . . . diis Amorrhæorum . . . ; ego autem et domus mea serviemus Domino."—*Jos.* xxiv. 15.

so that the will, as it were suspended and placed in the middle, may choose whichever it likes of the two objects."[1]

The same is said in other parts of Scripture: *I call heaven and earth to witness this day, that I have set before you life and death, blessing and cursing.—Choose, therefore, life, that both thou and thy seed may live.*[2] *God made man from the beginning, and left him in the hand of his own counsel. He added His commandments and precepts. . . . Before man is life and death, good and evil; that which he shall choose shall be given him.*[3] On the latter passage Petavius says: " If the teacher had now to decide the present point, how could he more clearly express the freedom from necessity which man enjoys? If he lived among us, and judged from our point of view, he could not describe in more precise terms the nature and property of human liberty and of free will than he has done here."[4]

There are other texts to the same purpose: *I called, and you refused.*[5] *They have been rebellious to the light.*[6] *I looked that it should bring forth grapes, and it hath brought forth wild grapes.*[7] *You always resist the Holy Ghost.*[8]

[1] " Plena utriusvis potestas ostenditur, ut, quasi suspensa et in medio posita, voluntas alterum quod volet e duobus adsciscat."—*De Op. sex d.* l. 3, c. 2.

[2] " Testes invoco hodie cœlum et terram, quod proposuerim vobis vitam et mortem, benedictionem et maledictionem; elige ergo vitam, ut et tu vivas et semen tuum."—*Deut.* xxx. 19.

[3] " Deus ab initio constituit hominem et reliquit illum in manu consilii sui. Adjecit mandata et præcepta sua. . . . Ante hominem vita et mors, bonum et malum; quod placuerit ei, dabitur illi."—*Ecclus.* xv. 14.

[4] " Non poterat expressioribus uti vocibus, si inter nos viveret ac de lite nostra judicaret, quam isthic fecit, ut libertatis humanæ arbitriique liberi naturam ac proprietatem describeret."—*Loco sup. cit.*

[5] " Vocavi et renuistis."—*Prov.* i. 24.

[6] " Ipsi fuerunt rebelles lumini."—*Job*, xxiv. 13.

[7] " Expectavi, ut faceret uvas, et fecit labruscas."—*Isa.* v. 2.

[8] " Vos semper Spiritui Sancto resistitis."—*Acts*, vii. 51.

It is certainly the work of the Holy Spirit to call men, to enlighten their minds, and to move the will to good; but how can it be said that *he* refuses the call, that *he* rebels against the light, that *he* resists grace, who is destitute of preponderating grace, and therefore must necessarily yield to the prevailing concupiscence?

II.

True Doctrine of St. Augustine on the " Victorious Delectation" and on Free Will.

"But what," says Jansenius, "if Augustine before me has maintained this same theory, that we must necessarily do that which pleases us most, according to the well-known passage, 'It is necessary that we act according to that which delights us most?'[1] Now, before we answer Jansenius, we must premise that St. Augustine, who had to confute several heresies of his time, all on the subject of grace, and all contrary to one another, had to speak of it diffusely and upon different points of view, and is therefore in several places obscure. Hence it has come to pass that not only each of the Catholic schools boasts of having him on its side, though their opinions are quite different, but also Calvin and Jansenius, whose errors have been condemned by the Church, have presumed to call him their patron. Calvin, writing against Pighius, says, "We follow nothing but Augustine. . . . Pighius may squeak as he pleases, he will never make us allow that Augustine is not on our side."[2] And Jansenius puts forward Augustine as his sole teacher, so that he even called his book by the title of

[1] "Quod amplius nos delectat, secundum id operemur necesse est." *In Gal.* n. 49.

[2] "Nos nihil quam Augustinum sequimur. . . . Etiamsi crepet Pighius, nobis hoc extorquere non potest, quin Augustinus sit noster." —*Adv. Pigh.* l. 3.

"Augustinus." And the Jansenists only call themselves Augustinians. From these premises we only wish to infer that many passages of St. Augustine require explanation by comparison with other passages of his works, where he declares his true opinion, if we would not be misled. Now let us come to the point.

We have already explained at the beginning of the chapter that this sentence of St. Augustine ought not and cannot be understood of indeliberate pleasure, antecedent to any co-operation of the will, but ought to be understood of deliberate and consequent pleasure; for in cases where man freely consents to the pleasure, then, certainly, it is necessary that he should act upon it. And this is proved by what Augustine says in other places, where he confounds pleasure with love, or, rather, explains that the superior pleasure is nothing else than that deliberate love, and that affection, which, by our own free choice, predominates in us; in which pleasure, if we deliberately take delight, then it is necessary that we act upon it. So, that in substance, he simply says that the will must act upon that which it deliberately loves the most; for in one place he says that the pleasure is, as it were, the weight of the soul, which drags it along with it—"for pleasure is, as it were, the weight of the soul;" [1] and in another place, that this weight which draws each man's soul is his love—"My love is my weight." [2] This he explains more clearly in another place, where he says we ought to be careful, " by God's help, to be so disposed as not to be tripped up by inferior things, and to take pleasure only in the higher things." [3] See how clearly he speaks of deliberate pleasure, freely accepted. In another place, " What is it to

---

[1] " Delectatio quippe quasi pondus est animæ."—*De Mus.* l. 6, c. 11.

[2] " Pondus meum, amor meus."—*Conf.* l. 13, c. 9.

[3] " Nos ita, Deo opitulante, ordinemus, ut inferioribus non offendamur, solis autem superioribus delectemur."—*De Mus.* l. 6, c. 11.

be drawn by pleasure? To delight in the Lord; and he will give thee the petitions of thy heart."[1] Again, "See how the Father draws! He delights us by teaching, not by laying us under necessity."[2] Again, "If we wish to enjoy the pleasures of heaven, we must bridle unlawful pleasure; as when we fast, the appetite rises against us; this it does by pleasure (i.e., indeliberate), but we restrain it by the law of the governing reason."[3] So that, according to St. Augustine, the pleasure which incites us to break the law may be freely repressed by man by means of the dominant reason, and by the help of grace. Hence he exhorts us: "Let justice so delight you as to conquer even lawful pleasures."[4]

This is made still clearer by the context of the passage on which we are now disputing, where, after saying, "We must needs act upon the greater pleasure," he adds, "It is clear that our life must be according to our pursuits, and our pursuits must be according to our affections (mark this). Therefore, if there are two contradictory things, the command of justice and the carnal habit, and both of them are loved, we shall pursue that which we love most."[5] So that when he says we must needs act according to that which delights us most, he only means

[1] "Quid est trahi voluptate? 'Delectare in Domino, et dabit tibi petitiones cordis tui.'"—*Ps.* xxxvi. 4.

[2] "Videte quomodo trahit Pater: docendo delectat, non necessitatem imponendo."—*In Joan. tr.* 26.

[3] "Si frui delectaverit, delectatio illicita refrenanda est; velut cum jejunamus, et visis cibis palati appetitus assurgit, non fit nisi delectatione, sed eam dominantis rationis jure cohibemus."—*De Serm. Dom. in monte,* l. 1, c. 12.

[4] "Justitia sic delectet, ut vincat etiam licitas delectationes."—*Serm.* 159, *E. B.*

[5] "Quod amplius nos delectat, secundum id operemur necesse est. Manifestum est certe secundum id nos vivere quod sectati fuerimus; sectabimur autem quod dilexerimus. Itaque, si ex adverso existant duo, præceptum justitiæ et consuetudo carnalis, et utrumque diligitur, ibi sectabimur quod amplius dilexerimus."—*In Gal.* n. 54.

that the will must necessarily act on that which it loves best; nor will it do to say, with Jansenius, that what gives most pleasure is most loved; for this is not always true, and St. Augustine expressly contradicts it when, in his *Confessions*, he says of himself, "I did not do that in which my affections took incomparably more pleasure, and which as soon as I would, I could do;"[1] by which he means that he was already moved by God with an indeliberate affection, which made virtue incomparably more pleasant to him than vice, and that he might easily have been virtuous if he would; but that he resisted grace, and refused to be virtuous, and abandoned himself to vice.

Further, if St. Augustine had believed that it was necessary for us to act upon the greater pleasure, he could never have said, "When the unlawful pleasure of concupiscence tickles you, fight, resist, do not consent; and the saying is fulfilled, Go not after thy desires."[2] Still further, he says elsewhere that of two persons who have the same temptation to impurity, it sometimes happens that one consents to it and the other resists; and why? because, he says, one wills to observe chastity, the other wills not: "If both are tempted by the same (mark the word *same*) temptation, and one yields and consents to it, while the other perseveres; what else is shown, but that one willed to fail, the other willed not to fail in chastity?"[3]

Moreover, when he says that it is necessary that we should act upon that which best pleases us, it may be

[1] "Non faciebam quod et incomparabili affectu amplius mihi placebat, et mox ut vellem, possem."—*Conf.* l. 8, c. 8.

[2] "Titillat delectatio illicitæ concupiscentiæ? pugna, resiste, noli consentire; et impletur hic: ' Post concupiscentias tuas non eas.' "—*Ecclus.* xviii. 30.—*Serm.* 155, *E. B.*

[3] "Si eadem tentatione ambo tententur, et unus ei cedat, atque consentiat, alter perseveret; quid aliud apparet, nisi unum voluisse, alterum noluisse a castitate deficere ?"—*De Civ. D.* l. 12, c. 6.

asked whether he speaks of deliberate or indeliberate
pleasure. Now, we say that if he had meant indeliberate pleasure, he would have been obliged, in consequence,
to deny that the will, in order to be truly free, need be
free not only from violence, but also from necessity.
But there are a thousand places where he teaches the
reverse, and says that man, whether in good or in evil,
acts without necessity; therefore, when he speaks of the
predominant pleasure overcoming, he must necessarily
mean the deliberate or consequent pleasure. To quote
a few of these numerous passages:

"Our will would be no will at all if it were not in our
own power; for that is not free to us which we have not
in our power." [1]

In another place, speaking of the passage of St.
Matthew where our Lord talks of good fruit springing
from a good tree, and bad fruit from a bad tree, [2] he
says, "When, therefore, our Lord says this, do this or
do that, he shows that it is in the power of man to do
it; for he that will not keep the law can keep it if he
will." [3] Calvin objects that Augustine is here speaking
of man in the state of innocence; but Bellarmine well
observes that St. Augustine is here explaining a passage
where our Lord is speaking against the Jews, and says
of them, *Ye shall know them by their fruits.* [4] So that it
can never be supposed that St. Augustine meant to apply the remark to Adam. Moreover, he repeats what he
had said against the Manichees, when writing against

---

[1] "Voluntas nostra nec voluntas esset, nisi esset in nostra potestate; non enim est nobis liberum quod in potestate non habemus."—
De Lib. Arb. l. 3, c. 3.

[2] Ch. vii. 17.

[3] "Hoc ergo Dominus dicens: Facite hoc, aut, Facite illud,—ostendit esse in potestate (hominum) quid facerent; . . . qui enim servare
legem non vult, in potestate ejus est, si velit."—*De act. cum Fel. man.*
l. 2, c. 4.

[4] "A fructibus eorum cognoscetis eos."

the Pelagians: "Whenever it is said, 'Do not this and do not that,' and whenever an act of will is required of us to do or not to do something which God commands or forbids, in such places the will is shown to be sufficiently free."[1] Here Jansenius replies (like a partisan of Calvin, as he is) that St. Augustine is speaking of necessity violently imposed on us, not of simple necessity. But here again Jansenius is mistaken; for on this point St. Augustine agreed with the Pelagians, and conceded to them that the will was free both from coercive and from simple necessity; hence in his book against Julian he did not scruple to say, "Both of us affirm that the will in man is free. But you say that any one is free to do good without God's help; hence you are a Pelagian"[2] When St. Augustine says, "Both of us affirm,"[3] he admitted the same liberty to do or not to do which the Pelagians maintained, and they certainly maintained it to be exempt from any necessity whatever; so that there is no doubt that he held the will to be free not only from violence, but from any necessity whatever; he only contradicted the Pelagians in this point, that they maintained the will to be free to do good even without grace.

Further, St. Augustine says that it is difficult to reconcile the liberty of the will with the efficacy of grace: "This question, wherein we discuss the choice of the will, and the grace of God, is so difficult to determine that when we defend free will we seem to deny the grace of God; and when we assert the grace of God, we are

[1] "Ubi dicitur: Noli hoc, et Noli illud;—et ubi ad aliquid faciendum vel non faciendum in divinis monitis opus voluntatis exigitur, satis liberum demonstratur arbitrium."—*De Gr. et Lib. Arb.* c. 2.

[2] "Liberum in hominibus esse arbitrium, utrique dicimus; liberum autem esse quemquam ad agendum bonum sine adjutorio Dei, . . . vos dicitis; hinc estis Pelagiani."—*De Nupt. et Conc.* l. 2, c. 3.

[3] "Utrique dicimus."

supposed to destroy free will." [1]   If St. Augustine had
supposed that the will was not free from simple necessity, but only from violence, it would not have been
difficult, but the easiest thing possible, to understand
how grace acted; when, therefore, he said that it was
difficult to understand, it was because he held that
efficacious grace certainly produced its effect in good
acts; and, on the other hand, that the will did these acts
freely, working without any necessity to prevent it from
being able to do or to wish any acts different from
those to which it was moved by grace.   For the rest, the
holy Father held it as certain that man, with the help of
ordinary grace, was able to fulfil the commandments, or,
at any rate, to procure by prayer greater help to enable
him to fulfil them; otherwise (as he said) God would
not have imposed these commandments on him: " Nor
would he have commanded us to do this if he had considered it impossible to be done by man." [2]

We will quote some more passages of St. Augustine,
where he reiterates the doctrine that the will of man is
free from any necessity: "For that would not be sin
which was not done by the will; and therefore punishment would also be unjust, if man had not free will;
that is, if he acted well or ill through necessity." [3]
Again, " Who would not exclaim that it is folly to give
commands to a man who is not free to do what is commanded ; and that it is injustice to condemn the man

[1] "Ista quæstio, ubi de arbitrio voluntatis et de Dei gratia dis-
putatur, ita est ad discernendum difficilis, ut, quando defenditur
arbitrium, negari Dei gratia videatur, quando asseritur Dei gratia,
liberum arbitrium putetur auferri."—*De Gr. Chr.* c. 47.

[2] "Neque imperaret hoc Deus ut faceremus, si impossibile judicaret
ut hoc ab homine fieret."—*In Ps.* lvi.

[3] "Non enim peccatum esset quod non fieret voluntate; ac per
hoc pœna injusta esset, si homo voluntatem non haberet liberam."—
De Lib. Arb. l. 2, c. 1.

who had no power to fulfil the command?"[1] Again, "If
the motion whereby the will turns aside from the un-
changeable good is natural and necessary, it can by no
means be culpable."[2] Then, after saying that previous
grace is necessary to enable us to do good, he adds,
"But to consent to the call of God, or to dissent from
it, is in the power of our own will."[3] Here he plainly
teaches that the will can freely obey grace or resist it.
Nor does it avail to say with Jansenius that St. Augustine only means that to consent and dissent is the
proper office of the will; for we can never believe that
the holy Doctor would have taken such useless pains to
prove that consent and dissent belong to the will and
not to the intellect, a thing which any illiterate man can
tell. Especially as St. Augustine's words, just before
the last quoted sentence, are as follows: "No one has it
in his power to determine what shall come into his mind,
but to consent, etc."[4] So that it is clear that he is speaking of the free power of the will to consent or dissent
from that which comes into the head. In another place
he says, "No one but God can make the tree" (he is
speaking of the good trees that produce good fruit, and
of the bad trees which produce bad fruit); "but every
man's will has power to choose either good or bad.
When, therefore, our Lord says, Do this or do that, he
shows that it is in men's power to choose what to do."
Elsewhere, in explanation of the help *sine quo*, he says,

[1] "Quis enim non clamet stultum esse præcepta dare ei cui liberum
non est quod præcipitur facere, et iniquum esse eum damnare cui non
fuit potestas jussa complere?"—*De Fide cont. Man.* c. 10.

[2] "Motus quo voluntas avertitur ab incommutabili bono, si natura
vel necessitate existit, culpabilis esse nullo pacto potest."—*De Lib.
Arb.* l. 3, c. 1.

[3] "Consentire autem vocationi Dei, vel ab ea dissentire, propriæ
voluntatis est."—*De Sp. et Litt.* c. 34.

[4] "Neminem habere in potestate quid ei veniat in mentem."

"Without it the will cannot will; but still it is left to the free will either to will or not to will, to use the help or not to use it."[1]

From all this it is very clearly seen how far St Augustine was from the opinion of Jansenius, that the will of man in its action is not free from necessity, much less that it is obliged to follow the preponderating pleasure, which by its impulse invincibly moves and determines it.

III.

Continuation of the Refutation of Jansenius and of His Adherents.

Now, let us apply this to the point we have in view, namely, to prove that God gives every one either proximate grace, or the remote grace of prayer, to enable him to observe the precepts; since otherwise the transgression of the law could never be imputed to him as a fault. Let us then see what are the two propositions that are exactly opposite to those of Jansenius.

His first is, "Some precepts of God are impossible to the just man who wishes and tries to fulfil them with his present strength; nor does God give him grace to make them possible."[2] Hence the Catholic proposition, contradictory of this, is as follows: "Not any of the precepts of God is impossible, at least to the just man, who wishes to observe them, and who endeavors to do so; nor, even with his present strength, is he without the grace (either proximate, or at least remote) whereby he may at least obtain greater assistance to enable him to

[1] "Sine quo voluntas velle non possit; sic tamen ut velle et nolle, uti vel non uti, in ejus libero arbitrio relinquatur."

[2] "Aliqua Dei præcepta hominibus justis, volentibus et conantibus, secundum præsentes quas habent vires, sunt impossibilia; deest quoque illis gratia qua possibilia fiant."

fulfil them. And here we must again observe that to avoid the condemned error it is not enough to grant the absolute possibility of observing the precept, for the Jansenists themselves admit this possibility; but we must also admit the possibility (relatively to the actual carnal delectation which preponderates over the delectation of grace) to fulfil the commandment when it is incumbent on us to do so, or at least to obtain grace to keep it; since the error of Jansenius consists precisely in denying, not the absolute, but the relative possibility.

Jansenius' third proposition is that "in order to merit ill or well in the state of fallen nature, man need not have freedom from necessity, but only freedom from compulsion."[1] Hence the Catholic proposition is the contradictory: to merit ill or well, even in the state of fallen nature, man, whether just or unjust, requires freedom, not only from compulsion, but also from simple necessity; since, according to the Catholic doctrine, the voluntary, whenever it is necessary, is not free in such a sense as is sufficient to merit ill or well in this life; but to merit ill or well the will must be free from any necessity whatever of being obliged to consent to either of two things determinately.

Moreover, F. Fortunato da Brescia (a man universally celebrated by the learned of these days, especially by Muratori), in his late work entitled *Confutation of the System of Cornelius Jansenius*, says that if this system could possibly be true, God's law would be either foolish or unjust; for, according to it, if the heavenly pleasure predominates, then the will, quite independently of the law, is obliged to follow the precise impulse of the pleasure, and thus the law is useless; or, if the earthly pleasure predominates, then the law is unjust, for God imposes a commandment which it is physically impossible for man

[1] " Ad merendum et demerendum in statu naturæ lapsæ, non requiritur in homine libertas a necessitate, sed sufficit libertas a coactione."

to obey, since the will must necessarily yield to the temptation.

And in this way all the threats and admonitions of the Scriptures would be useless, and there would be no human action which could merit reward or punishment, since all the actions of man would be done through necessity. So that whenever any one exhorted us to do well, we might answer with Eusebius against the Fatalists, "These powers are not mine, O Doctor; for they will do it if the fates so desire" (*i.e.*, if the carnal delight does not preponderate); "that which is fated will necessarily come to pass."[1] I must necessarily follow the pleasure that prevails.

The same author says, further, that if we admit this system, we must also admit Manicheism, which supposed two principles, a good and an evil; and says that as all the acts of men were derived from one or the other principle, the man was obliged to follow that which prevailed. Nor does it do to say that the necessity in the system of the preponderating pleasure is not derived from a good or evil principle, as the Manicheans held, but depends on the sin of Adam, which is its cause; for the question is not through what principle the will acts necessarily when it is moved, but whether the will after Adam's fall has remained free from necessity in its actions. And this is what the Jansenists deny, who hold that the will merits well and ill, though it is necessitated to will that to which the preponderating pleasure determines it. But, as F. Fortunato well observes, the books of Arnold, Irénée, Ventrochio, and the other Jansenists, were condemned for this very error of maintaining Jansenius' principle of the invincibility of the pleasure which is superior in degree. And we know that it was for this reason that the theology of Gio-

[1] "Non sunt potestates hæ meæ, O Doctor ! Faciam enim, si fata volunt . . . aderit necessario quod fatatum est."—*Præp. ev.* l. 6, c. 6.

venino was prohibited; for though he did not expressly hold the system we are discussing, yet he imprudently spoke too obscurely on the point: "The physical nature of efficacious grace consists simply in the preponderance of the pleasure which the mind takes in goodness."[1] Still he did not use the phrase "relatively preponderating," though he proves his proposition by the often-quoted text of St. Augustine: "We must act according to that which pleases us most." And for this cause his work was so long prohibited, and has at last been allowed because of the addition of a compendium, entitled *The True Doctrine of the Church*, extracted from the theology of Tourneley, who has amply and well confuted the system.

F. Fortunato concludes: "It is clear, then, that the system of Jansenius is favorable to them (Luther and Calvin), and so cannot be maintained by a Catholic without violating his faith. For we cannot preserve our faith and religion while defending a system on the admission of whose fundamental principles the reception of condemned doctrines necessarily follows."[2] Tourneley meant the same when he said, "Since the Church condemned the five propositions in the sense of Jansenius, they must be condemned as parts of Jansenius' theory of the superior and relatively preponderating pleasure, which is the foundation of his whole system."[3]

[1] "Natura physica gratiæ efficacis non in alio posita est quam in victrici delectatione qua mens circa bonum afficitur."—*Instit.* p. 6, d. I, q. 4, c. 7.

[2] "Manifestum relinquitur et Jansenianum systema illis (Luthero et Calvino) plane favere, indeque a viro Catholico sine crimine violatæ fidei propugnari nullatenus posse; non enim tuta fide, salvaque religione, defendi potest systema, cujus fundamentalibus admissis principiis, damnata dogmata necessum est approbare."

[3] "Cum Ecclesia quinque propositiones damnaverit in sensu Jansenii, necesse est illas damnatas fuisse in ipso Jansenii systemate, delectationis scilicet superioris ac relative victricis, quæ totius systematis fundamentum est."—*De Gr. Chr.* q. 3 *in prop.* 5 *Jans.*

Nor will it avail to say that the system of Jansenius is one thing, which supposes that the pleasure which relatively preponderates is indeliberate, that is, that it comes to us without any assent of the will; but that it is quite a different thing to say that the pleasure, though it relatively preponderates by the superiority of its degree, yet is deliberate; that is, it preponderates not by itself and by its own strength (as the maintainers of this system say), but it preponderates by being reinforced by the power of the consenting will. And hence they say that though the preponderating pleasure certainly and infallibly overcomes, yet it does not do so necessarily, as Jansenius maintained.

This will not avail, because, as Tourneley well replies, that grace, or that pleasure which is infallibly efficacious, and invincibly determines the will by its preponderating power, cannot but necessitate the will to consent. And he proves it thus, "That grace necessitates which supposes the will to be destitute of real power to resist it; but of this nature is grace, which is infallibly efficacious, because of the superiority of the degree of its strength. For grace of this kind supposes that the will has only inferior strength to resist; but it is a contradiction to say that superior strength, acting as such, can be overcome by inferior; otherwise it would be necessary that the inferior strength should act beyond the degree of its power of acting."[1] Nor does it avail to reply, that though the power of grace relatively preponderating is superior to that of the concupiscence taken by itself, it is not

---

[1] "Ea gratia est necessitans quæ supponit voluntatem destitutam vera potentia resistendi; atqui talis est gratia infallibiliter efficax ex virium graduali superioritate. Nam hujusmodi gratia supponit voluntatem non habere ad resistendum nisi vires inferiores. Repugnat autem ut vires superiores, quæ agunt ut superiores, vincantur ab inferioribus; alias necesse esset ut inferiores operarentur ultra suæ activitatis gradus."

superior to that of the concupiscence joined with that of the will, because, as Tourneley says, such a power of the will could only be admitted with respect to evil which a man can do by himself, as when he overcomes one vice by another, or at least with respect to good of the natural order; but not with respect to supernatural good, such as the conquest of a strong concupiscence, which cannot be effected without God's grace.

Hence the Fathers of Diospolis required every Pelagian, among other things, "to confess that when we fight against temptations and unlawful concupiscence, the victory comes not from our own will, but from the help of God." [1] And the reason is, as St. Thomas teaches, that no active principle can produce an effect exceeding the sphere of its activity; so that no natural principle or cause can produce a supernatural effect: "No act exceeds the proportion of its active principle; and hence we see that in natural things nothing can by its own operation produce an effect which exceeds the power of its activity, but can only by its own operation produce an effect proportionate to its power." [2] So that the natural power of the human will, although united to the power of grace, cannot, when the latter is inferior to the power of the concupiscence, contribute to produce a supernatural effect, such as the conquest of a violent concupiscence that preponderates over grace. And, in fact, the Jansenists say, we are contented if you grant to us that the delectation certainly overcomes by reason of

---

[1] "Ut fateatur, quando contra tentationes concupiscentiasque illicitas dimicamus, non ex propria voluntate, sed ex adjutorio Dei provenire victoriam."—*Cath. conf.*

[2] "Nullus actus excedit proportionem principii activi. Et ideo videmus in rebus naturalibus quod nulla res potest perficere effectum per suam operationem qui excedat virtutem activam, sed solum potest producere per operationem suam effectum suæ virtuti proportionatum."—I. 2. q. 109, a. 5.

its superior power. See how one of them, the Abbot de Bourzéis, speaks: "It is sufficient for us if this single truth be granted, that as often as we consent to the grace of God, it always arises from the right love which God inspires, being superior in strength to the perverse love; and in consequence of this superiority always most certainly overcoming it."[1] Hence Tourneley, speaking of the two systems, of pleasure absolutely preponderating, and of pleasure relatively preponderating, concludes, "We have known orthodox theologians who test efficacious grace by its pleasure being absolutely and simply preponderating over all other pleasures; and who call that sufficient grace which has just power enough to overcome the lust actually opposed to it. But we have only met with Jansenists who maintain that no grace can overcome unless it is relatively preponderating in degree, and who admit no other sufficient grace than one that is inferior in strength to the superior concupiscence which opposes it."[2]

So that, to conclude, we do not intend now to blame the opinion that the will, even when it follows the greater delectation, yet always acts freely, that is, without necessity, and with true power (not merely nominal or hypothetical power) to act in a contrary way; but we only

---

[1] " Nobis enim sufficit quod hæc sola nobis veritas concedatur, nimirum quoties gratiæ Dei consentimus, id oriri semper ex eo quod rectus amor, quem Deus nobis inspirat, viribus superior est perverso amori, et, quia viribus superior est, idcirco eum certissime superare." —*Collat.* 4, c. 30.

[2] " Novimus quidem orthodoxos theologos qui vim gratiæ efficacem colligunt ex ipsius delectatione absolute et simpliciter victrice; quique in gratia sufficiente pares vires agnoscunt ad oppositam actualem cupiditatem superandam. Verum qui gratiam velint esse victricem relative, seu ex superioritate graduum, quique non aliam sufficientem admittunt gratiam quam viribus inferiorem oppositæ superiori concupiscentiæ, non alios quam Janseniani systematis defensores novimus."—*De Gr. Chr.* q. 9, a. 2, obj. 6.

reject the opinion of those who say that when one of the two pleasures, the carnal or the heavenly, preponderates by being greater in degree than the other, then man has no more power to resist and to overcome it, because the greater force always overcomes the less.

Nevertheless, I cannot in this place neglect to mention the difficulty that I find in this system of the preponder‑ating delectation. Its defenders say, as also F. John Laurence Berti, that the efficacy of grace, as they main‑tain it, does not differ in substance from the efficacy as taught by the Thomists, though founded on different principles; for the Thomists make the efficacy of grace consist in a physical predetermination, but the Jansenists in the preponderating pleasure. That which is done by physical premonition according to the Thomists, the same is done by victorious delectation according to the Au‑gustinians; namely, the liberty of the will is moved to give consent *in actu secundo.* Further, both opinions teach that man still has the power, *in actu primo,* to act in opposite directions; so that the will always acts freely and without necessity.*

But I observe that, as the principles and the reasons of these two opinions are different, so also are their con‑sequences.

According to the Thomists, the reason of the efficacy of grace is because the created will is in a state of pas‑sive potentiality, able to receive the motions of grace ; so that to come to actual operation it must be moved by God, as the first agent and first free cause, who, by his

---

* Berti. August. *Syst. Vindic. Diss.* 5, c. 3, n. 4. " In actu primo," " in actu secundo." " In actu primo" is much the same with our English expression *in power*, or *in liability;* " in actu secundo," *in act.* Thus, at every moment we are subject to concupiscence *in actu primo*, because we are *liable* to be tempted by passion to disobey God's will; but we are only subject to it "in actu secundo" when we are *at this moment* tempted by passion to disobey God's will.—ED.

predetermination, adapts and determines the potentiality (of the will) into actuality. This only relates to the act; but as for the power of capability, the Thomists say that man has the grace of potentiality wholly complete, and in proximate preparation, so as to be able to act virtuously. Thus F. Gonet, "The grace which gives the power gives the full complement, and all the strength or sufficiency which is requisite, so far as the *actus primus* is concerned."[1] So, also, Cardinal Gotti: "Sufficient grace gives proximate power, and complete power within the limits of potentiality."[2]* And thus all other Thomists in general; and if any of them apparently speak otherwise, it is only of the *actus secundus*, not *primus.*

On the other hand, the reason of the principle of those who maintain the opinion of the pleasure superior in degree is because (as they say) whereas at first, in the state of innocence, man only required "sufficient grace" to do well, since his will, being then sound and in perfect balance, could easily act with only sufficient grace, without needing efficacious grace,—now, on the other hand, since the fall of Adam, the will, being injured and inclined to evil, has need of "efficacious grace," which, by means of the victorious pleasure, adapts it for acting virtuously. But (I say) according to this reason for the system, granting that the will of man has become so weak that, in its present state, it cannot act without

---

[1] "Gratia quæ dat posse, dat totum complementum et totam virtutem seu sufficientiam quæ requiritur ex parte actus primi."—*Man. Thom.* tr. 7, c. 10.

[2] "Gratia sufficiens dat posse proximum et expeditum in ratione potentiæ."—*De Gr.* q. 2, d. 4, § 2.

---

* Gotti t. ii. tr. vi. *de Grat.* q. 2, dub. 4, n. 4, p. 286. "In sensu composito," "in sensu diviso." The meaning of these phrases will best be shown by illustrations. I have full moral power to avoid *all* venial sins "in sensu *diviso*,"—that is, I can avoid *each one* of them; there is no *one* which I cannot avoid,—but not "in sensu *composito*," for I have *not* moral power to avoid *all* venial sins collectively.—ED.

efficacious grace, it is impossible to say that man still has, by virtue of sufficient grace, not even in the *actus primus*, nor either in the *sensus compositus*, nor *sensus divisus*, the complete and proximately prepared power to observe the commandments, or to be able to do any good work, even though it be mediate, by means of which he can place himself in a position to obtain greater help to enable him to fulfil the law.

I know that the supporters of this opinion have no objection to grant this, and to say that, in our present state, sufficient grace does not give complete and prepared power. "Sufficient grace," says F. Macedo, one of this school, " does not give power proximately complete and prepared." [1] And elsewhere, speaking of the grace of Adam innocent and of Adam fallen, he says, " The first supposed (a power) prepared and free; the second a power crippled, hindered, and enslaved." [2]

So, supposing that grace, when inferior to the concupiscence, does not give complete and prepared power to observe the commandments, it can, in truth, be no longer called sufficient. So that, in fact, F. Berti, who defends such a system of the relatively victorious delectation, finds no difficulty in further granting that such inferior grace ought properly to be called inefficacious, and not sufficient. So that on this system, they who do not receive from God grace that is efficacious, by means of the delectation relatively victorious over that of the concupiscence, have not even grace sufficient to enable them to fulfil the commandments. F. Berti thus writes in defence of his opinion: first, he states the three objections of his opponents, which are as follows: "There are three things which savor of the Jansenist dogma, and

[1] " Gratia sufficiens non dat potentiam proxime completam et expeditam."

[2] " Prima supponebat potentiam expeditam et liberam, secunda impeditam et servam."—*Cort. D. Aug.* tr. 2, q. 3, a. 2.

13

are the fountain and source of the five condemned propositions; to which the new Jansenists, the chief of whom are two (doubtless pretended) Augustinians, make no objection" (these two are F. Bellelli and F. Berti, against whom the Archbishop of Vienne wrote). "The first of these three things is, that they do not make efficacious grace consist simply in a victorious delectation, but in a delectation relatively preponderating, etc. The second is, that they deny the existence of a power proximately prepared in the case of a delectation of a lower grade, requiring for this, as regards the power and the *actus primus,* a stronger delectation; and therefore inefficacious grace (or the assistance *sine quo,* which they preach about) is not really sufficient grace, either in the Molinist sense or the Thomist sense; since sufficient grace, by the common consent of Catholics, confers power proximately prepared. The third thing that follows from this is, that they deny the existence of such a thing as sufficient grace; the very name of which they fraudulently abstain from using, and call it rather inefficacious than insufficient."[1] Such are the objections. Now for F. Berti's answer: "I most firmly and unhesitatingly declare that the three doctrines just cited are noway erroneous, nor principles of the five condemned proposi-

[1] "Tria sunt quæ Jansenianum redolent dogma, et quinque damnatarum propositionum sunt fons et origo, a quibus novi Janseniani, quos inter eminent duo haud dubie spurii Augustinenses minime abhorrent. Horum primum est, quod non tantum in delectatione victrici reponunt gratiam efficientem, sed in delectatione victrici relativa. Alterum, quod negant in delectatione inferioris gradus potentiam proxime expeditam, ad hanc requirentes ex parte potentiæ et actus primi robustiorem delectationem; ideoque gratia inefficax, sive adjutorium sine quo ab ipsis deprædicatum, non est vera gratia sufficiens, neque Molinistico sensu neque Thomistico, cum gratia sufficiens communi sensu Catholicorum conferat ipsam potentiam proxime expeditam. Tertium, quod hinc consequitur, veram gratiam sufficientem e medio tollunt, illam potius inefficacem quam sufficientem appellantes."

tions; but that some people, moved indeed by a laudable zeal for refuting Jansenius, but nevertheless carried away by the prejudice of their private judgment, have made no distinction between what is Catholic and what is erroneous and condemned; and that from these people's lucubrations, some anonymous sciolist" (the Archbishop of Vienne, to wit), "and some other men of scanty learning and fat wits, have taken occasion to calumniate the unshaken doctrines of Augustine (which, whether they admit it or not, are the same as ours) as monstrous heresies."[1]

Now I confess myself also to be precisely one of these scantily learned and gross-minded men; for I cannot understand how the propositions of F. Berti hold together; since in their consequences they appear clearly repugnant to one another. If he had said that to observe the divine law we have need of efficacious grace, but that sufficient grace, which is given to all, gives the proximate power to enable us to pray, and by prayer to obtain the greater assistance necessary for the actual observance of the commandments, we should quite agree; for this is our opinion, which we shall set forth and prove in the next chapter.

But we cannot agree; because, while speaking of prayer, he says well that every one of the faithful, by means of this sufficient grace, if he puts no impediment in the way, can pray, and by prayer obtain the immedi-

[1] " Ego vero firmissime et absque ulla hæsitatione pronuntio, tria doctrinæ capita nuperrime commemorata nequaquam erronea esse nec damnatarum propositionum principia; sed aliquos Jansenii quidem refutandi zelo permotos, sed propriæ sententiæ præjudicio abreptos, quid catholicum sit, quid erroneum et damnatum minime distinxisse, atque ex horum lucubrationibus ansam arripuisse sciolum anonymum, et si qui alii sunt curtæ eruditionis et pinguis minervæ homines, inconcussa Augustini dogmata, quæ, velint nolint, sunt eadem ac nostra, tamquam portenta hæresum calumniandi."—*Aug. syst. vind.* d. 4, c. 1, § 2.

ate assistance to enable him actually to fulfil the commandments. " To each of the faithful " (these are his words), " unless he freely puts an obstacle in the way, the grace of prayer is given, by which he may obtain the aid immediately sufficient to fulfil the commandments." [1]   And, further, he says in another place that the said sufficient grace, common to all the faithful, although only remotely sufficient for the observance of the precepts, is, nevertheless, proximately sufficient for prayer, by which efficacious grace is then obtained: " In him who has the little will (that is, the will which is furnished by the sufficient grace) there is a power proximately sufficient for prayer, and remotely sufficient for the observance of the commandments, which he will be able proximately to fulfil, when by prayer he has obtained a strong will " (which strong will is furnished by efficacious grace).[2]   He says then, and says wisely, that for the observance of the commandments, it cannot be said that sufficient grace gives to all the proximate power actually to fulfil them; for (as he well observes in the place just cited, § 4) the proximate power to observe the precepts is that which needs nothing further to enable it to act; hence he writes in the same section (4), near the beginning, that the complete and prepared power can only be had from efficacious grace: " Efficacious grace alone gives the complete and ready power." [3] Hence he adds that, in order that the sufficient grace may be said to be proximately sufficient for actual operation, " it is requisite that it should not need any fur-

---

[1] " Cuilibet fideli, nisi libere ponat obicem adest gratia orationis, qua impetrare potest auxilium immediate sufficiens ad implenda mandata."—*De Theol. Disc.* l. 18, c. 8, p 4.

[2] " In eo qui habet voluntatem parvam est potentia proxime sufficiens ad orandum et sufficiens remote ad observantiam præceptorum, quæ poterit proxime implere, dum per orationem obtinuerit robustam voluntatem."—*Aug. syst. vind.* d. 4, c. 1, § 9.

[3] " Gratia efficax sola dat potentiam completam et expeditam."— *Ibid.* § 4.

ther means in order to act." [1] So that, according to the
reasoning of F. Berti, though the sufficient grace does
not supply all the faithful with proximate power to keep
the commandments, yet it supplies all with power proximately sufficient to pray. Therefore each of the faithful, by the aid of "sufficient grace" alone, can actually
pray, without the need of any further assistance, that is,
of efficacious grace.

But then I do not know how this agrees with what he
says in another place: " No one without grace, efficacious in itself, has the power of praying united with the
act." [2] Therefore, according to this second proposition,
the "sufficient grace" does not give really, but only in
name, the power proximately sufficient for prayer. It
only gives the power remotely sufficient, if there is need
of efficacious grace to make the power of praying issue
in act. Either, therefore, for actual prayer, "efficacious
grace" is requisite, and then it cannot be said that the
sufficient grace gives the power proximately sufficient;
or else "sufficient grace" gives the power proximately
sufficient for actual prayer; and then there is no need
of the efficacious grace of the preponderating pleasure,
which he seeks to establish. But St. Augustine also,
says F. Berti, requires an overpowering pleasure to enable us to pray: "Augustine teaches that for prayer a
certain knowledge is requisite, and an overpowering
pleasure." [3] I have examined the passage referred to,
which is as follows: " Let us understand, if we can, that
the good Lord God sometimes does not give even to his
saints either the certain knowledge of some good work,
or an overpowering delight in it, in order that they may

---

[1] " Requiritur ut alio medio non egeat ut exeat in actum."

[2] " Nullus absque gratia per se efficaci, habet potentiam orandi
conjunctam cum actu."—*De Theol. Disc.* l. 18, c. 8, p. 5.

[3] " Augustinus docet necessariam esse ad orandum certam scientiam
et victricem delectationem."

understand that the light wherewith their darkness is enlightened comes not from themselves, but from him, and so also the sweetness by which their land yields its fruit." [1] St. Augustine does not say that an overpowering delight is requisite for prayer; he only says that sometimes God does not give even to his saints either the certain knowledge or the overpowering delight of some just work, in order that they may know that from him, and not from themselves, they have the light to illumine them, and the sweetness to make them bear fruit.

Therefore St. Augustine does not here primarily speak of the sufficient grace by which a man can work, but does not always work; nor does he say that man with only sufficient grace, and without efficacious grace, cannot actually pray; but he speaks only of efficacious grace, which, by means of an overpowering delight, infallibly causes him to do well. Secondly, he does not speak here of prayer, but of just works; which properly means the observance of the precepts or of the counsels; since prayer, though it is a good work, of its own nature is not a work, but the means of obtaining the aid necessary to execute good works.

We also hold, as we said before, that efficacious grace is necessary for the observance of the commandments; but we say that for actual prayer, whereby we may obtain efficacious grace, the sufficient grace which God gives to all the faithful is enough. And thus we do no violence to the truth that God's commandments are not impossible to any one; since every man, by means of the sufficient grace only, can perform such an easy thing as

---

[1] "Intelligamus, si possumus, Dominum Deum bonum ideo etiam sanctis suis alicujus operis justi aliquando non tribuere vel certam scientiam vel victricem delectationem, ut cognoscant non a seipsis, sed ab illo sibi esse lucem qua illuminentur tenebræ eorum, et suavitatem qua det fructum suum terra eorum."—*De Pecc. mer.* l. 2, c. 19.

prayer; and by means of prayer he will obtain the assistance of gratuitous efficacious grace, which is necessary for the actual performance of difficult things—such as the observance of the commandments. Thus says Cardinal Noris, whose words I will quote in the next chapter, and before him St. Augustine: "By the fact that we most firmly believe that God does not command impossibilities, we are admonished in easy matters what to do, and in difficult matters what to ask for."[1] Otherwise, if sufficient grace were not enough for actual prayer, and the addition of efficacious grace were always necessary, and if this were denied to any man—as, in fact, efficacious grace is denied to many—I cannot see how the commandments of God could be said to be possible to such a person, and how God could demand of him the observance of his law (at the time when he denies him even the efficacious grace to enable him actually to pray), and how with justice he could condemn him to hell for not observing it. This is precisely that which made Jansenius say that some precepts were impossible even from the first; because he erroneously said that some men want the grace to make the precepts possible to them. But it is not so; because God gives to all men (we are not here considering the case of infidels and obstinate sinners) the proximate grace to enable them actually to pray, as we shall prove in the next chapter. And so no one will be able to make the excuse that the observance of the precepts was impossible to him; for though he had not efficacious grace for their actual observance, he had, nevertheless, grace proximately sufficient for actual prayer, by means of which he would have obtained from God efficacious grace, according to his promise of hearing whoever prays to him;

---

[1] " Eo ipso quo firmissime creditur Deum justum et bonum impossibilia non præcipere, hinc admonemur, et in facilibus quid agamus, et in difficilibus quid petamus."—*De Nat. et Gr.* c. 69.

and with this he certainly might have observed the precepts. And the Council of Trent has expressly declared this against Luther, who asserted that the observance of God's law was impossible even to the faithful. "God," it says, "does not command impossibilities; but by commanding, he admonishes you to do what you can, and to ask for what you cannot do; and by his help he enables you to do it."[1]

[1] "Deus impossibilia non jubet; sed jubendo monet, et facere quid possis, et petere quod non possis; et adjuvat ut possis."—*Sess.* 6, *cap.* II.

CHAPTER IV.

GOD GIVES ALL MEN THE GRACE TO PRAY IF THEY CHOOSE, AS THE "SUFFICIENT GRACE" WHICH IS COMMON TO ALL MEN IS BY ITSELF ENOUGH FOR PRAYER.

I.

The Principal Theologians who teach this Doctrine.

Assuming, then, that God wills all men to be saved, and that, as far as he is concerned, he gives to all the graces necessary for their salvation, we must say that all men have given to them the grace to enable them actually to pray (without needing a further grace); and by prayer to obtain all further aid necessary for the observance of the commandments and for salvation. But it must be remarked that when we say "without needing a further grace," we do not mean that the common grace gives the power of prayer without the aid of assisting grace, since, in order to exercise any act of piety, besides the exciting grace, there is doubtless required the assisting or co-operating grace. But we mean that the common grace gives every man the power of actual prayer, without a further preventing grace, which, physically or morally, determines the will of man to exercise the act of prayer. We will first mention the names of the famous theologians who teach this opinion as certain, and then we will prove it by authorities and arguments.

It is held by Isambert, Cardinal du Perron, Alphonsus le Moyne, and others whom we shall presently quote, and at greater length as a set proposition by Honoratus

Tourneley. All these authors prove that every man, by means of the ordinary sufficient grace alone, can actually pray, without need of further aid; and by prayer can obtain all the graces requisite for the performance of the most difficult things.

It was also held by Cardinal Noris, who proves the proposition, that man, when the commandment urges (*urgendo il precetto*), can pray if he will; and he proves it thus: "It is clear that the power to pray should be proximate in the just man or the faithful; for if the faithful has only a remote power for a simple act of prayer (I am not here speaking of fervid prayer), he will not have another proximate power to obtain the grace of prayer, otherwise the series would be infinite."[1] Assuming that, in order to keep the commandments and to be saved, prayer is necessary, as we proved in the beginning, when we spoke of the necessity of prayer, this learned author says well that every one has the proximate power of prayer, in order that by prayer he may obtain the proximate power to do good; and therefore all can pray with only the ordinary grace, without other assistance. Otherwise, if, in order to obtain the proximate power for the act of prayer we required another power, we should still want another power of grace to obtain this power, and so on *ad infinitum*, and it would no longer be in the power of man to co-operate in his salvation.

The same author in another place maintains this doctrine more clearly: "Even in the state of fallen nature the assistance *sine quo* (*i.e.*, the sufficient grace which is common to all) is given, though Jansenius denies it; and this assistance produces in us weak acts, namely, prayer

[1] "Manifestum est potentiam ad orandum debere esse proximam in justo sive fideli; nam, si fidelis sit in potentia remota ad simpliciter orandum (non enim hic loquor de fervida et diuturniore oratione), non habet is aliam potentiam proximam pro impetranda oratione; alias procederetur in infinitum."—*Jans. err. cal. subl.* c. 2, § 1.

not very fervid, for fulfilling the commandments; but for the actual observance of these, the assistance *sine quo* is only a remote help, by which we can, however, obtain by prayer the assistance *quo*, or efficacious grace, by which the commandments are fulfilled."[1] So that Cardinal Noris held it as certain that in the present state all men have the assistance *sine quo, i.e.*, ordinary grace, which, without need of further assistance, produces prayer, by which we can then obtain efficacious grace to enable us to observe the law. And hence we can easily understand the axiom universally received in the schools: "To him who does what in him lies, God does not refuse his grace."[2] That is, to the man who prays, and thus makes good use of the sufficient grace which enables him to do such an easy thing as prayer, God does not refuse the efficacious grace to enable him to execute difficult things.

Thus, also, Louis Thomassin, who expresses astonishment at those who say that "sufficient assistance" is not enough to do any actual good work, nor to avoid any sin: "For if," he says, "this assistance is truly assistance, and gives proximate power, how is it that, out of the innumerable quantity of men who are thus assisted, none keep the commandments ? Or how is it truly sufficient, if, besides it, efficacious grace is necessary ? That man has not a sufficient power who wants a necessary assistance which is not in his own power."[3] He means that

---

[1] "Etiam in statu naturæ lapsæ datur adjutorium *sine quo non*, secus ac Jansenius contendit, quod quidem adjutorium efficit in nobis . . . actus debiles, nempe orationes minus fervidas pro adimplendis mandatis; in ordine ad quorum executionem adjutorium *sine quo non* est tantum auxilium remotum, impetratorium tamen auxilii *quo*, sive gratiæ efficacis qua mandata implentur."—*Jans. err. cal. subl.* c. 2, § 1.

[2] "Facienti quod in se est, Deus non denegat gratiam."

[3] "Si hæc enim auxilia vere auxilia sunt, et proximam vere dant potestatem, quî fit ut, ex innumerabili tamdiu hominum qui ita juvantur multitudine, præceptum observet nemo ? Aut quomodo vere

" sufficient grace," to be really sufficient, ought to give a man the proximate and ready power to execute a good act; but since, in order to perform such an act, another grace—namely, efficacious grace—is wanted, unless a man has (at least mediately) this efficacious grace which is necessary for salvation, how can it be said that the "sufficient grace" gives this proximate and ready power? Since, says St. Thomas, "God does not neglect to do that which is necessary to salvation." [1] On the one hand, it is true that God is not bound to give us his grace, because what is *gratis* is not of obligation; but, on the other hand, supposing that he gives us commandments, he is obliged to give us the assistance necessary for observing them. And as God obliges us actually to observe every precept whenever it applies, so ought he also actually to supply us (at least mediately or remotely) with the assistance necessary for the observance of the precept, without the necessity of a further grace, which is not common to all. Hence Thomassin concludes, that in order to reconcile the proposition that "sufficient grace" is enough for a man's salvation with the statement that efficacious grace is requisite to observe the whole law, it is necessary to say that sufficient grace is enough to pray, and to perform similar easy acts, and that by means of these we then obtain efficacious grace to fulfil the difficult acts. And this is without doubt in conformity with the doctrine of St. Augustine, who teaches: "By the very fact that God is most firmly believed not to command impossibilities, we are admonished both what to do in easy things, and in difficult things what to ask for." [2] On this

sufficientia sunt, si præterea gratia efficax est necessaria ? Non is habet potestatem sufficientem cui deest aliud auxilium necessarium, quod in ejus potestate non est."—*Cons. sch. de gr. tr.* 3, c. 8.

[1] " Deus non deficit ab agendo quod est necessarium ad salutem."— *P.* 1, q 49. a. 2.

[2] " Eo ipso quo firmissime creditur Deum justum et bonum impos-

passage Cardinal Noris observes, " Therefore, we are able to do easy or less perfect works without asking God for further help; for which, however, we must pray in more difficult works." [1] Thomassin also brings forward the authority of St. Bonaventure, Scotus, and others on this subject, and says, " All these considered the sufficient grace to be truly sufficient, whether the will consents to it or not." [2] And this he demonstrates in four parts of his book, adducing the authorities of the schoolmen for a long series of years, beginning from the year 1100.

Habert, Bishop of Vabres and Doctor of the Sorbonne, who was the first to write against Jansenius, says: " We think, first, that 'sufficient grace' has only a contingent or mediate connection with the actual effect of the complete consent. . . . We think, further, that 'sufficient grace' is a grace that disposes for efficacious grace, since from a good use of it God afterwards grants to the created will the grace that performs the complete effect." [3] He had said before that " all Catholic Doctors, of all schools, have professed, and do profess, that a real inward grace is given, which is capable of persuading the will to consent to good, though, on account of the free resistance of the will, it sometimes does not persuade it thus

sibilia non præcipere, hinc admonemur, et in facilibus quid agamus, et in difficilibus quid petamus."—*De Nat. et Gr.* c. 69.

[1] "Igitur opera facilia seu actus bonos minus perfectos facere possumus, absque eo quod majus auxilium a Deo postulemus, quod tamen in actibus difficilioribus petendum est."—*Loco sup. cit.*

[2] "Omnibus ea placuere sufficientia auxilia, vere sufficientia, quibus assentitur quandoque voluntas, quandoque non."—*Cons. sch.* p. 2, *ad fin.*

[3] "Censemus primo, quod immediate cum ipso effectu consensus completi (gratia) sufficiens non habet habitudinem, nisi contingenter vel mediate. . . . Arbitramur proinde gratiam sufficientem esse gratiam dispositionis ad efficacem, utpote ex cujus bono usu Deus postea gratiam completi effectus effectivam creatæ voluntati concedat."—*Theol. Gr. Patr.* l. 2, c. 15.

to consent,"[1] and for this doctrine be quotes Gamaches, Duval, Isambert, Perez, Le Moyne, and others. Then he goes on: "The assistance, therefore, of sufficient grace disposes us for the reception of efficacious grace; and is in some sort efficacious, namely, of an incomplete effect, obtained first remotely, then more nearly, and at last proximately—such as is an act of faith, hope, love, and, mixed with these, one of prayer. Hence the famous Alphonsus Le Moyne taught that this sufficient grace was the grace of asking, or of prayer, of which St. Augustine so often speaks."[2] So that, according to Habert, the difference between efficacious and sufficient grace is, that the former produces its effect completely, while the latter produces it either contingently (*i.e.*, sometimes, but not always) or mediately (*i.e.*, by means of prayer). Moreover, he says that sufficient grace, according to the good use we make of it, prepares us to obtain efficacious grace; hence he calls sufficient grace "in some sort efficacious" (*secundum quid*), because of its effect commenced but not completed. Lastly, he says that sufficient grace is the grace of prayer, of which it is in our power to avail ourselves, as St. Augustine teaches. So that a man has no excuse if he does not do that which he already has sufficient grace to enable him to perform; by which grace, without further assistance, he may either act, or at least obtain more help to enable him to act. And Habert

---

[1] "Catholici Doctores omnes, dari gratiam aliquam vere intrinsecam, quæ possit consensum voluntatis ad bonum salutis elicere, nec tamen propter liberam voluntatis resistentiam eumdem aliquando eliciat, omnibus in scholis professi sunt et profitentur."—*Theol. Gr. Patr.* l. 2, c. 6.

[2] "Auxilia igitur gratiæ sufficientis sunt dispositiva ad efficacem, et efficacia secundum quid, effectus videlicet incompleti, impetrantis primo remote, propius, ac tandem proxime, qualis est actus fidei, spei, timoris, atque inter hæc omnia orationis. Unde celeberrimus Alphonsus Lemoinus gratiam illam sufficientem docuit esse gratiam petendi, seu orationis, de qua toties beatus Augustinus."—*Ibid.* c. 15.

asserts that this was the common doctrine of the Sorbonne.

Charles du Plessis d'Argentré, another theologian of the Sorbonne, quotes more than a thousand theologians who teach directly that with sufficient grace easy works are accomplished; and that a man who makes use of it obtains thereby a more abundant assistance for his thorough conversion. And precisely in this sense, as we said before, he says the celebrated axiom of the schools is to be understood: "To those who do what is in their power" (that is, by means of sufficient grace) "God does not deny grace;"[1] that is, more abundant and efficacious grace.

The learned Dionysius Petavius proves at great length that man works with simple sufficient grace; and he even asserts that it would be monstrous to say otherwise; and that this is the doctrine not only of theologians, but also of the Church. Hence he says that the grace of observing the precepts follows prayer; and that the gift of prayer is given by God at the time when he imposes the precept: "This gift, by which God grants us power to do justly, follows the act of prayer; and this act is given contemporaneously with the law."[2] So that as the law is imposed upon all, so the gift of prayer is given to all.

The author of the *Theology for the Use of the Seminary of Peterkau* says that with sufficient grace alone "a man can do well, and sometimes does so;" so that "there is nothing to hinder that, of two persons furnished with the same assistance, one should very often perform the mere acts (which precede full conversion), the other

---

[1] Facienti quod in se est, Deus non denegat gratiam.

[2] "Donum istud, quo Deus dat ut jussa faciamus, affectum orationis subsequitur,—et talis affectus legi comes datur."—*De Deo*, l. 10, c. 20.—19.

[3] "Aliquis potest bene agere, et aliquando bene agit."

not." [1] And this, he says, is in conformity with the doctrine of St. Augustine and St. Thomas, and of his first disciples, especially of Father Bartholomew Medina, who says, "Sometimes a man is converted only with sufficient grace." [2] And I find that also Father Louis of Granada asserts this to be the common doctrine of theologians: "Theologians reckon two kinds of assistance—one sufficient, the other more than sufficient; by the former of which men are sometimes converted, sometimes refuse to be converted." [3] And, shortly afterwards, "And theologians define how universally this assistance is open to men." [4] Hence Petrocorensis says: "So man can do some acts of piety, such as to pray to God with humility with the sufficient grace only, and sometimes actually does them, and so prepares himself for further graces." [5] This, he says, is the order of God's Providence with regard to graces, "that the succeeding should follow the good use of the former." [6] And he concludes that thorough conversion and final perseverance "are infallibly obtained by prayer, for which the sufficient grace which is given to every one abundantly suffices." [7]

---

[1] "Nihil vetat ut, ex duobus æquali auxilio præventis, faciliores actus, plenam conversionem sæpissime præcedentes, unus faciat, alius non."—*Lib.* 6, q. 3.

[2] "Cum sola gratia sufficienti aliquando homo convertitur.—*In* I. 2. q. 109, a. 10.

[3] "Duo auxiliorum genera theologi statuunt, alterum sufficiens, alterum superabundans; et quidem priori auxilio excitati homines aliquando convertuntur, aliquando converti renuunt."

[4] "Et quidem prius illud auxilium ad omnes homines quam latissime patere theologi definiunt."—*In fest. S. Matt. conc.* I, p. 1.

[5] "Si quosdam pietatis actus (nempe humiliter Deum deprecari) cum solo auxilio sufficienti (homo) facere potest, et aliquando facit, quibus se ad ulteriores gratias præparat."

[6] "Ut priorum bono usui posteriores succedant."—*Loco sup. cit.*

[7] "Infallibiliter (homines) promerentur oratione, pro qua sufficiens gratia, quæ nulli non præsto est, plenissime sufficit."

The same is held by Cardinal d'Aguirre, who in all things follows St. Augustine.[1]

Father Antonio Boucat, of the order of St. Francis of Paula, defends the position that every one is *now* able, without new assistance, to obtain by prayer the grace of conversion. And after quoting Gamaches, Duval, Habert, Le Moyne, he cites in favor of this opinion Peter of Tarantasia, Bishop of Tulle, Godert de Fonté, and Henry of Ghent, Doctors of the Sorbonne, together with the Regius Professor Lygné, who, in his tract *De Gratia*, demonstrates that "sufficient grace" not only gives prayer, as Le Moyne and Professor Elias said, but also gives the power to do some works that are not difficult.

Gaudenzio Bontempi in like manner demonstrated that sufficient grace obtains efficacious grace by means of prayer, which is given to all who will avail themselves of it.

Cardinal Robert Pullo asserts two kinds of grace—one always victorious, the other one by which man sometimes works, sometimes does not: "The other by the assistance of which man can do which he chooses of these two things, either to co-operate with grace, or to despise it, and to continue sinning."[2]

Father Fortunato da Brescia is also of the same opinion, and holds that all men have the mediate grace of prayer to enable them to observe the precepts; and has no doubt that St. Augustine held the same.

Richard of St. Victor similarly teaches that there is a sufficient grace which a man sometimes consents to, sometimes resists.

Dominic Soto asks, "Why of two persons whom God

[1] *Theol. S. Ans.* t. 3, d. 125, 126, 127.
[2] "Utrumlibet aut gratiæ cooperans agit, aut ea spreta, malum agere non desistit."—*Sent.* l. 6, c. 50.

14

is most ready and desirous to convert, one is drawn by grace, and not the other?" And he answers: "No other reason can be given, except that one consents and co-operates, while the other does not co-operate."[1]

Matthias Felicio, who wrote against Calvin, thus defines ordinary or sufficient grace: "It is a divine motion, or instinct, which moves a man to good, and is denied to none. Men behave differently to this instinct; for some acquiesce in it, and are disposed *de congruo* for habitual grace; for we believe that God will not desert those who do what they can. Others, on the contrary, oppose it."[2]

Andreas Vega likewise says: "These helps, which are given to all men, are by most called inefficacious, because they do not always produce their effect, but are sometimes frustrated by sinners."[3] Therefore, sufficient grace sometimes produces its effect, and sometimes does not.

Cardinal Gotti in one place of his *Theology* apparently agrees with us; for where he discusses the difficulty, how a man can persevere if he will, when it is not in his power to have the special assistance which is requisite for perseverance, he answers that although this special assistance is not in a man's power, "yet it is said to be in a man's power, because he can by the grace of God ask for it and obtain it; and in this way it may be said

[1] "Alia ratio reddi non potest, nisi quod alter præbet assensum et cooperatur, alter vero minime."—*De Nat. et Gr.* l. 1, c. 15.

[2] "Est motio divina sive instinctus quo movetur homo ad bonum, nec alicui denegatur. Homines deversimode se ad istum habent instinctum: aliqui namque illi acquiescunt, sicque ad gratiam habitualem de congruo disponuntur, quia facientibus quod in se est, non defore Deus creditur; alii repugnant."—*Inst. chr.* d. 24, c. 20.

[3] "Hæc autem auxilia, quæ omnibus dantur, a plerisque inefficacia vocantur, quia non semper habent suum effectum, sed plerumque a peccatoribus frustrantur."—*De Justif.* l. 13, c. 13.

to be in a man's power to have the assistance necessary for perseverance, because it can be obtained by
prayers." [1] So, to verify the proposition that it is in a
man's power to persevere, it is necessary to grant both
that he can, without needing any further grace, obtain
by prayer the assistance requisite for perseverance; and,
also, that with only the sufficient grace common to all,
without need of any special grace, he can actually pray,
and by prayer obtain perseverance; otherwise it could
not be said that every man had the grace necessary for
perseverance, at least remotely or mediately, by means
of prayer.

But if Cardinal Gotti did not mean this, at any rate
St. Francis de Sales did, when he said that the grace of
actual prayer is given to every one who will avail himself of it, and thence deduced that perseverance is in
the power of everybody. The saint says this clearly in
his *Theotimus*, where, after proving that constant prayer
is necessary to obtain from God the gift of final perseverance, he adds: "Now, since the gift of prayer is
freely promised to all those who will consent to the
heavenly inspirations, consequently it is in our power
to persevere."

Cardinal Bellarmine teaches the same thing: "An assistance, then and there, sufficient for salvation, is given
mediately or immediately to all men. . . . We say mediately or immediately, because to those who have the use
of reason we believe that holy inspirations are given by
God, and that by this they have immediately the exciting
grace; by which, if they will acquiesce in it, they can

[1] "In potestate tamen hominis aliquo modo dicitur esse quod ipse
per Dei gratiam potest ab eo petere ac obtinere; et hoc modo in
hominis justi potestate dici potest esse ut habeat auxilium ad perse-
verandum necessarium, illud impetrando orationibus."—*De Grat.* q.
1, d. 13, § 3.

be disposed to be justified, and at last to obtain salvation." [1]

II.

Authority upon which this Doctrine is based.

Let us now proceed to examine the proofs of this doctrine. It is proved, first from authority. We shall cite Scripture, the Council of Trent, and the Holy Fathers.

I. HOLY SCRIPTURE.

We have first the authority of the Apostle, who assures us that God is faithful, and will not permit us to be tempted beyond our strength, since he always gives us assistance (whether immediate or mediate, by means of prayer) to resist the assaults of our enemies: *God is faithful, who will not suffer you to be tempted above that ye are able; but will make with the temptation issue, that ye may be able to bear it.* [2] Jansenius says that this text refers only to the predestinate, but this comment of his is completely unfounded; for St. Paul is writing to all the faithful of Corinth, all of whom he certainly did not consider to be predestinate. So that St. Thomas has good reason for understanding it generally of all men, and for saying that God would not be faithful if he did not grant us (so far as in him lies) those graces by means of which we can obtain salvation: " But he would

---

[1] " Auxilium sufficiens ad salutem, pro loco et tempore, mediate vel immediate omnibus datur. . . . Dicimus: Mediate vel immediate;—quoniam, iis qui usu rationis utuntur, immitti credimus a Deo sanctas inspirationes, ac per hoc immediate illos habere gratiam excitantem, cui si acquiescere velint, possint ad justificationem disponi et ad salutem aliquando pertingere."—*De Gr. et Lib. Arb.* l. 2, c. 5.

[2] " Fidelis autem Deus est, qui non patietur vos tentari supra id quod potestis; sed faciet etiam cum tentatione proventum, ut possitis sustinere."—1 *Cor.* x. 13.

not appear to be faithful were he to refuse us (so far as he is concerned) those things which are requisite to enable us to come to him." [1]   It is proved, moreover, by all those texts in which God exhorts us to convert our-selves, and to have recourse to him to ask him for the graces necessary for our salvation, and promises to hear us when we have recourse to him. *Wisdom preacheth aloud, . . . saying, O children, how long will ye love child-ishness, and fools covet those things which are hurtful to them-selves, etc.? Turn ye at My reproof: behold, I will utter My Spirit to you. . . . Because I called, and you refused, etc., I also will laugh in your destruction, and will mock at you.*[2] This exhortation, *Turn ye,* would be simple mock-ery, says Bellarmine, if God did not give to sinners at least the mediate grace of prayer for their conversion. Besides, we find in the passage mention made of the internal grace by which God calls sinners, and gives them actual assistance for conversion, if they will accept it, in the words, *Behold, I will bring forth My Spirit to you.*[3] *Come to Me, all you that labor and are heavy laden, and I will refresh you.*[4] *Come, and accuse me, saith the Lord ; if your sins be as scarlet, they shall be made white as snow.*[5] *Ask, and it shall be given you.*[6] And so in hun-

[1] " Non autem videretur esse fidelis Deus, si nobis denegaret, quan-tum in ipso est, ea per quæ pervenire ad eum possemus."—*In* 1 *Cor.* i. *lect.* 1.

[2] " Sapientia foris prædicat . . , dicens: Usquequo, parvuli, diligi-tis infantiam, et stulti ea quæ sibi sunt noxia cupient . . .? Conver-timini ad correptionem meam: en, proferam vobis spiritum meum. . . . Quia vocavi, et renuistis . . .; ego quoque in interitu vestro ridebo et subsannabo."—*Prov.* i. 20.

[3] " En, proferam vobis spiritum meum."

[4] " Venite ad me omnes, qui laboratis et onerati estis, et ego refi-ciam vos."—*Matt.* xi. 28.

[5] " Venite et arguite me, dicit Dominus, si fuerint peccata vestra ut coccinum, quasi nix dealbabuntur."—*Isa.* i. 18.

[6] " Petite, et dabitur vobis."—*Matt.* vii. 7.

dreds of other texts already quoted. Now, if God did not give every one grace actually to have recourse to him, and actually to pray to him, all these invitations and exhortations, *Come all, and I will refresh you ; seek, and it shall be given you*, would be vain.

2. THE COUNCIL OF TRENT.

' It is clearly proved by the passage of the Council of Trent so often quoted.[1] I beg the reader to give his best attention to this proof; which, if I am not mistaken, is perfectly decisive. There were innovators who said that as man was deprived of free-will by the sin of Adam, the will of man at present does nothing in good actions, but is induced to receive them passively from God, without producing them itself; and hence they inferred that the observance of the commandments was impossible to those who are not efficaciously moved and predetermined by grace to avoid evil and to do good. Against this error the Council pronounced sentence in words borrowed from St. Augustine: "God does not command impossible things; but by commanding, admonishes you both to do what you can, and to pray for what you cannot do; and he helps you, so that you may be able."[2]

The Council, then, in order to prove against the heretics that God's commandments are not impossible to any one, has declared that all men have assistance to enable them to do good, or at least have the grace of prayer whereby to obtain greater assistance. The meaning of this is, that every man can, by means of the common grace, do easy things (such as pray) without need of further extraordinary grace; and can by prayer obtain strength to do

---

[1] *Sess.* 6, *cap.* 4.

[2] "Deus impossibilia non jubet; sed jubendo monet, et facere quod possis, et petere quod non possis; et adjuvat ut possis."

difficult things, according to the teaching of St. Augustine, already quoted: "By the very fact that we most firmly believe that the good and just God could not have commanded impossible things, we are admonished in easy matters what to do, and in difficult matters what to pray for."[1] So that, according to the Council, the divine precepts are possible to all men, at least by means of prayer, by which greater help may be obtained to enable us to observe them. If, therefore, God has imposed his commands on all men, and has rendered their observance possible to all, at least mediately by means of prayer, we must necessarily conclude that all men have the grace to enable them to pray; otherwise, the commandments would not be possible to him who was without this grace. And as God grants to prayer actual grace to do good, and thereby renders all his commandments possible, so also he gives all actual grace to pray; otherwise, if there were any man who had not actual grace to pray to him, the commandments would be impossible, as he could not even by means of prayer obtain the assistance necessary for their observance.

This being settled, it is of no use to say that the words, "God admonishes you to do what you can, and to ask for what you cannot do,"[2] are only to be understood of possible, not of actual, prayer; because, we reply, if the common and ordinary grace gave only possible and not actual prayer, the Council would not have said, "He admonishes you to do what you can, and to ask for what you cannot do;"[3] but, "He admonishes you that you can do, and that you can pray."[4] Moreover, if the Council had

---

[1] "Eo ipso quo firmissime creditur Deum justum et bonum impossibilia non potuisse præcipere, hinc admonemur, et in facilibus quid agamus, et in difficilibus quid petamus."—*De Nat. et Grat.* c. 69.

[2] "Monet (Deus) et facere quod possis, et petere quod non possis."

[3] "Monet et facere quod possis."

[4] "Monet et petere quod non possis."

not intended to declare that every one can observe the precepts, or can pray to obtain grace to observe them, and had not meant to speak of actual grace, it would not have said "He admonishes," because this word properly refers to actual operation, and imports not the instruction of the mind, but the movement of the will to do that good which it can actually do. When, therefore, it said, "He admonishes you to do what you can, and to ask for what you cannot do," it most clearly expressed, not only possible operation and possible prayer, but actual operation and actual prayer. For if man had need of another extraordinary grace, which as yet he has not, in order actually to work or to pray, how could God admonish him to do or to ask that which he cannot actually either do or ask without efficacious grace? Father Fortunato Brescia speaks wisely on this point: If the actual grace of prayer were not given to all, but if for prayer we had need of efficacious grace, which is not common to all, prayer would be impossible to the great number who are without this efficacious grace; so that it could not be said with propriety that "God admonishes you to ask for that which you cannot do," because he would then admonish us to do a thing requiring a grace which we did not possess. So that God's admonition to work and to pray must be understood of actual operation and prayer, without need of a further extraordinary grace. And this is exactly what St. Augustine means: "Hence we are admonished in easy things what to do, and in difficult things what to pray for;"[1] because he supposes that though all have not grace to enable them to do difficult things, all have at least grace to pray, prayer being an easy thing for everybody, as he also propounds in the words afterwards adopted by the Council of Trent, "God

---

[1] "Hinc admonemur et in facilibus quid agamus, et in dificilibus quid petamus."

admonishes you to do what you can, and to ask for what you cannot do."

To recapitulate the argument: the Council says that God does not impose impossible commands, because he either gives assistance to observe them, or gives the grace of prayer to obtain this assistance, which he always grants when it is prayed for. Now, if it could ever be true that God does not give all men grace, at least the mediate grace of prayer, actually to observe all his precepts, Jansenius' proposition would be true, that even the just man is without grace to enable him actually to observe some of the commandments.

I do not know how else the text of the Council of Trent can be understood and explained, unless the "sufficient grace" gave to all men the power of actually praying without the "efficacious grace" which our opponents suppose to be necessary for the actual performance of any pious work. And supposing this necessity of a further grace for actual prayer, I cannot understand how this other text of the same Council can be true: "God does not leave those who have been once justified without grace, unless they first leave him."[1] If, I say, the ordinary sufficient grace would not be enough for actual prayer, but if for this purpose efficacious grace, which is not common to all men, would be required, it would be true that when the just man would be tempted to commit his first mortal sin, and God would not give him efficacious grace at least to enable him to pray, and so to obtain strength to resist, then his succumbing to temptation might rather be said to result from the just man being abandoned by God before he had abandoned God, and from being left without the efficacious grace necessary to enable him to resist.

---

[1] "Deus namque sua gratia semel justificatos non deserit, nisi ab eis prius deseratur."—*Sess.* 6, *cap.* 11.

Our opponents object to us a passage of St. Augustine where he appears to maintain that the grace of prayer is not granted to all men: "Is not our prayer itself at times so tepid, or rather so cold, and almost null—so null, indeed, that we do not notice its nullity with any sorrow; for if this coldness is against our will, it does not prejudice our prayer?"[1]   But Cardinal Sfondrati well replies, "It is one thing to say that sinners do not pray, another to say that they have not grace to enable them to pray."[2]   St. Augustine does not say that any persons are without grace to pray as they ought, but only that at times our prayer is so cold as to be almost null, not for want of God's assistance to enable us to pray better, but simply through our fault, which renders our prayer null.   Tourneley answers in the same way, where he says of the first condemned proposition of Jansenius: "The just do not always pray as they ought. It is their own fault that they do not pray so, since they have by grace sufficient strength to pray.   St. Augustine says that our prayer is sometimes cold and almost null; but he does not say that we have not grace to enable us to pray more fervently."[3]   Moreover, Cardinal Noris observes on this same passage, that by means of tepid prayer we can at least obtain grace to pray more fervently, and then by this we obtain efficacious grace to keep the commandments: "I conclude that even tepid

[1] "Nonne aliquando ipsa oratio nostra sic tepida est, vel potius frigida et pene nulla, imo interdum ita nulla ut neque hoc in nobis cum dolore advertamus, quia, si vel hoc dolemus, jam oramus?"—*Ad Simpl.* l. 1, q. 2.

[2] "Aliud est peccatores non orare, aliud non habere gratiam qua orare possint."—*Nod. præd.* p. 1, § 2.

[3] "Justi non semper orant ut oportet; eorum culpa est quod ita non orent, cum habeant ex gratia sufficientes vires ad orandum. Unde Sanctus Augustinus ait quidem orationem nostram aliquando frigidam ac pene nullam esse, at non ait desse gratiam per quam oratio possit ardentior fieri."—*De Gr. Chr.* q. 3, p. 1.

prayer is made with the assistance *sine quo non*, and by the ordinary help of God, since they are weak acts, etc. . . . And yet by tepid prayer we obtain the spirit of more fervent prayer, which is given to us by the assistance *quo*."[1] And he confirms this by the authority of St. Augustine, who writes thus on Ps. xvi.: "I have directed my prayers unto Thee with a free and strong intention; for Thou didst hear me when I prayed more weakly, and didst grant me strength for this."[2]

Nor can a valid objection be drawn from St. Augustine's observation on the text of St. Paul: "*The Spirit beseeches for us with groans not to be uttered,*"[3] that it is the Holy Spirit that makes us intercede, and inspires us with the disposition to intercede,[4] since the saint here simply says, against the Pelagians, that no one can pray without grace. And thus he himself explains it in his commentary on Ps. lii., where he says, "What thou doest by His gift, He is said to do; because without Him thou couldst not do it."[5]

3. THE HOLY FATHERS.

In the third place, our opinion is proved by the sayings of the holy Fathers.

St. Basil says: "When, however, any one is allowed to

---

[1] "Colligo ipsammet tepidam orationem fieri a nobis cum adjutorio *sine quo non* ac ordinario concursu Dei, cum sint actus debiles et minus perfecti. Ea tamen tepida oratione impetramus spiritum ferventioris orationis, qui nobis adjutorio *quo* donatur."—*Jans. err. cat. subl.* c. 3.

[2] "Ego libera et valida intentione preces ad te direxi, quoniam, ut hanc habere possem, exaudisti me infirmius orantem."—*In Ps.* xvi.

[3] "Spiritus postulat pro nobis gemitibus inenarrabilibus."—*Rom.* viii. 26.

[4] "Interpellare nos facit, nobisque interpellandi inspirat affectum."—*Ep.* 194. c. 4, *E. B.*

[5] "Quod dono ipsius tu facis, ille facere dicitur, quia sine illo tu non faceres."—*In Ps.* lii.

fall into temptation, it happens that he may be able to endure it, and to ask in prayer that the will of God may be done."[1] The saint then says that when God permits a man to be tempted, he does it in order that the man may resist by asking for God's will, *i.e.*, the grace to overcome. He therefore supposes that when a man has not sufficient assistance to overcome the temptation, he at least has the actual and common grace of prayer, by which he may obtain whatever further grace he needs.

St. John Chrysostom says, "He gave a law which might make their wounds manifest, in order that they might desire a physician."[2] And again: "Nor can any one be excused who, by ceasing to pray, has voluntarily abstained from overcoming his adversary.[3] If such a man had not the grace necessary for actual prayer, whereby he might obtain grace to resist, he might excuse himself when he is overcome.

So also St. Bernard: "Who are we, or what is our strength? This is what God wanted, that we, seeing our weakness, and that we have no other help, should, with all humility, have recourse to his mercy."[4] God, then, has imposed on us a law impossible to our own strength, in order that we should go to him, and by prayer obtain strength to observe it; but if any one were without the grace of actual prayer, to him the law would be utterly impossible. "Many persons," says the same

---

[1] "Ubi quis permissus est in tentationem incidere, eventum ut sufferre possit et voluntatem Dei per orationem petere."—*Mor. reg.* 62, c. 2.

[2] "Legem dedit quæ vulnera patefaceret, ut medicum optarent."—*In Gall.* iii. 22.

[3] "Nec quisquam poterit excusari, qui hostem vincere noluit, dum orare cessavit."—*Hom. de Moys.*

[4] "Qui sumus nos? aut quæ fortitudo nostra? hoc quærebat Deus, ut videntes defectum nostrum, et quod non est nobis auxilium aliud, ad ejus misericordiam tota humilitate curramus."—*In Quad.* s. 5.

St. Bernard, "complain that they are deserted by grace; but grace could much more justly complain of being deserted by them." [1] God has much more reason to complain of us for not corresponding to the grace he gives us, than we have to complain of not having grace to which we may correspond.

But no Father is more clear on this point than St. Augustine in several places. In one he says: "The Pelagians think themselves very knowing when they say, God would not command that which he knows man could not do. Who is ignorant of this? But God does command some things that we cannot do, in order that we might know that for which we ought to ask him." [2]

Again, "It is not reckoned your fault, if you are ignorant without wishing to be so; but only if you neglect to inquire into that of which you are ignorant; nor that you do not cure your wounded members, but that you despise him who is willing to heal you. These are your own sins; for no man is deprived of the knowledge of how to seek with advantage." [3] So that, according to St. Augustine, no one is deprived of the grace of prayer, whereby he may obtain help for his conversion; otherwise, if this grace were wanting, it could not be his fault if he were not converted.

Again: "What else, then, is shown us, but that it is

---

[1] "Omnes nobis causamur deesse gratiam; sed justius forsitan ipsa sibi queritur gratia deesse nonnullos."—*De Div.* s. 17.

[2] "Magnum aliquid Pelagiani se scire putant, quando dicunt: Non juberet Deus quod sciret non posse ab homine fieri.—Quis hoc nesciat? sed ideo jubet aliqua quæ non possumus, ut noverimus quid ab illo petere debeamus."—*De Gr. et Lib. Arb.* c. 16.

[3] "Non tibi deputatur ad culpam quod invitus ignoras, sed quod negligis quærere quod ignoras; neque illud quod vulnerata membra non colligis, sed quod volentem sanare contemnis. Ista tua propria peccata sunt: nulli enim homini ablatum est scire utiliter quærere."—*De Lib. Arb.* l. 3, c. 19.

God who gives us power both to ask, and to seek, and to knock, who commands us to do these things?"[1]

Again: "Once for all, receive this and understand it. Art thou not yet drawn? Pray that thou mayest be drawn."[2]

Again: "That the soul, then, knows not what it ought to do comes from this, that it has not yet received it; but it will receive this also, if it has made a good use of what it has received; and it has received power to seek piously and diligently if it will."[3]

Mark the words "it has received power to seek diligently and piously." Every one, then, has the grace necessary for prayer; and if he makes a good use of this, he will receive grace to do that which before he was unable to do immediately. Again: "Let the man who is willing, but cannot do what he wills, pray that he may have such a measure as suffices for fulfilling the commandments; for he is so far assisted as to be able to do what is commanded."[4] Again: "Free will is admonished by command to seek the gift of God; but it would be admonished without fruit to itself, unless it had first received some little love, to induce it to seek such aid as would enable it to fulfil what was commanded."[5]

---

[1] "Quid ergo aliud ostenditur nobis, nisi quia et petere et quærere et pulsare ille concedit, qui ut hæc faciamus jubet?"—*Ad Simpl.* l. 1, q. 2.

[2] "Semel accipe et intellige: nondum traheris? ora ut traharis."—*In Jo.* tr. 26.

[3] "Quod ergo ignorat (anima) quid sibi agendum sit, ex eo est quod nondum accepit; sed hoc quoque accipiet si hoc quod accepit bene usa fuerit: accepit autem ut pie et diligenter quærat, si volet."—*De Lib. Arb.* l. 3, c. 22.

[4] "Homo qui voluerit, et non potuerit, oret ut habeat tantam voluntatem, quanta sufficit ad implenda mandata: sic quippe adjuvatur, ut faciat quod jubetur."—*De Gr. et Lib. Arb.* c. 15.

[5] "Præcepto admonitum est liberum arbitrium, ut quæret Dei donum; quod quidem sine suo fructu prorsus admoneretur, nisi prius

Mark the words, "some little love ;" this means "suffi-cient grace" whereby man is able to obtain by prayer actual grace to keep the commandments, whereby " he is induced to seek such aid as would enable him to fulfil what was commanded." [1]

Again: " He gives us commandments for this reason, that when we have tried to do what we are com-manded, and are wearied through our infirmity, we may know how to ask the help of grace." [2] Here the saint supposes that with ordinary grace we are not able to do difficult things, but can by means of prayer obtain the aid necessary to accomplish them. Hence he goes on to say, *The Law entered that sin might abound*, when men do not implore the aid of God's grace; but when, by God's vocation, they understand to whom they must groan, and thereupon invoke him, the succeeding words will be fulfilled : *Where sin abounded, grace superabounded.* [3] Here, as Petavius says, we see in express terms the want of abundant grace; and, on the other hand, the presence of ordinary and common grace which enables men to pray, and which St. Augustine here calls "God's voca-tion."

In another place he says: " Free-will is left to man in this mortal life, not to enable him to fulfil justice when he pleases, but to enable him to turn with pious suppli-cations to Him by whose gift he can fulfil it." [4] When,

acciperet aliquid dilectionis, ut addi sibi quæreret unde, quod jube-batur, impleret."—*De Gr. et Lib. Arb.* c. 18.

[1] " Ut addi sibi quæreret unde, quod jubebatur, impleret."

[2] " Jubet ideo ut, facere jussa conati et nostra infirmitate fatigati, adjutorium gratiæ poscere noverimus."—*Ep.* 157, *E. B*.

[3] "Lex subintravit ut abundaret delictum, cum homines adjutorium gratiæ non implorant; cum autem vocatione divina intelligunt cui sit ingemiscendum, et invocant eum, fiet quod sequitur: ' Ubi abundavit delictum, superabundavit gratia.' "—*Rom.* v. 20.

[4] " Hoc restat in ista mortali vita libero arbitrio, non ut impleat homo justitiam cum voluerit, sed ut se supplici pietate convertat ad eum cujus dono eam possit implere."—*Ad Simpl.* l. 1, q. 1.

therefore, Augustine says that man is unable to fulfil the whole law, and that prayer is the only means given him to obtain help to fulfil it, he certainly supposes that God gives every man the grace of actual prayer, without need of a further extraordinary aid, not common to all men; otherwise, where this special aid was wanting, "nothing would be left to the will" to observe all the commandments, or at least the more difficult of them. And when the saint speaks thus, he certainly cannot mean that "sufficient grace" gives only the power, not the act of prayer; for so far as relates to power, it is certain that "sufficient grace" gives power for even the most difficult works. Hence the holy Father evidently means (as he teaches elsewhere) that easy things, such as prayer, may well be actually accomplished by any man with the "sufficient grace;" and difficult things with the help which is obtained by means of prayer.

But there are two texts of St. Augustine which are peculiarly to the point.

The first is this: "It is certain that we can keep the commandments if we will; but since the will is prepared by God, we must ask him that we may have such a will as is sufficient to enable us to perform what we will." [1] Here he says that it is certain we could observe the law if we would; on the other hand, he says that in order to will to do so, and actually to do so, we must pray. Therefore all men have grace given tnem to pray, and by prayer to obtain the abundant grace which makes us keep the commandments; otherwise, if for actual prayer, efficacious grace, which is not common to all, were requisite, those to whom it was not given would not be able to keep the commandments, nor to have the will to keep them.

---

[1] "Certum est nos mandata servare si volumus; sed, quia præparatur voluntas a Domino, ab illo petendum est ut tantum velimus, quantum sufficit ut volendo faciamus."—*De Gr. et Lib. Arb.* c. 16.

The second text is that where the holy Doctor answers the monks of Adramyttium, who said that " if grace was necessary, and if we can do nothing without it, why blame when we cannot work, and have not grace to do so ? You should rather pray God for us, that he would give us this grace." St. Augustine answers: You must be blamed, not because you do not work when you have not strength, but because you do not pray to obtain strength: "He who will not be admonished, and says, Do you rather pray for me, must on that very account be admonished to do it (*i.e.*, to pray) for himself."[1] Now if the saint had not believed that every man has grace, to pray (if he will) without need of further aid, he never could have said that these people were to be blamed for not praying; for they could have answered, that if they were not to be blamed for not working, when they had not special grace to enable them to work, in like manner they could not be blamed for not praying, when they had not special grace for actual prayer. This is what St. Augustine elsewhere says: "Let them not deceive themselves who say, why are we commanded to abstain from evil and do good, if it is God who works in us both to will and to do it?"[2] And he answers, that when men do good they should thank God for it, who gives them strength to do it; and when they do it not, they should pray to have the strength which they lack: "But when they do it not (these are his words), let them pray that they may receive that which as yet they have not."[3] Now, if these people had not even the grace for the act

---

[1] " Qui corripi non vult, et dicit: Ora potius pro me,—ideo corripiendus est ut faciat (oret) etiam ipse pro se."—*De Corr. et Gr.* c. 5.

[2] "Non se fallant qui dicunt: Ut quid nobis præcipitur ut declinemus a malo et faciamus bonum, si id velle et operari Deus operatur in nobis?"—*De Corr. et Gr.* c. 2.

[3] "Quando autem non agunt, orent ut, quod nondum habent, accipiant."

of prayer, they might answer, "Why are we commanded to pray, if God does not work in us to make us pray?"[1] How are we to will to pray, if we do not receive the grace necessary for actual prayer?

St. Thomas does not speak expressly of prayer, but assumes the certainty of our proposition, when he says, "It belongs to God's Providence to provide every individual with what is necessary for salvation, provided he puts no impediment in the way."[2] Since, then, it is true, on the one hand, that God gives to all men the graces necessary for salvation, and, on the other, for prayer,—we require the grace which enables us actually to pray, and thereby to obtain further and greater assistance to enable us to do that which we cannot compass with ordinary grace,—it follows, necessarily, that God gives all men sufficient grace actually to pray if they will, without need of efficacious grace.

Here we may add the answer of Bellarmine to the heretics, who inferred from the text, *No one can come to Me, unless My Father draw him*,[3] that no one could go to God who was not properly drawn by him. "We answer," he says, "that the only conclusion from this text is, that all men have not the efficacious grace to make them really believe; but we cannot conclude that all men have not at least assistance which confers the possibility of believing, or, at any rate, the possibility of asking for grace."[4]

---

[1] "Ut quid nobis præcipitur ut oremus, si orare Deus non operatur in nobis?"

[2] "Hoc ad divinam Providentiam pertinet, ut cuilibet provideat de necessariis ad salutem, dummodo ex parte ejus non impediatur."—*De Verit*. q. 14, a. 11.

[3] "Nemo potest venire ad me, nisi Pater, qui misit me, traxerit eum."—*John*, vi. 44.

[4] "Respondemus eo solum concludi non habere omnes auxilium efficax quo reipsa credant; non tamen concludi non habere omnes auxilium quo possint credere, vel certe quo possint auxilium petere."—*De Gr. et Lib. Arb*. l. 2 c. 8.

III.

Reasons that justify this Doctrine.

Let us now proceed, in the third and last place, to examine the reasons of this opinion. Petavius, Duval, and other theologians ask why God imposes on us commands which we cannot keep with the common and ordinary grace? Because, they answer, he wishes us to have recourse to him in prayer, according to the general consent of the Fathers, as we have seen above. Hence they infer that we ought to hold it to be certain that every man has grace actually to pray, and by prayer to obtain greater grace to enable him to do that which is impossible to him with the ordinary grace; otherwise God would have imposed an impossible law.

This reason is very strong; another is, that if God imposes on all men the duty of actual observance of his commandments, we must necessarily suppose that he also gives to all men the grace necessary for this actual observance, at least mediately, by means of prayer. In order, therefore, to uphold the reasonableness of the law, and the justice of the punishment of the disobedient, we must hold that every man has sufficient power, at least mediately, by means of prayer, for the actual satisfaction of the law; and that at times he prays without need of an unusual and additional grace; otherwise, if he had not this mediate or remote power of actually keeping the commandments, it could never be said that all men had from God sufficient grace for the actual observance of the law.

Thomassin and Tourneley accumulate many other reasons for this opinion; but I pass them over to attend to one that seems to me demonstrative. It is founded on the precept of hope, which obliges us all to hope in God with confidence for eternal life; and I say that if we were not certain that God gives us all grace to enable us actually to pray, without need of another particular and unusual grace, no one without a special revelation could hope for salvation as he ought. But I must first explain the grounds of this argument.

The virtue of hope is so pleasing to God that he has declared that he feels delight in those who trust in him: *The Lord taketh pleasure in them that hope in His mercy.*[1] And he promises victory over his enemies, perseverance in grace, and eternal glory, to the man who hopes, because he hopes: *Because he hoped in Me, I will deliver him; I will protect him. . . . I will deliver him and I will glorify him.*[2] *Preserve me, for I have put my trust in Thee.*[3] *He will save them, because they have hoped in Him.*[4] *No one hath hoped in the Lord, and hath been confounded.*[5] And let us be sure that the heaven and earth will fail, but the promises of God cannot fail: *Heaven and earth shall pass away, but My words shall not pass away.*[6] St. Bernard, therefore, says that all our merit consists in reposing all our confidence in God: "This is the whole merit of man, if he places all his hope in him."[7] The reason is, that he who hopes in God honors him much: *Call upon Me in the day of trouble, I will deliver thee, and thou shalt glorify Me.*[8] He honors the power, the mercy, and the faithfulness of

[1] "Beneplacitum est Domino . . . in eis qui sperant super misericordiam ejus."—*Ps.* xlvi. 11.

[2] "Quoniam in me speravit, liberabo eum, protegam eum, . . . eripiam eum, et glorificabo eum."—*Ps.* xc. 14.

[3] "Salvabit eos, quia speraverunt in eo."—*Ps.* xxxvi. 40.

[4] "Conserva me, Domine, quoniam speravi in te."—*Ps.* xv. 1.

[5] "Nullus speravit in Domino, et confusus est."—*Ecclus.* ii. 11.

[6] "Cœlum et terra transibunt, verba autem mea non præteribunt."—*Matt.* xxiv. 35.

[7] "Hoc totum hominis meritum, si totam spem suam ponat in eo."—*In Ps.* xc. s. 15.

[8] "Invoca me in die tribulationis; eruam te, et honorificabis me."—*Ps.* xlix. 15.

God; since he believes that God can and will save him; and that he cannot fail in his promises to save the man who trusts in him. And the Prophet assures us that the greater is our confidence, the greater will be the measure of God's mercy poured out upon us: *Let Thy mercy, O Lord, be upon us, as we have hoped in Thee.*[1]

Now, as this virtue of hope is so pleasing to God, he has willed to impose it upon us by a precept that binds under mortal sin, as all theologians agree, and as is evident from many texts of Scripture. *Trust in Him, all ye congregations of people.*[2] *Ye that fear the Lord, hope in Him.*[3] *Hope in thy God always.*[4] *Hope perfectly for that grace which is offered to you.*[5] Then this hope of eternal life ought to be sure and firm in us, according to the definition of St. Thomas: "Hope is the certain expectation of beatitude.[6] And the sacred Council of Trent has expressly declared, "All men ought to place and repose a most firm hope in the help of God; for God, unless they fail to correspond to his grace, as he has begun the good work, so will he finish it, working in them both to will and to perform."[7] And long before St. Paul had said of himself: *I know whom I have believed, and I am certain that He is able to keep what I have committed to Him.*[8] And herein is the difference between Christian and worldly hope. Worldly

---

[1] "Fiat misericordia tua, Domine, super nos, quemadmodum speravimus in te."—*Ps.* xxxii. 22.

[2] "Sperate in eo, omnis congregatio populi."—*Ps.* lxi. 9.

[3] "Qui timetis Dominum, sperate in illum."—*Ecclus.* ii. 9.

[4] "Spera in Deo tuo semper."—*Os.* xii. 6.

[5] "Perfecte sperate in eam, quæ offertur vobis, gratiam."—1 *Pet.* i. 13.

[6] 'Spes est certa expectatio futuræ beatitudinis."—2. 2. q. 18, a. 4.

[7] "In Dei auxilio firmissimam spem collocare et reponere omnes debent: Deus enim, nisi ipsi illius gratiæ defuerint, sicut cœpit opus bonum, ita perficiet, operans velle et perficere."—*Sess.* 6, *cap.* 13.

[8] "Scio enim cui credidi, et certus sum qui potens est depositum meum servare."—2 *Tim.* i. 12.

hope need only be an uncertain expectation: nor can it
be otherwise; for it is always doubtful whether a man
who has promised a favor may not hereafter change his
mind, if he has not already changed it. But the Christian hope of eternal salvation is certain on God's part;
for he can and will save us, and has promised to save
those who obey his law, and to this end has promised us
all necessary graces to enable us to obey this law, if we
ask for them. It is true that hope is accompanied by
fear, as St. Thomas says; but this fear does not arise
from God's part, but from our own; since we may at any
time fail, by not corresponding as we ought, and by putting an impediment in the way of grace by our sins.
Reasonably, then, did the Council of Trent condemn the
innovators, who, because they entirely deprive man of
free will, are obliged to make every believer have an infallible certitude of perseverance and salvation. This
error was condemned by the Council; because, as we
have said, in order to obtain salvation, it is necessary for
us to correspond; and this correspondence of ours is uncertain and fallible. Hence God wills that we should,
on the one hand, always fear for ourselves, lest we should
fall into presumption, in trusting to our strength; but, on
the other, that we should be always certain of his good
will, and of his assistance to save us; provided always
that we ask him for it; in other words, that we might
always have a secure confidence in his goodness. St.
Thomas says that we ought to look with certainty to
receive from God eternal happiness, confiding in his
power and mercy, and believing that he can and will
save us. " Whoever has faith, is certain of God's power
and mercy."[1]

Now, as the hope of our salvation by God ought to be

---

[1] " De potentia Dei et misericordia ejus certus est quicumque fidem
habet."

certain (as St. Thomas defines it), "the certain expectation of beatitude," [1] consequently the motive of our hope must also be certain; for if the foundation of our hope were uncertain, and admitted a doubt, we could not with any certainty hope and expect to receive salvation, and the means necessary for it, from the hands of God. But St. Paul will have us to be nothing less than firm and immovable in our hope, if we would be saved: *If so ye continue in the faith, grounded, and settled, and immovable from the hope of the Gospel, which you have heard.* [2] In another place he repeats that our faith ought to be as immovable as an anchor securely fixed; since it is grounded on the promises of God, who cannot lie: *And we desire that every one of you should show forth the same carefulness to the accomplishing of hope unto the end. . . . That by two immutable things, in which it is impossible for God to lie, we may have the strongest comfort, who have fled for refuge to hold fast the hope set before us, which we have as an anchor of the soul, sure and firm.* [3] Hence St. Bernard says that our hope cannot be uncertain, as it rests on God's promises: "Nor does this expectation seem to us vain, or this hope doubtful, since we rely on the promises of the eternal truth." [4] In another place he says of himself that his hope depends on three things,—the love which induced God to adopt us as his children, the truth of his promises, and his power to fulfil them: "Three things I see in

---

[1] "Certa expectatio beatitudinis."

[2] "Si tamen permanetis in fide fundati, et stabiles, et immobiles a spe Evangelii, quod audistis."—*Col.* i. 23.

[3] "Cupimus autem unumquemque vestrum eamdem ostentare sollicitudinem ad expletionem spei usque in finem; . . . ut per duas res immobiles, quibus impossibile est mentiri Deum, fortissimum solatium habeamus, qui confugimus ad tenendam propositam spem, quam sicut anchoram habemus animæ tutam ac firmam."—*Heb.* vi. 11-18.

[4] "Neque enim vana nobis hæc expectatio, aut dubia spes videtur, innixa nimirum æternæ promissionibus Veritatis."—*In Ps.* xc. s. 7.

which my hope consists,—the love of adoption, the truth of promise, the power of performance."[1]

And therefore the Apostle St. James declares that the man who desires the grace of God must ask for it, not with hesitation, but with the confident certainty of obtaining it: *Let him ask in faith, nothing wavering.*[2] For if he asks with hesitation, he shall obtain nothing: *For he that wavereth is like a wave of the sea, that is moved and carried about by the wind; therefore, let not that man think that he shall receive anything of the Lord.*[3] And St. Paul praises Abraham for not doubting God's promise; as he knew that when God promises, he cannot fail to perform: *In the promise, also, of God, he staggered not by distrust; but was strengthened in faith, giving glory to God; most fully knowing that whatsoever He has promised, He is able also to perform.*[4] Hence, also, Jesus Christ tells us that we shall then receive all the graces that we desire when we ask them with a sure belief of receiving them: *Therefore I say to you, all things whatsoever you ask when ye pray, believe that you shall receive them, and they shall come unto you.*[5] In a word, God will not hear us, unless we have a sure confidence of being heard.

Now let us come to the point. Our hope of salvation, and of receiving the means necessary for its attainment, must be certain on God's part. The motives on which

[1] " Tria considero in quibus spes mea consistit; charitatem adoptionis, veritatem promissionis, potestatem redditionis."—*Dom.* 6 p. *Pent.* s. 3.

[2] " Postulet autem in fide, nihil hæsitans."

[3] " Qui enim hæsitat, similis est fluctui maris, qui a vento movetur et circumfertur; non ergo æstimet homo ille quod accipiat aliquid a Domino."—*James,* i. 6.

[4] " In repromissione etiam Dei non hæsitavit diffidentia, sed confortatus est fide, dans gloriam Deo, plenissime sciens quia, quæcumque promisit Deus, potens est et facere."—*Rom.* iv. 20.

[5] " Propterea dico vobis: omnia quæcumque orantes petitis, credite quia accipietis, et evenient vobis."—*Mark,* xi. 24.

this certainty are founded, as we have seen, are the power, the mercy, and the truth of God; and of these the strongest and most certain motive is God's infallible faithfulness to the promise which he has made to us, through the merits of Jesus Christ, to save us, and to give us the graces necessary for our salvation; because, though we might believe God to be infinite in power and mercy, nevertheless, as Giovenino well observes, we could not feel confident expectation of God's saving us, unless he had surely promised to do so. But this promise is conditional, if we actively correspond to God's grace and pray, as is clear from the Scriptures: *Ask, and ye shall receive; if ye ask the Father anything in My name, He will give it you. He will give good things to those that ask Him. We ought always to pray. Ye have not, because ye ask not. If any one wanteth wisdom, let him ask of God;*[1] and many other texts which we have quoted before. For this cause the Fathers and theologians, as we showed in Part I., Chapter I., maintain that prayer is a necessary means of salvation.

Now, if we were not certain that God gives to all men grace to enable them actually to pray, without need of a further, special, and unusual grace, we could have no certain and firm foundation for a certain hope of salvation in God, but only an uncertain and conditional foundation. When I am certain that by prayer I shall obtain eternal life, and all the graces necessary to attain it; and when I know that God will not deny me the grace of actual prayer, if I will (because he gives it to all men), then I have a sure foundation for hoping in God for salvation, unless I fail on my part. But when I am in doubt whether or not God will give me that particular grace

---

[1] "Petite et accipietis.—Si quid petieritis Patrem in nomine meo, dabit vobis.—Dabit bona petentibus se.—Oportet semper orare.— Non habetis, propter quod non postulatis.—Si quis indiget sapientia, postulet a Deo, etc."

which he does not give to all, but which is necessary for actual prayer, then I have not a certain foundation for my hope of salvation, but only a doubtful and uncertain one; since I cannot be sure that God will give me this special grace, without which I cannot pray, since he refuses it to so many. And in this case the uncertainty would not be only on my part, but also on God's part; and so Christian hope would be destroyed, which, according to the Apostle, ought to be immovable, firm, and secure. I really cannot see how a Christian can fulfil the precept of hope—hoping, as he ought, with sure confidence for salvation from God, and for the graces necessary for its attainment—unless he holds it as an infallible truth that God commonly gives to every individual the grace actually to pray, if he chooses, without need of a further special assistance.

So that, to conclude, our system or opinion (held by so many theologians, and by our humble Congregation) well agrees, on the one hand, with the doctrine of grace intrinsically efficacious, by means of which we infallibly, though freely, act virtuously.

It cannot be denied that God can easily, with his omnipotence, incline and move men's hearts freely to will that which he wills, as the Scriptures teach: *The heart of the king is in the hand of the Lord; whithersoever He will, He shall turn it;*[1] *I will put My Spirit in the midst of you, and I will cause you to walk in My commandments;*[2] *My counsel shall stand, and all My will shall be done;*[3] *He changeth the heart of the princes of the people of the earth;*[4] *May the God of peace make you perfect in every good work, that you may do*

[1] "Cor regis in manu Domini: quocumque voluerit, inclinabit illud."—*Prov.* xxi. 1.

[2] "Spiritum meum ponam in medio vestri, et faciam ut in præceptis meis ambuletis."—*Ezek.* xxxvi. 27.

[3] "Consilium meum stabit, et omnis voluntas mea fiet."—*Isa.* xlvi. 10.

[4] "Qui immutat cor principum populi terræ."—*Job.* xii. 24.

His will; working in you that which is well-pleasing in His sight, through Jesus Christ.[1]

And it cannot be denied that St. Augustine and St. Thomas have taught the opinion of the efficaciousness of grace in itself, by its own nature. This is evident from many passages, and specially from the following:

St. Augustine says: " Yet God did not this, except by the will of the men themselves; since he, no doubt, has the most almighty and absolute power of inclining the hearts of men."[2] Again: " Almighty God works in the hearts of men, that he may do by their means that which he has determined to do."[3] Again: " Although they all do what is right in the service of God, yet he causes them to do what he commands."[4] Again: " It is certain that we act when we act; but he causes us to act, by bestowing most efficacious powers on the will, according to his words, *I will make you to walk in my justifications.*[5] Again, on the text *For it is God that worketh in you, both, to will and accomplish according to His good will,* he says " We therefore will; but God worketh in us, both to will and to perform."[6] Again: " As the will is prepared by God, we must pray that we may have as much will as

---

[1] " Deus autem pacis . . . aptet vos in omni bono, ut faciatis ejus voluntatem: faciens in vobis quod placeat coram se per Jesum Christum."—*Heb.* xiii. 21.

[2] " Qui (Deus) tamen hoc non fecit nisi per ipsorum hominum voluntates, sine dubio habens humanorum cordium inclinandorum omnipotentissimam potestatem."—*De Cor. et Gr.* c. 14.

[3] " Agit Omnipotens in cordibus hominum, ut per eos agat quod per eos agere voluerit."—*De Gr. et Lib. Arb.* c. 21.

[4] " Et si faciunt homines bona quæ pertinent ad colendum Deum, ipse facit ut illi faciant quæ præcepit."—*De Præd. SS.* c. 10.

[5] " Certum est nos facere cum facimus; sed ille facit ut faciamus, præbendo vires efficacissimas voluntati, qui dixit: ' Faciam ut in præceptis meis ambuletis' (*Ezek.* xxxvi. 27)."—*De Gr. et Lib. Arb.* c. 16.

[6] " Deus est enim (inquit Apostolus) qui operatur in vobis et velle et perficere pro bona voluntate. Nos ergo volumus; sed Deus in nobis operatur et velle."—*Phil.* ii. 13; *De Dono. pers.* c. 13.

is sufficient to make us act when we will."[1]   Again:
"God knows how to work in men's hearts, not so as to
make them believe against their will, which is impossible,
but so as to make them willing instead of unwilling."[2]
Again: "He works in men's hearts, not only true revela-
tions, but also good-will."[3]   Again: "Our acts of will
have just so much power as God chooses them to have."[4]
Again: "The wills which preserve the system of creation are in such sort in God's power, that he makes them
incline where he will and when he will."[5]   So St.
Thomas: "God infallibly moves the will by the efficacy
of the moving power, which cannot fail."[6]   Again:
"Love has the character of impeccability, from the power of the Holy Spirit, who infallibly works whatever he
will; hence it is impossible that these two things should
be at the same time true,—that the Holy Spirit wills to
move a person to an act of love, and that at the same
time the person should lose love by an act of sin."[7]

---

[1] "Quia præparatur voluntas a Domino, ab illo petendum est, ut
tantum velimus quantum sufficit, ut volendo faciamus."—*De Gr. et
Lib. Arb.* c. 16.

[2] "Novit (Deus) in ipsis hominum cordibus operari, non ut homines, quod fieri non potest, nolentes credant, sed ut volentes ex nolentibus fiant."—*Ad Bonif.* l. 1, c. 19.

[3] "Operatur in cordibus hominum, non solum veras revelationes,
sed bonas etiam voluntates."—*De Gr. Chr.* c. 24.

[4] "Voluntates nostræ tantum valent, quantum Deus eas valere
voluit."—*De Civ. D.* l. 5, c. 9.

[5] "Voluntates, quæ conservant sæculi creaturam, ita esse in Dei
potestate, ut eas, quo voluerit, quando voluerit, faciat inclinari."—*De
Gr. et Lib. Arb.* c. 20.

[6] "Deus movet voluntatem immutabiliter propter efficaciam virtutis
moventis, quæ deficere non potest."—*De Mal.* q. 6, ad 3.

[7] "Charitas impeccabilitatem habet ex virtute Spiritus Sancti, qui
infallibiliter operatur quodcumque voluerit; unde impossibile est hæc
duo simul esse vera: quod Spiritus Sanctus velit aliquem movere ad
actum charitatis, et quod ipse charitatem amittat peccando."—2. 2.
q. 24, a. 11.

Again: "If God moves the will to anything, it is impossible to say that the will is not moved to it."[1]

On the other hand, our opinion is quite consonant to the doctrine of truly sufficient grace being given to all, by corresponding to which a man will gain efficacious grace; while by not corresponding, but resisting, he will deservedly be refused this efficacious grace. And thus all excuse is taken away from those sinners who say that they have not strength to overcome their temptations; because if they had prayed, and made use of the ordinary grace which is given to all men, they would have obtained strength, and would have been saved. Otherwise, if a person does not admit this ordinary grace, by which every one is enabled at least to pray (without needing a further special and unusual grace), and by prayer to obtain further assistance to enable him to fulfil the law, I do not know how he can explain all those texts of the Scripture, in which souls are exhorted to return to God, to overcome temptation, and to correspond to the divine call: *Return, ye transgressors, to the heart;*[2] *Return and live; Be converted, and do penance;*[3] *Loose the bonds from off thy neck;*[4] *Come to Me, all you that labor and are burdened;*[5] *Resist, strong in faith;*[6] *Walk whilst you have the light.*[7] I cannot tell, I say, supposing it were true that the grace of prayer were not given to all, to enable them thereby to obtain the further assistance necessary for salvation, how these texts could be

---

[1] "Si Deus movet voluntatem ad aliquid, impossibile est huic positioni quod voluntas ad illud non moveatur."—1. 2. q. 10, a. 4.

[2] "Redite, prævaricatores, ad cor."—*Isa.* xlvi. 8.

[3] "Revertimini, et agite pœnitentiam . . . . Revertimini, et vivite." *Ezek.* xviii. 30, 32.

[4] "Solve vincula colli tui."—*Isa.* lii. 2.

[5] "Venite ad me omnes, qui laboratis et onerati estis."—*Matt.* xi. 28.

[6] "Resistite fortes in fide."—1 *Pet.* v. 9.

[7] "Ambulate dum lucem habetis."—*John,* xii. 35.

explained, and how the sacred writers could so forcibly exhort all men, without any exception, to be converted, to resist the enemy, to walk in the way of virtue, and, for this end, to pray with confidence and perseverance—if the grace of doing well, or at least of praying, were not granted to all, but only to those who have the gift of efficacious grace.   And I cannot see where would be the justice of the reproof given to all sinners without exception, who resist grace and despise the voice of God: *You always resist the Holy Ghost;*[1] *Because I called and you refused; I stretched out my hand, and there was none that regarded; you have despised all my counsel, and have neglected my reprehensions.*[2]   If they were without even the remote but efficacious grace of prayer, which our opponents consider necessary for actual prayer, I cannot tell how all these reproofs could be justly made against them.*

CONCLUSION.

I have done.   Some, perhaps, will wish that I had given more space to the distinct examination of the question so much controverted, wherein consists the effi-

---

[1] "Vos semper Spiritui Sancto resistitis."—*Acts*, vii. 51.

[2] "Quia vocavi, et renuistis; extendi manum meam, et non fuit qui aspiceret. Despexistis omne consilium meum, et increpationes meas neglexistis."—*Prov.* i. 24.

---

* It may be of benefit to the reader to sum up here in a few simple words the teaching of St. Alphonsus about actual grace and about prayer. His teaching seems to us to dissipate all the doubts and difficulties that we meet with in the different systems.

In what God requires of us there are easy things that we can do with the ordinary grace common to all men—the grace *really* sufficient for acting, without the need of special help. But as soon as a soul wishes to correspond to the first grace that invites it to do the good by enlightening its intellect and fortifying its will, the Holy Ghost does not fail to unite himself to it and to aid it. Now, among the easy things that require no other help than the common grace given to all men is necessarily *prayer*, by means of which we certainly obtain all the graces of which we stand in need in every state in

caciousness of grace, and which the systems of different schools attribute to a physical premotion, to congruous grace, to concomitant grace, to a delectation which overcomes by reason of a moral action, or to a delectation which overcomes by reason of its superiority in degree. But for this, such a book as this, which I deliberately intended should be small and easily readable, would not have been enough. To explore this vast sea, many volumes would have been required. But this work has been sufficiently performed by others, and, moreover, it was beside my purpose. Still, I wished to establish the point treated of in my second part, for the honor of God's providence and goodness, and to be of assistance to sinners, to prevent them from giving themselves up to despair, because they think themselves deprived of grace; and also to take from them all excuse, if they say that they have not strength to resist the assaults of the senses and of hell. I have shown them, that of those who are lost, no one is damned for the original sin of Adam, but solely for his own fault, because God refuses

which we may find ourselves. There are also difficult things which we cannot do without a special grace that is not common to all, but surely granted to every one that asks for it as he should by means of the common grace which is never wanting to any one.

This is conformable to the celebrated saying of St. Augustine, adopted and sanctioned by the Council of Trent: "*Deus impossibilia non jubet, sed jubendo monet, et facere quod possis, et petere quod non possis; et adjuvat ut possis*" (pages 30, 214). "God does not command impossible things: but by commanding, admonishes you both to do what you can, and to pray for what you cannot do; and he helps you, so that you may be able." God, who is just, in imposing his law, joins to it the necessary grace—light and force—that admonishes the conscience and furnishes the means: *Jubendo monet.* We must therefore admit a first grace given to all men:—a grace that makes them capable of doing easy things: *Facere quod possis*, and, consequently, to think of praying and to wish to pray. Now, as soon as we wish to pray, we are already united with God, we have already begun to ask and to obtain: *Petere quod non possis, et adjuvat ut possis.* In this all is contained.—Ed.

to no one the grace of prayer, whereby we may obtain his assistance to overcome every concupiscence, and every temptation.

For the rest, my principal intention was to recommend to all men the use of prayer as the most powerful and necessary means of grace, in order that all men should more diligently and earnestly attend to it, if they wish to be saved; for many poor souls lose God's grace, and continue to live in sin, and are finally damned, for this very reason, that they do not pray, nor have recourse to God for assistance. The worst of the matter is (I cannot help saying so), that so few preachers and so few confessors have any definite purpose of indoctrinating their hearers and penitents with the use of prayer, without which it is impossible to observe the law of God, and to obtain perseverance in his grace.

Having observed that so many passages, both of the Old and the New Testament, assert the absolute necessity of prayer, I have made it a rule to introduce into all the missions, as given by our Congregation for several years, a sermon on prayer; and I say, and repeat, and will keep repeating as long as I live, that our whole salvation depends on prayer; and, therefore, that all writers in their books, all preachers in their sermons, all confessors in their instructions to their penitents, should not inculcate anything more strongly than continual prayer. They should always admonish, exclaim, and continually repeat, Pray, pray, never cease to pray; for if you pray, your salvation will be secure; but if you leave off praying, your damnation will be certain. All preachers and directors ought to do this; because, according to the opinion of every Catholic school, there is no doubt of this truth, that he who prays, obtains grace and is saved; but those who practise it are too few, and this is the reason why so few are saved.

Devout Practices.

I.

Prayer to obtain Final Perseverance.

Eternal Father, I humbly adore and thank Thee for having created me, and for having redeemed me by means of Jesus Christ. I thank Thee for having made me a Christian by giving me the true faith, and by adopting me for Thy child in holy baptism. I thank Thee for having given me time for repentance after my many sins, and for having, as I hope, pardoned all my offences against Thee. I renew my sorrow for them, because I have displeased Thee. O Infinite Goodness! I thank Thee also for having preserved me from falling again as often as I should have done if Thou hadst not held me up and saved me. But my enemies do not cease to fight against me, nor will they until death, that they may again have me for their slave; if Thou dost not keep and help me continually by Thine assistance, I shall be wretched enough to lose Thy grace anew. I therefore pray Thee, for the love of Jesus Christ, to grant me holy persever-ance till death. Thy Son Jesus has promised that Thou wilt grant us whatever we ask for in his name. By the merits, then, of Jesus Christ, I beg of Thee for myself, and for all those who are in Thy grace, the grace of never more being separated from Thy love, but that we may always love Thee in this life and in the next.

Mary, Mother of God, pray to Jesus for me.

16

II.

Prayer to Jesus Christ, to obtain His Holy Love.

My crucified Love, my dear Jesus! I believe in Thee, and confess Thee to be the true Son of God and my Saviour. I adore Thee from the abyss of my own nothingness, and I thank Thee for the death Thou didst suffer for me, that I might obtain the life of divine grace. My beloved Redeemer, to Thee I owe all my salvation. Through Thee I have hitherto escaped hell; through Thee have I received the pardon of my sins. But I am so ungrateful that, instead of loving Thee, I have repeated my offences against Thee. I deserve to be condemned, so as not to be able to love Thee any more. But no, my Jesus, punish me in any other way, but not in this. If I have not loved Thee in time past, I love Thee now; and I desire nothing but to love Thee with all my heart. But without Thy help I can do nothing. Since Thou dost command me to love Thee, give me also the strength to fulfil this Thy sweet and loving precept. Thou hast promised to grant all that we ask of Thee: *You shall ask whatever you will, and it shall be done unto you.*[1] Confiding, then, in this promise, my dear Jesus, I ask, first of all, pardon of all my sins; and I repent, above all things, because I have offended Thee, O Infinite Goodness! I ask for holy perseverance in Thy grace till my death. But, above all, I ask for the gift of Thy holy love. Ah, my Jesus, my Hope, my Love, my All, inflame me with that love which Thou didst come on earth to enkindle![2] For this end, make me always live in conformity with Thy holy will. Enlighten me, that I may understand more and more how worthy Thou art of our love, and that I may know the immense love Thou hast borne me, especially in giving Thy life for me. Grant, then, that I may love Thee with all my

[1] "Quodcumque volueritis, petetis, et fiet vobis."—*John* xv. 7.
[2] "Tui amoris in me ignem accende."

heart and may love Thee always, and never cease to beg of Thee the grace to love Thee in this life; that living always, and dying in Thy love, I may come one day to love Thee with all my strength in heaven, never to leave off loving Thee for all eternity.

O Mother of beautiful love, my advocate and refuge, Mary, who art of all creatures the most beautiful, the most loving, and the most beloved of God, and whose only desire it is to see him loved ! ah, by the love thou bearest to Jesus Christ, pray for me, and obtain for me the grace to love him always, and with all my heart ! This I ask and hope for from thee. Amen.

III.
Prayer to obtain Confidence in the Merits of Jesus Christ and in the Intercession of Mary.

Eternal Father, I thank Thee for myself, and on behalf of all mankind, for the great mercy that Thou hast shown us, in sending Thy Son to be made man, and to die to obtain our salvation; I thank Thee for it, and I should wish to offer Thee in thanksgiving all that love which is due for such an inestimable benefit. By his merits our sins are pardoned, and Thy justice is satisfied for the punishment we had merited; by these merits Thou dost receive us miserable sinners into Thy grace, while we deserve nothing but hatred and chastisement: Thou dost receive men to reign in Paradise. Finally, Thou hast bound Thyself, in consideration of these merits, to grant all gifts and graces to those who ask for them in the name of Jesus Christ.

I thank Thee also, O Infinite Goodness, that, in order to strengthen our confidence, besides giving us Jesus Christ as our Redeemer, Thou hast also given us Thy beloved daughter Mary as our advocate; so that, with that heart full of mercy which Thou hast given her, she may never cease to succor by her intercession any sinner who may have recourse to her; and this intercession is so powerful with Thee that Thou canst not deny her any grace which she asks of Thee.

Hence it is Thy will that we should have a great confidence in the merits of Jesus, and in the intercession of Mary. But this confidence is Thy gift, and it is a great gift which Thou dost grant to those only who ask Thee for it. This confidence, then, in the blood of Jesus Christ, and in the patronage of Mary, I beg of Thee, through the merits of Jesus and Mary. To Thee, also, my dear Redeemer, do I turn; it was to obtain for me this confidence in Thy merits that Thou didst sacrifice Thy life on the cross for me, who was worthy only of punishment. Accomplish, then, the end for which Thou hast died; enable me to hope for all things, through confidence in Thy Passion. And thou, O Mary, my Mother, and my hope after Jesus, obtain for me a firm confidence, first in the merits of Jesus thy Son, and then in the intercession of thy prayers,—prayers which are all-powerful in gaining all they ask !

O my beloved Jesus! O sweet Mary! I trust in you. To you do I give my soul; you have loved it so much, have pity on it, and save it.

IV.

Prayer to obtain the Grace of being Constant in Prayer.

O God of my soul, I hope in Thy goodness that Thou hast pardoned all my offences against Thee, and that I am now in a state of grace. I thank Thee for it with all my heart, and I hope to thank Thee for all eternity.[1] I know that I have fallen, because I have not had recourse to Thee when I was tempted, to ask for holy perseverance. For the future, I firmly resolve to recommend myself always to Thee, and especially when I see myself in danger

---

[1] " Misericordias Domini in æternum cantabo."—*Ps.* lxxxviii. 2.

of again offending Thee. I will always fly to Thy mercy, invoking always the most holy names of Jesus and Mary, with full confidence that when I pray Thou wilt not fail to give me the strength which I have not of myself to resist my enemies. This I resolve and promise to do. But of what use, O my God, will all these resolutions and promises be, if Thou dost not assist me with Thy grace to put them in practice; that is, to have recourse to Thee in all dangers? Ah, Eternal Father! help me, for the love of Jesus Christ; and let me never omit recommending myself to Thee whenever I am tempted. I know that Thou dost always help me when I have recourse to Thee; but my fear is, that I should forget to recommend myself to Thee, and so my negligence will be the cause of my ruin, that is, the loss of Thy grace, the greatest evil that can happen to me. Ah, by the merits of Jesus Christ, give me grace to pray to Thee; but grant me such an abundant grace that I may always pray, and pray as I ought!

O my Mother Mary, whenever I have had recourse to thee, thou hast obtained for me the help which has kept me from falling! Now I come to beg of thee to obtain a still greater grace, namely, that of recommending myself always to thy Son and to thee in all my necessities. My Queen, thou obtainest all thou dost desire from God by the love thou bearest to Jesus Christ; obtain for me now this grace which I beg of thee,—namely, to pray always, and never to cease praying till I die. Amen.

V.

Prayer to be said Every Day, to obtain the Graces Necessary for Salvation.

Eternal Father, Thy Son has promised that Thou wilt grant us all the graces which we ask Thee for in his name. In the name, therefore, and by the merits of

Jesus Christ, I ask the following graces for myself and for all mankind. And, first, I pray Thee to give me a lively faith in all that the holy Roman Church teaches me. Enlighten me also, that I may know the vanity of the goods of this world, and the immensity of the infinite good that Thou art; make me also see the deformity of the sins I have committed, that I may humble myself and detest them as I ought; and, on the other hand, show me how worthy Thou art by reason of Thy goodness, that I should love Thee with all my heart. Make me know also the love Thou hast borne me, that from this day forward I may try to be grateful for so much goodness. Secondly, give me a firm confidence in Thy mercy of receiving the pardon of my sins, holy perseverance, and, finally, the glory of paradise, through the merits of Jesus Christ and the intercession of Mary. Thirdly, give me a great love towards Thee, which shall detach me from the love of this world and of myself, so that I may love none other but Thee, and that I may neither do nor desire anything else but what is for Thy glory. Fourthly, I beg of Thee a perfect resignation to Thy will, in accepting with tranquillity sorrows, infirmities, contempt, persecutions, aridity of spirit, loss of property, of esteem, of relatives, and every other cross which shall come to me from Thy hands. I offer myself entirely to Thee, that Thou mayest do with me and all that belongs to me what Thou pleasest. Do Thou only give me light and strength to do Thy will; and especially at the hour of death help me to sacrifice my life to Thee with all the affection I am capable of, in union with the sacrifice which Thy Son Jesus Christ made of his life on the Cross on Calvary. Fifthly, I beg of Thee a great sorrow for my sins, which may make me grieve over them as long as I live, and weep for the insults I have offered Thee, the Sovereign Good, who art worthy of infinite love, and who hast loved me so much. Sixthly, I pray Thee to give me the spirit of true humility and meekness, that I may accept with peace, and even with joy, all the contempt, ingratitude, and ill-treatment that I may receive. At the same time, I also pray Thee to give me perfect charity, which shall make me wish well to those who have done evil to me, and to do what good I can, at least by praying, for those who have in any way injured me. Seventhly, I beg of Thee to give me a love for the virtue of holy mortification, by which I may chastise my rebellious senses and cross my self-love; at the same time, I beg Thee to give me holy purity of body, and the grace to resist all bad temptations, by ever having recourse to Thee and Thy most holy Mother. Give me grace faithfully to obey my spiritual Father and all my Superiors in all things. Give me an upright intention, that in all I desire and do I may seek only Thy glory, and to please Thee alone. Give me a great confidence in the Passion of Jesus Christ, and in the intercession of Mary Immaculate. Give me a great love towards the most Adorable Sacrament of the Altar, and a tender devotion and love to Thy holy Mother. Give me, I pray Thee, above all, holy perseverance, and the grace always to pray for it, especially in time of temptation and at the hour of death.

Lastly, I recommend to Thee the holy souls of Purgatory, my relatives and benefactors; and in an especial manner I recommend to Thee all those who hate me or who have in any way offended me; I beg of Thee to render them good for the evil they have done, or may wish to do me. Finally, I recommend to Thee all infidels, heretics, and all poor sinners; give them light and strength to deliver themselves from sin. O most loving God, make Thyself known and loved by all, but especially by those who have been more ungrateful to Thee than others, so that by Thy goodness I may come one day to

sing Thy mercies in paradise; for my hope is in the merits
of Thy blood, and in the patronage of Mary.

O Mary, Mother of God, pray to Jesus for me! So I
hope; so may it be!

VI.

Thoughts and Ejaculations.

O God! who knows what fate awaits me?
I shall be either eternally happy or eternally miserable.
Of what worth is all the world without God?
Let all be lost, but let not God be lost.
I love Thee, my Jesus, who didst die for me!
Would that I had died before I ever offended Thee!
I will rather die than lose God.
Jesus and Mary, you are my hope.
My God, help me, for the love of Jesus Christ!
My Jesus, Thou alone art sufficient for me!
Suffer me not to separate myself from Thee.
Give me Thy love, and then do with me what Thou pleasest.
Whom shall I love, if I love not Thee, my God?
Eternal Father, help me, for the love of Jesus!
I believe in Thee, I hope in Thee, I love Thee!
Here I am, O Lord; do with me what Thou wilt!
When shall I see myself altogether Thine, my God?
When shall I be able to say to Thee, My God, I can lose Thee
    no more?
Mary, my hope, have pity on me!
Mother of God, pray to Jesus for me!
Lord, who am I, that Thou shouldst desire to be loved by me?
My God, I desire Thee alone, and nothing more.
I desire all that Thou dost will, and that alone.
Oh, that I might be annihilated for Thee, who wast annihilated
    for me!
Towards Thee alone, my God, have I been ungrateful!
I have offended Thee enough, I will no longer displease Thee.
If I had died then, I could not have loved Thee any more.
Let me die before again offending Thee.
Thou hast waited for me that I might love Thee. Yea, I will
    love Thee.

I consecrate the remainder of my life to Thee.

O my Jesus, draw me entirely to Thyself!

Thou wilt not leave me; I will not leave Thee. I hope that we shall always love each another, O God of my soul!

My Jesus, make me all Thine before I die!

Grant that when Thou shalt come to judge me, I may see Thee with a benign countenance.

Thou hast done more than enough to oblige me to love Thee. I love Thee, I love Thee!

Deign to accept the love of a sinner who has so often offended Thee.

Thou hast given Thyself all to me; I give myself all to Thee.

I desire to love Thee exceedingly in this life, that I may love Thee exceedingly in the next.

Teach me to know Thy great goodness, that I may love Thee very much.

Thou lovest those that love Thee. I love Thee; do Thou also love me.

Give me the love Thou requirest of me.

I rejoice that Thou art infinitely happy.

Oh that I had always loved Thee, and had died before I had offended Thee.

Grant that I may overcome all things to please Thee.

I give Thee my whole will; dispose of me as thou pleasest.

My pleasure is to please Thee, O Infinite Goodness!

I hope to love Thee for all eternity, O eternal God!

Thou art omnipotent; make me a saint.

Thou didst seek me while I was flying from Thee; Thou wilt not drive me away now that I seek after Thee.

I thank Thee for giving me time to love Thee. I thank Thee, and love Thee!

Let me give myself entirely to Thee this day,

Punish me in any way, but deprive me not of the power of loving Thee.

I will love Thee, my God, without reserve.

I accept all sufferings and all contempt, provided I may love Thee.

I desire to die for Thee, who didst die for me.

I wish that all could love Thee, who didst die for me.

I wish that all could love Thee as Thou meritest.

I wish to do everything that I know to be Thy pleasure.
I care more to please Thee than for all the pleasures of the world.
O holy will of God, you are my love!
O Mary, draw me entirely to God!
O my Mother, make me always have recourse to thee; it is for
thee to make me a saint; this is my hope.

HYMN.

Invocation of the Blessed Virgin in Time of Temptation.

Haste, my Mother, run to help me;
   Mother, haste, do not delay;
See from hell the envious serpent
   Comes my troubling soul to slay.

Ah! his very look affrights me,
   And his cruel rage I fear;
Whither fly, if he attacks me?
   See him, see him coming near!

Lo! I faint away with terror,
   For if yet thou dost delay,
He will dart at me his venom;
   Then, alas! I am his prey.

Cries and tears have nought availed me,
   Spite of all, I see him there;
Saints I call till I am weary,
   Still he stands with threat'ning air.

Now his mighty jaws are open,
   And his forkèd tongue I see;
Ah! he coils to spring upon me,—
   Mother! hasten, make him flee.

Mary! yes, the name of Mary
   Strikes with dread my cruel foe,
Straight he flees, as from the sunbeam
   Swiftly melts the winter's snow.

Now he's gone, but do thou ever
   Stay beside me, Mother dear;
Then the hellish fiend to tempt me
   Nevermore will venture near.

Mental Prayer and the Exercises of a Retreat.

I. *MENTAL PRAYER.**

I.

Mental Prayer is Morally Necessary for Salvation.

I. IT ENLIGHTENS THE MIND.

In the first place, without mental prayer the soul is without light. They, says St. Augustine, who keep their eyes shut cannot see the way to their country. The eternal truths are all spiritual things that are seen, not with the eyes of the body, but with the eyes of the mind; that is, by reflection and consideration. Now, they who do not make mental prayer do not see these truths, neither do they see the importance of eternal salvation, and the means which they must adopt in order to obtain it. The loss of so many souls arises from the neglect of considering the great affair of our salvation, and what we must do in order to be saved. *With desolation*, says the prophet Jeremias, *is all the land made desolate: because there is none that considereth in the heart.*[1] On the other

[1] " Desolatione desolata est omnis terra, quia nullus est qui re-cogitet corde."—*Jer.* xii. 11.

---

* We have made up this treatise from different extracts; the greatest part is taken from the True Spouse of Christ, Chapter XV., and the rest from other works that are indicated. The whole offers a complete exposition of the teaching of St. Alphonsus on mental prayer, and fills a very important gap that we could not leave in the methodical plan that we have followed; for mental prayer is unquestionably one of the greatest means of salvation and of perfection. To this treatise we add the Spiritual Retreat, which is but an extraordinary exercise of prayer.—ED.

hand, the Lord says that he who keeps before his eyes the truths of faith—that is, death, judgment, and the happy or unhappy eternity that awaits us—shall never fall into sin. *In all thy works remember thy last end, and thou shalt never sin.*[1] Draw near to God, says David, and you shall be enlightened. *Come ye to Him and be enlightened.*[2] In another place, our Saviour says, *Let your loins be girt, and lamps burning in your hands.*[3] These lamps are, according to St. Bonaventure, holy meditations;[4] for in prayer the Lord speaks to us, and enlightens, in order to show us the way of salvation. *Thy word is a lamp to my feet.*[5]

St. Bonaventure also says that mental prayer is, as it were, a mirror, in which we see all the stains of the soul. In a letter to the Bishop of Osma, St. Teresa says, "Although it appears to us that we have no imperfections, still when God opens the eyes of the soul, as he usually does in prayer, our imperfections are then clearly seen."[6] He who does not make mental prayer does not even know his defects, and therefore, as St. Bernard says, he does not abhor them.[7] He does not even know the dangers to which his eternal salvation is exposed, and, therefore, he does not even think of avoiding them. But he who applies himself to meditation instantly sees his faults, and the dangers of perdition, and, seeing them, he will reflect on the remedies for them. By meditating on eternity, David was excited to the practice of virtue, and to sorrow and works of penance for his sins. *I*

---

[1] "Memorare novissima tua, et in æternum non peccabis."—*Ecclus.* vii. 40.

[2] "Accedite ad eum, et illuminamini."—*Ps.* xxxiii. 6.

[3] "Sint lumbi vestri præcincti, et lucernæ ardentes in manibus vestris."—*Luke,* xii. 35.

[4] "Oratio est lucerna."

[5] "Lucerna pedibus meis, verbum tuum."—*Ps.* cxviii. 105.

[6] Letter 8.

[7] "Seipsum non exhorret, quia nec sentit."—*De Cons.* l. 1, c. 2.

thought upon the days of old, and I had in my mind the eternal years . . . and I was exercised, and I swept my spirit.[1] The spouse in the Canticles says, *The flowers have appeared in our land: the time of pruning is come: the voice of the turtle is heard in our land.*[2] When the soul, like the solitary turtle, retires and recollects itself in meditation to converse with God, then the flowers—that is, good desires—appear: then comes the time of pruning, that is, the correction of faults which are discovered in mental prayer. "Consider," says St. Bernard, "that the time of pruning is at hand, if the time of meditation has gone before."[3] For (says the saint in another place) meditation regulates the affections, directs the actions, and corrects defects.[4]

2. IT DISPOSES THE HEART TO THE PRACTICE OF VIRTUES.

Moreover, without meditation there is not strength to resist the temptations of our enemies, and to practise the virtues of the Gospel.

Meditation is like fire with regard to iron, which, when cold, is hard, and can be wrought only with difficulty. But placed in the fire it becomes soft, and the workman gives it any form he wishes,[5] says the venerable Bartholomew à Martyribus. To observe the divine precepts and counsels, it is necessary to have a tender heart, that is, a heart docile and prepared to receive the impressions

[1] "Cogitavi dies antiquos, et annos æternos in mente habui . . . et exercitabar, et scopebam spiritum meum."—*Ps.* lxxvi. 6.

[2] "Flores apparuerunt in terra nostra, tempus putationis advenit; vox turturis audita est in terra nostra."—*Cant.* ii. 12.

[3] "Puta tempus putationis adesse, si meditatio præivit."—*De Cons.* l. 2, c. 6.

[4] "Consideratio regit affectus, dirigit actus, corrigit excessus."—*Ibid.* l. 1, c. 7.

[5] "Faber ignitum ferrum ictibus mollire satagit."—*De grad. Doctr. Spir.* c. 26.

of celestial inspirations, and ready to obey them. It was this that Solomon asked of God: *Give, therefore, to thy servant an understanding heart*[1] Sin has made our heart hard and indocile; for, being altogether inclined to sensual pleasures, it resists, as the Apostle complained, the laws of the spirit: *But I see another law in my members, fighting against the law of my mind.*[2] But man becomes docile and tender to the influence of grace which is communicated in mental prayer. By the contemplation of the divine goodness, the great love which God has borne him, and the immense benefits which God has bestowed upon him, man is inflamed with love, his heart is softened, and made obedient to the divine inspirations. But without mental prayer, his heart will remain hard and restive and disobedient, and thus he will be lost: *A hard heart shall fare evil at the last.*[3] Hence, St. Bernard exhorted Pope Eugene never to omit meditations on account of external occupations. "I fear for you, O Eugene, lest the multitude of affairs (prayer and consideration being intermitted) may bring you to a hard heart, which abhors not itself, because it perceives not."[4]

Some may imagine that the long time which devout souls give to prayer, and which they could spend in useful works, is unprofitable and lost time. But such persons know not that in mental prayer souls acquire strength to conquer enemies and to practise virtue. "From this leisure," says St. Bernard, "strength comes forth."[5] Hence, the Lord commanded that his spouse

[1] "Dabis ergo servo tuo cor docile."—3 *Kings*, iii. 9.

[2] "Video autem aliam legem in membris meis, repugnantem legi mentis meæ."—*Rom.* vii. 23.

[3] "Cor durum habebit male in novissimo; et qui amat periculum, in illo peribit."—*Ecclus.* iii. 27.

[4] "Timeo tibi, Eugeni, ne multitudo negotiorum, intermissa oratione et consideratione, te ad cor durum perducat, quod seipsum non exhorret, quia nec sentit."—*De Cons.* l. 1, c. 2.

[5] "Ex hoc otio vires proveniunt."

should not be disturbed. *I adjure you . . . that you stir
not up, nor awake my beloved till she please.*[1] He says, *until
she please;* for the sleep or repose which the soul takes in
mental prayer is perfectly voluntary, but is, at the same
time, necessary for its spiritual life. He who does not
sleep has not strength to work nor to walk, but goes
tottering along the way. The soul that does not repose and acquire strength in meditation is not able to
resist temptations, and totters on the road. In the life
of the Venerable Sister Mary Crucified, we read that,
while at prayer, she heard a devil boasting that he had
made a nun omit the common meditation, and that
afterwards, because he continued to tempt to her, she
was in danger of consenting to mortal sin. The servant
of God ran to the nun, and, with the divine aid, rescued
her from the criminal suggestion. Behold the danger to
which one who omits meditation exposes his soul! St.
Teresa used to say that he who neglects mental prayer,
needs not a devil to carry him to hell, but that he brings
himself there with his own hands. And the Abbot
Diocles says that " the man who omits mental prayer
soon becomes either a beast or a devil."

3. IT HELPS US TO PRAY AS WE SHOULD.

Without petitions on our part, God does not grant the
divine helps; and without aid from God, we cannot
observe the commandments.[2] From the absolute necessity of the prayer of petition arises the moral necessity
of mental prayer; for he who neglects meditation, and
is distracted with worldly affairs, will not know his
spiritual wants, the dangers to which his salvation is exposed, the means which he must adopt in order to con-

[1] " Ne suscitetis neque evigilare faciatis Dilectam, donec ipsa
velit."—*Cant.* iii. 5.
[2] See Necessity of Prayer, page 23.

quer temptations, or even the necessity of the prayer of petition for all men; thus, he will give up the practice of prayer, and by neglecting to ask God's graces he will certainly be lost. The great Bishop Palafox, in his Annotations to the letters of St. Teresa, says:[1] "How can charity last, unless God gives perseverance? How will the Lord give us perseverance, if we neglect to ask him for it? And how shall we ask him without mental prayer? Without mental prayer, there is not the communication with God which is necessary for the preservation of virtue." And Cardinal Bellarmine says, that for him who neglects meditation, it is morally impossible to live without sin.

Some one may say, I do not make mental prayer, but I say many vocal prayers. But it is necessary to know, as St. Augustine remarks, that to obtain the divine grace it is not enough to pray with the tongue, it is necessary also to pray with heart. On the words of David, *I cried to the Lord with my voice,*[2] the holy Doctor says, "Many cry not with their own voice (that is, not with the interior voice of the soul), but with that of the body. Your thoughts are a cry to the Lord.[3] Cry within, where God hears."[4] This is what the Apostle inculcates: *Praying at all times in the spirit.*[5] In general, vocal prayers are said distractedly with the voice of the body, but not of the heart, especially when they are long, and still more especially when said by a person who does not make mental prayer; and, therefore, God seldom hears them, and seldom grants the graces asked. Many say the Rosary, the Office of the Blessed Virgin,

---

[1] Letter 8.

[2] "Voce mea ad Dominum clamavi."—*Ps.* cxli. 2.

[3] "Multi clamant, non voce sua, sed corporis. Cogitatio tua clamor est ad Dominum."—*Ennarr. in Ps.* cxli.

[4] "Clama intus, ubi audit Deus."—*In Ps.* xxx. en. 4.

[5] "Orantes omni tempore in spiritu."—*Eph.* vi. 18.

17

and perform other works of devotion; but they still continue in sin. But it is impossible for him who perseveres in mental prayer to continue in sin: he will either give up meditation or renounce sin. A great servant of God used to say that mental prayer and sin cannot exist together. And this we see by experience: they who make mental prayer rarely incur the enmity of God; and should they ever have the misfortune of falling into sin, by persevering in mental prayer they see their misery and return to God. Let a soul, says St. Teresa, be ever so negligent, if it persevere in meditation, the Lord will bring it back to the haven of salvation.

II.

Mental Prayer is Indispensable in order to attain Perfection.

All the saints have become saints by mental prayer. Mental prayer is the blessed furnace in which souls are inflamed with the divine love. *In my meditation,* says David, *a fire shall flame out.*[1] St. Vincent of Paul used to say that it would be a miracle if a sinner who attends at the sermons in the mission, or in the spiritual exercises, were not converted. Now, he who preaches, and speaks in the exercises, is only a man; but it is God himself that speaks to the soul in meditation. *I will lead her into the wilderness; and I will speak to her heart.*[2] St. Catharine of Bologna used to say, " He who does not practise mental prayer deprives himself of the bond that unites the soul with God; hence, finding her alone, the devil will easily make her his own." " How," she would say, " can I conceive that the love of God is found in the soul that cares but little to treat with God in prayer ?" Where, but in meditation, have the saints been inflamed

---

[1] " In meditatione mea exardescet ignis."—*Ps.* xxxviii. 4.
[2] " Ducam eam in solitudinem, et loquar ad cor ejus."—*Osee,* ii. 14.

with divine love? By means of mental prayer, St. Peter of Alcantara was inflamed to such a degree that in order to cool himself, he ran into a frozen pool, and the frozen water began to boil like water in a caldron placed on the fire. In mental prayer, St. Philip Neri became inflamed, and trembled so that he shook the entire room. In mental prayer, St. Aloysius Gonzaga was so inflamed with divine ardor that his very face appeared to be on fire, and his heart beat as strongly as if it wished to fly from the body.

St. Laurence Justinian says: "By the efficacy of mental prayer, temptation is banished, sadness is driven away, lost virtue is restored, fervor which has grown cold is excited, and the lovely flame of divine love is augmented."[1] Hence, St. Aloysius Gonzaga has justly said that he who does not make much mental prayer will never attain a high degree of perfection.

A man of prayer, says David, is like a tree planted near the current of waters, which brings forth fruit in due time; all his actions prosper before God. *Blessed is the man . . . who shall meditate on his law day and night! And he shall be like a tree which is planted near the running waters, which shall bring forth its fruit in due season, and his leaf shall not fall off: and all whatsoever he shall do shall prosper.*[2] Mark the words *in due season;* that is, at the time when he ought to bear such a pain, such an affront, etc.

St. John Chrysostom[3] compared mental prayer to a

---

[1] "Ex oratione fugatur tentatio, abscedit tristitia, virtus reparatur, excitatur fervor, et divini amoris flamma succrescit."—*De Casto Conn.* c. 22.

[2] "Beatus vir qui . . . in lege ejus meditabitur die ac nocte. Et erit tamquam lignum quod plantatum est secus decursus aquarum, quod fructum suum dabit in tempore suo; et folium ejus non defluet, et omnia quæcumque faciet, prosperabuntur."—*Ps.* i. 3.

[3] *Ad pop. Ant. hom.* 79.

fountain in the middle of a garden. Oh! what an abundance of flowers and verdant plants do we see in the garden which is always refreshed with water from the fountain! Such, precisely, is the soul that practises mental prayer: you will see, that it always advances in good desires, and that it always brings forth more abundant fruits of virtue. Whence does the soul receive so many blessings? From meditation, by which it is continually irrigated. *Thy plants are a paradise of pomegranates with the fruits of the orchard. . . . The fountain of gardens, the well of living waters, which run with a strong stream from Libanus.*[1] But let the fountain cease to water the garden, and, behold, the flowers, plants, and all instantly wither away; and why? Because the water has failed. You will see that as long as such a person makes mental prayer, he is modest, humble, devout, and mortified in all things. But let him omit meditation, and you will instantly find him wanting in modesty of the eyes, proud resenting every word, indevout, no longer frequenting the sacraments and the church; you will find him attached to vanity, to useless conversations, to pastimes, and to earthly pleasures; and why? The water has failed, and, therefore, fervor has ceased. *My soul is as earth without water unto thee. . . . My spirit hath fainted away.*[2] The soul has neglected mental prayer, the garden is therefore dried up, and the miserable soul goes from bad to worse. When a soul abandons meditation, St. Chrysostom regards it not only as sick, but as dead. "He," says the holy Doctor, "who prays not to God, nor desires to enjoy assiduously his divine conversation, is dead. . . .

---

[1] "Emissiones tuæ, paradisus malorum punicorum cum pomorum fructibus. . . . Fons hortorum, puteus aquarum viventium, quæ fluunt impetu de Libano."—*Cant.* iv. 13.

[2] "Anima mea sicut terra sine aqua tibi, . . . defecit spiritus meus."—*Ps.* cxlii. 6.

The death of the soul is not to be prostrated before God."[1]

The same Father says that mental prayer is the root of the fruitful vine.[2] And St. John Climacus writes, that "prayer is a bulwark against the assault of afflictions, the spring of virtues, the procurer of graces."[3] Rufinus asserts, that all the spiritual progress of the soul flows from mental prayer.[4] And Gerson goes so far as to say that he who neglects meditation cannot, without a miracle, lead the life of a Christian.[5] Speaking of mental prayer, Jeremias says, *He shall sit solitary, and hold his peace; because he hath taken it up upon himself.*[6] That is, a soul cannot have a relish for God, unless it withdraws from creatures, and *sits*, that is, stops to contemplate the goodness, the love, the amiableness of God. But when solitary and recollected in meditation—that is, when it takes away its thoughts from the world—it is then raised above itself; and departs from prayer very different from what it was when it began it.

St. Ignatius of Loyola used to say that mental prayer is the short way to attain perfection. In a word, he who advances most in meditation makes the greatest progress in perfection. In mental prayer the soul is filled with holy thoughts, with holy affections, desires, and holy resolutions, and with love for God. There man sacri-

---

[1] "Quisquis non orat Deum, nec divino ejus colloquio cupit assidue frui, is mortuus est. . . . Animæ mors est non provolvi coram Deo." —*De or. D.* l. 1.

[2] "Radix vitis frugiferæ."—*De or. D.* l. 1.

[3] "Oratio est propugnaculum adversus impetum afflictionum, virtutum scaturigo, gratiarum conciliatrix."—*Scala sp. gr.* 28.

[4] "Omnis profectus spiritualis ex meditatione procedit."—*In Ps.* xxxvi.

[5] "Absque meditationis exercitio, nullus, secluso miraculo Dei, ad Christianæ religionis normam attingit."—*De Med. cons.* 7.

[6] "Sedebit solitarius, et tacebit, quia levavit super se."—*Lam.* iii. 28.

fices his passions, his appetites, his earthly attachments, and all the interests of self-love. Moreover, by praying for them, in mental prayer, we can save many sinners, as was done by St. Teresa, St. Mary Magdalene de Pazzi, and is done by all souls enamoured of God, who never omit, in their meditations, to recommend to him all infidels, heretics, and all poor sinners; begging him also to give zeal to priests who work in his vineyard, that they may convert his enemies. In mental prayer we can also, by the sole desire of performing them, gain the merit of many good works which we do not perform. For, as the Lord punishes bad desires, so, on the other hand, he rewards all our good desires.

PRAYER.

My Jesus, Thou hast loved me in the midst of pains; and in the midst of sufferings, I wish to love Thee. Thou hast spared nothing, Thou hast even given Thy blood and Thy life, in order to gain my love; and shall I continue, as hitherto, to be reserved in loving Thee? No, my Redeemer, it shall not be so: the ingratitude with which I have hitherto treated Thee is sufficient. To Thee I consecrate my whole heart. Thou alone dost deserve all my love. Thee alone do I wish to love. My God, since Thou wishest me to be entirely Thine, give me strength to serve Thee as Thou deservest, during the remainder of my life. Pardon my tepidity and my past infidelities. How often have I omitted mental prayer, in order to indulge my caprice! Alas! how often, when it was in my power to remain with Thee in order to please Thee, have I remained with creatures, so as to offend Thee! Oh, that so many lost years would return! But, since they will not return, the remaining days of my life must be entirely Thine, O my beloved Lord! I love Thee, O my Jesus! I love Thee, O my Sovereign Good! Thou art and shalt be forever the only love of my soul. O Mother of fair love, O Mary! obtain for me the grace to love thy Son, and to spend the remainder of my life in his love. Thou dost obtain from Jesus whatsoever thou wishest. Through thy prayer I hope for this gift.

III.

The Ends of Mental Prayer.*

In order to practise well mental prayer, or meditation, and to make it truly profitable to the soul, we must well ascertain the ends for which we attempt it.

TO UNITE OURSELVES TO GOD.

We must meditate in order to unite ourselves more completely to God. It is not so much good thoughts in the intellect as good acts of the will, or holy desires, that unite us to God; and such are the acts which we perform in meditation,—acts of humility, confidence, self-sacrifice, resignation, and especially of love and of repentance for our sins. Acts of love, says St. Teresa, are those that keep the soul inflamed with holy love.

But the perfection of this love consists in making our will one with that of God; for the chief effect of love, as Dionysius the Areopagite says, is to unite the wills of those who love, so that they have but one heart and one will. St. Teresa also says, "All that he who exercises himself in prayer should aim at, is to conform himself to the divine will, and he may be assured that in this consists the highest perfection; he who best practises this will receive the greatest gifts from God, and will make the greatest progress in an interior life." [1]

There are many, however, who complain that they go to prayer and do not find God; the reason of which is, that they carry with them a heart full of earth. "Detach the heart from creatures, says St. Teresa; seek God, and you will find him." *The Lord is good to the soul that seeketh Him.*[2] Therefore, to find God in prayer, the soul

[1] *Interior Castle*, d. 2, ch. 1.
[2] "Bonus est Dominus . . . animæ quærenti illum."—*Lam.* iii. 25.

---

* *Pious Reflections*, § 15; *Preparation for Death*, consid. xxxvi.; *The Love of God*, § 3.

must be stripped of its love for the things of earth, and
then God will speak to it: *I will lead her into the wilder-*
ness, and I will speak to her heart.[1]   But in order to find
God, solitude of the body, as St. Gregory observes, is
is not enough; that of the heart is necessary too.   The
Lord one day said to St. Teresa: "I would willingly speak
to many souls; but the world makes such a noise in their
heart that my voice cannot make itself heard."   Ah!
when a detached soul is engaged in prayer, truly does
God speak to it, and make it understand the love which
he has borne it; and then the soul, says St. Laurence
Justinian, burning with holy love, speaks not; but in
that silence, oh, how much does it say!   The silence of
charity, observes the same writer, says more to God than
could be said by the utmost powers of human eloquence;
each sigh that it utters is a manifestation of its whole
interior.[2]   It then seems as if it could not repeat often
enough, *My Beloved to me, and I to Him.*

TO OBTAIN GRACE FROM GOD.

We must meditate in order to obtain from God the
graces that are necessary to advance in the way of salvation, and especially to avoid sin, and to use the means
which will lead us to perfection.

The best fruit which comes from meditation is the
exercise of prayer.   Almighty God, ordinarily speaking,
does not give grace to any but those who pray.   St.
Gregory writes: "God desires to be entreated; he desires
to be constrained; he desires to be, as it were, conquered
by importunity."   It is true that at all times the Lord is
ready to hear us, but at the time of meditation, when we
are most truly in converse with God, he is most bounti-
ful in giving us his aid.

[1] "Ducam eam in solitudinem, et loquar ad cor ejus."—*Osee*, ii.
14.

[2] *De Disc. mon.* c. 24.

Above all, should we, in meditation, ask God for perseverance and his holy love.

Final perseverance is not a single grace, but a chain of graces, to which must correspond the chain of our prayers. If we cease to pray, God will cease to give us his help, and we shall perish. He who does not practise meditation will find the greatest difficulty in persevering in grace till death. Let us remember what Palafox says: "How will the Lord give us perseverance if we do not ask it? And how shall we ask for it without meditation? Without meditation there is no communion with God."

We must also be urgent with prayers to obtain from God his holy love. St. Francis de Sales says that all virtues come in union with holy love. *All good things came to me together with her.*[1]

Let us, therefore, pray continually for perseverance and love; and, in order to pray with greater confidence, let us ever bear in mind the promise made us by Jesus Christ, that whatever we seek from God through the merits of his Son, he will give it us.[2] Let us, then, pray, and pray always, if we would that God should make us abound in every blessing. Let us pray for ourselves, and, if we have zeal for the glory of God, let us pray also for others. It is a thing most pleasing to God to be entreated for unbelievers and heretics, and all sinners. *Let the people confess to Thee, O God; let all the people confess to Thee.*[3] Let us say, O Lord, make them know Thee, make them love Thee. We read in the lives of St. Teresa and St. Mary Magdalene of Pazzi how God inspired these holy women to pray for sinners. And to

---

[1] "Venerunt autem mihi omnia bona pariter cum illa."— *Wisd.* vii. 7.

[2] 'Amen, amen, dico vobis: si quid petieritis Patrem in nomine meo, dabit vobis."— *John.* xvi. 23.

[3] "Confiteantur tibi populi, Deus, confiteantur tibi populi omnes." —*Ps.* lxvi. 6.

prayer for sinners let us also add prayers for the holy souls in purgatory.

WE OUGHT NOT TO SEEK IN MENTAL PRAYER SPIRITUAL CONSOLATIONS.

We must apply ourselves to meditation, not for the sake of spiritual consolations, but chiefly in order to learn what is the will of God concerning us. *Speak, Lord,* said Samuel to God, *for Thy servant heareth.*[1] Lord, make me to know what Thou wilt, that I may do it. Some persons continue meditation as long as consolations continue; but when these cease, they leave off meditation. It is true that God is accustomed to comfort his beloved souls at the time of meditation, and to give them some foretaste of the delights he prepares in heaven for those who love him. These are things which the lovers of the world do not comprehend; they who have no taste except for earthly delights despise those which are celestial. Oh, if they were wise, how surely would they leave their pleasures to shut themselves in their closets, to speak alone with God ! Meditation is nothing more than a converse between the soul and God; the soul pours forth to him its affections, its desires, its fears, its requests, and God speaks to the heart, causing it to know his goodness, and the love which he bears it, and what it must do to please him.

But these delights are not constant, and, for the most part, holy souls experience much dryness of spirit in meditation. "With dryness and temptations," says St. Teresa, "the Lord makes proof of those who love him." And she adds, "Even if this dryness lasts through life, let not the soul leave off meditation; the time will come when all will be well rewarded." The time of dryness is the time for gaining the greatest rewards; and when

---

[1] " Loquere, Domine, quia audit servus tuus."—1 *Kings,* iii. 9.

we find ourselves apparently without fervor, without good desires, and, as it were, unable to do a good act, let us humble ourselves and resign ourselves, for this very meditation will be more fruitful than others. It is enough then to say, if we can say nothing more, " O Lord, help me, have mercy on me, abandon me not !" Let us also have recourse to our comforter, the most holy Mary. Happy he who does not leave off meditation in the hour of desolation.

IV.

Principal Subjects of Meditation. *

The Holy Spirit says, *In all thy works remember thy last end, and thou shalt never sin.*[1] He who often meditates on the four last things—namely, death, judgment, and the eternity of hell and paradise will not fall into sin. But these truths are not seen with the eye of the body; the soul only perceives them. If they are not meditated on, they vanish from the mind; and then the pleasures of the senses present themselves, and those who do not keep before themselves the eternal truths are easily taken up by them; and this is the reason why so many abandon themselves to vice, and are damned. All Christians know and believe that they must die, and that we shall all be judged; but because they do not think about this, they live far away from God.

If we, moreover, do not meditate especially on our obligation to love God on account of his infinite perfections and the great blessings that he has conferred upon us, and the love that he has borne us, we shall hardly detach ourselves from the love of creatures in order to fix our whole love on God. It is in the time of prayer that God gives

---

[1] " Memorare novissima tua, et in æternum non peccabis."—*Ecclus.* vii. 40.

* *Rule of Life*, ch. i. § 2 ; *The Love of God*, § 3.

us to understand the worthlessness of earthly things, and the value of the good things of heaven; and then it is that he inflames with his love those hearts that do not offer resistance to his calls.

After all, the good rule is that we preferably meditate on the truths and mysteries that touch us more and procure for our soul the most abundant nourishment. Yet the subject most suitable for a person that aspires to perfection ought to be the Passion of our Lord. Louis Blosius relates that our Lord revealed to several holy women—to St. Gertrude, St. Bridget, St. Mechtilde, and St. Catharine of Sienna—that they who meditate on his Passion are very dear to him. According to St. Francis de Sales, the Passion of our Redeemer should be the ordinary subject of the meditation of every Christian. Oh, what an excellent book is the Passion of Jesus! There we understand, better than in any other book, the malice of sin, and also the mercy and love of God for man. To me it appears that Jesus Christ has suffered so many different pains—the scourging, the crowning with thorns, the crucifixion, etc.—that, having before our eyes so many painful mysteries, we might have a variety of different subjects for meditating on his Passion, by which we might excite sentiments of gratitude and love.

V.

The Place and the Time Suitable for Meditation.

THE PLACE.*

We can meditate in every place, at home or elsewhere, even in walking, in working. How many are there who, not being able to do otherwise, raise their hearts to God and apply their minds to mental prayer without leaving for this purpose their occupations, their work,

---

* *Homo Apost.* app. 4. § 3; *Pious Reflections*, § 32–34.

or meditate even when travelling! He who seeks God will find him everywhere and at all times.

The essential condition to converse with God is the solitude of the heart, without which prayer would be worthless, and, as St. Gregory says, it would profit us little or nothing to be with the body in a solitary place, while the heart is full of worldly thoughts and affections.[1] But to enjoy the solitude of the heart, which consists in being disengaged from worldly thoughts and affections, deserts and caves are not absolutely necessary. Those who from necessity are obliged to converse with the world, whenever their hearts are free from worldly attachments, even in the public streets, in places of resort, and public assemblies, can possess a solitude of heart, and continue united with God. All those occupations that we undertake in order to fulfil the divine will have no power to prevent the solitude of the heart. St. Catharine of Sienna truly found God in the midst of the household labors in which her parents kept her employed in order to draw her from devotional exercises; but in the midst of these affairs she preserved a retirement in her heart, which she called her cell, and there ceased not to converse with God alone.

However, when we can, we should retire to a solitary place to make our meditation. Our Lord has said, *When thou shalt pray, enter thy chamber, and, having shut the door, pray to thy Father in secret.*[2] St. Bernard says that silence, and the absence of all noise, almost force the soul to think of the goods of heaven.[3]

But the best place for making mental prayer is the church; for Jesus Christ especially delights in the medi-

---

[1] "Quid prodest solitudo corporis, si solitudo defuerit cordis?"—*Mor.* l. 30, c. 23.

[2] "Tu autem, cum oraveris, intra in cubiculum tuum, et, clauso ostio, ora Patrem tuum in abscondito."—*Matt.* vi. 6.

[3] "Silentium, et a strepitu quies, cogit cælestia meditari."—*Epist.* 78.

tation that is made before the Blessed Sacrament, since there it appears that he bestows light and grace most abundantly upon those who visit him. He has left himself in this sacrament, not only to be the food of souls that receive him in Holy Communion, but also to be found at all times by every one who seeks him. Devout pilgrims go to the holy town of Loreto, where Jesus Christ dwelt during his life; and to Jerusalem, where he died on the cross ; but how much greater ought to be our devotion when we find him before us in the tabernacle, in which this Lord himself now dwells in person, who lived among us, and died for us on Calvary ! It is not permitted in the world for persons of all ranks to speak alone with kings; but with Jesus Christ, the King of kings, both nobles and plebeians, rich and poor, can converse at their will, setting before him their wants, and seeking his grace; and there Jesus gives audience to all, hears all, and comforts all.

THE TIME.

We have here to consider two things—namely, the time of the day most suitable for mental prayer, and the time to be spent in making it.

1. According to St. Bonaventure, the morning and the evening are the two parts of the day which, ordinarily speaking, are the fittest for meditation.[1] But, according to St. Gregory of Nyssa, the morning is the most seasonable time for prayer, because, says the saint, when prayer precedes business, sin will not find entrance into the soul.[2] And the Venerable Father Charles Carafa, founder of the Congregation of the *Pious Workers,* used to say that a fervent act of love, made in the morning

[1] " Mane et vespere tempus est orationis opportunum."—*Spec. disc.* p. 1, c. 12.

[2] " Si oratio negotium præcesserit, peccatum aditum non inveniet." —*De orat. Dom. or.* 1.

during meditation, is sufficient to maintain the soul in fervor during the entire day. Prayer, as St. Jerome has written, is also necessary in the evening. Let not the body go to rest before the soul is refreshed by mental prayer,[1] which is the food of the soul. But at all times and in all places we can pray; it is enough for us to raise the mind to God, and to make good acts, for in this consists mental prayer.

2. With regard to the time to be spent in mental prayer, the rule of the saints was, to devote to it all the hours that were not necessary for the occupations of human life. St. Francis Borgia employed in meditation eight hours in the day, because his Superiors would not allow him a longer time; and when the eight hours had expired, he earnestly asked permission to remain a little longer at prayer, saying, "Ah! give me another little quarter of an hour." St. Philip Neri was accustomed to spend the entire night in prayer. St. Anthony the Abbot remained the whole night in prayer; and when the sun appeared, which was the time assigned for terminating his prayer, he complained of it for having risen too soon.

Father Balthassar Alvarez used to say that a soul that loves God, when not in prayer, is like a stone out of its centre, in a violent state; for in this life we should, as much as possible, imitate the life of the saints in bliss, who are constantly employed in the contemplation of God.

But let us come to the particular time which a religious who seeks perfection should devote to mental prayer. Father Torres prescribed an hour's meditation in the morning, another during the day, and a half-hour's meditation in the evening, when they should not be hindered by sickness, or by any duty of obedience.

[1] "Non prius corpusculum requiescat, quam anima pascatur."—*Ad Eust. de Virgin.*

If to you this appears too much, I counsel you to give at least two hours to mental prayer. It is certain that a half hour's meditation each day would not be sufficient to attain a high degree of perfection; for beginners, however, this would be sufficient.*

Sometimes the Lord wishes you to omit prayer in order to perform some work of fraternal charity; but it is necessary to attend to what St. Laurence Justinian says: "When charity requires it, the spouse of Jesus goes to serve her neighbor; but during that time she continually sighs to return to converse with her Spouse in the solitude of her cell."[1] Father Vincent Carafa, General of the Society of Jesus, stole as many little moments of time as he could, and employed them in prayer.

Mental prayer is tedious to those who are attached to the world, but not to those who love God only. Ah! conversation with God is not painful nor tedious to those who truly love him. *His conversation has no bitterness, his company produces not tediousness, but joy and gladness.*[2] Mental prayer, says St. John Climacus, is nothing else than a familiar conversation and union with God.[3] In prayer, as St. Chrysostom says, the soul converses with God, and God with the soul. No, the life of holy persons who love prayer, and fly from earthly amusements, is not a

[1] "Cum charitas urget, se exponit proximo, sic tamen ut continue anhelet ad cubile Sponsi reditum."—*De Casto Conn.* c. 12.

[2] "Non enim habet amaritudinem conversatio illius, nec tædium convictus illius, sed lætitiam et gaudium."—*Wisd.* viii. 16.

[3] "Oratio est familiaris conversatio et conjunctio cum Deo."—*Scala sp. gr.* 28.

* *Homo apost. App.* 4, § 3. Pope Benedict XIV. grants to all the faithful who make mental prayer devoutly for half an hour, or at least for a quarter of an hour, every day, for a month, a *plenary* indulgence when truly penitent, after confession and Communion they devoutly pray to the intentions of the Church. This indulgence is applicable to the souls in purgatory.

life of bitterness. If you do not believe me, *Taste and see that the Lord is sweet.*[1] Try it, and you shall see how sweet the Lord is to those who leave all things in order to converse with him only. But the end which we ought to propose to ourselves in going to meditation should be, as has been said several times, not spiritual consolation, but to learn from our Lord what he wishes from us, and to divest ourselves of all self-love. "To prepare yourself for prayer," says St. John Climacus, "put off your own will."[2] To prepare ourselves well for meditation, we must renounce self-will, and say to God, *Speak, Lord, for thy servant heareth.*[3] Lord, tell me what Thou wishest me to do; I am willing to do it. And it is necessary to say this with a resolute will, for without this disposition the Lord will not speak to us.

VI.

Manner of making Mental Prayer.

Mental prayer contains three parts: the preparation, the meditation, and the conclusion.

I. THE PREPARATION.

Begin by disposing your mind and body to enter into pious recollection.

Leave at the door of the place where you are going to converse with God all extraneous thoughts, saying, with St. Bernard, O my thoughts! wait here: after prayer we shall speak on other matters. Be careful not to allow the mind to wander where it wishes; but should a distracting thought enter, act as we shall tell you to do in § 7.

The posture of the body most suitable for prayer is to

---

[1] "Gustate, et videte quoniam suavis est Dominus."—*Ps.* xxxiii. 9.
[2] "Ad præparandum te ad orationem, exue voluntates tuas."
[3] "Loquere, Domine, quia audit servus tuus."—1 *Kings,* iii. 10.

be kneeling; but if this posture becomes so irksome as to cause distractions, we may, as St. John of the Cross says, make our meditation while modestly sitting down.

The preparation consists of three acts: 1. Act of faith in the presence of God; 2. Act of humility and of contrition; 3. Act of petition for light. We may perform these acts in the following manner:

Act of Faith in the Presence of God, and Act of Adoration.

My God, I believe that Thou art here present, and I adore Thee with my whole soul.

Be careful to make this act with a lively faith, for a lively remembrance of the divine presence contributes greatly to remove distractions. Cardinal Carracciolo, Bishop of Aversa, used to say that when a person is distracted in prayer there is reason to think that he has not made a lively act of faith.

Act of Humility and of Contrition.

Lord, I should now be in hell in punishment of the offences I have given Thee. I am sorry for them from the bottom of my heart; have mercy on me.

Act of Petition for Light.

Eternal Father, for the sake of Jesus and Mary, give me light in this meditation, that I may draw fruit from it.

We must then recommend ourselves to the Blessed Virgin by saying a *Hail Mary,* to St. Joseph, to our guardian angel, and to our holy patron.

These acts, says St. Francis de Sales, ought to be made with fervor, but should be short, that we may pass immediately to the meditation.

II. THE MEDITATION.

When you make meditation privately you may always use some book,* at least at the commencement, and stop

---

* *Rule of Life*, ch. 2, § 2.

It may be useful to mention here what the author himself wrote to his religious in a circular dated February 26, 1771: "I recommend that, for the most part, the meditations should be taken from my books, *The Preparation for Death, Meditations on the Passion, Darts of Fire,*—the meditations from Advent to the octave of the Epiphany. I say this, not in order to put forward my own poor books, but because these meditations are made up of devout affections, and, what is of more importance, are full of holy prayers, of which I do not find many in other books ; hence I make the request that the second part of the *Meditations,* consisting of affections and prayers, be always read."

Let us remark that St. Alphonsus renders the practice of meditation extremely simple, clear, easy, and not less profitable. Thanks to the method that he teaches, this exercise, which is indispensable to every one that wishes to sanctify himself, is, in fact, adapted to the comprehension of all. The Saint wishes that every one should learn how to meditate; he earnestly recommends that special instructions should be given to the people for this purpose; and that every day mental prayer should be made in the church, in common for persons in every condition of life, and particularly for those who do not know how to read. He moreover explains the method that should be followed in its exercise, that it may produce lasting fruits. (See Missions, ch. 7–9.)

Pope Benedict XIV. grants *an indulgence of seven years and seven times forty days,* every time, to all those who, in a church or, elsewhere, either in public or in private, shall teach the manner of making mental prayer, as well as to those who attend such instruction, provided that each time, being truly penitent, they confess their sins and receive Holy Communion. To those who shall teach assiduously the way to make mental prayer, as well as to those who shall, with the same assiduity, learn how to make it, the same Pope grants a plenary indulgence once a month, on any day, when, being truly penitent, after confession and Communion, they shall pray for peace and union among Christian princes, for the extirpation of heresy, and for the triumph of the Church. These indulgences are applicable to the souls in Purgatory.—ED.

when you find yourself most touched. St. Francis de Sales says that in this we should do as the bees that stop on a flower as long as they find any honey on it, and then pass on to another. St. Teresa used a book for seventeen years; she would first read a little, then meditate for a short time on what she had read. It is useful to meditate in this manner, in imitation of the pigeon that first drinks and then raises its eyes to heaven.

When mental prayer is made in common, one person reads for the rest the subject of meditation and divides it into two parts: the first is read at the beginning, after the preparatory acts; the second, towards the middle of the half hour, or after the Consecration if the meditation is made during the Mass. One should read in a loud tone of voice, and slowly, so as to be well understood.

It should be remembered that the advantage of mental prayer consists not so much in meditating as in making affections, petitions, and resolutions: these are the three principal fruits of meditation. " The progress of a soul," says St. Teresa, " does not consist in thinking much of God, but in loving him ardently; and this love is acquired by resolving to do a great deal for him." [1] Speaking of mental prayer, the spiritual masters say that meditation is, as it were, the needle which, when it has passed, must be succeeded by the golden thread, composed, as has been said, of affections, petitions, and resolutions; and this we are going to explain.

I. THE AFFECTIONS.

When you have reflected on the point of meditation, and feel any pious sentiment, raise your heart to God and offer him acts of humility, of confidence, or of thanksgiving; but, above all, repeat in mental prayer acts of contrition and of love.

---

[1] *Book of the Foundations*, ch. 5.

The act of love, as also the act of contrition, is the golden chain that binds the soul to God. An act of perfect charity is sufficient for the remission of all our sins: *Charity covereth a multitude of sins.*[1] The Lord has declared that he cannot hate the soul that loves him: *I love them that love Me.*[2] The Venerable Sister Mary Crucified once saw a globe of fire, in which some straws that had been thrown into it were instantly consumed. By this vision she was given to understand that a soul, by making a true act of love, obtains the remission of all its faults. Besides, the Angelic Doctor teaches that by every act of love we acquire a new degree of glory. " Every act of charity merits eternal life." [3]

Acts of love may be made in the following manner :

My God, I esteem Thee more than all things.

I love Thee with my whole heart.

I delight in Thy felicity.

I would wish to see Thee loved by all.

I wish only what Thou wishest.

Make known to me what Thou wishest from me, and I will do it.

Dispose as Thou pleasest of me and of all that I possess.

This last act of oblation is particularly dear to God.

In meditation, among the acts of love towards God, there is none more perfect than the taking delight in the infinite joy of God. This is certainly the continual exercise of the blessed in heaven; so that he who often rejoices in the joy of God begins in this life to do that which he hopes to do in heaven through all eternity.*

---

[1] "Charitas operit multitudinem peccatorum."—1 *Peter*, iv. 8.

[2] " Ego diligentes me diligo."—*Prov.* viii. 17.

[3] "Quilibet actus charitatis meretur vitam æternam."—1. 2. q. 114. a. 7.

* *Pious Reflections,* § 33.

It may be useful here to remark, with St. Augustine, that it is not the torture, but the cause, which makes the martyr.[1] Whence St. Thomas[2] teaches that martyrdom is to suffer death in the exercise of an act of virtue. From which we may infer, that not only he who by the hands of the executioner lays down his life for the faith, but whoever dies to comply with the divine will, and to please God, is a martyr, since in sacrificing himself to the divine love he performs an act of the most exalted virtue. We all have to pay the great debt of nature; let us therefore endeavor, in holy prayer, to obtain resignation to the divine will—to receive death and every tribulation in conformity with the dispensations of his Providence. As often as we shall perform this act of resignation with sufficient fervor, we may hope to be made partakers of the merits of the martyrs. St. Mary Magdalene, in reciting the doxology, always bowed her head in the same spirit as she would have done in receiving the stroke of the executioner.*

Remember that we here speak of the ordinary mental prayer; for should any one feel himself at any time united with God by supernatural or infused recollection, without any particular thought of an eternal truth or of any divine mystery, he should not then labor to perform any other acts than those to which he feels himself sweetly drawn to God. It is then enough to endeavor, with loving attention, to remain united with God, without impeding the divine operation, or forcing himself to make reflections and acts. But this is to be understood when the Lord calls the soul to this supernatural prayer; but until we receive such a call, we should not depart from the ordinary method of mental prayer, but should,

---

[1] "Martyres veros, non pœna facit, sed causa."—*Epist.* 89, *E. B.*
[2] 2. 2. q. 124, a. 5.

* *Vict. of the Martyrs,* Introd. § 2.

as has been said, make use of meditation and affections. However, for persons accustomed to mental prayer, it is better to employ themselves in affections than in consideration.

2. PETITIONS.

Moreover, in mental prayer it is very profitable, and perhaps more useful than any other act, to repeat petitions to God, asking, with humility and confidence, his graces; that is, his light, resignation, perseverance, and the like; but, above all, the gift of his holy love. St. Francis de Sales used to say that by obtaining the divine love we obtain all graces; for a soul that truly loves God with its whole heart will, of itself, without being admonished by others, abstain from giving him the smallest displeasure, and will labor to please him to the best of its ability.

When you find yourself in aridity and darkness, so that you feel, as it were, incapable of making good acts, it is sufficient to say:

My Jesus, mercy. Lord, for the sake of Thy mercy, assist me. And the meditation made in this manner will be for you perhaps the most useful and fruitful.

The Venerable Paul Segneri used to say that until he studied theology, he employed himself during the time of mental prayer in making reflections and affections; but "God" (these are his own words) "afterwards opened my eyes, and thenceforward I endeavored to employ myself in petitions; and if there is any good in me, I ascribe it to this exercise of recommending myself to God." Do you likewise do the same; ask of God his graces, in the name of Jesus Christ, and you will obtain whatsoever you desire. This our Saviour has promised, and his promise cannot fail: *Amen, amen, I say to you, if you ask the Father anything in My name, He will give it you.*

In a word, all mental prayer should consist in acts

and petitions. Hence, the Venerable Sister Mary Crucified, while in an ecstasy, declared that mental prayer
is the respiration of the soul; for, as by respiration, the
air is first attracted, and afterwards given back, so, by
petitions, the soul first receives grace from God, and
then, by good acts of oblation and love, it gives itself
to him.

3. RESOLUTIONS.

In terminating the meditation it is necessary to make
a particular resolution; as, for example, to avoid some
particular defect into which you have more frequently
fallen, or to practise some virtue, such as to suffer the
annoyance which you receive from another person, to
obey more exactly a certain Superior, to perform some
particular act of mortification. We must repeat the
same resolution several times, until we find that we have
got rid of the defect or acquired the virtue. Afterwards
reduce to practice the resolutions you have made, as
soon as an occasion is presented. You would also do
well, before the conclusion of your prayer, to renew the
vows or any particular engagement by vow or otherwise
that you have made with God. This renewal is most
pleasing to God; we multiply the merit of the good
work, and draw down upon us a new help in order to
persevere and to grow in grace.

III. THE CONCLUSION.

The conclusion of meditation consists of three acts:
1. In thanking God for the lights received.
2. In making a purpose to fulfil the resolutions made.
3. In asking of the Eternal Father, for the sake of
Jesus and Mary, grace to be faithful to them.
Be careful never to omit, at the end of meditation, to
recommend to God the souls in purgatory and poor sin-

ners. St. John Chrysostom says that nothing more clearly shows our love for Jesus Christ than our zeal in recommending our brethren to him.

St. Francis de Sales remarks that in leaving mental prayer we should take with us a nosegay of flowers, in order to smell them during the day; that is, we should remember one or two points in which we have felt particular devotion, in order to excite our fervor during the day.

The ejaculations which are dearest to God are those of love, of resignation, of oblation of ourselves. Let us endeavor not to perform any action without first offering it to God, and not to allow at the most a quarter of an hour to pass, in whatever occupations we may find ourselves, without raising the heart to the Lord by some good act. Moreover, in our leisure time, such as when we are waiting for a person, or when we walk in the garden, or are confined to bed by sickness, let us endeavor, to the best of our ability, to unite ourselves to God. It is also necessary by observing silence, by seeking solitude as much as possible, and by remembering the presence of God, to preserve the pious sentiments conceived in meditation.

VII.

Distractions and Aridities.

I. DISTRACTIONS.

If, after having well prepared ourselves for mental prayer, as has been explained in a preceding paragraph, a distracting thought should enter, we must not be disturbed, nor seek to banish it with a violent effort; but let us remove it calmly and return to God.

Let us remember that the devil labors hard to disturb us in the time of meditation, in order to make us abandon it. Let him, then, who omits mental prayer on account of distractions, be persuaded that he gives delight to the devil. It is impossible, says Cassian, that our minds should be free from all distractions during prayer.

Let us, then, never give up meditation, however great our distractions may be. St. Francis de Sales says that if, in mental prayer, we should do nothing else than continually banish distractions and temptations, the meditation would be well made. Before him St. Thomas taught that involuntary distractions do not take away the fruit of mental prayer.[1]

Finally, when we perceive that we are deliberately distracted, let us desist from the voluntary defect and banish the distraction, but let us be careful not to discontinue our meditation.

2. ARIDITIES.*

The greatest pain of souls in meditation is to find themselves sometimes without a feeling of devotion, weary of it, and without any sensible desire of loving God; and with this is joined the fear of being in the wrath of God through their sins, on account of which the Lord has abandoned them; and being in this gloomy darkness, they know not how to escape from it, it seeming to them that every way is closed against them.

When a soul gives itself up to the spiritual life, the Lord is accustomed to heap consolations upon it, in order to wean it from the pleasures of the world, but afterwards, when he sees it more settled in spiritual ways, he draws back his hand, in order to make proof

---

[1] "Evagatio mentis, quæ fit præter propositum, orationis fructum non tollit."—2. 2. q. 83, a. 13.

* *Pious Reflections,* § xxxiv.; *Conformity to the Will of God,* § 5.

of its love, and to see whether it serves and loves God unrecompensed, while in this world, with spiritual joys. Some foolish persons, seeing themselves in a state of aridity, think that God may have abandoned them; or, again, that the spiritual life was not made for them; and so they leave off prayer, and lose all that they have gained.

In order to be a soul of prayer, man must resist with fortitude all temptations to discontinue mental prayer in the time of aridity. St. Teresa has left us very excellent instructions on this point. In one place she says, "The devil knows that he has lost the soul that perseveringly practises mental prayer." In another place she says, "I hold for certain that the Lord will conduct to the haven of salvation the soul that perseveres in mental prayer, in spite of all the sins that the devil may oppose." Again, she says, "He who does not stop in the way of mental prayer reaches the end of his journey, though he should delay a little." Finally she concludes, saying, "By aridity and temptations the Lord proves his lovers. Though aridity should last for life, let not the soul give up prayer: the time will come when all shall be well rewarded."

The Angelic Doctor says that the devotion consists not in feeling, but in the desire and resolution to embrace promptly all that God wills. Such was the prayer that Jesus Christ made in the Garden of Olives; it was full of aridity and tediousness, but it was the most devout and meritorious prayer that had ever been offered in this world. It consisted in these words: My Father, not what I will, but what Thou wilt.

Hence, never give up mental prayer in the time of aridity. Should the tediousness which assails you be very great, divide your meditation into several parts, and employ yourself, for the most part, in petitions to God, even though you should seem to pray without confidence

and without fruit. It will be sufficient to say and to
repeat: *My Jesus, mercy. Lord, have mercy on us.* Pray,
and doubt not that God will hear you and grant your
petition.

In going to meditation, never propose to yourself your
own pleasure and satisfaction, but only to please God,
and to learn what he wishes you to do. And, for this
purpose, pray always that God may make known to you
his will, and that he may give you strength to fulfil it.
All that we ought to seek in mental prayer is, light to
know, and strength to accomplish, the will of God in our
regard.

PRAYER.

Ah ! my Jesus, it appears that Thou couldst do nothing more,
in order to gain the love of men. It is enough to know that
Thou hast wished to become man ; that is, to become, like us, a
worm. Thou hast wished to lead a painful life, of thirty-three
years, amid sorrow and ignominies, and in the end to die on an
infamous gibbet. Thou hast also wished to remain under the
appearance of bread, in order to become the food of our souls ;
and how is it possible that Thou hast received so much ingratitude, even from Christians who believe these truths, and still
love Thee so little ? Unhappy me ! I have hitherto been among
those ungrateful souls ; I have attended only to my pleasures,
and have been forgetful of Thee and of Thy love. I now know
the evil I have done ; but I repent of it with my whole heart :
my Jesus, pardon me. I now love Thee ; I love Thee so ardently that I choose death, and a thousand deaths, rather than
cease to love Thee. I thank Thee for the light which Thou
givest me. Give me strength, O God of my soul ! always to advance in Thy love. Accept this poor heart to love Thee. It is
true that it has once despised Thee, but now it is enamoured of
Thy goodness ; it loves Thee and desires only to love Thee. O
Mary, mother of God, assist me : in thy intercession I place
great confidence.

II. *THE EXERCISES OF A RETREAT.*

Advantages of the Spiritual Exercises made in Retreat.

A LETTER TO A YOUNG MAN WHO IS DELIBERATING ON THE CHOICE OF A STATE OF LIFE.*

I have received your last favor, in which you tell me that you are still undecided as to the state of life you should choose, and that, having communicated to your pastor the counsel I gave you,—namely, to go for that purpose to perform the spiritual exercises in that house which your father has in the country,—the said pastor answered you that it was not necessary for you to go to that house to torture your brains during eight days in solitude, but that it was enough for you to attend the exercises he would soon give to the people in his own church. Since, then, on this last point of the exercises, you again ask my advice, it is necessary that I should answer you more at length, and show you, first, how much greater the fruit of the spiritual exercises is, when they are performed in silence, in some retired place, than when performed whilst they are given in public, when one is obliged during that time to go to one's own house, and continues to converse with one's parents and friends ; and the more so in your case, as you write to me, you have in your house no room to which you may retire. On the other hand, I am very much in favor of those exercises when performed in solitude, as I know it is to such I owe my own conversion and my resolution

---

* St. Alphonsus wrote this letter, as also the meditations that follow it, during the last years of his life, according to Tannoia, book 4, ch. 18.

to leave the world. I will then, in the second place, suggest to you the means and precautions to be taken during the exercises, in order to derive from them the fruit you desire. I beg you, when you have read this letter yourself, to give it to your Rev. Pastor, that he may read it also.

I.

Let us then speak first of the great benefit of the exercises, when they are performed in solitude, where one treats with no person but God; and, first of all, let us see the reason for it.

The truths of eternal life, such as the great affair of our salvation, the value of the time that God gives us that we may amass merits for a happy eternity, the obligations under which we are to love God for his infinite goodness and the immense love he bears towards us,—these and similar things are not seen with the eyes of the flesh, but with the eyes of the mind. It is, on the contrary, certain that, unless our intellect represents to the will the value of a good or the greatness of an evil, we shall never embrace that good nor reject that evil. And this is the ruin of those who are attached to the world. They live in darkness ; whence it happens that, not knowing the greatness of eternal good and evil, and allured by the senses, they give themselves up to forbidden pleasure and miserably perish.

Wherefore the Holy Ghost admonishes us that in order to avoid sin, we must keep before our eyes the last things which are to come upon us; that is, death, with which all the goods of this earth will come to an end for us, and the divine judgment, in which we shall have to give an account of our whole life. *Remember thy last end, and thou shalt never sin.*[1] And in another place he says,

---

[1] "Memorare novissima tua, et in æternum non peccabis."—*Ecclus.* vii. 40.

Oh, that they would be wise and would understand, and would provide for their last end.[1] By which words he wishes to give us to understand that if men would consider the things of the other life, they would all certainly take care to sanctify themselves, and would not expose themselves to the danger of an unhappy life through all eternity. They shut their eyes to the light and thus, remaining blind, precipitate themselves into so great evils. For this reason the saints always prayed the Lord to give them light. *Enlighten my eyes, that I never sleep in death.*[2] *May God cause the light of His countenance to shine upon us.*[3] *Make the way known to me wherein I should walk.*[4] *Give me understanding and I will learn Thy command-ments.*[5]

But to obtain this divine light, we must go near to God. *Come ye to Him and be enlightened.*[6] "For," says St. Augustine, "as we cannot see the sun without the light of the sun itself, so we cannot see the light of God but by the light of God himself."[7] This light is obtained in the spiritual exercises; by them we approach to God, and God enlightens us with his light. The spiritual exercises mean nothing else than that we retire for that time from intercourse with the world, and go to converse with God alone, where God speaks to us by his inspira-tions, and we speak to God in our meditations by acts of love, by repenting of our sins by which we have displeased

---

[1] "Utinam saperent, et intelligerent, ac novissima providerent!"— *Deut.* xxxii. 29.

[2] "Illumina oculos meos, ne unquam obdormiam in morte."—*Ps.* xii. 4.

[3] "Deus illuminet vultum suum super nos."—*Ps.* lxvi. 2.

[4] "Notam fac mihi viam, in qua ambulem."—*Ps.* cxlii. 8.

[5] "Da mihi intellectum, et discam mandata tua."—*Ps.* cxviii. 73.

[6] "Accedite ad eum, et illuminamini."—*Ps.* xxxiii. 6.

[7] "Sicut solem non videt oculus. nisi in lumine solis, sic lumen verum et divinum non poterit intelligentia videre, nisi in ipsius lumine."—*De Sp. et An.* c. 12.

him, by offering ourselves to serve him for the future with all our heart, and by beseeching him to make known to us his will, and to give us strength to accomplish it.

Holy Job says, *Now I should have rest in my sleep with kings and consuls of the earth, who build themselves solitudes.*[1] Who are those kings that build themselves solitudes? They are, as St. Gregory says, those despisers of the world, who go from its tumults to render themselves fit to talk alone with God. "They build solitudes, that is, they separate themselves as far as possible from the tumult of the world, in order to be alone and to become fit to speak with God."[2]

When Arsenius was reflecting on the means that he should take to become a saint, God caused him to hear these words: "Fly, be silent, and rest."[3] Fly from the world, be silent, cease to talk with men, and talk alone with me, and thus rest in peace and solitude. In conformity with this, St. Anselm wrote to one worried by many worldly occupations, who complained that he had no moment of peace, the following advice: "Leave a little your occupations; hide yourself for a while from your tumultuous thoughts; apply yourself a little to contemplate God and rest in him; say to God, Now teach my heart where and how I may seek Thee, where and how I shall find Thee."[4] Words that are applicable each and all to yourself. Fly, says he, for a short time from those earthly occupations which render you so unquiet, and

---

[1] "Nunc enim . . . requiescerem cum regibus et consulibus terræ, qui ædificant sibi solitudines."—*Job*, iii. 13.

[2] "Ædificant solitudines, id est, se ipsos a tumultu mundi quantum possunt, elongant, ut soli sint, et idonei loqui cum Deo."—*In Job, loc. cit.*

[3] "Fuge, tace, quiesce."

[4] "Fuge paululum occupationes terrenas, absconde te modicum a tumultuosis cogitationibus tuis; vaca aliquantulum Deo, et requiesce in eo. Dic Deo: Eia, nunc doce cor meum, ubi et quomodo te quærat, ubi et quomodo te inveniat."—*Medit.* 21.

rest in retirement with God ; say to him, O Lord, show me where and how I may find Thee, that I may speak alone to Thee, and at the same time hear Thy words.

God speaks indeed to those who seek him, but he does not speak in the midst of the tumult of the world. *The Lord is not in the commotion of the earthquake,*[1] as was said to Elias, when God called him to solitude. The voice of God, as it is said in the same place, is as *the whistling of a gentle air,*[2] which is scarcely heard, not, however, by the ear of the body, but by that of the heart, without noise and in a sweet rest. This is exactly what the Lord says through Osee: *I will lead her into solitude, and I will speak to her heart.*[3] When the Lord wishes to draw a soul to himself, he leads it into solitude, far from the embarrassment of the world and intercourse with men, and there speaks to it with words of fire.[4] The words of God are said to be of fire, because they melt a soul, as the sacred Spouse says: *My soul melted, when He* (my Beloved) *spoke.*[5] In fact, they prepare the soul to submit readily to the direction of God, and to take that form of life which God wishes it to take; they are words exceedingly efficacious, and so efficient that at the very time they are heard they operate in the soul that which God requires of it.

One day the Lord said to St. Teresa: "Oh, how willingly would I speak to many souls, but the world makes so great a noise in their hearts that my voice cannot be heard ! Oh, if they would but separate themselves a little from the world!" Thus, then, my very dear friend, the Lord wishes to speak to you, but alone and in soli-

---

[1] "Non in commotione Dominus."—3 *Kings,* xix. 11.

[2] "Sibilus auræ tenuis."—*Ibid.*

[3] "Ducam eam in solitudinem, et loquar ad cor ejus."—*Os.* ii. 14.

[4] "Ignitum eloquium tuum."—*Ps.* cxviii. 140.

[5] "Anima mea liquefacta est, ut (Dilectus meus) locutus est."—*Cant.* v. 6.

tude; since if he should speak to you in your own house, your parents, your friends, and your domestic occupations would continue to make a noise in your heart, and you would be unable to hear his voice. The saints have for this reason left their homes and their country, and gone to hide themselves in caverns or deserts, or at least in a cell of a religious house, there to find God and hear his words. St. Eucherius[1] relates that a certain person seeking a place in which he could find God, went for this purpose to ask counsel from a master of the spiritual life. The man of God led him to a solitary place and then said: " Behold, here God may be found," without saying anything more. By this he wished to give him to understand that God is not to be found in the midst of the noise of the world, but in solitude. St. Bernard says that he learned to know God among the beech-trees and oaks better than in all the learned books he had read.

The inclination of worldlings is to be in company with friends, to talk and divert themselves; but the desire of the saints is to be in solitary places, in the midst of forests, or in caverns, there to converse alone with God, who in solitude familiarly converses with souls, as a friend with his friend. " Oh, solitude !" exclaims St. Jerome, " in which God familiarly converses with his servants."[2] The Venerable Vincent Caraffa said that if it had been free to him to wish for anything in this world, he would have asked for nothing but a little grotto with a piece of bread and a spiritual book; there always to live far from men and conversing alone with God. The Spouse of the Canticles, praising the beauty of a soul living in solitude, compares it to the beauty of the turtle-dove: *Thy cheeks are beautiful as the turtle-dove's.*[3]

[1] *Epist. ad Hilar.*

[2] "O solitudo, in qua Deus cum suis familiariter loquitur et conversatur!"

[3] " Pulchræ sunt genæ tuæ sicut turturis."—*Cant.* i. 9.

Precisely because the turtle-dove avoids the company of other birds, and always lives in the most solitary places. Hence it is that the holy angels admire with joy the beauty and splendor which embellish on its flight to heaven a soul, that in this life has lived hidden and solitary as in a desert: *Who is this that cometh up from the desert, flowing with delights?* [1]

I have wished to write all these things to you in order to inspire you with a love for holy solitude, for I hope that in the exercises which you will perform, you will not have to torture your brains, as your pastor said, but that the Lord will make you taste so great a spiritual delight, that you will come out of your retreat with such an affection for them that you will not fail hereafter to go through them every year; a thing which will be of immense advantage to your soul, whatever state of life you may choose, because in the midst of the world, the various occupations, disturbances, and distractions always produce dryness of spirit, so that it is necessary from time to time to irrigate, as it were, and renew it, as St. Paul exhorts: *Be ye renewed in the spirit of your mind.* [2]

King David, troubled by earthly cares, wished to have wings and to fly away from the bustle of the world in order to find rest: *Who will give me wings, and I will fly away, and be at rest?* [3] But being unable to leave the world with his body, he at least sought from time to time to disengage himself from the affairs of the realm he governed, and dwell in solitude conversing with God, and thus his spirit found peace. *I have gone far off flying away, and I abode in the wilderness.* [4]

---

[1] " Quæ est ista quæ ascendit de deserto, deliciis affluens?"—*Cant.* viii. 5.

[2] "Renovamini autem spiritu mentis vestræ."—*Ephes.* iv. 23.

[3] "Quis dabit mihi pennas, sicut columbæ, et volabo et requiescam?"—*Ps.* liv. 7.

[4] "Ecce, elongavi fugiens, et mansi in solitudine."—*Ibid.* v. 8.

Jesus Christ also, who had no need of solitude to be recollected and united with God, but wished to set us an example, often retired from intercourse with man and went away to mountains or into deserts to pray: *Having dismissed the multitude, He went into a mountain alone to pray;*[1] and *He retired into a desert and prayed.*[2] And he desired that his disciples, after the fatigue of their missions, should retire to some solitary place to rest in spirit: *Come apart into a desert place and rest a little;*[3] declaring by this that the spirit, even amidst spiritual occupations, being obliged to treat with men, becomes somewhat relaxed, whence it becomes necessary to renew it in solitude.

Worldlings, who are accustomed to divert themselves in conversations, at banquets and plays, believe that in solitude, where no such things are found, one must suffer an insupportable tediousness. This is really the case with those who have a conscience defiled by sin; for when they are occupied in the affairs of this world, they do not think of the things of the soul; but when they are disengaged and in solitude, as they do not seek God, they feel at once the remorse of their conscience, and thus find not peace, but tediousness and pain. But give me one who seeks God; and he will find in solitude not tediousness, but contentment and joy. This the Wise Man assures us of: *For her* (wisdom's) *conversation hath no bitterness, nor her company any tediousness, but joy and gladness.*[4] Oh no! to converse with God causes no bitterness, no tediousness, but joy and peace.

[1] "Dimissa turba, ascendit in montem solus orare."—*Matt.* xiv. 23.

[2] "Ipse autem secedebat in desertum, et orabat."—*Luke*, v. 16.

[3] "Venite seorsum in desertum locum, et requiescite pusillum."—*Mark*, vi. 31.

[4] "Non enim habet amaritudinem conversatio illius, nec tædium convictus illius, sed lætitiam et gaudium."—*Wisd.* viii. 16.

The venerable Cardinal Bellarmine used, during the season, when the other cardinals went to divert themselves in country-seats and villas, to go to some solitary house to make the exercises during a month, and these he called his country diversions, and certainly his heart found more delight in them than all the others did in their amusements.

St. Charles Borromeo made the exercises every year and found in them his paradise on earth; and it was whilst he was one year engaged in these exercises on Mount Varalla that his last illness came upon him and brought him to his blessed end. For this reason St. Jerome says that solitude was a paradise which he had discovered on earth: " Solitude is a paradise to me." [1]

But, perhaps, some one will say, What contentment can a person find, being alone and having no one to converse with ? St. Bernard answers, " He who seeks God is by no means alone in solitude, for God himself is there with him, and renders him more content than if he had the company of the first princes of the world." " I was never less alone," writes the holy abbot, " than when I was alone." [2]

The prophet Isaias, describing the sweetness which God gives those to taste who go to seek him in solitude, says: *The Lord therefore will comfort Sion, and will comfort all the ruins thereof; and He will make her desert as a place of pleasure, and her wilderness as the garden of the Lord. Joy and gladness shall be found therein, thanksgiving and the voice of praise.* [3] The Lord well knows how to comfort a soul who retires from the world; he recom-

---

[1] " Solitudo mihi paradisus est."—*Epist. ad Rust.*

[2] " Nunquam minus solus, quam cum solus."—*De Vita sol.*

[3] " Consolabitur Dominus Sion, et consolabitur omnes ruinas ejus: et ponet desertum ejus quasi delicias, et solitudinem ejus quasi hortum Domini: gaudium et lætitia invenietur in ea, gratiarum actio et vox laudis."—*Isa.* li. 3.

penses a thousand-fold all the pleasures of the world it foregoes, and makes solitude become for it a garden of delight, where all the tumult of the world being excluded and there being only thanksgiving and praise to that God who treats it so lovingly, it finds a peace that satiates it. If there were no other contentment in solitude than that of knowing the eternal truths, this alone should be sufficient to induce us to desire it. Divine truth, when known, truly satiates the soul, and not the vanities of the world, which are but lying and deceitful things; and this is precisely that great delight which is found in the exercises made in solitude and silence. In them we see in their purest light the Christian maxims, the importance of eternal salvation, the ugliness of sin, the value of grace, the love of God towards us, the vanity of the goods of this world, and the foolishness of those who, in order to acquire them, lose eternal goods and prepare for themselves an eternity of pains. Whence it happens that man, at the sight of these truths, takes the most efficacious means to secure his eternal salvation, and rises above himself, as Jeremiah says: *He shall sit solitary and hold his peace, because he raised himself above himself.*[1] There man disengages himself from earthly affections, and unites himself to God in prayer, by the desire of belonging to him altogether, by offering himself to him, and by other repeated acts of sorrow, love, and resignation, and thus finds himself raised so high above all created things that he laughs at those who so much prize the goods of this world which he despises, knowing them to be too little and too unworthy of the love of a heart created to love the infinite good, which is God.

It is certain that he who comes out of the exercises, comes out of them much changed and better than he

[1] " Sedebit solitarius et tacebit, quia levavit se supra se."—*Lam.* iii. 28.

was when he began them. It was the sentiment of St. John Chrysostom that retirement is a great help towards the acquisition of perfection.[1] Therefore a learned author speaking of the exercises, writes thus : "Happy the man whom Christ leads from the noise of the world to the spiritual exercises, and into the solitude filled with heavenly sweetness."[2] Happy indeed is the man who, flying from the tumult of the world, lets the Lord lead him to the spiritual exercises, where he enjoys a solitude which gives him a foretaste of the delights of paradise. The sermons preached in churches are good ; but if the hearers do not apply themselves to reflect on them, little will be the fruit they will derive from them. Our reflections on them will never be made as they ought, if we do not make them in solitude. The sea-shell, after having received the dew of heaven, suddenly shuts itself and goes down to the bottom of the sea, and there the pearl is formed. It is an undoubted fact that what makes the fruit of the exercises perfect is the reflecting in silence (treating alone with God) on the truths heard in the sermon or read in a book. Therefore St. Vincent of Paul, in the missions he gave, always invited the hearers to perform the exercises, retired in some solitary place. One single holy maxim, well ruminated, is sufficient to make a saint. St. Francis Xavier left the world in consequence of the impression made on him by that sentence of the Gospel : " *What doth it profit a man, if he gain the whole world and suffer the loss of his own soul ?* "[3] A certain student in consequence of one single sentiment on death, suggested to him by a good religious, changed his bad life and became virtuous. St. Clement of Ancyra was

[1] " Ad adipiscendam perfectionem, magnum in secessu subsidium."
[2] " Felix homo, quem Christus e mundi strepitu in spiritualia exercitia et solitudinem cœlesti amœnitate florentem inducit."
[3] " Quid prodest homini, si mundum universum lucretur, animæ vero suæ detrimentum patiatur ?"—*Matt.* xvi. 26.

encouraged by another consideration on eternity suggested to him by his mother, namely, "The thing we contend for is life eternal,"[1] and joyously suffered for Jesus Christ many torments inflicted on him by the tyrant.

To conceive, then, a just idea of the fruit which the exercises produce when performed in solitude, read a book on this subject, if you have one, and see there the stupendous conversions occasioned by them. I will here mention a few.

Father Maffei relates that there was in Sienna a priest who gave public scandal. This priest having made the exercises with a missionary who passed by accident through Sienna, was not only converted and made a good confession, but on a certain day, whilst a great number of people was present in the church, he went into the pulpit weeping and having a cord round his neck, and asked pardon for all the scandals he had given, and after this he went away to become a Capuchin and died as a saint. On his death-bed he confessed that for all the graces he had received he was indebted to those spiritual exercises.

Moreover, Father Bartoli relates of a certain German knight who had given himself up to all kinds of vice, so far as to give his soul to the devil by a written contract signed with his own blood, that, having afterwards performed the exercises, he conceived so great a sorrow for his sins that he fainted several times, and thenceforth he continued to lead a penitential life as long as he lived.

F. Rossignoli relates that, in Sicily, a son of a certain Baron became so debauched that his father, after having tried without effect many means to correct him, was obliged to put him in chains in a galley with the slaves. But a certain good religious, moved by compassion, went

" Negotium pro quo contendimus, vita æterna est."

to see him, and by his winning manners and good advice induced him to meditate on certain eternal truths in the galley where he was confined. The young man having done so, wished to make a general confession, and showed such a change in his conduct that his father with much joy received him again into his house, and never afterwards had any reason to be displeased with him.

Another youth of Flanders, having made the exercises and being converted by them from a most wicked life he had been leading, said afterwards to his companions who were wondering at this : "You wonder at me, but I tell you that the devil himself, if he could make the exercises, would be brought to penance."

Another, a religious, but of so bad conduct that he had rendered himself insupportable to all, was by his Superiors sent to make the exercises. Being about to leave, he jestingly said to his friends, "Keep your beads ready to touch my body when I come back." But after the exercises he was so much changed that he became an example to all the other religious, who, seeing this change, wished to make them also.

Certain young men seeing other young men, their friends, going to make the exercises, wished to accompany them, not to profit, but to jest afterwards in their conversations about their devotions. But exactly the contrary happened ; for during the exercises they were filled with such compunction that they all began to sigh and weep, confessed their sins, and changed their lives.

I could adduce such facts by thousands, but I shall relate only one more, that of a nun in the monastery of Torre di Specchi in Rome, who pretended to learning, but led a very imperfect life. This nun began, though with a bad will, to assist at the exercises that were given in the monastery; but the first meditation she made on the end of man made such an impression on her that she began to weep, went to her spiritual Father and said to him " Father, I wish to become a saint, and this promptly." She wanted to say more, but the tears prevented her from speaking. Having then retired to her cell, she made a writing by which she gave herself entirely to Jesus Christ, and began to live a penitent and retired life, in which she persevered until death.

But when we see the esteem in which the exercises have been held by so many holy men, this, if we had no other reason, should be enough to make us prize them highly. St. Charles Borromeo, from the first time he made the spiritual exercises in Rome, began to lead a perfect life. St. Francis de Sales confessed that it was to the exercises he owed the beginning of his holy life. Father Louis of Granada, a holy man, said that his whole life would not suffice to explain the knowledge of heavenly things that he had received in making the spiritual exercises. Father Avila called the exercises a school of heavenly wisdom, and wished that all his spiritual children should go to make them. Father Louis Blosius, a Benedictine, said that we should give to God special thanks for having in these latter times made known to his Church this treasure of the exercises.

II.

But if the exercises are of a great help to persons in every state or condition, they are of an especial help to him who wishes to make the choice of the state of life he should embrace. For I find it stated that the first end for which the exercises were instituted was that of making the choice of a state of life, because upon this choice depends the eternal salvation of each one. We cannot expect that an angel from heaven should come to assure us of the state which, according to the will of God, we should choose. It is sufficient to place before our eyes the state we think of choosing, and then we ought to consider the end we have in view in that choice, and weigh all the circumstances of the case.

This is the principal reason for which I wish you to make the exercises in silence; namely, for making the choice of the state of life. When, then, you have entered upon the exercises, as I hope you will, I beg of you to follow the advice I am going to subjoin:

1. The only intention you should have in making these exercises is that you may know what God will have you to do; and, therefore, in going to that solitary house, say within yourself, *I will hear what the Lord God shall speak in me.*[1] I go to know what the Lord will tell me and what he wishes from me.

2. Besides, it is necessary that you have a determined will to obey God and to follow without reserve the vocation he will make known to you.

3. It is, moreover, necessary that you pray earnestly to the Lord, that he may make known to you his will, namely, in what state of life he wishes you to live. But remember that in order to obtain this light you ought to pray with indifference of mind. He who prays to God to enlighten him on his state of life, but does so without this indifference, and, instead of wishing to conform to the will of God, wishes rather that God should conform to his own will, is like a pilot who feigns to will, but indeed wills not that his vessel should advance, since he casts the anchor and then hoists the sail. God does not enlighten or speak to such a person. But if you will supplicate him with this indifference and the resolution to accomplish his will, he will make you see clearly the state which is best for you. And if you should then feel any repugnance to it, you ought to place before your eyes the hour of your death, and reflect which state you would in that hour wish to have embraced, and then embrace it.

[1] " Audiam quid loquatur in me Dominus Deus."—*Ps.* lxxxiv. 9.

4. Take with you to your house of retreat a book containing the meditations which are commonly made during the exercises; read these meditations and let them be instead of sermons, reflecting on them for half an hour, as well in the morning as in the evening. Take also with you the Life of some saint or some other spiritual books out of which to make your spiritual reading; and these ought to be your only companions in solitude during the eight days. It is also necessary, in order to obtain that light and to hear what the Lord will speak to you, to avoid every distraction: *Be still, and see that I am God.*[1] To hear the divine voice, we must cease all intercourse with the world. To a sick man no remedies will be of any use if he does not take them with the proper precaution, as avoiding exposure to the cold air, unwholesome food, or too much application of mind. In the same manner, in order that the exercises may be useful for the health of your soul, you must remove hurtful distractions, such as the receiving of visits from friends, messages from without, or letters which are sent to you. St. Francis de Sales, when he was engaged in the exercises, laid aside all the letters he received, and did not read them until after the exercises. It is also necessary to read no books of amusement, and not even of study; for then we ought only to study the crucifix. Therefore, have in your room none but spiritual books, and, reading in them, read not for curiosity's sake, but only for this one end,—namely, to decide on the state of life which God will make known to you as the one that he wishes you to embrace.

6. Moreover, it is not enough to avoid distractions from without, you must also avoid those from within, for if you should there deliberately allow your mind to think on the things of the world, or of study, or the like, the exercises and the solitude will be of little use to you. St. Gregory says, " What avails the solitude of the body

---

[1] " Vacate, et videte quoniam ego sum Deus."—*Ps.* xlv. 11.

if the solitude of the heart is wanting?"[1] Peter Ortiz, an envoy of Charles V., wished to go to the monastery of Monte Cassino, to make the exercises. Having arrived at the door of the monastery, he said to his thoughts what our Lord said to his disciples: *Sit ye here till I go yonder and pray.*[2] Thoughts of the world, wait here outside; having finished the exercises, I shall again see you, and we will again talk together. Whilst one is engaged in the exercises, one ought to make use of the time only for the good of his soul, without losing any moment of it.

7. I beg of you to recite during the exercises the following short prayer:

My God, I am that miserable one who in the past have despised Thee; but now I esteem and love Thee above everything, nor will I love any other but Thee. Thou wouldst have me belong entirely to Thee, to Thee I will belong entirely. *Speak, O Lord; for thy servant heareth.*[3] Let me know what Thou wishest from me, and I will do all; and let me especially know in what state Thou wishest me to serve Thee : *Make Thou known to me the way in which I should walk.*[4]

During the exercises recommend yourself also in an especial manner to the divine Mother Mary, praying her to obtain for you the grace perfectly to accomplish the will of her Son.

And do not forget, when you make the exercises, to recommend me to Jesus Christ, as I will not omit to do in a particular manner for you, that he may make you a saint, as I heartily wish. In which sentiment I sign myself to be your most devoted and obliged servant, etc.

---

[1] " Quid prodest solitudo corporis, si desit solitudo cordis ?"—*Mor.* l. 30, c. 23.

[2] "Sedete hic. donec vadam illuc, et orem."—*Matt.* xxvi. 36.

[3] "Loquere, Domine, quia audit servus tuus."—1 *Kings*, iii. 10.

[4] "Notam fac mihi viam in qua ambulem."—*Ps.* cxlii. 8.

HYMN.

"I will lead her into solitude, and I will speak to her heart."—Osee, ii. 14.

Fly hither from the storm that rages round ;
Fly, where true peace in solitude is found ;
Where cares and strife and worldly troubles cease,
Here I invite thee to repose in peace.
A gift awaits thee here : My light divine,
To loving souls so dear, on thee shall shine ;
Here thou shalt see how vile is all the earth,
How sweet My love to those who know its worth.

Then from My lips that sweet inviting word,
That bids thee love Me, shall by thee be heard ;
How much I always loved thee thou shalt see,
And how ungrateful thou hast been to Me.
Sweet contrite tears thy wounds of sin shall heal,
The ardor of My love thou then shalt feel.
And here I wait thee to bestow in love
A foretaste of the joys of heaven above.

Meditations for a Private Retreat of Eight Days.

INTRODUCTION.*

1. There can be no doubt that retreats made in community, in which meditations and instructions are given by the clergy, are very profitable; but for persons who desire to advance in divine love, one great means is to go through the same spiritual exercises in private retreats. It is in total solitude that God speaks most efficaciously to the souls of his beloved; and it is impossible for a Christian to make such retreats, and not, each time, come out a different man from what he was when he entered into them. The saints, in order the more to enjoy God, who in solitude communicates himself more familiarly to those who seek him, retired into caves and deserts. St. Bernard says that he learned more of divine things amidst the beeches and oaks of the desert than he ever learned from masters and from books. You may have the same desert, if you will, in your own house; strive to avail yourself of it for at least eight days. But others do not make such retreats. What then? If others do not make them, do you at least make them; and by so doing, you may induce others to follow your example. Such singularities are pleasing to God. No one, says St. Bernard, can become a saint, if he leads not a singular life in the practice of virtue and in the availing himself of the means of salvation: "That cannot be perfect which is not singular."[1]

[1] "Non potest esse perfectum nisi singulare."

* For a method of making a retreat, see Appendix at the end of this treatise.—ED.

It is necessary, in order to make these retreats in a proper manner, to relinquish, during the time, all temporal affairs and worldly thoughts; to keep silence as much as possible, and to remain only in the church or in your own house. You may, however, take a walk occasionally for the sake of recreation.

For the purpose of such retreats I here add the following meditations, which are not in the way of discourses, but only collections of eternal maxims, of devout sentiments and affections, in order that you may stay on any point from which the soul seems to derive most nourishment, without obliging yourself to read the whole meditation. Sometimes our Lord will enlighten you at the first or second sentiment that you read; if so, stop there, without going farther, in order that the mind and heart may find that on which to feed.

Take care not to enter into these retreats with an anxiety for sensible tenderness and devotion, but solely to learn and to accomplish what God desires of you. If you have purely this object in view, although you should experience nothing but tediousness and aridity, God will not fail to enlighten you and to inflame you with his holy love; and the greater your fidelity in desolation, the greater will be the divine graces with which your soul will be enriched.

As to the distribution of time and the different exercises, you may make use of the following, which every person may adapt to his circumstances.

In the Morning.—After rising, first meditation for half an hour. Recitation of the office. Preparation for Communion for half an hour. Communion, after which, an hour's thanksgiving, and during this time hear one or more masses. Work for half an hour. Spiritual reading for half an hour, to be followed by the second meditation. Particular examination of conscience, and dinner.

After Dinner.—Vespers and Complin. Second lecture of the Lives of the saints, for half an hour. Third meditation. Work for half an hour. Visit to the Most Holy Sacrament and to the Blessed Virgin.

In the Evening.—Fourth meditation for half an hour. The noting-down of resolutions. The Rosary. Supper. General examination of conscience. The Litany of the Blessed Virgin, and other vocal prayers.

FIRST DAY.

The Importance of Salvation.*

MEDITATION I.

Salvation is our only Business in this World.

I. Of all our affairs there is none more important than that of our eternal salvation, on which depends our happiness or misery for eternity.

One thing is necessary.[1] It is not necessary that we should be rich, honored, or in the enjoyment of good health, but it is necessary that we should be saved. For this end alone has God placed us in the world; and woe to us if we do not attain it!

St. Francis Xavier said that the only good to be obtained in this world is salvation; and the only evil to be dreaded, damnation. What matter if we are poor, despised, or infirm? If saved, we shall be happy forever. On the contrary, what does it avail to be great, or to be monarchs? If lost, we shall be miserable for eternity.

O God, what will become of me? I may be saved,

---

[1] " Porro unum est necessarium."—*Luke*, x. 42.

* We have divided these meditations into three points, according to the usual method of the saintly Author. Though these meditations have been composed for the time of a retreat, yet they may be used at any other time.—ED.

20

and I may also be lost. And if I may be lost, why do I
not resolve to adhere more closely to Thee?

My Jesus, have pity on me. I will amend my life.
Give me Thy assistance. Thou hast died to save me,
and shall I, notwithstanding, forfeit my salvation?

II. Have we already done enough to secure salvation?
Are we already secure of not falling into hell?

What shall a man give in exchange for his soul? [1] If he
lose his soul, what will compensate him for its loss?

What have not the saints done to secure their salvation? How many kings and queens have renounced
their kingdoms and shut themselves up in cloisters!
How many young men have left their country, and have
gone to live in deserts! How many young virgins have
renounced marriage with the great ones of the world,
to go and give their lives for Jesus Christ? And what
do we do?

O my God, how much has Jesus Christ done for our
salvation! He spent thirty-three years in toil and labor;
he gave his blood and his life: and shall we, through our
own fault, be lost?

O Lord! I give Thee thanks for not having called me
out of the world when I had forfeited Thy grace. Had
I then died, what would have become of me for all
eternity?

III. God desires that all should be saved: "He will
have all men to be saved." [2] If we are lost, it will be
entirely our own fault. And this will be our greatest
torment in hell.

St. Teresa says that even the loss of a trifle, of an orna-
ment, of a ring, when it has happened through our own
carelessness, occasions us the greatest uneasiness. What

---

[1] "Quam dabit homo commutationem pro anima sua?"—*Matt.* xvi.
26.

[2] "Omnes homines vult salvos fieri."—1 *Tim.* ii. 4.

a torment, then, will it be to the damned to have wilfully lost all,—their souls, heaven, and God!

Alas! death approaches; and what have I done for life eternal?

O my God! for how many years have I deserved to dwell in hell, where I could not repent, nor love Thee! Now, that I can do both, I will repent and will love Thee.

MEDITATION II.

Damnation is an Irreparable Evil.

I. And how long shall we delay? Until we weep with the damned, saying, *We therefore have erred,*[1] and there is now no longer, nor will there ever be, any remedy for us?

For every other error in this world there is a remedy, but for the loss of the soul there is none.

What pains and trouble do men take to obtain wealth, dignities, or pleasures! But what do they do to save their souls? Nothing: as though the loss of the soul were but of little consequence.

How much diligence in preserving bodily health! The best physicians, the best remedies, the best climate are sought after. And as regards the health of the soul, what great negligence!

O my God! I will no longer resist Thy calls. Who knows but that the words which I am now reading may be my last call from God?

II. Can we be sensible of the danger of being lost forever and not tremble? and do we delay to apply a remedy to the disorders of our consciences?

My soul, how many graces has our Lord bestowed upon you that you might be saved! he has caused you to be born in the bosom of the true Church. How many

[1] "Ergo erravimus."—*Wisd.* v. 6.

advantages for becoming a saint! sermons, confessions, the good example of companions. How many lights, how many loving calls in spiritual exercises, in meditation, in holy Communion! How many mercies has he shown you! how long has he waited for you! how many times has he pardoned you!—graces which he has not bestowed on so many others.

What is there that I ought to do more for My vineyard that I have not done to it?[1] What more, says the Almighty, ought I to do for your soul? For how many years have you been in the world, and what fruit have you hitherto brought forth?

If we had been allowed to choose the means of salvation, what more easy and effectual means could we have chosen?

Alas! if we do not avail ourselves of so many graces, they will serve only to render our death the more miserable.

To become a saint it is not necessary to have ecstasies and visions; sufficient for you are the ordinary means which you possess. Meditate, communicate frequently, read spiritual books, fly all sinful occasions, and you will become a saint.

O God, already have I lived many years in the world, and what have I hitherto gained? O Jesus! Thy precious blood, Thy death upon the cross, are my hope.

III. If this night I were to die, should I be satisfied with my past life? No; and why do I delay? that death may arrive, and I may lament and say, Alas! my life is now at an end, and I have done nothing?

What a grace would it be for a sick man, already despaired of by his physicians, to be allowed another year, or even another month! And God grants me this time; and in what shall I employ it for the future?

[1] "Quid est quod debui ultra facere vineæ meæ, et non feci?"—*Isa.*
v. 4.

O Lord ! since Thou hast waited for me until now, I will no longer disregard Thee. Behold me; tell me what Thou requirest of me, and I will do it. I will not wait to give myself to Thee until that time when time for me will be no more. O Jesus ! I will nevermore offend Thee. I will spend the remainder of my life in bewailing my past sins, and in loving Thee, the God of my soul.

MEDITATION III.

We must, before all, secure our Salvation.

I. Let us proceed quickly, for death is at hand. What we can do to-day let us not put off till to-morrow. To-day passes on and returns not.

Every one says, at the hour of death, Oh that I had been a saint ! But of what avail will such regrets be, when the lamp will soon be extinguished for want of oil ?

We shall say when death comes, What would it have cost me to have avoided that occasion, to have borne with that person, to have broken off that correspondence, to have yielded that punctilio ? But I did not do so; and now what will become of me ?

O Lord, help me. I will say to Thee, with St. Catharine of Genoa, "My Jesus, no more sins, no more sins!" I renounce all things to please Thee.

II. Let us not think that we can do too much to gain eternal salvation. "No security can be too great," says St. Bernard, "where eternity is at stake." [1]

To secure our salvation, we must be resolved to adopt the means. Inclination will not be sufficient; nor will it serve us to say, I will do it by and by. Hell is filled with souls who said by and by, by and by. Death came in the mean time, and they were lost.

---

[1] "Nulla nimia securitas, ubi periclitatur æternitas."

The Apostle says, *With fear and trembling work out your salvation.*[1] He who trembles at the thought of being lost, always recommends himself to God, avoids the occasions of sin, and will be saved.

To be saved we must use violence. Heaven is not given to indolent cowards. *The violent bear it away.*[2]

O Lord! how many promises have I made Thee? but my promises have all been treasons. I will never betray Thee more; help me, grant that I may die rather than offend Thee.

III. *Ask*, says our Lord, *and you shall receive;*[3] by which he manifests to us his great desire that we should be saved. If any one should say to his friend, Ask of me what you please, he could say nothing more. Let us, then, ever pray to God, and we shall be enriched with graces, and secure of salvation.

My dear Jesus, cast Thine eyes on my miseries and have pity on me. I have been forgetful of Thee, but Thou hast not forgotten me. I love Thee, my love, with all my soul; I detest all the offences that I have committed against Thee above every evil. Pardon me, my God, and forget my many ingratitudes. And since Thou knowest my weakness, do not abandon me; enlighten me, and strengthen me to conquer all things to please Thee. Grant that I may forget all, that I may think only of Thy love, and the mercies by which Thou hast so powerfully obliged me to love Thee. Mary, Mother of God, pray to Jesus for me.

[1] "Cum metu et tremore vestram salutem operamini."—*Phil.* ii. 12.

[2] "Violenti rapiunt illud."—*Matt.* xi. 12.

[3] "Petite et accipietis."—*John*, xvi. 24.

SECOND DAY.

The Vanity of the World.

MEDITATION I.

The Goods of this World are False Goods.

I. *What doth it profit a man, if he gain the whole world and suffer the loss of his own soul.*[1] O great maxim, which has conducted so many souls to heaven, and bestowed so many saints on the Church! What doth it profit to gain the whole world, which passes away, and lose the soul, which is eternal?

The world! And what is this world but outside show a scene which quickly passes away? *The fashion of this world passeth away.*[2] Death approaches, the curtain falls, the scene closes, and thus all things come to an end.

Alas! at the hour of death, how will all worldly things appear to a Christian—those vases of silver, those heaps of money, that rich and vain furniture—when he must leave them all forever?

O Jesus! grant that henceforward my soul may be wholly Thine; grant that I may love no other but Thee. I desire to renounce all things before death tears me away from them.

II. St. Teresa says, " Nothing ought to be considered of consequence which must have end." Let us, therefore, strive to gain that fortune which will not fail with time. What does it avail a man to be happy for a few days (if anything can be called happiness without God), if he must be unhappy forever.

David says that earthly goods, at the hour of death,

---

[1] "Quid prodest homini, si mundum universum lucretur, animæ vero suæ detrimentum patiatur?"—*Matt.* xvi. 26.

[2] "Præterit enim figura hujus mundi."—1 *Cor.* vii. 31.

will seem as a dream to one waking from sleep: *As the dream of them that awake.*[1] What disappointment does he feel who, having dreamt that he was a king, on awaking, finds himself still lowly and poor as ever?

O my God! who knows but that this meditation which I am now reading may be the last call for me? Enable me to root out of my heart all earthly affections, before I enter into eternity. Grant that I may be sensible of the great wrong that I have done Thee, by offending Thee, and by forsaking Thee for the love of creatures. *Father, I am not worthy to be called Thy Son.*[2] I am grieved for having turned my back upon Thee; do not reject me, now that I return to Thee.

III. No posts of honor, no pomps, no riches, no amusements, no punctilios, will console a Christian at the hour of death; the love of Jesus Christ, and the little that he has suffered for his love, will alone console him.

Philip II., while dying, said, "Oh that I had been a lay brother in some monastery, and not a king!" Philip III. said, "Oh that I had lived in a desert! for now I shall appear but with little confidence before the tribunal of God." Thus, at the hour of death, do those express themselves who have been esteemed the most fortunate in this world.

In short, all earthly goods acquired during life, at the hour of death, generally end in remorse of conscience and fears of eternal damnation. O God! will the dying sinner say, I have had sufficient light to direct me to withdraw myself from the world, but yet I have followed the world, and the maxims of the world; and now what sentence will be pronounced upon me? He will say, Fool that I have been! I might have been a saint, with the means and advantages that I enjoyed! I might have led a happy life in union with God; and now what do I

---

[1] "Velut somnium surgentium."—*Ps.* lxxii. 20.
[2] "Pater, . . . non sum dignus vocari filius tuus."—*Luke,* xv. 21.

find from my past life? But when will he say this? when the scene is about to close, and himself about to enter into eternity, at that moment on which will depend his happiness or misery forever.

O Lord, have pity on me! For the past I have not been so wise as to love Thee. From this day forward Thou alone shalt be my only good : *My God and my all.* Thou alone deservest all my love, and Thee only will I love.

MEDITATION II.
The Goods of this World are of Short Duration.

I. Ye great ones of the world, who are now tormented in the flames of hell, what remains of your honors and riches? They answer, weeping, Nothing, nothing ; we have nothing but torments and despair. All is passed but our punishment, which will never end.

They will say, *What hath pride profited us? or what advantage hath the boasting of riches brought us? All those things are passed away like a shadow.*[2] Alas! the remembrance of the good things which we have enjoyed in this world will not, at the hour of death, inspire us with confidence, but will fill us with terror and confusion.

Woe to me! how many years have I been in the world, and what have I hitherto done for God? O Lord, have pity on me, and *cast me not away from Thy face.*[3]

The time of death is the time of truth : then do all worldly things appear as they really are,—vanity, smoke, and dust.

O my God! how frequently have I exchanged Thee for nothing! I should not dare to hope for pardon, were it not that Thou hast died in order to pardon me. Now

[1] "Deus meus, et omnia."

[2] "Quid nobis profuit superbia? aut divitiarum jactantia quid contulit nobis? Transierunt omnia illa tamquam umbra."—*Wisd.* v. 8.

[3] "Ne projicias me a facie tua."—*Ps.* l. 13.

will I love Thee above all things, and will esteem Thy grace of greater value than all the kingdoms of the earth.

II. Death is compared by St. Paul to a thief,[1] because it robs us of all things,—possession, beauty, dignity, parents, even of our own flesh. The day of death is called also *the day of destruction.*[2] Then shall we lose all that we have ever acquired, and all that we can hope for from this world. O my Jesus! I am not concerned about the loss of earthly goods, but only lest I should lose Thee, the infinite good.

We extol the saints, who, for the love of Jesus Christ, despise the goods of this earth; and do we continue to be attached to them at the imminent danger of our salvation?

We have a great esteem for the advantages of this life; and why do we make so little account of the advantages of eternity?

Enlighten me, O my God! and make me sensible that all creatures are nothing, and that Thou art my all, the infinite good. Grant that I may leave all things to gain only Thee. My God, my God, Thee only do I desire, and besides Thee nothing.

III. St. Teresa says that all our faults and attachments to the goods of this earth arise from a want of faith. Let us then reanimate our faith, that we shall one day have to leave all and to go into eternity. And hence let us leave all now, while we can obtain merit by so doing, which we shall one day be forced to leave. What are riches, honors, parents? God, God, let us seek only God, and God will be our all.

That eminent servant of God, Sister Margarite of St. Ann, daughter of the Emperor Rudolf II., and a discal-

---

[1] " Dies illa tamquam fur."—1 *Thess.* v. 4.
[2] " Dies perditionis."—*Deut.* xxxii. 35.

ceated nun, said, "What will kingdoms avail at the hour of death?"

The death of the Empress Isabella induced St. Francis Borgia to renounce the world, and to give himself entirely to God; at the sight of her corpse he said, It is thus, then, that the grandeurs and the crowns of this world terminate?

O my God! Thou hast always loved me! Grant that I may become wholly Thine before death overtakes me.

MEDITATION III.

Death discloses the Vanity of the World.

I. O the great secret of death! how does it destroy all worldly desires! how does it expose all worldly grandeur as smoke and deceit! Things the most desired of this earth lose all their splendor when beheld from the bed of death. The shadow of death obscures the beauty of all things here below.

Of what avail are riches when nothing remains but a winding-sheet? Of what avail is bodily beauty, when all is reduced to a heap of worms? Of what avail is authority, when nothing remains but to be thrown into the grave, and be forgotten by all?

St. Chrysostom says, "Go to a sepulchre, contemplate dust and worms; and sigh." Look on the graves of the dead; see those skeletons gnawed by worms and crumbling into dust, and say, with a sigh, Such must I become, and why do I not think of this? why do I not give myself to God? Alas! who knows but that the sentiments which I am now reading may be the last call for me?

My dear Redeemer, I accept of my death, and I accept of it in whatever way it may please Thee to send it to me; but I beseech Thee, before Thou judgest me, to allow me time to bewail the offences which I have committed against Thee. I love Thee, O my Jesus! and I am truly sorry for having despised Thee.

II. O God! how many miserable beings, to obtain worldly things, pleasures, or vanities, have lost their souls, and, by losing their souls, have lost all!

Do we believe or not believe that we must die? and that only once? And why do we not leave all, to secure a happy death? Let us leave all, to secure all.

Is it possible to know that the remembrance of a disorderly life will at the hour of death be an insufferable torment, and still continue to live on in sin?

O my God! I thank Thee for the light which Thou affordest me. But, O Lord! what have I done? Have I multiplied my sins, and hast Thou augmented Thy graces? Woe to me, if I do not avail myself of them!

He who reflects that in a short time he must leave the world will not be attached to it.

Oh, with what peace of soul do those live and die who, despoiled of all things, are contented to say, *My God and my all!*

Solomon said that all the goods of this earth are only vanity and affliction of spirit; since the more any one possesses of them, the more he suffers.

St. Philip Neri called those fools whose hearts are attached to this world. Fools, because even here they lead miserable lives.

O my God! what now remains of the many offences of which I have been guilty, but the pain and remorse which now torment me, and will torment me still more at the hour of death? Oh, do Thou make haste to pardon me. Thou desirest that I should be all Thine, and such do I desire to be. Behold, from this moment, I give myself to Thee, and I desire nothing in return but Thyself.

III. Let us not imagine that to be detached from all, in order to love only God, is to live a disconsolate life. Who on this earth is so contented and happy as the man that loves Jesus Christ with his whole heart? Find me one amongst all the kings of the world who is more happy than the soul that gives itself wholly to God.

My soul, if now thou wert to depart out of this world, wouldst thou die satisfied with thy past life? And for what dost thou delay? that the light which God in his mercy now affords thee may serve to reproach thee at the great accounting day?

O Jesus! I renounce all to give myself to Thee. Thou didst seek me when I fled from Thee; and now that I seek Thee, do not reject me. Thou didst love me when I did not love Thee, nor even desire that Thou shouldst love me: and now that I have no other desire but to love Thee, and to be loved by Thee, cast me not away from Thy face. O my God! I am now convinced that Thou desirest to save me, and I desire to work out my salvation to please Thee. I leave all, and give my whole self to Thee. Mary, Mother of God, pray to Jesus for me.

THIRD DAY.

Our Journey to Eternity.

MEDITATION I.

We are Travellers on this Earth.

I. *We have not here a lasting city, but we seek one that is to come.*[1] In this world we are not citizens, but pilgrims; we are on our way to eternity: *Man shall go into the house of his eternity.*[2]

Soon, therefore, must we be dislodged from this world. The body must soon go down into the grave, and the soul into eternity.

Would not that traveller be guilty of great folly, who

---

[1] " Non habemus hic manentem civitatem, sed futuram inquirimus." —*Heb*. xiii. 14.

[2] " Quoniam ibit homo in domum æternitatis suæ."—*Eccles*. xii. 5

should consume all he had in building himself a dwelling in a place which he must soon leave?

O my God! my soul is eternal; I must, then, either enjoy Thee or lose Thee for eternity.

In eternity there are two places of abode,—one overflowing with all delights, the other replete with every torment. And these delights and torments will be eternal. *If the tree fall to the south, or to the north, in what place soever it shall fall, there shall it be.*[1] If the soul go to the place of salvation, it will be happy there forever; but if it fall into hell, it will remain there to weep and lament as long as God shall be God.

There is no medium: either forever a king in heaven, or forever a slave of Lucifer; either forever blessed in heaven, or forever in despair in hell.

Which of these abodes will fall to the lot of each one of us? That which each one voluntarily chooses. *Man shall go.*[2] He who goes to hell, goes of his own accord. Every one that is damned, is damned because he wills his own damnation.

O my Jesus, would that I had always loved Thee! Too late have I known Thee; too late have I loved Thee, O Thou, *the God of my heart, and the God that is my portion forever!*[3]

II. Every Christian, in order to live well, ought always to keep eternity before his eyes. Oh, how well regulated is the life of that man who lives and sees all things in the light of eternity!

If heaven, hell, and eternity were doubtful things, surely we ought to do all in our power not to run the risk of being lost forever. But no; they are not doubtful things, but articles of faith.

[1] " Si ceciderit lignum ad austrum aut ad aquilonem, in quocumque loco ceciderit, ibi erit."—*Eccles.* xi. 3.

[2] " Ibit homo."

[3] "Deus cordis mei, et pars mea Deus in æternum."—*Ps.* lxxii. 26.

To what will all the fortunes of this world come? To a funeral, to a descent into the grave. Blessed is he who obtains eternal life!

O Jesus! Thou art my life, my riches, my love. Grant me a great desire to please Thee during the remainder of my life; and give me Thy assistance to fulfil it.

III. One thought of eternity is sufficient to make a saint. St. Augustine called it the "great thought." It is this thought that has sent so many young persons into cloisters, so many anchorites into deserts, and so many martyrs to cruel deaths.

Father Avila converted a lady who was attached to the world, by only saying, "Consider, *always, forever.*"

Oh, how much depends on the last moment of our lives! On our last breath depends an eternity, either of happiness or misery; a life of eternal bliss, or of eternal woe. Jesus Christ died upon the cross, in order to secure for us his grace at this last moment.

My dear Redeemer, if then Thou hadst not died for me, should I have been lost forever? I thank Thee, O my love! I confide in Thee, and love Thee.

MEDITATION II.

Folly of those who do not think of Eternity.

I. Either we believe or we do not believe. If we do not believe, we do too much for things which we regard as fables. But if we do believe, we do too little to obtain a happy eternity, and to avoid eternal misery.

Father Vincent Carafa said that if men thoroughly knew the truths of eternity, and compared the goods and evils of this life with those of the next, the world would become a desert, because there would be none that would attend to the affairs of this life.

When the last moment of life is near at hand, how shall

we tremble at the thought that on that moment will depend our eternal happiness or misery!

O God! months and years pass away; we are approaching eternity, and we think not of it! And who knows but that this year or month may be my last? Who knows but that this may be the last warning I may receive from God?

O my God! I will no longer abuse Thy graces. Behold me; make known to me what Thou wouldst have me do, and in all things I will obey Thee.

II. And why should we delay after so many lights and calls from God? Unless we desire to lament with the damned, saying, *The summer is ended, and we are not saved.*[1] Now is the time for reconciliation with God; after death no remedy will be left us.

With good reason did Father Avila say that Christians who believe eternal life, and live at a distance from God, ought to be shut up within an asylum as insane.

The business of eternity is indeed a great point. It is not whether we shall inhabit a house less commodious or lightsome; but whether we shall dwell in a palace of all delights, or in an abyss of the worst of torments.

It is whether we shall be happy with the saints and angels, or live in despair with the multitude of the enemies of God. And for how many years? For a thousand? No, forever, forever, as long as God shall be God.

If then, O God, I had died in my sins, should I have lost Thee forever? If as yet, O Lord, Thou hast not pardoned me, pardon me now, I beseech Thee. I love Thee with all my soul, and I am sorry above every other evil for having offended Thee. I will never lose Thee more. I love Thee with all my heart, and will forever love Thee. Have pity on me.

[1] " *Finita est æstas, et nos salvati non sumus.*"—*Jer.* viii. 20.

III. Upon many, during life, it makes little impression to hear of judgment, hell, or eternity. But in death, what dread and terror do these truths excite ! but, alas ! with but little fruit; because then they serve only to increase their remorse and confusion.

St. Teresa said to her religious, "Daughters, one soul, one eternity;" by which she meant that if the soul is lost, all is lost, and that the soul once lost is lost forever.

O Lord ! wait yet awhile, that I may weep for my sins. Too many years have I spent to Thy displeasure; the time which yet remains to me shall be given all to Thee. Accept of me, that I may serve Thee, my God, my God !

The Lord waits for us; let us highly prize the time which, in his mercy, he bestows upon us, that we may not have to regret it when it will be no more for us.

O God ! what would not a dying man give for another day, or even another hour ! but another day or hour, with his sound senses, for the time which remains to the dying is but little adapted to the settling of affairs of conscience. Giddiness of head, pains of body, oppressions at the chest, hinder the mind from doing anything in a proper manner. Then the soul, as it were, buried in obscurity, is alive to nothing but the distress which overpowers it, and which it cannot alleviate; it would that there were time, but sees that there is no more time for it.

At what hour you think not, the Son of Man will come.[1] God conceals from us the time of death, that we may always be ready. The time of death is not the time to prepare ourselves to give in our accounts, but the time when we should find ourselves prepared to do so. St. Bernard said, "In order to die well, we must be ever prepared to die."

---

[1] "Qua hora non putatis, Filius hominis veniet."—*Luke*, xii. 40.

21

O Jesus! too long have I offended Thee. It is surely now time that for the future I should prepare for death. I will no longer abuse Thy patience. I desire to love Thee with all my power. I have very much offended Thee; I desire now in like manner to love Thee.

MEDITATION III.

We must profit by the Time.

Oh, what a torment, to repent of our carelessness when there is no longer time to do what has been left undone!

St. Laurence Justinian says that worldlings, in death, will willingly give all their riches to obtain but one more hour of life. But it will be said to them, *Time shall be no more.*[1] It will be intimated to them to depart without delay: *Go forth, Christian soul, out of this world.*[2]

St. Gregory relates that a certain Crisorius, being at the point of death, cried out to the demons, "Give me time until to-morrow." But they replied, "Fool! thou hast had it, and why didst thou lose it? Now there is no more time for thee."

Ah, my God, how many years have I lost! The remainder of my time shall be entirely devoted to Thee. Grant that Thy holy love may abound in me, in whom sin has long abounded.

St. Bernardine of Sienna said that every moment of time in this life is as precious as God; because at every moment, by an act of love or contrition, we may acquire new degrees of grace.

St. Bernard says that time is a treasure to be found only in this life. In hell, the lamentation of the damned is: "Oh, if one hour were given us!"[3] Oh, if we had

---

[1] "Tempus non erit amplius."—*Apoc.* x. 6.

[2] "Proficiscere, anima Christiana, de hoc mundo."

[3] "Oh! si daretur hora."

but one hour in which to escape from eternal ruin! In heaven there is no weeping; but if the blessed could weep it would be at the thought of having lost, during their lives, portions of time in which they might have acquired higher degrees of glory.

My beloved Redeemer, I do not deserve Thy pity; but Thy Passion is my hope. Help me, therefore, and stretch out Thy hand to a miserable sinner, who now desires to become wholly Thine.

II. And who knows but that a sudden death may surprise us, and deprive us of all time for the making-up of our accounts? The many who have died suddenly did not expect so to die; and if they were in sin, what has become of them for all eternity?

The saints thought that they did but little, in preparing themselves during their whole lives to secure a good end. Father Avila, when it was announced to him that he was about to die, said: "Oh that I had but a little more time to prepare myself!"

And we, why do we delay? That we may make a wicked and miserable end, and leave to others an example of the divine justice?

No, my Jesus, I will not oblige Thee to abandon me. Tell me what Thou requirest of me, and in all things I will do it. Grant that I may love Thee, and I ask for nothing more.

III. *He will call against me the time.*[1] Let us tremble, and let us not so live that God may hereafter, as judge of our ingratitude, call against us the time which, in his mercy, he now bestows upon us. *Walk,* says our Lord, *whilst you have the light.*[2] *The night cometh when no man can work.*[3]

St. Andrew Avellino trembled, saying, "Who knows

---

[1] "Vocavit adversum me tempus."—*Lam.* i. 15.
[2] "Ambulate, dum lucem habetis."—*John*, xii. 35.
[3] "Venit nox quando nemo potest operari."—*John*, ix. 4.

whether I shall be saved or lost?" But so saying, he ever united himself the more closely to God. But we, what do we do? How is it possible that he who believes that he must die and go into eternity should not give himself wholly to God?

My beloved Redeemer, my crucified love, I will not wait to embrace Thee until Thou consignest me to death: from this moment I embrace Thee, I bind Thee to my heart, and leave all to love Thee alone, my only good. O Mary, my Mother, unite me to Jesus, and obtain for me, that I may never more separate myself from his love.

FOURTH DAY.

Sin.

MEDITATION I.

Malice of Mortal Sin.

I. What is mortal sin? According to St. Thomas and St. Augustine, *it is a turning-away from God;* an act of contempt for his grace and love; and a throwing-off of all respect for him before his face, by which the sinner declares, I will not serve Thee; I will do as I please, and it matters not to me if by so doing I displease Thee, and forfeit thy friendship.

To understand how great is the malice of mortal sin, we must first know what God is, and what man is who contemns him. Before God all the saints and angels are as nothing, and shall a worm of the earth have the insolence to contemn him?

But what more? Man by committing sin, not only contemns a God of infinite majesty, but a God who has so loved him as to die for the love of him. An eternity, therefore, would not be sufficient to bewail but one mortal sin.

He who commits it, dishonors God by preferring a

vapor, a fit of madness, a wretched gratification before him. A God so great! a God so good!

O Lord! if Thou hadst not sacrificed Thyself on the cross for the love of me, I should lose all hope of pardon; but Thy death gives me confidence. *Into thy hands I commend my spirit.*[1] I commend to Thee my soul for which thou hast been pleased to shed Thy blood and sacrifice Thy life; grant that it may love Thee and never more lose Thee. I love Thee, my Jesus, my love, and my hope. And how shall I ever be able, after having learned how much Thou hast loved me, to separate myself from Thee, my only good?

II. What an affliction is it to us to be injured by one for whom we have done much? God is not capable of grief; but could he grieve, he would die of grief and sorrow, at being despised by a creature for whom he has given even his own life.

O my accursed sins! a thousand times do I detest and abhor you: you have caused me to offend my Redeemer, who has so much loved me.

Unhappy souls, who are now confined in hell, you who, during life, said that sin was a slight evil, acknowledge now that all your torments are not equal to what you have deserved.

It must be that sin is a great evil, since God, who is mercy itself, is obliged to punish it with an eternal hell. But what more? In order to satisfy divine justice for sin, a God was obliged to sacrifice his own life.

O God, we know that hell is the most horrible punishment, and have we no fear of sin, which may cast us into hell? We know that God has died, in order that he might be able to pardon our sins; and do we continue to commit sin.

The loss of the least worldly good makes us uneasy

[1] "In manus tuas commendo spiritum meum; redemisti me, Domine."—*Ps.* xxx. 6.

and sad; and does the loss of God by sin fail to over-whelm us with affliction and grief for the remainder of our lives?

I give Thee thanks, O Lord! for having given me time to bewail my offences against Thee. O Jesus! I abhor them with the greatest hatred: give me still greater sorrow, still greater love, that I may lament all my sins, not so much on account of the punishments which I have deserved by them, as for having offended Thee, my most amiable God.

III. What disquiet and fears agitate a courtier who is afraid of having offended his prince? And do we, who know for certain that we have displeased God, and have for a time forfeited his friendship, live tranquil and without being in continual grief?

What care do not men take to avoid poison, which destroys the body? And yet what great negligence in avoiding sin, which is the poison of the soul, and robs us of God!

Let us not be ensnared to commit sin by that fraud of the devil, by which he suggests to us that we may afterwards confess it. Oh, how many has the enemy drawn into hell by this stratagem!

O my God! for how many years have I deserved to dwell in hell! Thou hast waited for me, that I may for-ever bless Thy mercy and love Thee. Yes, my Jesus, I bless Thee and love Thee; and I trust in Thy merits that I shall nevermore be separated from Thy love. But if after so many graces I should again offend Thee, how shall I be able to presume that Thou wilt not aban-don me, but again forgive me? Permit it not, O Lord.

MEDITATION II.

Abuse of the Divine Mercy.

I. God has pity on them that fear him, but not on them that despise him. To offend God because he shows mercy is to provoke him in the highest degree to chastise us.

Again, to offer an outrage to God, because God is forgiving, is to deride him; but *God is not mocked.*[1]

The devil will say to you: "But who knows? even with this sin it may be that you may still be saved." But meanwhile, if you sin, you yourself may condemn yourself to hell. Who knows? It may be that as yet you may be saved; but it may also be, and that more easily, that you may be lost. And is the affair of eternal salvation to be risked on a *who knows?* If in the mean time death should come upon you! if God should abandon you! What will become of you?

No, my God, I will nevermore offend Thee. How many are now suffering in hell for fewer sins than mine? I will no longer be devoted to self, but will be Thine and entirely Thine. To Thee I consecrate my whole liberty and will. *I am Thine; do Thou save me.*[2] Save me from hell, but first save me from sin. I love Thee, my Jesus, I will nevermore forsake Thee.

II. The holy Fathers say, that God has determined the number of sins which he will forgive each one. Hence, as we know not this number, we ought to fear lest at every additional sin God should abandon us. This fear—Who knows whether God will any more pardon me?—ought to be a great restraint upon us to keep us from again offending God: with this fear we should be secure.

And he who has been the more favored by God with his lights and graces ought to be the more afraid of being abandoned by him. The Angelic Doctor says that the grievousness of sin increases in proportion to the ingratitude with which sin is committed. Woe, then,

---

[1] "Deus non irridetur."—*Gal.* vi. 7.
[2] "Tuus sum ego, salvum me fac."—*Ps.* cxviii. 94.

to the Christian who, after having been enriched with the graces of God, offends him mortally!

O my Jesus, while Thou hast shown me numberless mercies, I have repaid them by multiplied offences! Thou hast bestowed favors upon me, and I, in return, have despised Thee! But now I love Thee with my whole heart, and I desire to make amends by my love for all the offences that I have committed against Thee. O do Thou enlighten and strengthen me.

III. "Sin," said Sister Mary Strozzi, "in a religious person, strikes heaven with horror, and obliges God to turn himself away."

He who has not a great dread of mortal sin is not far from falling into it. Hence it is necessary to fly from dangerous occasions as much as possible.

It is necessary also to fly from all deliberate venial sins. Father Alvarez said, "Little negligences, but voluntary, do not kill the soul, but they weaken it; so that, on occasion of a grievous temptation, it will not have strength to resist, and will fall." [1]

St. Teresa has written: "From known sin, however small it be, may God deliver us!" [2] Because, said the saint, a deliberate venial sin does us more harm than all the devils in hell can do.

No, my Jesus, no, I will no more offend Thee; neither in great nor in small things. Thou hast done too much to oblige me to love Thee. I desire rather to die than to give Thee the least offence. Thou hast not deserved it; but hast deserved all my love, and I desire to love Thee with all my strength. Give me Thy assistance.

[1] *De Perf.* l. 5. p. 2, c. 16.
[2] *Way of Perf.* ch. 42.

MEDITATION III.

Venial Sins.

I. Unhappily, venial sins are regarded as slight evils: but how can that be called a slight evil which is an offence against God !

He who commits venial sins without restraint says: I may do this and still be saved. But I say: by continuing such a course, you will not be saved; for, says St. Gregory: " The soul never remains where it falls, but always descends lower." St. Isidore[1] writes that he who makes no account of venial sins is permitted by Almighty God to fall into mortal sins, in punishment of his want of love. And our Lord himself said to the Blessed Suso, that those who make no account of venial sins expose themselves to much greater danger than they are aware of; because it thus becomes much more difficult for them to persevere in grace.

The Council of Trent[2] teaches that we cannot persevere in grace without the special assistance of God; but he is too undeserving of such special assistance who offends God by voluntary venial sins, without any thought of amendment.

Chastise me not, O Lord ! as I have deserved. Remember not the many offences which I have committed against Thee, and deprive me not of Thy light and assistance. I desire to amend, I desire to be Thine. O omnipotent God, accept of me and change me. This is my hope.

II. Our Lord said to Blessed Angela de Foligni, " Those who are enlightened by me to aim at perfection, but, debasing their souls, walk in the ordinary way, will be abandoned by me."

---

[1] *Sent.* l. 2, c. 19.　　　[2] *Sess.* 6, *can.* 22.

He who serves God, but is not afraid of offending him by venial indulgences, would seem to think that God is not worthy of being served with greater attention. He declares, in fact, that God is not deserving of so much love as to oblige us to prefer his pleasure to our own satisfaction.

Habitual defects, says St. Augustine,[1] are a kind of leprosy, which renders the soul so disgusting as to deprive it of God's embraces.

I am sensible, O Lord! that Thou hast not as yet abandoned me, as I have deserved; strengthen me, therefore, to shake off tepidity. I desire nevermore deliberately to offend Thee. I desire to love Thee with my whole soul. O Jesus! help me; in Thee do I confide.

III. St. Francis says that it is the devil's art to bind souls first with a hair, that he may afterwards bind them with a chain, and secure them. Let us therefore be on our guard not to be entangled by any of the passions. A soul that is entangled by passion is either lost, or in great danger of being lost.

"The devil," said Mary Victoria Strada, "when he cannot have much, is content with little, but by that little he gains much."

Our Lord declares that the lukewarm are loathsome and disgusting to him: *Because thou art lukewarm, . . . I will begin to vomit thee out of my mouth.*[2] This means abandonment on the part of God.

Tepidity is a hectic fever, which is scarcely perceived, but if neglected becomes fatal; inasmuch as tepidity renders the soul insensible to remorse of conscience.

O Jesus! do not cast me off, as I have deserved; look not on my ingratitude, but on the sufferings which Thou hast endured for my sake. I am sorry for all my offences

---

[1] *Serm.* 351, *E. B.*

[2] "Quia tepidus es, . . . incipiam te evomere ex ore meo."—*Apoc.* iii. 16.

against Thee. I love Thee, O my God! and from this day forward I desire to do my utmost to please Thee. O love of my soul! I have very much offended Thee; grant that for the remainder of my life I may very much love Thee. O Mary, my hope, help me by thy holy intercession.

FIFTH DAY.

Death.

MEDITATION I.

The Worldling at the Approach of Death.

I. We must die. Sooner or later we must die. In every age, houses and cities are filled with new inhabitants, and their predecessors consigned to the grave.

We are born but to die. However long our life may be, a day, an hour, will come which will be our last, and this hour is already determined.

I thank Thee, O God! for the patience with which Thou hast borne me. Oh that I had died rather than have ever offended Thee! But since Thou givest me time to repair what is past, make known to me what Thou requirest of me, and I will obey Thee in all things.

In a few years, neither I who write, nor Thou that readest, will be living on this earth. As we have heard the bell toll for others, so will others one day hear it toll for us. As we now read the names of others inscribed in the lists of the dead, so will others read ours.

In a word, there is no alternative; we must die. And, what is more terrible, we can die but once; and if once lost, we shall be lost forever.

What will be your alarm when it is announced to you that you must receive the last sacraments, and that there is no time to be lost! Then will you see your relatives and friends leave your room, and none remain but your confessor, and the servants to attend you.

O Jesus! I will not wait until death to give myself to Thee. Thou hast said that Thou knowest not how to reject the soul that seeks Thee: *Seek and you shall find.*[1]

Now, therefore, do I seek Thee; grant that I may find Thee. I love Thee, O infinite goodness! Thee alone do I desire, and besides Thee, nothing.

II. In the midst of his schemes and intrigues the man of the world shall hear it said to him: "Christian Brother, you are fatally ill, and must prepare to die." He would put his accounts in order; but, alas! the terror and confusion which agitate him render him incapable of doing anything.

Whatever he sees or hears adds to his fears and distress. All worldly things become to him as thorns; the remembrance of past pleasures, punctilios of honor, vanities, ostentation, friends who have withdrawn him from God, vain apparel, and all such things, alarm and torment him.

What will be his terror when he reflects: "In a short time I shall be no more; and I know not whether I shall be happy, or miserable, for eternity!" O God, what consternation will the bare words judgment, hell, eternity, strike into the souls of poor dying worldlings.

My Redeemer, I believe that Thou hast died for me. From Thy precious blood do I hope for salvation. I love Thee, O infinite goodness! and I am grieved for having offended Thee. O Jesus, my hope, my love! have pity on me.

III. Imagine to yourself a man seized with his last illness. He who but a little while ago went about slandering, threatening, and ridiculing others is suddenly paralyzed, and deprived of his strength and bodily senses, so that he cannot speak, nor see, nor hear.

Alas! the unhappy man thinks now no more of his engagements, or his schemes of vanity; the thought of

[1] 'Quærite et invenietis."—*Matt.* vii. 7.

the account which he must soon render to God alone
occupies his mind. His relatives, weeping, sighing, or
in sad silence surround him, and his confessor tries to
assist him.

Physicians consult together and increase his alarm.
In such a state, he thinks no longer of his amusements ;
he thinks only of the news which is brought him, that his
malady is mortal.

But there is no remedy ; in this state of confusion, in
this tempest of pain, affliction, and fear, he must prepare
himself to depart out of this world. But how is he to
prepare himself in so short a time ? His mind is almost
gone. But there is no remedy, he must depart. What
is done is done.

O God ! what will my death be ? No, I desire not to
die in so great uncertainty as to my salvation. I will
change my life. O Jesus ! help me, for I am resolved to
love Thee henceforward, with my whole heart. Unite
me to Thyself, and never suffer me to be separated from
Thee.

MEDITATION II.

Last Preparations.

I. If you were about to die, what would you not give
for another year, or another month ? Resolve, therefore,
to do now what you will not be able to do at the hour of
death.

Who knows but that this year, or this month, or even
this day, may be your last ?

You would not wish to die in the state in which you
now are ; and will you dare to continue to live on in the
same state ? You lament over those who die suddenly,
because they have no time to prepare themselves for
death ; and have you time, and will not prepare yourself ?

O my God ! I will not oblige Thee to forget me. I thank Thee for the mercies which Thou hast bestowed upon me ; assist me in my endeavors to change my life. I see that Thou desirest to save me ; and I desire to be saved that I may praise and love Thee for all eternity.

At the approach of death the crucifix will be presented to you, and you will be admonished that Jesus Christ must be your only refuge and consolation. To those who have had but little love for the crucifix, it will be a subject of fear rather than of encouragement. On the contrary, what a consolatiou will it be to those who have left all for the love of their crucified Jesus !

My beloved Jesus, Thou shalt be my only love in life and in death : *My God and my all.*

II. How are the dying, whose consciences reproach them, filled with terror at the sole mention of eternity ! Hence they will not hear anything else spoken of but their malady, physicians, and remedies; and if the affairs of their souls be mentioned, they soon grow tired, change the subject, and beg of you to let them rest.

The sinner will exclaim : "Oh that I had time to amend my life !" But it will be said to him,[1] *Depart out of this world.** "Call in additional medical aid," will he answer; "try other remedies." But of what avail will these be ? His hour is come; he must depart and go into eternity.

To him who loves God how consoling will it be to hear it said, *Depart !* He will not be terrified, but rejoice at the thought of being soon out of all danger of losing his sovereign and beloved good.

Let thy place be this day in peace, and thy abode in holy Sion.[2] What a joyful announcement to him who dies in a well-grounded confidence of being in the grace of God !

[1] " Proficiscere de hoc mundo."

[2] " Hodie sit in pace locus tuus, et habitatio tua in sancta Sion."

* This and the following texts are taken from the prayers of the Church for the recommendation of a soul departing.—ED.

O Jesus! in Thy precious blood do I place my hope, that Thou wilt conduct me into that place of peace, where I shall be able to say, My beloved God, I have now no longer any fear of losing thee.

Have compassion, O Lord, on his sighs: have compassion on his tears.[1] My God, I will not wait until death to bewail my offences against Thee ; I now detest and abhor them, and am sorry for them with my whole heart, and would willingly die of sorrow for having committed them. I love Thee, O infinite goodness! I desire to live and to die in sorrow and in love.

Remember, O Lord, he is Thy creature; not made by strange gods, but by Thee, the only living and true God.[2] O my God, Thou who hast created me for Thyself, cast me not away from Thy face. If I have despised Thee, I now love Thee more than myself, and I desire to love only Thee.

III. He who has had but little love for Jesus Christ will tremble at the appearance of the holy Viaticum ; but he, on the contrary, who has loved only Jesus, will be filled with confidence and love, when he beholds his Lord at hand to accompany him in his passage to eternity.

While Extreme Unction is received, the devil will remind the dying man of all the sins committed by means of the senses. Let us therefore be careful to bewail them before the approach of death.

When he has received all the sacraments, his relatives and friends will retire, and he will be left alone with the crucifix.

O Jesus! when all have abandoned me, do not Thou depart from me. *In Thee, O Lord, have I hoped, let me never be confounded.*[3]

---

[1] "Miserere, Domine, gemituum, miserere lacrymarum ejus."

[2] "Agnosce, Domine, creaturam tuam, non a diis alienis creatam, sed a te solo Deo vivo et vero."

[3] "In te, Domine, speravi; non confundar in æternum."—*Ps.* xxx. 2.

MEDITATION III.

The Agony of Death.

I. A cold sweat spreads itself over him, his eyes become dim, his pulse intermits, his extremities become cold, he stretches himself out like a corpse, and his agony begins. Alas! he is already rapidly passing away into eternity.

His breath fails him, his respirations become much less frequent, and death is near at hand. The priest lights a blessed candle and places it in his hand, and begins to repeat for him acts suitable for the soul's immediate departure. O light, enlighten now our souls, for then thou wilt be of but little service to us when the time has gone for repairing the evil which we have done.

O God! how will our offences and the vanities of this world appear by this last light?

The dying man expires; and in the same moment in which he breathes his last, time for him concludes and eternity begins. O moment which will decide our happiness or misery for eternity!

O Jesus! have mercy; pardon me and unite me to Thee, that I may not at my last moment be lost forever.

II. The soul being departed, the priest says to the bystanders, He is gone.—Is he dead? Yes, he is dead.— May he rest in peace. He rests in peace if he has died in peace with God; but if not, he will never enjoy peace so long as God shall be God.

As soon as he is dead the news spreads abroad. One says, He was a man of address, but not very devout. Another, Who knows whether he is lost? His relatives and friends, to save their feelings, will not hear him spoken of, and say to those who mention his name, "For pity's sake, do not mention him."

Thus, he who was the life of conversation becomes the

horror of all. Go into his house, he is no longer there; his room, his bed, his furniture, are divided amongst others. And he, where is he? His body is in the grave, his soul in eternity.

If you wish to see him, open that grave; he is no longer blooming and feasting, but a heap of corruption, in which are engendered multitudes of worms, which will soon eat away the lips and the cheeks, so that in a little while nothing more will remain of him but a fetid skeleton, which, in time, will fall to pieces, the head from the trunk, and the bones from one another.

See then to what this body of ours will one day be reduced, on account of which we so often offend God!

O saints of God! you remembered this, and kept your bodies in subjection by mortification; now are your bones venerated upon altars, and your souls are enjoying the sight of God, waiting for the day of final retribution, when your bodies will become your companions in glory, as they were formerly your companions in suffering.

III. Were I now in eternity, what should I not wish to have done for God?

St. Camillus de Lellis, looking on the graves of the dead, was accustomed to say: "Oh, if these were alive, what would they not now do for eternal life? And I who am alive, what do I do?"

O Lord! do not condemn me with the reprobate on account of my ingratitude. Others have offended Thee in the midst of darkness and ignorance, but I have offended Thee in the midst of light. Thou hast more than sufficiently enlightened me to know the wrong which I did in committing sin; and yet I closed my eyes to Thy lights, trampled on Thy graces, and turned my back upon Thee. *O Thou who art my hope, be not to me a subject of dread, in the day of affliction.*[1]

[1] " Non sis tu mihi formidini; spes mea tu in die afflictionis."—*Jer.* xvii. 17.

22

MEDITATION IV.

The Death of the Just.

I. *Precious. . . . the death of His saints.*[1] St. Bernard says that the death of the just is called precious, because it is the end of labor and the gate of life. To the saints death is a reward, because it is the end of sufferings, pains, struggles, and the fear of losing God.

That word *Depart*, which is such a terror to worldlings, alarms not the just; because to them it is not painful to leave all worldly goods, for God has been their only riches: nor honors, for they have despised them: nor relatives, for they have loved them only in God. Hence, as they frequently repeated in life, so now with re-doubled joy do they exclaim in death, *My God and my all.*

Nor do the pains of death afflict them; they rejoice in offering to God the last moments of life in testimony of their love for him, uniting the sacrifice of their lives to the sacrifice of Jesus Christ offered on the cross, for the love of them.

II. Oh, what a consolation for the saints is the thought that now the time is over when they might have offended God, and were in constant danger of losing him! Oh, what joy to be able then to embrace the crucifix, and to say, *In peace, in the self same, I will sleep and I will rest!*[2]

The devil will endeavor at that time to disquiet us by the sight of our sins; but if we have bewailed them, and have loved Jesus Christ with our whole heart, Jesus will console us. God is more desirous of our salvation than the devil is for our perdition.

Moreover, death is the gate of life. God is faithful, and will indeed at that time console those who have

---

[1] " Pretiosa . . . mors sanctorum."—*Ps.* cxv. 15.

[2] " In pace, in idipsum, dormiam et requiescam."—*Ps.* iv. 9.

loved him. Even in the sorrows of death he will bestow upon them foretastes of heaven. Their acts of confidence, of love of God, of desire soon to behold him, will begin for them that peace which they will enjoy throughout eternity. What joy, in particular, will the holy Viaticum afford to those who can say, with St. Philip Neri, "Behold my love, behold my love."

III. We ought therefore not to fear death, but sin, which alone makes death so terrible. A great servant of God, Father Colombiere, said, "It is morally impossible for one who in life has been faithful to God to die unhappily."

He who loves God is desirous of death, which will unite him eternally to God. It is a sign of but little love for God, not to desire soon to behold him.

Let us accept of the hour of death with the loss of worldly things. We may do this now meritoriously, but then, it must be done forcibly and with danger of being lost. Let us live as though every day were to be the last of our lives. Oh, how well does he live who lives always with the remembrance of death present to his mind!

O my God! when will the day arrive, in which I shall see Thee and love Thee face to face? I do not deserve it; but Thy wounds, O my Redeemer! are my hope. I will say to Thee with St. Bernard: *Thy wounds are my merits.* And hence I will take confidence, and will also say to Thee with St. Augustine: *Would that I may die, O Lord, that I may behold Thee!* [1] O Mary, Mother, in the blood of Jesus Christ, and in thy holy intercession, do I hope for salvation, and to come to praise thee, thank thee, and love thee forever in heaven.

[1] "Eia, Domine! moriar, ut te videam."—*Sol. an.* c. I.

SIXTH DAY.

Judgment.

MEDITATION I.
Particular Judgment.

I. Place yourself, in imagination, in the same situation in which you will be when dying and in your agony, when not more than an hour or less will remain for you. Imagine that in a very short time you will have to be presented before your Judge, Jesus Christ, to render an account of your whole life. Nothing will then so much alarm you as remorse of conscience. Put, therefore, your accounts in order, before the arrival of the great accounting day.

When you are on the point of entering into eternity, how will remorse for past sins, diffidence, increased by the suggestions of the devil, and uncertainty as to our future lot, cast us into a tempest of confusion and fear! Let us therefore now unite ourselves to Jesus Christ, and to Mary. that at that critical moment they may not abandon us.

How terrified shall we be at the thought, that in a few moments we shall be judged by Jesus Christ! St. Mary Magdalen of Pazzi, being ill, and being asked by her director why she trembled, answered: "How terrible is the thought of being obliged to appear before Christ as our Judge."

O Jesus! remember that I am one of those whom Thou hast redeemed with Thy blood. *We beseech Thee, there-fore, help Thy servants, whom Thou hast redeemed with Thy precious blood.*[1]

II. It is the common opinion among divines that in

[1] "Te ergo quæsumus, tuis famulis subveni, quos pretioso sanguine **redemisti.**"

the same place and moment in which the soul departs, it is judged by Jesus Christ. So that in that same moment the trial is gone through, and the sentence passed and put in execution.

O fatal moment, in which is decided the happy or miserable lot of each one for eternity !

The Ven. Father da Ponte, when he thought of judgment, trembled to such a degree as to shake the room in which he was.

O Jesus ! if now Thou wert to judge me, what would become of me? Eternal Father, *look upon the face of thy Christ.*[1] I sincerely repent of all the sins that I have committed against Thee: look on the blood, the wounds of Thy Son, and have pity on me.

III. The soul goes forth and leaves the body, but it is some time doubtful whether the person is alive or dead. While the bystanders are doubting, the soul enters into eternity. The priest, satisfied at length that the man is dead, sprinkles the corpse with holy water and repeats the prayer of the Church: "Come to his assistance, all ye saints of God; meet him, ye angels of the Lord."[2] But if the soul be lost, the saints and angels can no longer assist it.

Jesus will come to judge us appearing with the same wounds that he received for us in his Passion. These wounds will be a source of great consolation to penitents, who with true sorrow have bewailed their sins during life, but will be a source of great terror to sinners who have died in their sins.

O God ! how painful will it be for man to behold him for the first time as his indignant Judge ! It will be more painful than hell itself.

Man will then behold the majesty of the Judge: he will see how much He has suffered for the love of him;

---

[1] " Respice in faciem Christi tui."—*Ps.* lxxxiii. 10.

[2] " Subvenite, Sancti Dei; occurrite, Angeli Domini."

he will see the many mercies which He has exercised toward him, the many and great means which He has afforded him of gaining salvation; he will see the vanity of all worldly things, and the greatness of those which are eternal; he will see, in a word, all these truths, but without any advantage. Then will there be no more time to repair past errors. What is done is done.

My beloved Redeemer! grant that when I first behold Thee, I may see Thee with an appeased countenance; and for this end give me now light, give me strength to reform my life. I desire always to love Thee. If hitherto I have despised Thy graces, I now esteem them above all the kingdoms of the world.

MEDITATION II.

The Sentence depends on us.

I. What great consolation will he enjoy at the hour in which he is to be judged, who, for the love of Jesus Christ, has been detached from all worldly things, who has loved contempt, and mortified the body; who, in a word, has loved nothing but God!

What joy will he experience in hearing it said to him: " Well done, thou good and faithful servant; enter thou into the joy of thy Lord. Be glad and rejoice, for now thou art saved, and there is no longer any fear of thy being lost."

On the contrary, the soul which leaves this life in a state of sin, before Jesus condemns it, will condemn itself, and will declare itself deserving of hell.

O Mary, my powerful advocate, pray to Jesus for me. Help me, now that thou art able to help me. Then thou wouldst behold me perish and wouldst not be able to assist me.

II. *What things a man shall sow, those also shall he reap.*[1]

---

[1] " Quæ seminaverit homo, hæc et metet."—*Gal.* vi. 8.

Let us examine what things we have hitherto sown. And let us do now what we shall then wish to have done.

If now, within an hour, we had to appear for judgment, how much should we be willing to give to purchase another year? And in what shall we spend the years which remain for us?

The abbot Agatho, after many years of penance, when he thought of judgment, said, "What will become of me when I shall be judged?" And holy Job exclaimed: *What shall I do when God shall rise to judge? and when He shall examine, what shall I answer Him?* [1] And what shall we answer when Jesus Christ calls us to account for the graces which he has bestowed upon us, and for the bad use which we have made of them?

O God, *deliver not up to beasts the souls that confess to Thee.* [2] I do not deserve pardon, but Thou wouldst not have me lose confidence in Thy mercy. Save me, O Lord! raise me up from the mire of my miseries. I desire to amend my life, do Thou assist me.

III. The cause to be decided at the hour of death will be one that will involve our eternal happiness or misery. Hence we should be most careful in using our utmost endeavors to secure a favorable issue. Each one, considering this, should say to himself, So it is. Why, therefore, do I not leave all things to give myself entirely to God? *Seek ye the Lord, while He may be found.* [3] He who at his judgment after death loses God will never again find him; but, in life, he who seeks him finds him.

O Jesus! if hitherto I have despised Thy love, I now seek for nothing but to love Thee and to be loved by

---

[1] "Quid faciam, cum surrexerit ad judicandum Deus? et cum quæsierit, quid respondebo illi?"—*Job,* xxxi. 14.

[2] "Ne tradas bestiis animas confitentes tibi."—*Ps.* lxxiii. 10.

[3] "Quærite Dominum, dum inveniri potest."—*Isa.* lv. 6.

Thee. Grant that I may find Thee, O Thou the God of my soul!

MEDITATION III.

General Judgment.

I. O the folly of worldlings! I look forward to your appearance in the valley of Josaphet. There you will change your sentiments, there you will bewail your folly; but to no purpose.

And you, who are afflicted in this world, be of good heart. On that last day all your pains will be changed into the delights and enjoyments of paradise: *Your sorrow shall be turned into joy.*[1]

What a glorious appearance will the saints then make who in this world were so much despised! And what a horrible appearance will so many nobles, kings, and princes make, who will then be condemned!

My crucified and despised Jesus, I embrace Thy cross. What is the world, what are pleasures, what are honors? O my God, Thee only do I desire, and besides Thee, nothing.

II. What horror will the reprobate in that day experience at being separated from Jesus Christ by that terrible sentence, publicly pronounced: *Depart from Me, ye cursed!*[2]

O my Jesus! I also at one time deserved such a sentence. But now I hope that Thou hast pardoned me. Oh, do not suffer me to be any more separated from Thee. I love Thee, and hope to love Thee forever.

What joy, on the other hand, will the elect experience, when they hear themselves invited by Jesus Christ to partake of the bliss of heaven in those sweet words: *Come, ye blessed!*

My beloved Redeemer, I hope in Thy precious blood

[1] " Tristitia vestra vertetur in gaudium."—*John*, xvi. 20.

[2] " Discedite a me, maledicti."—*Matt.* xxv. 41.

that I also shall be numbered with these happy souls, and, embracing Thy feet, shall love Thee for all eternity.

III. Let us reanimate our faith, and reflect that one day we shall meet in that valley, and be placed either on the right hand with the elect, or on the left with the reprobate. Let us cast ourselves at the feet of the crucifix, and turn our attention to the state of our souls; and if we find them unprepared to appear before Jesus Christ, let us correct and amend them now, whilst we have time. Let us detach ourselves from everything which is not God, and unite ourselves to Jesus Christ as much as we are able, by meditation, the holy Communion, mortification of the senses, and, above all, by prayer. The use of these means which God affords us for our salvation will be a great sign of our predestination.

O my Jesus and my Judge! I do not desire to lose Thee, but to love Thee forever. I love Thee, my Lord, I love Thee; and thus I hope to be able to address Thee when I shall first behold Thee as my Judge. I now say to Thee: Lord, if Thou desirest to chastise me, as I have deserved, chastise me, but do not deprive me of Thy love; grant that I may always love Thee, and may be always loved by Thee, and then do with me what Thou wilt.

SEVENTH DAY.

Remorse of the Christians in Hell.

MEDITATION I.

For very Little have those in Hell damned Themselves.

I. The greatest torment that the damned will have to endure in hell will be, themselves ever preying on themselves by remorse: *Their worm dieth not.* Alas! what a cruel worm will it be to Christians who are lost, to think for how very little they have condemned themselves! Have we then, will they say, for such trifling, transitory, and poisonous gratifications, lost heaven and God, and condemned ourselves to this prison of torments forever?

We had the happiness of being of the true faith; but, forsaking God, we led miserable lives, to be succeeded by others still more miserable in this pool of fire! God favored us with so many lights, so many means of salvation, and we miserably chose to damn ourselves.

O my Jesus! thus should I now have been bewailing my misery in hell, if Thou hadst caused me to die when I was in sin. I thank Thee for the mercies which Thou hast shown me, and detest all the sins that I have committed against Thee. Had I been in hell, I could no longer have loved Thee; but since I can still love Thee, I desire to love Thee with all my heart. I love Thee, my God, my love, my all.

II. At present what does our past life appear, but as a dream, a moment? But what will a life of forty or fifty years appear to the damned, when, after hundreds and thousands of millions of years have passed away, they will find that their eternity is still to come?

What will those miserable pleasures for which they have sacrificed their salvation appear to them? They will say, "Have we, then, for these accursed gratifications, which were scarcely tasted before they were ended, condemned ourselves to burn forever in this furnace of fire, abandoned by all, for all eternity?"

III. Another subject of remorse will be the thought of the little that they were required to do in order to be saved. They will say, "Had we pardoned those injuries, had we overcome those human respects, had we avoided those occasions, we should not have been lost."

What would it have cost us to avoid those conversations? to deprive ourselves of those accursed gratifications? to yield that punctilio? Whatever they have cost us, we ought to have been willing to do everything to obtain salvation; but we did not do so, and now there is no remedy for our eternal ruin.

Had we frequented the sacraments, had we not neglected meditation, had we recommended ourselves to God, we should not have fallen into sin. We frequently proposed to do this, but we did it not. We sometimes began a good course, but we soon discontinued it; hence we are lost.

O God of my soul! how many times have I promised to love Thee, and again turned my back upon Thee? Oh, by that love with which Thou didst die for me on the cross, grant me sorrow for my sins, grant me grace to love Thee, and ever to have recourse to Thee in the time of temptation!

MEDITATION II.

The Christian in Hell had very Many Graces to save Himself.

I. What cruel swords will the lights, the calls, and all the other graces of God be to the damned! Of these they will say, "We might have been saints and happy forever in heaven; but now we must be forever miserable!"

The greatest torment of the damned will be to reflect that they are lost wilfully, through their own fault, notwithstanding Jesus Christ died to save them. "God," will they say, "gave his life for our salvation, and we fools wilfully cast ourselves into this furnace of fire to burn forever! Heaven lost! God lost! ourselves eternally miserable!"

Such will be the eternal lamentations of the damned.

O my God! despised and forsaken by me, grant that I may now find Thee whilst time yet remains for me. For this end, grant me, O my Redeemer! to share in that sorrow which overwhelmed Thee in the garden of Gethsemani for my sins. I am sorry above every evil for having offended Thee. Receive me into Thy favor,

O Jesus ! now that I promise to love Thee, and to love no other but Thee.

II. Represent to yourself a sick man in great pain and suffering, who has none to pity him, but many to load him with injuries, to reproach him with his disorders, and to scorn him with great bitterness. The damned are treated much worse. They suffer all kinds of torments, without the slightest compassion from any one.

But, at least, cannot the damned love God who justly punishes them ? Ah, no; while they know that he is sovereignly amiable, they are constrained to hate him. This is hell, not to be able to love the sovereign good, which is God.

If the damned could resign themselves to the divine will, as pious souls in their sufferings are now able to do, hell would no longer be hell. But no; the damned shall rage like wild beasts under the scourge of divine justice, and their rage shall serve but to increase their torments.

If, then, O Jesus ! I were in hell, should I be incapable of loving Thee and hate Thee forever ? And what evil hast Thou done me, for which I should hate Thee ? Thou hast created me, Thou hast died for me; Thou hast bestowed upon me many special graces: these are the evils which Thou hast done me. Chastise me as Thou pleasest, but do not deprive me of the power of loving Thee. I love Thee, my Jesus, and I desire ever to love Thee.

III. Think of the horror of a soul on its first entrance into hell. " Am I then," will it say, " really damned ? or am I mistaken?" It will think whether there can be any remedy; but will find that there can be none for all eternity.

Millions of ages will pass away, as many as there are drops of water in the sea, or grains of sand on the earth, or leaves upon the trees; and hell will still be hell, eternity will be still to come.

At least, will not the damned be able to flatter them-selves saying, "Who knows but that hell may one day have an end?" No, for in hell there can be no one *who knows*. The damned will be most certain that all the tor-ments which they suffer every moment will continue throughout all eternity. O God! is hell believed, and are there any that commit sin?

Greater will be the torment of those who have often meditated on hell, and yet by sin have consigned them-selves to its torments. Ah! let us not lose time, let us renounce all and unite ourselves to Jesus Christ. All that we can do to avoid hell will be but little. And let us tremble; he that trembles not, will not be saved.

O my Jesus! Thy precious blood, Thy death, are my hope. All others may abandon me, but do not Thou abandon me. I see that Thou hast not as yet abandoned me, since Thou still invitest me to pardon, if I will but repent of my sins, and still offerest me Thy grace and Thy love, if I will but love Thee. Yes, my Jesus, my life, my treasure, my love, I will ever bewail my offences against Thee, and will ever love Thee with my whole heart. My God, if I have lost Thee, I will lose Thee no more. Tell me what Thou requirest of me, and I will endeavor to comply with Thy will in all things; grant that I may live and die in Thy grace, and then dispose of me as Thou pleasest. O Mary, my hope, be thou my protectress, and suffer me not any more to lose God.

EIGHTH DAY.

Love for Jesus Crucified.

MEDITATION I.

Our Ingratitude towards Jesus Crucified.

I. O my Jesus! what greater proof of Thy love couldst Thou have given me, than the sacrificing of Thy life upon the disgraceful gibbet of the cross, to make satisfaction for my sins, and to conduct me with Thee into paradise.

He humbled himself, becoming obedient unto death, even to the death of the cross.[1] The Son of God therefore, for the love of man, obedient to his Eternal Father, whose will it was that he should die for our salvation, humbled himself to die, and to die on a cross! and are there those to be found who believe this and love not such a God?

O Jesus! how much has it cost Thee to make me understand that Thou ardently lovest me; and I have basely repaid Thee with ingratitude. Oh, accept of me now and suffer me to love Thee, since now I will no more abuse Thy love. I love Thee, my sovereign good, and desire to love Thee forever. Remind me continually of the pains which Thou suffered for me, that I may never forget to love Thee.

II. O God! the Passion of Jesus Christ is spoken of, and is listened to as though it were a fable, or the sufferings of some one unknown to us, and not at all belonging to us.

O ye sons of men, why do ye not love Jesus Christ? Tell me, what more could our blessed Redeemer have done to make us love him than to die in the midst of grief and torments?

If the vilest of mankind had suffered for us the torments which Jesus Christ has suffered, could we help giving him our affection and showing him our gratitude?

But, my Jesus, why do I speak of others and not rather of myself? What has hitherto been my ingratitude towards Thee? Alas, I have repaid Thy love only with offences against Thee!

Pardon me; for, from this day, I desire to love Thee,

---

[1] "Humiliavit semetipsum, factus obediens usque ad mortem, mortem autem crucis."—*Phil.* ii. 8.

and to love Thee much. I should be too ungrateful, if, after so many favors and mercies, I loved Thee but little.

III. Let us reflect that this man of sorrows, nailed to the disgraceful wood of the cross, is our true God, and suffers and dies there for no other motive but love for us.

Do we, then, believe that Jesus Christ crucified is our God, and really dies for us, and can we love anything but him?

O beautiful flames of love which consumed the life of my Saviour on Calvary! come and consume in me all worldly affections; cause me ever to burn with love for such a God, who was pleased to die and to sacrifice his whole self for the love of me.

What a spectacle, for the angels of heaven to behold the divine Word fastened to a gibbet, and dying for the salvation of us his miserable creatures!

O my Saviour! Thou hast not refused me Thy blood and Thy life, and shall I refuse Thee my affections? Shall I refuse Thee anything that Thou askest of me? No; Thou hast given Thy whole self to me, and I will give my whole self without reserve to Thee.

MEDITATION II.

The Love of Jesus for us demands our Love.

I. My soul, behold on Calvary Thy God crucified and dying; see how much he suffers, and say to him,

Why, O Jesus! why dost Thou so much love me, why art Thou so much afflicted and tormented on the cross? Oh, Thou wouldst be less afflicted if Thou didst love me less!

Ah, my dear Redeemer! what a multitude of sorrows, ignominies, and internal afflictions torment Thee upon the cross! Thy most sacred body hangs from three nails, and bears only on Thy wounds; the people who surround

Thee deride and blaspheme Thee; and Thy immaculate soul is internally much more afflicted than Thy body. Tell me, why dost Thou suffer so much? Thou answerest me: I suffer all for the love of thee; remember, then, the affection which I have borne thee, and love Me.

Yes, my Jesus, I will love Thee. And whom shall I love, if not God who dies for me? Hitherto I have despised Thee, but now my greatest grief is the remembrance of my offences against Thee, and I desire nothing but to be entirely Thine. O my Jesus! pardon me, and draw my heart to Thee; pierce and inflame it thoroughly with Thy love.

II. Let us consider how loving were the sentiments of Jesus Christ, with which he presented his hands and feet to be nailed to the cross, offering at the same time his divine life to his Eternal Father for our salvation. My beloved Saviour, when I think how much my soul has cost Thee, I cannot despair of pardon. However great and numerous my sins, I will not despair of being saved, since Thou hast already superabundantly satisfied for me. My Jesus, my hope, and my love, as much as I have offended Thee, so much will I love Thee: I have exceedingly offended Thee, I desire also exceedingly to love Thee; Thou who givest me this desire, help me.

Eternal Father, *look on the face of thy Christ.*[1] Behold Thy dying Son upon the cross; look on that livid countenance, that head crowned with thorns, those hands pierced with nails, that body all bruised and wounded; behold the victim sacrificed for me, and which I now present to Thee; have pity on me.

III. *He hath loved us and washed us from our sins in his own blood.*[2] Why should we fear that our sins will hinder us from becoming saints, when Jesus Christ has instituted

---

[1] "Respice in faciem Christi tui."—*Ps.* lxxxiii. 10.

[2] "Dilexit nos. et lavit nos a peccatis nostris in sanguine suo."—*Apoc.* i. 5

a bath of his own blood, to wash our souls from them? It is sufficient that we repent of them and desire to amend.

Jesus, on the cross, had us in his thoughts, and thence prepared for us all those graces and mercies that he now bestows upon us, with as much love as though he had had to save only the soul of each one in particular.

O my Saviour! Thou didst foresee upon the cross the offences which I should commit against Thee, and instead of punishments Thou didst prepare for me lights, loving calls, and pardon. O my Jesus! shall I ever again, after so many graces, offend Thee and separate myself from Thee? O my Lord! permit it not. Grant that I may die rather than not love Thee. I will say to Thee, with St. Francis de Sales, "Either to die, or to love; either to love, or to die." [1]

[1] *Love of God,* book 12, ch. 13.

23

HYMN.

To God the Creator.

Why didst Thou not create my soul
  From all eternity,
Since from eternity, dear Lord!
  Thou always lovedst me?

For then to Thee a grateful love
  My heart could have returned
From that first moment all unsought
  Thy love for me thus burned.

I pine not now for the delights
  Of paradise above,
But only to behold Thy face,
  And gaze on Thee with love.

I long to be forever fixed
  In that blest changeless state,
Where I might love Thee with a love
  Immeasurably great.

I look around,—amazed, I cry,
  Is it, alas! for this—
This lump of earth, this ant-hill vile—
  Men lose eternal bliss?

To suffer or to die, my soul!
  For if thou canst not gain
The battle to be fought on earth,
  In heaven thou canst not reign.

God sees me—and he is my judge;
  The sentence, heaven or hell;
And there where'er my doom decides,
  Forever shall I dwell.

VARIOUS PRACTICES.

I.

Rules for leading a Good Life.*

1. In the morning, on rising from bed, make the Christian acts. Every day make mental prayer for half an hour; read at least for a quarter of an hour some spiritual book. To hear Mass. To make a visit to the Most Blessed Sacrament and to the Divine Mother. To say the Rosary. And in the evening to make the examination of conscience, with the act of contrition, and the Christian acts, together with the Litany of the Ever-Blessed Mary.

2. To go to confession and Communion at least every week, and oftener if possible, with the advice of your spiritual director.

3. To choose a good, learned, and pious confessor, and to be directed always by him, as well in your exercises of devotion, as in all affairs of importance; and not to leave him without a good reason.

4. To avoid idleness, bad companions, immodest conversations, and, above all, the occasions of sin, especially where there is danger of incontinency.

5. In temptations, of impurity particularly, to sign yourself immediately with the sign of the holy Cross, and to invoke the most holy names of Jesus and Mary as long as the temptation lasts.

6. When you commit any sin, to repent of it at once, and resolve to amend; and if it is a grievous sin, to confess it as soon as possible.

7. To hear sermons as often as you can, and to belong

---

* These rules are a summary of the *Rule of Life*, which is found entire in Volume I., and abridged in Volume II.—ED.

to some confraternity, with no other end than to attend to the affair of your eternal salvation.

8. To fast in honor of the Ever-Blessed Mary on Saturday, and on the vigils of her seven feasts, observing some other corporal mortification, according to the advice of your spiritual Father; to make the novenas of the above-named feasts of Mary, as well as of the Nativity, Pentecost, and that of your holy patron.

9. In adverse circumstances, as in sickness, losses, persecutions, you must unite yourself in all things to the will of God, and be resigned; saying always, "This is (or has been) the will of God; may his will be done !"

10. To make the spiritual exercises every year in some religious house, or in some place apart; or at least to make them in your own house, applying yourself during those days as much as possible to prayer, spiritual reading, and to silence. And in the same way to make a day of retreat every month, by going to Communion, and by avoiding all conversation.

II.

Devout Acts to be made Every Day.

I adore Thee, my God, Most Holy Trinity, Father, Son, and Holy Ghost, three Persons and one only God !

I humble myself in the abyss of my nothingness to the will of Thy infinite majesty.

I firmly believe all that Thou hast deigned to make known to me by means of the Holy Scripture and Thy holy Church, because Thou hast said so; and I am ready to give my life a thousand times for this faith.

I place all my hope in Thee. Whatever good I may have, whether spiritual or temporal, either in this life or in the next, I hope for from Thee, through the merits of Jesus Christ, O God, my life and my only hope !

I love Thee, Infinite Goodness, with all the affection of my heart and of my soul, because Thou dost merit

all my love. I wish I knew how to love Thee as the
angels, the saints, and just men love Thee. I unite my
imperfect love to that which all the saints, Most Holy
Mary, and Jesus Christ, bear to Thee.

My God, because Thou art the supreme good, infinitely
worthy of being loved and served, I am sorry and repent
of all my sins, detesting them as much as possible above
every other evil. I resolve for the future rather to die
than to consent to anything that may give Thee the
slightest displeasure.

I offer Thee now and forever my body, my soul, and
all my senses and faculties, my memory, my understanding, and my will. Do with me, Lord, and with all that
belongs to me, what Thou pleasest. Give me Thy love
and final perseverance, and grant that in all temptations
I may always have recourse to Thee.

I resolve to employ myself entirely in those things
which are pleasing to Thee, being ready to suffer any
pain and labor in order to please Thee, saying always,
Lord, may Thy will be done !

I desire that all should serve and love Thee. I would
gladly spend my time in persuading all mankind to love
and honor Thy Majesty.

I offer to Thy Majesty all the works I shall ever do,
steeping them in the blood of Jesus, my Redeemer.

I intend to gain all the indulgences that I can in my
actions this day, and to apply them by way of suffrage
to the souls in purgatory.

I recommend to Thee all the souls in purgatory, as
also all sinners; enlighten and strengthen these unhappy
creatures, that they may know and love Thee.

I rejoice exceedingly that Thy happiness is infinite,
and will never have an end.

I thank Thee for all the graces and benefits that Thou
hast bestowed upon all mankind, but especially upon
me, who have been more ungrateful than others.

My beloved Jesus, I take refuge within Thy sacred wounds: do Thou there defend me this day, and forever, from all temptations, till Thou shalt grant me to see Thee and love Thee eternally in paradise. Amen. This is my hope, and so may it be.

III.

Spiritual Maxims for a Christian.

Of what use will it be to gain the whole world and to lose one's soul?

Everything has an end; but eternity has no end.

All may be lost, provided God be not lost.

No sin, however small, is a light evil.

If we desire to please God, we must deny ourselves.

That which is done for our own satisfaction is all loss.

In order to save ourselves we must be in constant fear of falling.

Let me die, so that I may please God.

The only evil that we ought to fear is sin. All that God wills is good, and therefore to be desired.

He who desires nothing but God is happy and contented with everything that happens.

I ought to imagine to myself that there are no others in the world but God and myself.

The whole world cannot satisfy our heart; God alone can satisfy it.

All good consists in loving God. And loving God consists in doing his will.

All our riches are in prayer. He who prays obtains everything that he can desire.

Let us consider that day lost on which we omit our mental prayer. "He who leaves off praying," says St. Teresa, "casts himself into hell of his own accord."

Let us not pass a day without reading some spiritual book.

Points of honor are the plague of spirituality.

To be humble of heart, and not merely in word, it is not sufficient to say that we are deserving of all contempt, but we must also be glad when we are despised. And what has a Christian learnt to do, if he cannot suffer an affront for God's sake? When you are insulted, take it all cheerfully.

He who thinks of hell, which he has deserved, finds every trouble easy to bear.

He who loves poverty possesses all things. In the things of this world we must choose the worst; in the things of God we must choose the best.

An obedient soul is the delight of God.

True charity consists in doing good to those who do us evil, and in thus gaining them over.

Of what use are the riches and honors of this world at the hour of death?

It is a great grace of God to be called to his holy love.

God does not leave a single good desire unrewarded.

All attachment, even to good things (except to God), is bad.

Let us be grateful, and first of all to God. Let us therefore resolve to deny him nothing, making choice of those things which are most pleasing to him.

The most beautiful prayer is when in sickness we unite ourselves to the will of God.

A holy life and sensual pleasures cannot agree together.

He who trusts in himself is lost; he who trusts in God can do all things.

And what greater delight can a soul have than to know that it is pleasing God.

God is ready to give himself to those who leave all for his love.

The only way by which we can become saints is the way of suffering.

It is by aridity and temptations that God tries those who love him.

No one can be lost who loves God and trusts in him.

Let us beg of God to give us a tender devotion to his Divine Mother.

He who looks on Jesus crucified suffers everything in peace.

He who loves God most in this world is the happiest. All that is not done for God, turns to pain.

No kind of disquietude, although for a good end, comes from God.

It is enough that we do not stand still; we shall arrive in the end.

He who desires only God is rich and happy: he is in want of nothing, and may laugh at all the world.

Nothing can satisfy one whom God does not satisfy.

God, God, and nothing more.

We must overcome all to gain all.

IV.

An Epitome of the Virtues in which a Christian Soul, that desires to lead a Perfect Life and become a Saint, should exercise itself.

It would be useful to read this epitome every time you make your day's retreat, that you may see in what virtues you are wanting.

1. To desire always to increase in love towards Jesus Christ. Holy desires are wings with which souls fly to God. St. Aloysius Gonzaga made himself a saint in a short time, through the great desire he had of loving God ; and as he knew he should never be able to love him as much as he was worthy of being loved, he consumed himself in ardent desires. On this account, St. Mary Magdalene of Pazzi called St. Aloysius a martyr of love.

2. To meditate often on the Passion of Jesus Christ.

St. Bonaventure said that the wounds of Jesus Christ are wounds which pierce every heart, and inflame them with holy love.

3. Often during the day to make acts of love towards Jesus Christ, beginning from the time you wake in the morning, and trying to make an act of love as you fall asleep. Acts of love, says St. Teresa, are the fuel with which the fire of divine love is kept burning in our hearts.

4. Always to ask Jesus Christ to give you his holy love. The grace of loving God, says St. Francis de Sales, is the grace which contains and brings along with it all the other graces; because he who truly loves God will endeavor to avoid anything that might be displeasing to him, and will study how to please him in all things. It is, therefore, necessary above all things to ask of God the grace to love him.

5. To frequent Holy Communion. A soul can do nothing that is more pleasing to God than to communicate in a state of grace. The reason of this is, that love tends to perfect union with the object beloved; as then Jesus Christ loves a soul that is in grace with an immense love; he ardently desires to unite himself to it. This is what Holy Communion does; by it Jesus Christ is wholly united to the soul: *He that eats my flesh dwells in Me, and I in him.*[1] Consequently the soul can perform no action that is dearer to Jesus Christ than that of receiving him in the Holy Eucharist. For this reason let spiritual souls endeavor to communicate many times in the week, and if possible every day, but always with the permission of their director; for Communions and mortifications done out of a person's own head lead to pride rather than spirituality. For the rest, the penitent should earnestly ask his director both for Communions and

[1] " Qui manducat meam carnem, et bibit meum sanguinem, in me manet, et ego in illo."—*John*, vi. 57.

mortifications; because directors are induced to grant them, more or less frequently, according to the greater or less desire which they discover in their penitents.

6. To make during the day many spiritual Communions; at least three.

7. Often to visit the Most Holy Sacrament of the altar, at least once or twice a day; and in the visit, after the acts of faith, of thanksgiving, of love, and of contrition, to ask fervently for perseverance and holy love.

8. When disturbances, losses, affronts, or other adverse things happen, to have recourse to the ever-blessed Sacrament, at least in spirit, if you cannot go to the church.

9. Every morning on rising to offer yourself to God to suffer in peace, and to accept from his hands all the crosses that will befall you on that day; embracing also in peace all contradictions. "Fiat voluntas tua" is the word which is constantly in the mouths of the saints: Lord, may Thy will always be done!

10. To be glad, and to rejoice that God is infinitely happy and blessed. If we love God more than ourselves, as we are bound to love him, we ought to rejoice more at God's happiness than at our own.

11. To desire heaven and death, that we may be delivered from the danger in which we are of losing God, and to go and love Jesus Christ with all our strength and forever, without the fear of losing him again.

12. Often to speak with others of the love which Jesus Christ has borne us, and of the love we owe to him.

13. To go to God without reserve, not denying him anything that we know to be pleasing to him; but rather choosing such things as are most agreeable to him.

14. To desire and endeavor to persuade all to love Jesus Christ.

15. Always to pray for the souls in purgatory, and for poor sinners.

16. To drive away from your heart all affections that have not God for their object.

17. Often to have recourse to the saints, and especially to the Ever-blessed Mary, that they may obtain for you the love of God.

18. To honor Mary in order to please God.

19. To do all your actions with the sole end of pleasing Jesus Christ; saying at the commencement of each action, O Lord, let it be all for Thee!

20. To offer yourself many times during the day to God and to Jesus Christ, as willing to suffer any pain for his love, and say: My Jesus, I give myself all to Thee; here I am, do with me what Thou wilt.

21. To be resolved to die a thousand times rather than commit a deliberate sin, even though only a venial one.

22. To deny yourself even lawful satisfactions; doing so at least once or twice a day.

23. When we hear people talk of riches, honors, and amusements of the world, let us remember that all things have an end, and let us then say, My God, I wish only for Thee, and nothing more!

24. To make two hours of mental prayer, or at least one hour during the day.

25. To make use of all those external mortifications that obedience permits; but to pay particular attention to interior mortification, such as abstaining from gratifying our curiosity, from answering when we are reproached, from saying witty things, and the like, and never to do anything for your own satisfaction.

26. Whatever devout exercise you may perform, to do it as if it were the last time you had to do it. To this end in your meditation you should often think of death; and when you go to bed, think that you will one day there expire.

27. Not to leave off your usual devotions, or any other good work, on account of any aridity or weariness that

you may experience. He who begins to leave them off for a slight cause is in danger of giving them up entirely.

28. Not to leave undone any good action out of human respect. Not to complain in sickness of any want of attention on the part of the doctors, servants, or assistants, and to try and conceal even our sufferings as much as we can. To love solitude and silence, in order to be able to discourse only with God. And for this reason we must shun the conversations of this world.

29. To drive away sadness, preserving our tranquillity, and a cheerful countenance in all events with a constant uniformity. One who wills what God wills should never be afflicted.

30. To recommend yourself often to spiritual persons.

31. Always to have recourse immediately to Jesus and Mary with great confidence in your temptations ; continuing to pronounce the names of Jesus and Mary as long as the temptation lasts.

32. To have great confidence, first in the Passion of Jesus Christ, and then in the intercession of Mary; and to ask God every day to give you this confidence.

33. After a fault, not to be disturbed and never to despair, even though you should know yourself to be wanting in fidelity, and though you should fall again and again into the same fault; but to repent immediately, and to renew your promise of amendment, with confidence in God.

34. To render good to any one who does you evil, or at least to pray to the Lord for him.

35. To answer with meekness when any one says or does anything to injure you; and so you will gain him over to you. Moreover, when you feel yourself annoyed, it is well to be silent until you are composed, otherwise you will commit many faults without perceiving it.

36. When you have to correct any one, you should choose a time when neither you nor the person who is

to be corrected are excited, otherwise the correction will prove more hurtful than useful.

37. To speak well of all; and to excuse the intention, when you cannot justify the action.

38. To help your neighbor as much as you can, especially one who has been opposed to you.

39. Not to say or do anything that may be displeasing to any one ; and except it were necessary in order to please God rather than men.

40. And if sometimes you are wanting in charity towards any one, ask his pardon, or at least speak kindly to him.

41. To speak always with meekness and in a low voice.

42. To offer to God the contempt you meet with, and not to complain afterwards to others of it.

43. To observe carefully the rules given you by your director.

44. To consider and honor in your Superiors the person of Jesus Christ himself.

45. To love the most humble employments.

46. To choose the poorest things for yourself.

47. To obey without replying, and without showing repugnance; and, on the other hand, not to ask anything for your own satisfaction.

48. Not to speak of yourself, whether it be good or evil; sometimes to speak in disparagement of ourselves fosters pride.

49. To humble yourself even towards your inferiors.

50. Not to excuse yourself when you are reproved or calumniated, unless it should be absolutely necessary for the common good, or to avoid giving scandal to others.

51. To visit and assist the sick as much as possible, and especially the most abandoned.

52. Often to say to yourself, If I wish to become a saint, I must suffer; if I wish to please God, I must do his will, and not my own.

53. Always to renew your resolution of becoming a saint, and not to lose courage in whatever state of tepidity you may find yourself.

54. To renew each day the resolution that you have taken of advancing in perfection.

55. Let religious endeavor every day to renew the vows of their profession. The Doctors of the Church say that a person who renews his vows of religion gains a plenary indulgence, as he does the first time that he makes them.

56. The exercise which is most essential to be practised by a soul that desires to please God is to conform itself in all things to the divine will, and to embrace with peace all things that are contrary to the senses in pains, sicknesses, affronts, contradictions, loss of property, the death of relatives or of other persons who are dear to us; and to receive them each day when we awake as coming from God. Tribulations are those blessed treasuries in which the saints find such stores of merits. We cannot give greater glory to God than by conforming ourselves in all things to his holy will. This is the continual practice of devout souls. And it is the end to be attained by mental prayer. St. Teresa says that "all that a person who gives himself up to prayer ought to seek is conformity to the divine will; and let him be sure that in this consists the highest perfection." This, then, must be our only intention in all our actions, in our meditations, and in our prayers; we must always pray, *O Lord, teach me to do Thy will.*[1] *Tell me, Lord, what Thou dost desire of me, and I will do it all.*[2] "Thy will be done:" such is the prayer continually on the lips of the saints. And this is all that God requires of us: *My son, give me thy heart.*[3]

[1] "Doce me facere voluntatem tuam."—*Ps.* cxlii. 10.
[2] "Domine, quid me vis facere?"—*Acts,* ix. 6.
[3] "Præbe, fili mi, cor tuum mihi."—*Prov.* xxiii. 26.

But perfection consists in conforming ourselves to the will of God in those things which are disagreeable to us. The Ven. F. Avila says, "It is of more use to say once, 'Blessed be God,' in any contradiction, than to thank him six thousand times when we are pleased." We must also be conformed to those crosses which come to us by means of others, as in calumniations, deceptions, and contempt, because it all comes from God. Not that the Lord then wills the fault of the person who offends us, but he does will that we should be humble and mortified: *Good things and evil are from God.*[1] We call tribulations evils and misfortunes; and we make them so by suffering them with impatience; but if we received them with resignation, they would become graces and jewels to enrich our crown in heaven. In a word, he who is always united with the will of God becomes a saint, and enjoys even here on earth a perpetual peace: *Whatever shall befall the just man, it shall not make him sad.*[2]

57. To recommend ourselves to the prayers of devout people; but still more to recommend ourselves to the saints in heaven, and especially to the Ever-blessed Mary, setting great value on devotion towards this divine Mother; and not omitting any opportunity of inducing others to practise it. Those who have a great confidence in the patronage of Mary ought to be very grateful to God for it, for it is a great pledge of their salvation; and those who have it not, ought to pray that he would grant it to them.

V.

Prayer to obtain all Holy Virtues.

My Lord and my God, by the merits of Jesus Christ, I ask Thee first to enlighten me; make me know the vanity of the goods of this world, that there is no other

[1] " Bona et mala . . . a Deo sunt."—*Ecclus*. xi. 14.
[2] " Non contristabit justum, quidquid ei acciderit."—*Prov*. xii. 21.

good but to love Thee, the supreme and infinite good. Make me know my unworthiness, and how worthy Thou art of being loved by all, and especially by me for the love Thou hast borne me. Give me holy humility to embrace with cheerfulness all the contempt that I may receive from men. Give me a great sorrow for my sins. Give me the love of holy mortification, that by it I may curb my passions and punish my rebellious senses. Give me a love for the obedience I owe to my Superiors. Give me grace to direct all that I do to the sole end of pleasing Thee. Give me holy purity of mind and body, and a detachment from everything that does not tend to the love of Thee. Give me great confidence in the Passion of Jesus Christ, and in the intercession of the Ever-blessed Mary. Give me, above all, a great love towards Thee, and a perfect conformity to Thy divine will. I recommend to Thee also the souls of purgatory, my relatives, benefactors, and friends, and all those from whom I have received any affront or injury; I pray Thee shower down upon them all blessings. Finally, I recommend to Thee infidels, heretics, and all those who are in a state of sin. Since Thou, my God, art worthy of infinite love, make Thyself known and loved by all; but especially by me, who have been most ungrateful to Thee. I have offended Thee enough; make me love Thee exceedingly, and take me to Heaven, where I shall sing Thy mercies for all eternity. Blessed Mary, pray to Jesus for me! Amen.

VI.

Prayer to obtain Holy Perseverance.

My God, I thank Thee for having pardoned me, as I trust Thou hast, all the offences that I have committed against Thee. I love Thee above all things; and I am more sorry for having despised Thy infinite majesty than for any other evil that has happened to me. I resolve rather to die than ever to offend Thee again; but I fear lest through my weakness I should fall again, and lose Thy grace. Ah, by the merits of Jesus Christ, never permit me to fall again under Thy displeasure! And Thou, Jesus, my Redeemer, since Thou hast died on the cross to save me, never let me separate myself from Thee again. My Jesus, my Jesus, hear me! "Ne permittas me separari a Te; ne permittas me separari a Te." Such is my hope in that blood which Thou hast shed for me with so much grief. And thou, Mary, my mother and my hope, pray for me; and when thou seest me assailed by any temptation, obtain for me that I may always have recourse immediately to thy Son and thee, saying, Help me, my Jesus: My mother, come to my aid, that I may not lose God. Thus I hope to die loving God and thee, in order to love thee eternally in paradise.

VII.

Prayer of a Devout Soul to Mary and Jesus.

My Queen and my Mother, if thou protect me I fear not that I shall go to hell; because thou dost interpose thy prayers and thy merits for those whom thou dost protect, and Jesus Christ knows not how to deny anything that thou dost ask him. My dear Lady, for the love thou hast for thy Son, pray to him, and have pity on me! And Thou, my Jesus, by the prayers and merits of Thy Mother, and by the blood which Thou hast shed for me, deliver me from hell; because in hell I cannot love Thee. From this hell I pray Thee to deliver me, by that compassion which forced Thee even to die on the Cross for the love of me. Jesus and Mary, you are my love and my hope!

24

VIII.

Prayers to the Blessed Virgin.

I. TO OBTAIN THE FORGIVENESS OF OUR SINS AND HOLY PERSEVERANCE.

Behold, O Mother of God, at thy feet a miserable sinner, who has recourse to thee, and trusts in thee! O Mother of mercy, have pity on me! I hear thee called by all the refuge and the hope of sinners; thou art, then, my refuge and hope also. By thy intercession thou hast power to save me. Help me, for the love of Jesus Christ; lend thy hand to a fallen wretch, who recommends himself to thee, and who dedicates himself to thee as thy faithful servant. I offer myself, then, O Queen of Heaven, to serve thee all my life; accept me, and reject me not, as I deserve. O my Mother, in thy protection have I placed all my hopes. I bless and thank God a thousand times for having in his mercy given me this confidence in thee, which I consider as an earnest of my salvation. Ah, how many times have I not unhappily fallen because I had not recourse to thee! I hope now that, through the merits of Jesus Christ and thy prayers, these sins have been pardoned. I may still, notwithstanding, again lose the divine grace. Do thou, my Lady, protect me; never let me again become the slave of hell. Help me always. By thy help I know that I shall conquer; and I know that thou wilt surely assist me if I recommend myself to thee; but my fear is that, in the occasions of falling, I should omit to call upon thee, and so should be lost. This, then, is the grace I seek from thee, and which I beseech and conjure thee to obtain for me,—namely, that in the assaults of hell I should always have recourse to thee, and say, Mary, help me! help me, O Mary! my Mother, permit me not to lose my God!

2. TO OBTAIN A GOOD DEATH.

O Mary ! what death shall I die ? When I now think of my sins, and of that moment in which I shall expire and be judged, I am confounded and tremble ! O my Mother, in the blood of Jesus Christ, and in thy intercession, do I place my hopes ! O comforter of the afflicted, abandon me not at that moment, fail not to console me in that great affliction ! If thou help me not, I shall be lost. Ah, Lady, before death comes, obtain for me a great sorrow for my sins, a true amendment, and a constant fidelity to God during the remainder of my life. And when I come to the last stage of my existence, O Mary, my hope ! help me in those moments of misery; and comfort me, so that I may not despair at the sight of my sins, which the devil will then put before me. Obtain for me that I may then invoke thee more frequently, that I may die with thy name and that of thy divine Son on my lips. Pardon my boldness if I ask thee even to come thyself to console me by thy presence before I expire. I am a sinner, it is true, and I am not worthy of such a favor; but I am thy servant; I love thee, and have great confidence in thee. O Mary, I shall expect thee; leave me not without consolation ! At least, if I am unworthy of such a grace, assist me from heaven, that I may go forth from this life loving God and thee, and come to love you both eternally in paradise.

3. TO OBTAIN DELIVERANCE FROM HELL AND THE POSSESSION OF PARADISE.

O most dear Lady ! I thank thee that thou hast so many times delivered me from hell, which I have so often merited by my sins. I, a miserable wretch, was at one time condemned to that prison; already, perhaps at my first sin, the sentence would have been executed on me, if thou hadst not mercifully helped me. Without my even praying to thee, but out of thy pure compassion, thou didst restrain the divine justice, and then, overcoming my hardness of heart, thou didst encourage me to have confidence in thee. And, oh, into how many other sins should I not have fallen, in the many dangers which have occurred to me, if thou, most loving Mother, hadst not preserved me by the graces thou didst obtain for me. Ah, my Queen, keep me far from hell! O my Mother, leave me not to myself, for I shall then be lost, but make me always fly to thee! Save me, my hope! save me from sin, which can alone condemn me to hell. May I come to rejoice with thee in heaven for all eternity. I thank God above all things for having given me this confidence in the blood of Jesus Christ, and in thee. Yes, I hope that thou wilt save me; that thou wilt free me from sin, and wilt obtain for me light and strength to fulfil the divine will, and finally that thou wilt conduct me in safety to the gates of paradise. Thy servants have always had this hope, and none have been deceived. Neither shall I be. O Mary, it is so; thou must save me. Pray to thy Son (as I also pray to him by the merits of his passion), and he may ever keep and increase in me this confidence; and so I shall be saved.

IX.

Consecration to the Blessed Virgin.

Most holy Virgin Mary, Mother of God, I, N. N., although most unworthy of being thy servant, nevertheless, moved by thy wonderful compassion and by a desire to serve thee, choose thee this day, in presence of my angel guardian, and of all the heavenly court, for my special lady, advocate, and mother; and I firmly resolve to serve thee always, and to do everything in my power to make others serve thee also. I beseech thee, then, most merciful Mother, by the blood of thy Son, which was shed for me, to take me into the number of thy clients as thy servant forever. Protect me in my actions, and obtain for me grace so to measure my thoughts, words, and works, that I may never offend thy most pure eyes. nor those of thy divine Son, Jesus. Remember me, and abandon me not at the hour of my death.

X.

Protestation for a Happy Death.

My God, being certain that I shall die, and not knowing when it will be, I intend now to prepare myself for death; and I therefore declare that I believe all that the Holy Church believes, and especially the mystery of the Most Holy Trinity, the incarnation and death of Jesus Christ, paradise and hell; because Thou, who art truth itself, hast revealed all these truths.

I deserve a thousand hells: but I hope in Thy mercy, through the merits of Jesus Christ, to obtain pardon, final perseverance, and the glory of Paradise.

I protest that I love Thee above all things, because Thou art the infinite good; and because I love Thee, I am more sorry that I have so often offended Thee than for any other evil, and I resolve rather to die than offend Thee again. I pray Thee rather to take away my life than to permit me to lose Thee by another sin.

I thank Thee, my Jesus, for all the sufferings Thou hast undergone for me, and for the many mercies Thou hast shown me, after I had so greatly offended Thee.

My beloved Lord, I rejoice in that Thou art infinitely happy, and that Thou art loved by so many souls in heaven and on earth. I desire that all should know and love Thee.

I protest that if any one has offended me, I pardon

him for the love of Thee, O my Jesus; and I beg of Thee to do good to him !   .

I declare that I desire to receive the most holy sacraments, both in life and death: and I intend now to ask for absolution of my sins, in case I should not be able to give any sign of it at my death.

I accept my death, and all the pains that will accompany it, in union with the death and sorrows which Jesus suffered on the Cross. And I accept, my God, all the pains and tribulations which Thou shalt send me before my death. Do with me, and with all that belongs to me, what Thou pleasest. Give me Thy love and holy perseverance, and I ask nothing more.

My Mother Mary, assist me always, but especially at my death; in the mean time, help me and keep me in the grace of God. Thou art my hope. Under thy mantle I will live and die. St. Joseph, St. Michael Archangel, my guardian angel, help me always, but especially in the hour of my death.

And Thou, my dear Jesus, who to obtain for me a happy death didst give Thyself to suffer so bitter a death, abandon me not in my last hour. From this time I embrace Thee, that I may die in Thy arms. I deserve hell, but I throw myself on Thy mercy, hoping in Thy blood to die in Thy friendship, and to receive Thy blessing when I shall see Thee first as my judge. Into Thy hands, wounded for my love, I commend my soul.[1] I hope in Thee, that Thou wilt not then condemn me to hell. Ah, help me always, but especially at my death; grant me to die loving Thee, so that the last sigh of life may be an act of love, which shall transport me from this earth to love Thee forever in paradise.

Jesus, Mary, and Joseph, assist me in my agony ! Jesus, Mary, and Joseph, I give myself to you; do you receive my soul at that moment.

[1] " In te, Domine, speravi, non confundar in æternum."—*Ps.* xxx. 2.

APPENDIX.

The manner of making a retreat.

The spiritual exercises are made in public, in common, or in private. They are made in public, when all the people of a parish or of a town are invited without distinction to attend them, and then the exercises are properly called a mission. They are made in common when a certain number of persons—as, for example, the members of a confraternity, etc.—unite to make them together. Finally, the spiritual exercises are made in private when one makes them by one's self, and then they are called a retreat. In the first two, the exercises are directed by preachers. Here, however, we wish to give some supplementary instructions useful to persons who make a retreat in private.

I. THE ENDS OF A RETREAT.

A retreat being only an extraordinary exercise of mental prayer, it has the same ends as has prayer. We make a retreat in order to be enlightened; to know, purify, and correct ourselves; to be united with God and to pray to him; to renew our spirit; to maintain ourselves in virtue and to increase in fervor; to obtain some special grace, as when there is question of knowing one's vocation; to embrace a state of life; to enter upon the duties of an important office; to undertake a dangerous voyage, etc.

2. THE PLACE.

Strictly speaking, every one may make the spiritual exercises at home, if not in body, at least in spirit. But in order to be really in retreat, we must retire from all that may disturb silence and recollection, as St. Alphonsus explains this so well. The place most suitable is ordinarily a religious house; there we can find all desirable facilities.

3. ITS DURATION.

Let us at first say, in general, that to keep up the fire of divine love in the soul, it is advisable to devote to the spiritual exercises at least an hour every day, a day in every month, and a week every year. This is the summing-up of all that the Saint teaches on this subject in all his works. The annual retreat should there-fore last about eight days. The same thing holds good whenever we wish to make a regular retreat, though circumstances may exact of us a longer or a shorter time.

4. ORDER OF THE EXERCISES.

Each one may regulate the exercises of the day to suit his own convenience.

To serve as an example, we give the following order :

The Morning.

5 or 5.30 A.M.		Meditation on the eternal truths.
6 or 6.30 "		Mass. When we go to Communion, we make half an hour's preparation and an hour's thanksgiving.
7.30 "		Remission or mental rest, during which we make take breakfast, perform some manual work, or walk about in silence.

Before Dinner.

8.30 "		The Rosary.
9 "		The Way of the Cross.
10 "		A half hour's spiritual reading.
10.30 "		Meditation on the Blessed Sacrament or some other mystery, on the devotion to the Blessed Virgin, or on a virtue or a vice.
11.30 "		A quarter of an hour's remission, followed by the Particular Examination on a virtue or a predominant passion.
12. "		Dinner, followed by an hour's remission.

After Dinner.

1.30 P.M.		Vocal prayers, as Vespers and Compline, Of-fice of the Blessed Virgin, etc.
2 "		Visit to the Blessed Sacrament and to the Blessed Virgin.
3 "		Reading of the Life of a saint.
3.30 "		Meditation on the Passion of Jesus Christ.
4.30 "		Remission.

The Evening.

5	P.M.	Visit to the Blessed Sacrament and Protestation for a happy death.
6	"	Meditation on the eternal truths.
7	"	Supper and remission.
8	"	Recollection in the oratory or before the Blessed Sacrament.
8.30	"	Evening prayers, during which is made the examination of conscience on the faults of the day. At the end we read the principal points of the next day's meditation.

We employ the intervals that remain free according to our devotion, in praying, in conversing intimately with God, in reading, in briefly noting down good thoughts or a good resolution, in examining our conscience in order to make a good confession, etc.

5. SILENCE AND RECOLLECTION.

If we cannot keep strict silence during the whole retreat, as it is advisable for us to do, we should at least avoid everything that may disturb interior recollection, without which there would be no retreat. All mental strain is also hurtful; it is to the heart that God speaks in calmness and peace. A retreat is not a hardship, but a spiritual repose to which the Lord kindly invites us in order that we may sweetly commune with him: *Come apart into a desert place, and rest a little.—Mark*, vi. 31.

6. THE MEDITATIONS.

Each meditation should last at least half an hour, As for the subjects of meditation, let every one choose what best suits his own spiritual temperament. Besides the meditations on the eternal truths, mentioned above, the following are other plans of a retreat according to St. Alphonsus, the subjects of which are treated in the first two volumes:

I.

1st DAY.		True wisdom.
2d	"	Value of time.
3d	"	Abuse of the divine mercy.
4th	"	Sentiments of a dying person who has neglected his conscience.

5th DAY.   Judgment.
6th "   Pains of hell.
7th "   Confidence in the protection of the Blessed Virgin.
8th "   The love that Jesus Christ bears us, and our obliga-
            tion to love him.

II.

1st DAY.   Malice of mortal sin.
2d   "   Value of the grace of God.
3d   "   Importance of salvation.
4th "   Happiness of him who loves Jesus Christ.
5th "   What advantage it is to meditation on the Passion
            of Jesus Christ.
6th "   Fruits that are derived from frequent Communion.
7th "   Excellence of the devotion to the Blessed Virgin.
8th "   Necessity of perseverance in doing what is good.

7. MORTIFICATION.

Prayer is the soul of the retreat; but in order to make prayer well, we must practise not only exterior, but interior, mortification; to this we must add, according to our means, corporal and spiritual alms, according to the advice given by the angel Raphael to Tobias : *Prayer is good with fasting and alms.*[1]

8. THE SACRAMENTS.

It would be well to abstain from going to Holy Communion during the first days of the retreat, in order to prepare our-selves for a good general confession, if we have not yet made one, or for a review of the faults committed since the last re-treat. But we should consult our director in regard to this mat-ter, and conform to his advice. We should also take care to consult him about penances that we wish to impose on our-selves, and about any other important point. The road of obedience is always the most sure and the most meritorious road to walk on.—ED.

---

[1] "Bona est oratio cum jejunio et eleemosyna."—*Tob.* xii. 8.

In 1750, St. Alphonsus published the *Counsels concerning the Religious State*, followed by *Considerations on the Religious State*, having especially in view the young men who presented themselves to be admitted into the Congregation (Tannoia, book 2, ch. 34). In the *Counsels*, which we divide into five paragraphs instead of two, the author treats at first of the necessity of conforming to the designs of Divine Providence in the choice of a state of life, whatever it may be, and then enlarges upon vocation to religious perfection. To this little work, which is one of the first productions of the holy Author, we unite all that he afterwards wrote about this important matter, and we complete the collection by adding to it a short treatise on vocation to the priesthood, drawn from his well-known work entitled *Selva* (Volume XIII. Ch. 10).—ED.

The Choice of a State of Life, and the Vocation to the Religious State.

COUNSELS CONCERNING A RELIGIOUS VOCATION.

I.

We ought to conform to the Designs of God in the Choice of a State of Life, whatever it may be.

It is evident that our eternal salvation depends principally upon the choice of our state of life. Father Granada calls this choice the chief wheel of our whole life. Hence, as when in a clock the chief wheel is deranged, the whole clock is also deranged, so in the order of our salvation, if we make a mistake as to the state to which we are called, our whole life, as St. Gregory Nazianzen says, will be an error.

If, then, in the choice of a state of life, we wish to secure our eternal salvation, we must embrace that to which God calls us, in which only God prepares for us the efficacious means necessary to our salvation. For, as St Cyprian says: " The grace of the Holy Spirit is given according to the order of God, and not according to our own will;" [1] and therefore St. Paul writes, *Every one hath his proper gift from God.*" [2] That is, as Cornelius a Lapide explains it, God gives to every one his vocation, and chooses the state in which he wills him to be saved. And this is the order of predestination described by the same apostle: *Whom he predestinated, them he also called;*

[1] " Ordine suo, non arbitrio nostro, virtus Spiritus Sancti ministratur."—*De Sing. cler.*
[2] " Unusquisque proprium donum habet a Deo."—I *Cor.* vii. 7.

*and whom he called, them he also justified, . . . and them he
also glorified.*[1] *

We must remark that in the world this doctrine of the
vocation is not much studied by some persons. They
think it to be all the same, whether they live in the state
to which God calls them, or in that which they choose
of their own inclination, and therefore so many live a
bad life and damn themselves.

But it is certain that this is the principal point with
regard to the acquisition of eternal life. He who dis-
turbs this order and breaks this chain of salvation will
not be saved. With all his labors and with all the good
he may do, St. Augustine will tell him, "Thou runnest
well, but out of the way,"[2] that is, out of the way in
which God has called you to walk for attaining to salvation. The Lord does not accept the sacrifices offered
up to him from our own inclination, *But to Cain and his
offerings he had no respect.*[3] Rather he threatens with
great chastisement those who, when he calls them, turn
their backs on him in order to follow the whims of their

---

[1] " Quos prædestinavit, hos et vocavit; et quos vocavit, hos et justificavit: quos autem justificavit, illos et glorificavit."—*Rom.* viii. 30.

[2] " Bene curris, sed extra viam."

[3] " Ad Cain et ad munera ejus non respexit."—*Gen.* iv. 5.

---

* In another work (Volume XIII.) the holy Author expresses himself in these words: " God wills that all men should be saved, but
not in the same way. As in heaven he has distinguished different
degrees of glory, so on earth he has established different states of
life, as so many different ways of gaining heaven" (Ch. II. § 2). The
choice is not arbitrary: " To enter into any state of life, a divine vocation is necessary; for without such a vocation it is, if not impossible, at
least most difficult to fulfil the obligations of our state, and obtain salvation" (Ch. X.). The reason of this is evident; for it is God who in
the order of his Providence assigns to each one of us his state of life
and afterwards provides us with the graces and the help suitable to
the state to which he calls us. We ought to be persuaded and ought
never to forget that from all eternity God thinks with love of each
one of us, just as a good father thinks of his only son.—Ed.

own caprice. *Woe to you apostate children*, he says through Isaias, *that you would take counsel and not from me, and would begin a web and not by my spirit.*[1] *

II.

The Vocation to the Religious State. How Important it is to follow it promptly.

1. MISERY TO WHICH ONE EXPOSES ONE'S SELF BY NOT CORRESPONDING TO IT.

The divine call to a more perfect life is undoubtedly a special grace, and a very great one, which God does not give to all; hence he has much reason to be indignant against those who despise it. How greatly would not a prince think himself offended, if he should call one of his vassals to serve him near his person, and this vassal should refuse to obey the call! And should God not resent such conduct? Oh, he resents it but too much, and threatens such persons by saying, *Woe to him*

---

[1] "Væ, filii desertores, dicit Dominus, ut faceretis consilium, et non ex me; et ordiremini telam, et non per spiritum meum."—*Isa.* xxx. 1.

---

* From this it follows that the great and only affair which ought to preoccupy the minds of young persons of both sexes is to know the designs of God relatively to the state of life that they are to embrace, and to obtain from him the strength to conform to it. The *means* to adopt in order to be successful in this affair are indicated in an appendix to this treatise.

But we should know that God does not always call one all at once and suddenly to the most perfect state. Some he calls sooner, others later. There are some who are raised to it gradually, others who are led to it by a circuitous road, more or less long. Sometimes when we correspond well to a first vocation God grants us a better one; and occasionally our Lord is satisfied with making us understand the advantages of this or that vocation, in order that by esteeming it we may desire it, and by desiring it we may endeavor to obtain it by prayer and good works. We must conform to the will of God, and be united with it as well during life as at death.—ED.

that gainsayeth his maker.[1] The word *Woe* in Scripture signifies eternal damnation. The chastisement of the disobedient will begin even in this life, in which he will always be unquiet, for, says Job, *Who hath resisted Him and hath had peace?*[2] Therefore he will be deprived of those abundant and efficacious helps necessary to lead a good life. For which reason Habert, a divine, writes, " He will with great difficulty be able to work out his salvation."[3] He will with great difficulty save himself; for, being like a member out of his proper place, he will with great difficulty be able to live well. " In the body of the Church," adds the learned author, " he will be like a limb of the human body out of its place, which may be able to perform its functions, but only with difficulty and in an awkward manner." Whence he concludes, "And though, absolutely speaking, he may be saved, he will with difficulty enter upon and advance in the road, and use the means of salvation."[4] The same thing is taught by St. Bernard[5] and St. Leo.[6] St. Gregory,[7] writing to the Emperor Maurice, who by an edict had forbidden soldiers to become religious, says that this was an unjust law, which shut the gates of paradise to many, because many would save themselves in religion who would otherwise perish in the world.

Remarkable is the case related by F. Lancicius. There

---

[1] " Væ qui contradicit Fictori suo!"—*Isa.* xlv. 9.

[2] " Quis restitit ei, et pacem habuit ?"—*Job*, ix. 4.

[3] " Non sine magnis difficultatibus poterit saluti suæ consulere."— *De Ord.* p. 3, c. 1, § 2.

[4] " Manebitque in corpore Ecclesiæ, velut membrum in corpore humano suis sedibus motum, quod servire potest, sed ægre, et cum deformitate. Licet, absolute loquendo, salvari possit, difficile tamen ingredietur viam humilitatis et pœnitentiæ, qua sola ipsi patet ingressus ad vitam."—*Ibid.*

[5] *De Vit. Cler.* c. 5.

[6] *Epist.* 87.

[7] *Epist.* l. 2, c. 100.

was in the Roman college a youth of great talents. Whilst he was making the spiritual exercises, he asked his confessor whether it was a sin not to correspond with the vocation to the religious life The confessor replied that in itself it was no grievous sin, because this is a thing of counsel and not of precept, but that one would expose one's salvation to great danger, as it had happened to many, who for this reason were finally damned. He did not obey the call. He went to study in Macerata, where he soon began to omit prayer and holy Communion, and finally gave himself up to a bad life. Soon after, coming one night from the house of a wicked woman, he was mortally wounded by a rival; certain priests ran to his assistance, but he expired before they arrived, and, moreover, in front of the college. By this circumstance God wished to show that this chastisement came upon him for having neglected his vocation.

Remarkable also is the vision had by a novice, who, as F. Pinamonti relates in his treatise of the victorious vocation, had resolved on leaving his Order. He saw Christ on a throne in wrath, ordering his name to be blotted out of the book of life; by this vision he was so terrified that he persevered in his vocation.

How many other similar examples are there, not to be found in books! And how many unhappy youths shall we not see damned on the day of judgment for not having followed their vocation! Such are rebels to the divine light, as the Holy Ghost says: *They have been rebellious to the light, they have not known his ways,*[1] and they will be justly punished by losing the light; and because they would not walk in the way shown them by the Lord, they shall walk without light in that chosen by their own

[1] " Ipsi fuerunt rebelles lumini; nescierunt vias ejus."—*Job*, xxiv. 13.

caprice and perish. *Behold, I will utter my spirit to you.*[1]
Behold the vocation, but because they fail to follow it,
God adds: *Because I called and you refused . . . you have
despised all my counsel . . . I also will laugh in your destruction, and I will mock when that shall come upon you which
you feared.*[2] *Then shall they call upon me, and I will not hear:
they shall rise in morning and shall not find me. Because they
have hated instruction and received not the fear of the Lord.
Nor consented to my counsel, but despised all my reproof.*[3]*
And this signifies that God will not hear the prayers of
him who has neglected to obey his voice. St. Augustine
says, "They who have despised the will of God which
invited them, shall feel the will of God when it becomes
its own avenger.[4]

2. WE MUST OBEY THE VOICE OF GOD WITHOUT DELAY.

Whenever God calls to a more perfect state, he who
does not wish to expose his eternal salvation to great
danger must then obey, and obey promptly. Otherwise
he will hear from Jesus Christ the reproach he made to
that young man who, when invited to follow him, said,
I will follow Thee, Lord, but let me first take my leave of them

---

[1] "En, proferam vobis spiritum meum."—*Prov.* i. 23.

[2] "Quia vocavi, et renuistis . . . despexistis omne consilium meum.
. . . Ego quoque in interitu vestro ridebo et subsannabo, cum vobis
id, quod timebatis, advenerit."—*Ibid.* i. 24–26.

[3] "Tunc invocabunt me, et non exaudiam; mane consurgent, et non
invenient me. Eo quod exosam habuerint disciplinam, . . . nec
acquieverint consilio meo, et detraxerint universæ correptioni meæ."
—*Ibid.* i. 28–30.

[4] "Qui spreverunt voluntatem Dei invitantem, voluntatem Dei
sentient vindicantem."—*R. ad obj. Vinc.* 16.

---

* With these last words God reprimands those who set but little
value on vocation, and who pretend that one can save one's soul in-
differently in every state of life. (*Theol. mor.* l. 4. n. 78.)

that are at my house.[1] And Jesus replied to him that he was not fit for paradise: *No man putting his hand to the plough and looking back is fit for the kingdom of God.*[2]

The lights which God gives are transient, not permanent, gifts. Whence St. Thomas says that the vocation of God to a more perfect life ought to be followed as promptly as possible.[3] He proposes in his summary[4] the question whether it be praiseworthy to enter religion without having asked the counsel of many and without long deliberation? He answers in the affirmative, saying that counsel and deliberation are necessary in doubtful things, but not in this matter which is certainly good; because Jesus Christ has counselled it in the Gospel, since the religious state comprehends most of the counsels of Jesus Christ. How singular a thing it is, when there is question of entering religion to lead a life more perfect and more free from the dangers of the world, the men of the world say that it is necessary to deliberate a long time before putting such resolutions in execution, in order to ascertain whether the vocation comes from God or from the devil. But they do not talk thus when one is to accept of a place in the magistracy, of a bishopric, etc., where there are so many dangers of losing the soul. Then they do not say that many proofs are required whether there be a true vocation from God.

The saints, however, do not talk thus. St. Thomas says that if the vocation to religion should even come from the devil, we should nevertheless follow it, as a good counsel, though coming from an enemy. St. John

[1] "Sequar te, Domine; sed permitte mihi primum renuntiare his quæ domi sunt."—*Luke*, ix. 61.

[2] "Nemo mittens manum suam ad aratrum, et respiciens retro, aptus est regno Dei."—*Ibid*. 62.

[3] "Quanto citius."

[4] 2. 2. q. 189, a. 10.

Chrysostom, as quoted by the same St. Thomas, says that God, when he gives such vocations, wills that we should not defer even a moment to follow them. Christ requires from us such an obedience that we should not delay an instant.[1] And why this? Because as much as God is pleased to see in a soul promptitude in obeying him, so much he opens his hand and fills it with his blessings. On the contrary, tardiness in obeying him displeases him, and then he shuts his hand and withdraws his lights, so that in consequence a soul will follow its vocation with difficulty and abandon it again easily. Therefore, St. John Chrysostom says that when the devil cannot bring one to give up his resolution of consecrating himself to God, he at least seeks to make him defer the execution of it, and esteems it a great gain if he can obtain the delay of one day only, or even of an hour.[2] Because, after that day or that hour, other occasions presenting themselves, it will be less difficult for him to obtain greater delay, until the individual who has been thus called, finding himself more feeble and less assisted by grace, gives way altogether and loses his vocation. Therefore St. Jerome gives to those who are called to quit the world this advice: "Make haste, I beseech you, and rather cut than loosen the cable by which your bark is bound fast to the land."[3] The saint wishes to say that as a man who should find himself in a boat on the point of sinking, would seek to cut the rope, rather than to loosen it, so he who finds himself in the midst of the world ought to seek to get out of it as promptly as possible, in order to free himself

---

[1] "Talem obedientiam Christus quærit a nobis, ut neque instanti temporis moremur."—*In Matt. hom.* 14.

[2] "Si vel levem arripuerit prorogationem."—*Ad pop. Ant. hom.* 56.

[3] "Festina, quæso te, et hærentis in salo naviculæ funem magis præcide, quam solve."—*Ad Paulin. de St. Scr.*

from the danger, which is so great in the world, of losing his own soul.*

Let us also hear what St. Francis de Sales writes in his works, on religious vocation, because the whole of it will go to confirm what has already been said, and what will be said hereafter: "To have a sign of a true vocation, it is not necessary that our constancy be sensible, it suffices if it be in the superior part of our soul. And therefore we must not judge that a vocation is not a true one, if the individual thus called, before putting it in execution, does not feel any longer those sensible movements which he felt in the beginning. Even should he feel a repugnance and coldness, which sometimes bring him to waver, and make it appear to him that all is lost.

---

* We must here call to mind what the Author says in the *Christian Rule of Life*, chap. i.: "You should choose your director; consult him on all more important matters; and obey him in everything. He who obeys his confessor need not fear to go astray: *He that heareth you, heareth Me* (Luke, x. 16). The voice of the confessor is the voice of God." We should, therefore, consult at least the confessor, who may delay giving an opinion when he thinks fit to do so on account of the importance of the decision he has to render.

The following are, according to St. Alphonsus, the three principal signs of a true vocation to the religious state: "1. We should have a good end in view, such as to remove from the dangers of the world, the better to assure ourselves of salvation, and to become more closely united with God. 2. We should not be subject to any positive impediment, such as the want of health, or of talent, or parents who are necessitous ("in necessitate gravi"— *Theol mor.* l. 4. n. 66)—matters that should be submitted to the judgment of the Superiors, towards whom we should be frank in telling the truth. 3. We should be admitted by the Superiors of the Institute. (Counsels to Novices.)"

Moreover, in the Church there are different religious Institutes, different kinds of perfection. It is not enough to know that one is called to the religious state; one must also examine for what Institute, for what Community the Lord has destined us, and one must follow in every point the impulse of grace. (See *Homo apost. tr. ult.* n. 39.)
ED.

It is enough that the will remains constant in not abandoning the divine call, and also that there remains some affection for this call. To know whether God will have one become a religious, one ought not to expect that God himself should speak or send to one an angel from heaven to signify his will. And as little necessary is it that ten or twelve Doctors should examine whether the vocation is to be followed or not. But it is necessary to correspond with the first movement of the inspiration, and to cultivate it, and then not to grow weary if disgust or coldness should come on; for if one acts thus, God will not fail to make all succeed to his glory. Nor ought we to care much from what quarter the first movement comes. The Lord has many means to call his servants. Sometimes he makes use of a sermon, at other times of the reading of good books. Some, as St. Anthony and St. Francis, have been called by hearing the words of the Gospel; others by means of afflictions and troubles that came upon them in the world, and which suggested to them the motive for leaving it. These persons, although they come to God only because they are disgusted with the world or out of favor with it, nevertheless, failing not to give themselves to him with their whole will, become sometimes greater saints than those who entered religion with a more apparent vocation. Father Platus relates that a nobleman, riding one day on a fine horse, and striving to make a great display in order to please some ladies whom he saw, was thrown from the horse into the mire, from which he rose besmeared and covered with mud. He was so full of confusion at this accident that at the same moment he resolved to become a religious, saying, 'Treacherous world, thou hast mocked me, but I will mock thee. Thou hast played me a game, I will play thee another; for I will have no more peace with thee, and from this hour I resolve to forsake thee and to become a **friar.'**

And, in fact, he became a religious, and lived in religion a holy life." [1]

III.

Means to be Employed for Preserving a Religious Vocation in the World.

He, then, who wishes to be faithful to the divine call ought not only to resolve to follow it, but to follow it promptly, if he does not wish to expose himself to the evident danger of losing his vocation; and in case he should by necessity be forced to wait, he ought to use all diligence to preserve it, as the most precious jewel he could have.

The means to preserve vocation are three in number: secrecy, prayer, and recollection.

I. SECRECY.

First, generally speaking, he must keep his vocation secret from everybody except his spiritual Father, because commonly the men of the world scruple not to say to young men, who are called to the religious state, that one may serve God everywhere, and therefore in the world also. And it is wonderful that such propositions come sometimes out of the mouth of priests, and even of religious; but of such religious only as have either become so without vocation, or do not know what vocation is. Yes, without doubt, he who is not called to the religious state may serve God in every place, but not he who is called to it, and then from his own inclination wishes to remain in the world; such a one, as I have said above, can with difficulty serve God and lead a good life."

It is especially necessary to keep the vocation secret from parents.

[1] *Entret.* 17.

It was, indeed, the opinion of Luther, as Bellarmine relates,[1] that children entering religion without the consent of their parents commit a sin. For, said he children are bound to obey their parents in all things. But this opinion has generally been rejected by Councils and the holy Fathers. The tenth Council of Toledo expressly says: "It is lawful for children to become religious without the consent of their parents, provided they have attained the age of puberty;" these are the words: "It shall not be lawful for parents to put their children in a religious order after they have attained their fourteenth year. After this age, it shall be lawful for children to take upon themselves the yoke of religious observance, whether it be with the consent of their parents, or only the wish of their own hearts."[2] The same is prescribed in the Council of Tribur,[3] and is taught by St. Ambrose, St. Jerome, St. Augustine, St. Bernard, St. Thomas, and others, with St. John Chrysostom, who writes in general: "When parents stand in the way in spiritual things, they ought not even to be recognized."[4]

Some Doctors then say that when a child called by God to the religious state could easily and securely obtain the consent of his parents, without any danger on their part of hindering him from following his vocation, it is becoming that he should seek to obtain their blessing. This doctrine could be held speculatively, but not so in practice, because in practice such a danger always exists. It will be well to discuss this point fully, in

[1] *De Mon.* l. 2, c. 36.

[2] "Parentibus filios religioni contradere non amplius quam usque ad decimum quartum eorum ætatis annum licentia poterit esse; postea vero, an cum voluntate parentum, an suæ devotionis sit solitarium votum, erit filiis licitum religionis assumere cultum."—*Cap.* 6.

[3] *Can.* 24.

[4] "Cum spiritualia impediunt parentes, nec agnoscendi quidem sunt."—*In Jo. hom.* 84.

order to do away with certain pharisaical scruples which some entertain.

It is certain that in the choice of a state of life, children are not bound to obey parents. Thus the Doctors, with common accord, teach with St. Thomas, who says: " Servants are not bound to obey their masters, nor children their parents, with regard to contracting matrimony, preserving virginity, and such like things.[1] Nevertheless, with regard to the state of marriage, F. Pinamonti, in his treatise on religious vocation, is justly of the opinion of Sanchez, Comminchio, and others, who hold that a child is bound to take counsel of his parents, because in such matters they may have more experience than the young. But speaking then of religious vocation, the above-mentioned Pinamonti wisely adds that a child is not bound at all to take counsel of his parents, because in this matter they have not any experience, and through interest are commonly changed into enemies, as St. Thomas also remarks, when speaking of religious vocation. " Frequently," he says, " our friends according to the flesh are opposed to our spiritual good."[2] For fathers often prefer that their children should be damned with themselves, rather than be saved away from them. Whence St. Bernard exclaims, " O hard father, O cruel mother, whose consolation is the death of their son, who wish rather that we perish with them than reign without them !"[3]

God, says a grave author, Porrecta, when he calls one to a perfect life, wishes one to forget one's father, saying,

[1] " Non tenentur, nec servi dominis, nec filii parentibus, obedire de matrimonio contrahendo, vel virginitate servanda, vel aliquo alio hujusmodi."—2. 2. q. 104, a. 5.

[2] " Frequenter amici carnales adversantur profectui spirituali."— 2. 2. q. 189, a. 10.

[3] " O durum patrem, o sævam matrem, quorum consolatio mors filii est; qui me malunt perire cum eis, quam regnare sine eis!"—*Ep.* 111.

Hearken, O daughter, and see, and incline thine ear; and forget thy people and thy father's house.[1] "By this, then," he adds, "the Lord certainly admonishes us that he who is called ought by no means to allow the counsel of parents to intervene." "If God will have a soul, who is called by him, forget its father and its father's house, without doubt he suggests by this, that he who is called to the religious state ought not, before he follows the call, to interpose the counsel of the carnal friends of his household."[2]

St. Cyril, explaining what Jesus Christ said to the youth mentioned above, *No man putting his hand to the plough and looking back is fit for the kingdom of God,*[3] comments on it and says that he who asks for time to confer with his parents in reference to his vocation is exactly the one who is declared by our Lord to be unfit for heaven. "In order to confer with his parents, he looks back who seeks for delay."[4] Whence St. Thomas absolutely advises those who are called to religion, to abstain from deliberating on their vocation with their relatives: "From this deliberation, the relatives of the flesh are before all to be excluded; for it is said, *Treat thy cause with thy friend* (Prov. xxv. 9); but the relatives of the flesh are in this affair not our friends, but our enemies,

---

[1] "Audi, filia, et vide, et inclina aurem tuam; et obliviscere populum tuum, et domum patris tui."—*Ps.* xliv. 11.

[2] "Si Dominus vult animam ad se vocatam oblivisci patrem, domumque patris ejus, suggerit utique per hoc, quod vocatus ab ipso ad religionem non debet suorum carnalium amicorumque domesticorum consilium interponere talis vocationis exsecutioni."—*In* 2. 2. q. 189, a. 10.

[3] "Nemo mittens manum ad aratrum, et respiciens retro, aptus est regno Dei."—*Luke,* ix. 61.

[4] "Respicit retro, qui dilationem quærit, cum propinquis occasione conferendi."—*Ap. S. Thom. loc. cit.*

according to the saying of our Lord: *A man's enemies are those of his household*[1] (Matt. x. 36).

If, then, for following one's vocation it would be a great error to ask the counsel of parents, it would be a greater one still to ask their permission, and to wait for it, for such a demand cannot be made without an evident danger of losing the vocation, as often as there is a probable fear that parents would exert themselves to prevent it. And, in fact, the saints, when they were called to leave the world, left their homes without giving their parents so much as an intimation of it. Thus acted St. Thomas Aquinas, St. Francis Xavier, St. Philip Neri, St. Louis Bertrand. And we know that the Lord has even by miracles approved of these glorious flights.

St. Peter of Alcantara, when he went to the monastery to become a religious, and was fleeing from the house of his mother, under whose obedience he had lived since the death of his father, found himself prevented by a wide river from advancing any farther. He recommended himself to God, and at the same instant saw himself transported to the other side.

Likewise, when St. Stanislaus Kostka fled from home, without the permission of his father, his brother set out after him in great haste in a carriage, but having almost overtaken him, the horses, in spite of all the violence used against them, would not advance a step farther, till turning towards the city, they began to run at full speed.

In like manner the Blessed Oringa of Waldrano, in Tuscany, being promised in marriage to a young man, fled from the house of her parents in order to consecrate herself to God; but the river Arno opposing itself to her

---

[1] " Ab hoc consilio, primo quidem, amovendi sunt carnis propinqui; dicitur enim: 'Causam tuam tracta cum amico tuo.' Propinqui autem carnis, in hoc negotio, amici non sunt, sed inimici, juxta sententiam Domini: 'Inimici hominis, domestici ejus.' "

course, after a short prayer she saw it divide and form, as it were, two walls of crystal, to let her pass through with dry feet.

Therefore, my very beloved brother, if you are called by God to leave the world, be very careful not to make your resolution known to your parents, and, content to be thus blessed by God, seek to execute it as promptly as you can, and without their knowledge, if you would not expose yourself to the great danger of losing your vocation. For, generally speaking, relatives, as has been said above, especially fathers and mothers, oppose the execution of such resolutions; and although they may be endowed with piety, interest and passion nevertheless render them so blind that under various pretexts they scruple not to thwart with all their might the vocation of their children.

We read in the life of Father Paul Segneri the younger that his mother, though a matron much given to prayer, left nevertheless no means untried to prevent her son from entering the religious state to which he was called. We also read in the life of Mgr. Cavalieri, Bishop of Troja, that his father, although a man of great piety, used every means to prevent his son from entering the Congregation of Pious Workmen (which, notwithstanding, he afterwards did), and even went so far as to bring against him a lawsuit in the ecclesiastical court. And how many other fathers, notwithstanding they were men of piety and prayer, have not in such cases been seen to change, and to become possessed, as it were, of the devil! For under no other circumstance does hell seem to employ more formidable arms than when there is question of preventing those who are called to the religious state from executing their resolution.

For this reason be also very careful not to communicate your design to your friends, who will not scruple to dissuade you from it, or at least to divulge the secret, so that the knowledge of it will easily come to the ears of your parents.[1]

2. PRAYER.

In the second place, it is necessary to know that these vocations are only preserved by prayer; he who gives up prayer will certainly give up his vocation. It is necessary to pray, and to pray much; and therefore let him who feels himself called, not omit to make every morning after rising an hour of mental prayer, or at least half an hour, in his own room, if he can do so there without molestation, and if not, in the church, and likewise half an hour in the evening.

Let him not neglect also to make every day, without fail, a visit to the Most Holy Sacrament, as also to the Most Blessed Virgin Mary, in order to obtain the grace

---

[1] The grace of a religious vocation is not only a signal favor for him who receives it, but is also a great blessing for the whole family. Christian parents should wish it for their children as the most precious good, by giving thanks to God if he deigns to grant it, and should hasten to offer him with their whole heart the happy sacrifice that he requires of them. What may they not expect from Him who rewards so liberally the least action that we perform out of love for Him? On the other hand, to oppose a vocation is to oppose God. What would be the consequence of such an attempt?

Happily, we see parents who, giving the good example of an entire submission to God's will, have the wisdom to anticipate their children with the intention not to oppose their happiness and to leave them every liberty in reference to their vocation. Such parents do not run the risk of being deceived, and they acquire, moreover, great merit before the Lord.

St. Alphonsus, however, does not wish that young men should act thoughtlessly in a matter as important as it is delicate. He requires of them that they at least should consult a prudent director who will take care to weigh maturely before God all the circumstances, and to examine, among other things, whether the parents would not have some serious reason to allege; for instance, the grave necessity in which they found themselves, etc. We thus remove all danger of taking a rash step. (See note, page 388.)—ED.

of perseverance in his vocation. Let him likewise not omit to receive Holy Communion thrice, or at least twice, a week.

His meditations ought almost always to be on this point of the vocation, considering how great a favor from God he has received in being thus called by him; how much more easily he will secure his eternal salvation, if he be faithful to God in following his vocation; and, on the contrary, to how great a danger of being damned he exposes himself if he be unfaithful. Let him then especially place before his eyes the hour of death, and consider the contentment that he will then feel if he shall have obeyed God, and the pains and the remorse he would experience if he should die in the world. To this end I shall add at the end of this some considerations on which he may make his mental prayer.

It is, moreover, necessary that all his prayers to Jesus and Mary, and especially those after Communion and in the visits, be directed to obtain perseverance. In all his prayers and Communions let him always renew the offering of himself to God, by saying, " Behold, O Lord ! I am no more mine, I am Thine. Already have I given myself to Thee, and now I renew this my offering of my whole self. Accept of me and give me strength to be faithful to Thee and to retire as quickly as possible into Thy house."

3. RECOLLECTION.

In the third place, it is necessary that he be recollected, which will not be possible for him unless he withdraws from worldly conversations and amusements. What, in short, as long as we are in the world, is enough to cause the loss of vocation ? A mere nothing. One day of amusement, a word from a friend, a passion we do not mortify, a little attachment, a thought of fear, a resentment we do not overcome, suffices to bring to nought all our resolutions of retiring from the world, or of giving ourselves entirely to God. Wherefore we ought to keep perfectly recollected, detaching ourselves from everything of this world. We ought during this time to think of nothing but prayer and frequenting the sacraments, and to be nowhere but at home and in church. Let him who will not do so, but distracts himself by pastimes, be persuaded that he will without doubt lose his vocation. He will remain with the remorse of not having followed it, but he certainly will not follow it. Oh, how many by neglecting these precautions have lost, first their vocation, and afterwards their souls!

IV.

Disposition required for entering Religion.

He who feels himself to be called by God to a religious Institute in which reigns exact observance * ought to know that the end of every regular observance is, to follow as exactly as possible the footsteps and examples of the most holy life of Jesus Christ, who led a life entirely detached and mortified, full of suffering and contempt. He, then, who resolves to enter such a holy state must at the same time resolve to enter it for the sake of suffering and denying himself in all things, as Jesus Christ himself has declared to those who wish perfectly to follow him· *If any man will come after Me, let him deny himself, and take up his cross and follow Me.*[1]

---

[1] "Si quis vult post me venire, abneget semetipsum, et tollat crucem suam, et sequatur me."—*Matt.* xvi. 24.

---

* "I say 'in which reigns exact observance;' for it would be, perhaps, better to remain in the world than to enter a religious Institute in which relaxation has been introduced." We see that this remark is made by the author himself; he also says elsewhere, "Si institutum relaxatum est, melius erit alicui ordinarie loquendi, quod in sæculo remaneat." (*Hom. apost. tr. ult.* n. 39.)

He, then, who wishes to enter religion must firmly establish within himself this resolution to go to suffer, and to suffer much, so that afterwards he may not give way to temptations, when, having entered, he feels depressed under the hardships and privations of the poor and mortified life which is there led.

Many, on entering Communities of exact observance take not the proper means of finding peace therein, and of becoming saints, because they only place before their eyes the advantages of the Community life, such as the solitude, the quiet, the freedom from the troubles caused by relatives, from strife and other disagreeable matters, and from the cares consequent on being obliged to think of one's lodging, food, and clothing.

There is no doubt that every religious is only too much indebted to his Order, which delivers him from so many troubles, and thus procures for him so great a facility to serve God perfectly in peace, continually furnishing him with so many means for the welfare of his soul, so many good examples from his companions, so much good advice from his Superiors who watch for his benefit, so many exercises conducive to eternal salvation. All this is true; but with all this he must also, in order not to be deprived of so blessed a lot, resolve to embrace all the sufferings he may, on the other hand, meet with in the Order; for if he does not embrace them with love, he will never obtain that full peace which God gives to those who overcome themselves: *To him that overcomes I will give the hidden manna.*[1] For the peace which God gives his faithful servants to taste is hidden; nor is it known by the men of the world, who, seeing their mortified life, know not how to envy them, but pity them and call them the unhappy ones of this earth. But "they see the cross, the unction they do not see,"[2] says St.

---

[1] "Vincenti dabo manna absconditum."—*Apoc.* ii. 17.
[2] "Crucem vident, unctionem non vident."—*In Dedic.* s. 1.

Bernard; they see their mortification, but they do not see the contentment that God gives them to enjoy.

It is true that in the spiritual life one has to suffer, but, says St. Teresa, when one resolves to suffer, the pain is gone. Nay, the pains themselves turn into joy. " My daughter," so the Lord said one day to St. Bridget, " the treasure of my graces seems to be surrounded with thorns; but for him who overcomes the first stings, all is changed into sweetness." And then those delights which God gives to his beloved souls to enjoy in their prayers, in their Communions, in their solitude; those lights, those holy ardors and embraces, that quiet of conscience, that blessed hope of eternal life, who can ever understand them, if he does not experience them ? " One drop of the consolations of God," said St. Teresa, " is worth more than all the consolations and the pleasures of the world." Our most gracious God knows well how to give to him who suffers something for his sake, even in this valley of tears, the experience of the foretaste of the glory of the blessed; for in this is properly verified that which David says: *Thou who framest labor in commandment.*[1] In the spiritual life, God, announcing pains, tediousness, death, seems to frame labor, but, in fact, afterwards it is not so; for spiritual life brings to them who entirely give themselves to God that peace which, as St. Paul says, *Surpasseth all understanding.*[2] It surpasses all the pleasures of the world and of worldlings. Whence we see a religious more content in a poor cell than all the monarchs in their royal palaces. *O taste, and see that the Lord is sweet.*[3]

But, on the other hand, he must be persuaded that he who does not resolve to suffer and to overcome himself in the things contrary to his inclinations, will never be able

[1] " Qui fingis laborem in præcepto."—*Ps.* xciii. 20.

[2] " Exsuperat omnem sensum."—*Phil.* iv. 7.

[3] " Gustate, et videte quoniam suavis est Dominus."—*Ps.* xxxiii. 9.

26

to enjoy this true peace, though he should have already entered religion. *To him that overcomes, I will give the hidden manna.*[1] It is, then, necessary that he who wishes to be admitted into an Order of exact observance should enter with a mind determined to overcome himself in everything, by expelling from his heart every inclination and desire that is not from God, nor for God, so that he must detach himself from all things, and especially from the four following: 1. From his comforts. 2. From his parents. 3. From self-esteem. 4. From his own will.

I. DETACHMENT FROM HIS COMFORTS.

In religion, after the year of novitiate, one makes, besides the vows of chastity and obedience, also the vow of poverty, in consequence of which one can never possess anything as one's individual property, not even a pin, no income, no money or other things. The Community will provide him with all that he needs. But the vow of poverty does not suffice to make one a true follower of Jesus Christ if one does not afterwards embrace with joy of spirit all the inconveniences of poverty. "Not poverty, but the love of poverty is a virtue,"[2] says St. Bernard, and he means to say that for one to become a saint it is not enough to be poor only, if one does not love also the inconveniences of poverty. "Oh, how many would wish to be poor and similar to Jesus Christ!" says Thomas à Kempis; "they wish to be poor but without any want,"[3] but so that they be in want of nothing. In a word, they would wish the honor and the reward of poverty, but not the inconveniences of poverty.

It is easy to understand that in religion no one will seek for things that are superfluous,—cloths of silk, costly

---

[1] "Vincenti dabo manna absconditum."—*Apoc.* ii. 17.

[2] "Non paupertas, sed amor paupertatis virtus est."—*Epist.* 100.

[3] "Volunt esse pauperes, sed sine defectu."

food, furniture of value, and the like; but he may desire to have all things that are necessary, and these he may be unable to get. For then it is he gives proof that he truly loves poverty, when things that are needful,—such as his necessary clothing, bed-covering or food,—happen to be wanting, and yet he remains content and is not troubled. And what kind of poverty would that be to suffer if he were never in want of anything necessary? F. Balthasar Alvarez says that in order truly to love poverty we must also love the effects of poverty; that is, as he enumerates them, cold, hunger, thirst, and contempt.[1]

In religion, every one ought not only to be content with that which is given to him, without ever asking for anything of which, through the neglect of the stewards, he should be in want, which would be a great defect, but he ought also to prepare himself sometimes to bear the want even of those simple things that the Rule allows. For it may happen that sometimes he is in want of clothes, coverings, linen, or such-like things, and then he has to be satisfied with that little which has been given him, without complaining or being disquieted at seeing himself in want even of what is necessary. He who has not this spirit, let him not think of entering religion, because this is a sign that he is not called thereto or that he has not the will to embrace the spirit of the Institute. He who goes to serve God in his house, says St. Teresa, ought to consider that he is going not to be well treated for God, but to suffer for God.

2. DETACHMENT FROM HIS PARENTS.

He who wishes to enter religion must detach himself from his parents and forget them altogether. For, in religious houses of exact observance, detachment from

[1] " Frigus, famem, sitim, et contemptum."

parents is put in practice in the highest degree, in order perfectly to follow the doctrine of Jesus Christ, who said, *I came not to send peace, but the sword: I came to set a man at variance with his father,* etc.; [1] and then added the reason: *A man's enemies shall be they of his own household.*[2] And this is especially the case, as has been remarked above, in this point of religious vocation. When one's leaving the world is in question, there are no worse enemies than parents, who, either through interest or passion, prefer to become enemies of God, by turning their children away from their vocation, rather than to give their consent to it. Oh! how many parents shall we see in the valley of Josaphat damned for having made their children or nephews lose their vocation! and how many youths shall we see damned who, in order to please their parents, and by not detaching themselves from them, have lost their vocation and afterwards their souls! Whence Jesus declares to us, *If any man hate not his father,* etc., *he cannot be my disciple.*[3] Let him, then, who wishes to enter a religious Order of perfect observance, and to become a true disciple of Jesus Christ, resolve to forget his parents altogether.

When any one has already entered religion, let him remember that he must practise then the same detachment from parents. Let him know that he cannot go to visit his parents in their own house, except in the case of some dangerous illness of his father or mother, or of some other urgent necessity, though always with the permission of the Superior. Otherwise to go to the house of one's parents without the most express permis-

[1] "Non veni pacem mittere sed gladium; veni enim separare hominem adversus patrem suum et filiam adversus matrem suam."— *Matt.* x. 34.

[2] "Inimici hominis, domestici ejus."—*Ib.* 36.

[3] "Qui non odit patrem suum, et matrem, . . . etc., non potest esse meus discipulus."—*Luke*, xiv. 26.

sion would be considered in religion as a most notable and scandalous fault. In religion it is also considered a great defect even to ask permission or to show a desire of seeing parents or of speaking with them.

St. Charles Borromeo said that when he visited the house of his parents he always, after his return, found himself less fervent in spirit. And thus, let him who goes to the house of his parents by his own will and not through a positive obedience to his Superiors, be persuaded that he will leave it either under temptation or be cold and lukewarm.

St. Vincent of Paul could only be induced once to visit his country and his parents, and this out of pure necessity; and he said that the love of home and country was a great impediment to his spiritual progress. He said also that many, on account of having visited their country, had become so tender towards their relatives that they were like flies, which being once entangled in a cobweb, cannot extricate themselves from it. He added, "For that one time that I went, though it was for a short time only, and though I took care to prevent in my relatives every hope of help from me, notwithstanding, I felt at leaving them such a pain that I ceased not to weep all along the road, and was for three months harassed by the thought of succoring them. Finally, God in his mercy took that temptation from me."

Let him know, moreover, that no one may write to his parents without permission, and without showing the letter to the Superior. Otherwise, he would be guilty of a most grievous fault that is not to be tolerated in religion, and should be punished with severity; for from this might come a thousand disorders tending to destroy the religious spirit. Let especially the new-comer know that during the novitiate this is observed with the greatest rigor; for novices during their year of novitiate do not easily obtain permission to talk to their parents, or to write to them.

Finally, let him know that in case a subject should become sick, it would be a notable defect to ask or to show an inclination to go to his own house for his restoration to health, under the plea of being better taken care of, or of enjoying the benefit of his native air. The air of his own country becomes almost always, or rather always, hurtful, and pestilential to the spirit of the subject. And if he should ever say that he wishes to be cured at home in order not to subject the Order to expenses for remedies, let him know that the Order has charity enough to take sufficient care of the sick. As to the change of air, the Superiors will think of that; and if that of one house is not beneficial to him, they will send him to another. And as for remedies, they will even sell the books, if need be, to provide for the sick. And so let him be sure that divine Providence will not fail him. And if the Lord should decree against his recovery, he ought to conform to the will of God, without even mentioning the word " home." The greatest grace that he who enters an Order can desire is to die, when God wills it, in the house of God, assisted by the brethren of his Order, and not in a secular house in the midst of his relatives.

3. DETACHMENT FROM SELF-ESTEEM.

He must also be altogether detached from all self-esteem. Many leave their country, their comforts, and parents, but carry with them a certain esteem for themselves; but this is the most hurtful attachment of all. The greatest sacrifice that we can make to God is to give to him not only goods, pleasures, and home, but ourselves also, by leaving ourselves. This is that denying of one's self which Jesus Christ recommends above all to his followers. And in order to deny one's self, one must first place under foot all self-esteem, by desiring and embracing every imaginable contempt that he may meet with in religion; as, for instance, to see others, whom perhaps he thinks less deserving, preferred to himself, or to be considered unfit to be employed, or only employed in lower and more laborious occupations. He ought to know that in the house of God those charges are the highest and the most honorable that are imposed by obedience. God forbid that any one should seek for or aspire to any office or charge of pre-eminence. This would be a strange thing in religion, and he would be noted as proud and ambitious, and as such should be put in penance, and should especially be mortified in this point. Better would it be, perhaps, that a religious Order should be destroyed than that there should enter into it that accursed pest of ambition which, when it enters, disfigures the most exemplary Communities, and the most beautiful works of God.

But he ought to feel even consoled in spirit when he sees himself mocked and despised by his companions. I say consoled in spirit, for as to the flesh this will be impossible, nor need a subject be uneasy when he sees that he resents it; it is enough that the spirit embraces it, and that he rejoices at it in the superior part of the soul. Thus also seeing himself continually reprimanded and mortified by all, not only by Superiors, but also by equals and inferiors, he ought heartily, and with a tranquil mind, to thank those who thus reprimand him, and have the charity to admonish him, answering that he will be more attentive not to fall into that fault again.

One of the greatest desires of the saints in this world was to be contemned for the love of Jesus Christ. It was this that St. John of the Cross asked for, when Jesus Christ appeared to him with a cross on his shoulder, and said, " John, ask from me what thou wishest," and St. John answered, "O Lord, to suffer and to be despised for Thee." [1] The Doctors teach, with St. Francis de Sales, that the highest degree of humility we can have is to be pleased with abjections and humiliations. And in this consists also one of the greatest merits we can have with God. One contempt suffered in peace for the love of God is of greater value in his sight than a thousand disciplines and a thousand fasts.

It is necessary to know that to suffer contempt either from Superiors or from companions is a thing unavoidable even in the most holy Communities. Read the lives of the saints, and you will see how many mortifications were encountered by St. Francis Regis, St. Francis of Jerome, Father Torres, and others. The Lord sometimes permits that even among saints there should exist, though without their fault, certain natural antipathies, or at least a certain diversity of character among subjects of the greatest piety, which will cause them to suffer many contradictions. At other times false reports will be spread and believed. God himself will permit this, in order that the subjects may have occasion to exercise themselves in patience and humility.

In short, he will gain little in religion and lose much who cannot quietly put up with contempt and contradiction; and, therefore, he who enters religion to give himself entirely to God ought to be ashamed not to know how to bear contempt when he appears before Jesus Christ, who was "filled with opprobriums" [2] for love of us. Let every one be attentive to this, and resolve to be pleased in religion with all abjections, and to prepare himself to suffer many of them, for without the least doubt he will have many to bear. Otherwise, the disquiet caused by contradictions, and contempt badly

---

[1] "Joannes, pete a me, quid vis. . . . Domine, pati et contemni pro te."

[2] "Saturatus opprobriis."

borne with, might trouble him so much as to make him lose his vocation, and chase him out of religion. Oh, how many have lost their vocation on account of such impatience in humiliations! But of what service to the Order or to God can he be who does not know how to bear contempt for his sake? And how can one ever be said to be dead according to that promise which he made to Jesus Christ, on entering religion, to die to himself if he remained alive to resentment and disquiet, when he sees himself humbled? Out of the Order with such subjects, so attached to their own esteem! out with them! It is well for them to go as soon as possible, that they may not infect the rest also with their pride. In religion every one ought to be dead, and especially to his own self-esteem, otherwise it is better for him not to enter, or to depart again if he has already entered.

4. DETACHMENT FROM HIS OWN WILL.

He who enters religion must altogether renounce his own will, consecrating it entirely to holy obedience. Of all things, this is the most necessary. What does it avail to leave comforts, parents, and honors, if we still carry into religion our own will? In this principally consists the denial of ourselves, the spiritual death, and the entire surrender of ourselves to Jesus Christ. The gift of the heart—that is, of the will—is what pleases him most, and what he wishes from the children of religion. Otherwise, if we do not entirely detach ourselves from our own will and renounce it in all, all mortifications, all meditations and prayers, and all other sacrifices, will be of little avail.

It is, then, evident that this is the greatest merit we can have before God, and this is the only and sure way of pleasing God in all things, so that then we can, each one of us, say what Jesus our Saviour said: *I do always the things that please Him.*[1] Certainly, he who in religion lives without self-will may say and hope that in all that he does he pleases God, whether he studies or prays, or hears confessions, whether he goes to the refectory or to recreation, or to rest; for in religion not a step is made, not a breath drawn, but in obedience to the Rule, or to Superiors.

The world does not know, and even certain persons given to spirituality have little idea of, the great value of a Community life under obedience. It is true that outside of religious Communities there are to be found many persons who do much, and, may be, more than those who live under obedience; they preach, do penance, pray and fast, but in all this they consult more or less their own will. God grant that at the day of judgment they may not have to lament as those mentioned in Scripture: *Why have we fasted and Thou hast not regarded, have we humbled ourselves, and Thou hast not taken notice? Behold, in the day of your fast, your own will is found.*[2] On which passage St. Bernard remarks: "Self-will is a great evil, for through it that which is good in itself may be for you no good at all."[3] This to be understood when in all these exercises we seek not God, but ourselves. On the contrary, he who does all by obedience is sure that in all he pleases God. The Venerable Mother Mary of Jesus said that she prized so much her vocation to religion principally for two reasons: the first was that in the monastery she enjoyed always the presence and company of Jesus in the Blessed Sacrament, and the other was that there by

[1] " Ego, quæ placita sunt ei, facio semper."—*John*, viii. 29.

[2] " Quare jejunavimus, et non aspexisti? humiliavimus animas nostras, et nescisti? Ecce in die jejunii vestri invenitur voluntas vestra." —*Isa.* lviii. 3.

[3] "Grande malum, propria voluntas, qua fit, ut bona tua tibi bona non sint."—*In Cant.* s. 71.

obedience she entirely belonged to God, sacrificing to him her own will.

It is related by F. Rodriguez that after the death of Dositheus, the disciple of St. Dorotheus, the Lord revealed that in those five years he had lived under obedience, though by reason of his infirmities he could not practise the austerities of the other monks, yet by the virtue of obedience he had merited the reward of St. Paul the Hermit and of St. Anthony the Abbot.

He, then, who wishes to enter religion must resolve to renounce altogether his own will, and to will only what holy obedience wills. God preserve any religious from ever letting escape from his mouth the words, I will or I will not. But in all things, even when asked by Superiors what he desires, he should only answer, I wish that which holy obedience wills. And, provided there is no evident sin, he ought in every command imposed on him to obey blindly and without examination, because the duty of examining and deciding the doubts belongs not to him, but to his Superiors. Otherwise, if in obeying he does not submit his own judgment to that of the Superior, his obedience is imperfect. St. Ignatius of Loyola said that prudence in things of obedience is not required in subjects, but in Superiors; and if there is prudence in obeying, it is too bey without prudence. St. Bernard says, " Perfect obedience is indiscreet," [1] and in another place he says, " For a prudent novice to remain in the Congregation is an impossible thing;" and, adding the reason for it, he says, " To judge belongs to the Superior; and to obey, to the subject." [2]

But to make progress in this virtue of obedience, on which all depends, he must always keep his mind ready to do all that for which he feels the greatest repugnance,

---

[1] " Perfecta obedientia est indiscreta."—*De vita solit.* c. 5.

[2] " Novitium prudentem in congregatione durare impossibile est. . . . Discernere superioris est, subditi obedire."—*Ibid.*

and, on the contrary, he must be prepared to bear it quietly when he sees that all he seeks or desires is refused to him. It will happen that when he wishes to be in solitude, to apply himself to prayer or study, he will be the most employed in exterior occupations. For though it is true that in religion one leads as much as possible a solitary life when at home, and that for this end there are many hours of silence,—the retreat each year of ten days in perfect silence, and of one day each month, besides the fifteen days before the receiving of the habit, and one of fifteen before the profession, when the vows are made,—nevertheless, if it is an Order of priests called to work and to be employed for the salvation of souls, the subject, if he is continually employed in this by obedience, ought to be content with the prayers and exercises of the Community; he must be prepared sometimes to go even without these when obedience will have it so, without either excusing himself or being disquieted, being well persuaded of that of which St. Mary Magdalene of Pazzi was so confident when she said that "all the things which are done through obedience are but so many prayers."

V.

Trials which we must expect to have in the Religious Life.

When, then, any one has thus entered religion, however truly he may be called, and though he may have conquered all his passions and his earthly affections, let him not imagine that he will be exempt from other temptations and trials, which God himself will send him, such as tediousness, darkness, various fears, in order to establish him more firmly in his vocation. We must remember that even the saints, who have loved their vocation the most, have sometimes suffered great darkness with regard to it, and that it seemed to them as if they were deceived, and would not be able to save themselves in that state. So it happened with St. Teresa, St. John of the Cross, the Venerable Mother Frances de Chantal. But by recommending themselves to God, that darkness was dissipated, and they recovered their peace of mind. Thus the Lord tries his most beloved children, as it was said to Tobias: *Because thou wast acceptable to God, it was necessary that temptation should prove thee.*[1] And in the book of Deuteronomy, *The Lord, your God trieth you, that it may appear whether you love him or not.*[2] Let each one therefore prepare himself to suffer in religion this obscurity. It will sometimes appear to him that he cannot bear the observance of the Order, that he will have no more peace of mind, or will not even be able to save himself. But, most of all, every one must be on his guard when the temptation presents specious scruples or pretexts of greater spiritual good, in order to make him abandon his vocation.

The principal remedies in such temptations are two in number.

FIRST REMEDY: TO HAVE RECOURSE TO GOD.

The first is prayer, *Go ye to him and be enlightened.*[3] For as it will not be possible for temptation to overcome him who has recourse to prayer, so he who does not recommend himself to God will surely be overcome by it. And let it be remarked that sometimes it will not suffice to have recourse to God once, or for a few days, to become victorious. Perhaps the Lord will permit the temptation to continue, even after we have prayed for several weeks, months, and even years; but let us be as-

[1] " Quia acceptus eras Deo, necesse fuit ut tentatio probaret te."— *Tob.* xii. 13.

[2] " Tentat vos Dominus Deus vester, ut palam fiat, utrum diligatis eum, an non."—*Deut* xiii. 3

[3] " Accedite ad eum, et illuminamini."—*Ps.* xxxiii. 6.

sured that he who ceases not to recommend himself to God will certainly be enlightened and victorious, and thereafter he will have more peace and be more firm in his vocation.

Until we have gone through that storm, which for the most part comes over all, let none of us think himself secure. Let us be persuaded, however, that in this time of temptation we ought not to expect a fervor, and a clearness of reason sufficient to tranquillize ourselves; for in the midst of this darkness we see nothing but confusion. We have nothing then to do but to say to the Lord, O Lord, help me! O Lord, help me! and also to have frequently recourse to Most Holy Mary, who is the mother of perseverance, confiding in that divine promise: *Ask and you shall receive.*[1] And it is certain that he who, with the help of divine grace, is victorious in such a combat finds afterwards a double calm and peace in his vocation.

SECOND REMEDY: TO HAVE RECOURSE TO THE SUPERIORS.

The second remedy, and a principal and necessary one in such temptations, is to communicate to the Superiors, or to the spiritual Father of the Community, the temptation which afflicts you, and this at once, before the temptation becomes strong. St. Philip Neri said that when a temptation is thus manifested it is half vanquished. On the contrary, there is in such a case no greater evil than to conceal the temptation from Superiors; for then, on the one hand, God withdraws his light because of the little fidelity shown by the subject in not disclosing it, and, on the other, whilst the mine is not sprung, the temptation gains strength. Whence it may be held for certain that he will surely lose his vocation who, when he is tempted against it, does not disclose his temptations.

[1] " Petite et accipietis."—*John*, xvi. 24.

And let it be understood that in religion the most dangerous temptations that hell can bring against a subject are those against vocation, in which, if it should succeed and conquer, by that one stroke it will have gained many victories; for when a subject has lost his vocation and left religion, what good will he any more be able to do in the service of God ? Though the enemy may make him believe that out of religion he will have more peace and be able to do more good, nevertheless let him hold for certain that as soon as he is out of it he will feel such a remorse in his heart that he will nevermore have peace. And God grant that such a remorse may not torment him afterwards through all eternity in hell, into which, as has already been said, he who through his own fault loses his vocation falls so very easily. He will be so lukewarm and discouraged in doing good that he will not even have the courage to raise his eyes to heaven. It will be an easy thing for him to give up prayer altogether, because as often as he begins it he will feel a hell of remorse, hearing his conscience reproach him, and saying, "What hast thou done ? Thou hast abandoned God; thou hast lost thy vocation; and for what ? To follow thine own caprice, to please thy parents." Let him be certain that he will have to hear this reproach through his whole life, and still more shall he hear it made to him at the hour of his death, when, in sight of eternity, instead of dying in the house of God, and in the midst of good brethren in religion, he will have to die outside of the Community, perhaps in his own house, in the midst of his relatives, to please whom he has displeased God. Let religious always beseech God to let them die rather than to permit that greatest of disgraces, the greatness of which they will better understand at the point of death and to their greater torment, because then there will be no more any remedy for their error. For him, then, who is tempted against his vocation, this is the best meditation he can make in the time of the temptation,—namely, to reflect what torment the remorse of having lost his vocation, and of having to die outside of religion, through his own caprice, through his own fault, will cause him at the hour of death.

CONCLUSION.

Finally, let him who wishes to enter religion not forget to resolve to become a saint, and to suffer every exterior and interior pain, in order to be faithful to God, and not to lose his vocation. And if he be not resolved to this, I exhort him not to deceive the Superiors and himself, and not to enter at all, for this is a sign that he is not called, or, which is a still greater evil, that he wishes not to correspond, as he ought, with the grace of his vocation. Hence, with so bad a disposition it is better to remain without, in order to acquire a better disposition, to resolve to give himself entirely to God, and to suffer all for God. Otherwise he will do an injury both to himself and to the Order; for he will easily go back to the world, and then, being disgraced before the world, as well as before God, he will be guilty of a still further infidelity to his vocation, and will lose the confidence in the power of taking another step in the way of God. God only knows into what other misfortunes and sins he may afterwards fall.

On the other hand, a beautiful sight it is to see in religion souls wholly given to God, who live in the world as if out of the world, without any other thought than that of pleasing God.

In religion each one has to live only for eternal life. What happiness for us, if we spend these few days of our life for God! And to this he is most especially obliged who has perhaps already spent much of his life in the service of the world. Let us set eternity before our eyes, and then we shall suffer all with peace and joyfulness.

Let us thank God, who gives us so much light and so many means to serve him perfectly, since he has chosen us, from among so many, to serve him in religion, having bestowed on us the gift of his holy love. Let us make haste to please him in the practice of virtue, reflecting that, as St. Teresa said to her daughters, we have already by his grace done the principal thing necessary to become saints, by turning our backs on the world and all its goods, the least yet remains to be done, and we shall be saints. I hold it for certain that for those who die in religion, Jesus Christ has prepared a prominent place in paradise. On this earth we shall be poor, despised, and treated as fools, as imprudent men, but in the other life our lot will be changed.

Let us always recommend ourselves to our Redeemer hidden in the Sacrament, and to Most Holy Mary, because in religion all subjects must profess a most special love for Jesus in the Blessed Sacrament, and for the Immaculate Virgin Mary; and let us have great confidence. Jesus Christ has chosen us to be princes of his court, as we may confidently conclude from the protection he extends to all religious Orders, and to each member of them. *The Lord is my light and my salvation, whom shall I fear?* [1]

O Lord! finish Thy work, and, for Thy glory, grant us to be all Thine, so that all the members of Thy Orders may until the day of judgment, be pleasing to Thee, and gain over to Thee an immense number of souls. Amen. Amen.

[1] "Dominus illuminatio mea et salus mea; quem timebo?"—*Ps.* xxvi. 1.

27

CONSIDERATIONS FOR THOSE WHO ARE CALLED TO THE RELIGIOUS STATE.

CONSIDERATION I.

How the Salvation of the Soul is secured by entering the Religious State.

To know how important is the eternal salvation of our soul, it suffices to have faith, and to consider that we have but one soul, and when that is lost, all is lost. *What does it profit a man if he gain the whole world, and suffer the loss of his soul?*[1] This great maxim of the Gospel has induced many youths either to shut themselves up in cloisters or to live in deserts, or by martyrdom to give up their lives for Jesus Christ. For, said they, what does it profit us to possess the whole world, and all the goods of this world, in this present life, which must soon finish, and then be damned and be miserable in that life to come, which will never end? All those rich men, all those princes and emperors, who are now in hell, what have they now of all they enjoyed in this life, but a greater torment and a greater despair? Miserable beings, they lament now and say, *All those things are passed like shadows.*[2] For them all is passed like a shadow, like a dream, and that lamentation which is their lot has lasted already many years, and shall last throughout all eternity. *The fashion of this world passeth away.*[3] This world is a scene which lasts but a short time; happy he

[1] "Quid enim prodest homini, si mundum universum lucretur, animæ vero suæ detrimentum patiatur?"—*Matt.* xvi. 26.
[2] "Transierunt omnia illa tanquam umbra."—*Wisd.* v. 9.
[3] "Præterit figura hujus mundi."—1 *Cor.* vii. 51.

who plays on this scene that part which will afterwards make him happy in the life which will never end. When he shall then be contented, honored, and a prince in paradise, so long as God shall be God, little will he care for having been in this world poor, despised, and in tribulation. For this end alone has God placed us on this earth, and keeps us here in life, not to acquire transitory but eternal goods: *The end is life everlasting.*[1]

This is the sole end, which all men who live in the world ought to have in view. But the misfortune is, that in the world one thinks little or nothing of everlasting life. In the midst of the darkness of this Egypt, the greatest number of men bestow all their care on acquiring honor and pleasures; and this is the reason why so many perish. *With desolation is all the land made desolate, because there is none that considereth in his heart.*[2] How few are they who reflect on death, by which for us the scene is closed; on the eternity which awaits us; on what God has done for our sake! And thence it comes that these miserable beings live in blindness and at random, far from God, having their eyes, like the beasts, intent only on earthly things, without remembering God, without desiring his love, and without a thought of eternity. Therefore, they die afterwards an unhappy death, which will be the beginning of an eternal death and an endless misery. Having arrived there, they will open their eyes; but it will be only to lament for their own foolishness.

This is the great means of salvation which is found in religion, to wit: the continual meditation on the eternal truths. *Remember thy last end, and thou shalt never sin.*[3] In all well-regulated religious houses this is done every

---

[1] "Finem vero, vitam æternam."—*Rom.* vi. 22.

[2] "Desolatione desolata est omnis terra, quia nullus est qui recogitet corde."—*Jer.* xii. 11.

[3] "Memorare novissima tua, et in æternum non peccabis."—*Ecclus.* vii. 40.

day, and even several times a day. And therefore in this light of divine things, which there shines continually, it is morally impossible to live, at least for a long time, far from God, and without keeping one's account ready for eternity.

Prayer.

O my God! how have I ever deserved this great mercy, that, having left so many others to live in the midst of the world, Thou hast willed to call me, who have offended Thee more than others, and deserved, more than they, to be deprived of Thy divine light, to enjoy the honor of living as a friend in Thy own house! O Lord! grant that I may understand this exceeding grace which Thou hast bestowed on me, that I may always thank Thee for it, as I purpose and hope to do always during my life and throughout eternity, and do not permit me to be ungrateful for it. Since Thou hast been so liberal towards me, and hast in Thy love preferred me to others, it is but just that more than others I should serve and love Thee. O my Jesus! Thou wouldst have me to be wholly Thine, and to Thee I give myself wholly. Accept me, and henceforward keep me as Thy own, since I am no more mine. Finish Thou the work which Thou hast begun. Thou hast called me to Thy house, because Thou wilt have me become a saint. Make me then what Thou wilt have me. Do it, O eternal Father! for the love of Jesus Christ, in whom is all my confidence. I love Thee, my sovereign good, I love Thee. O infinite goodness! I love Thee alone, and will love Thee forever. O Mary, my hope, come to my assistance, and obtain for me to be always faithful and thankful to my Lord.

CONSIDERATION II.

The Happy Death of the Religious.

Happy are the dead who die in the Lord.[1] And who are those blessed dead who die in the Lord, but the religious, who at the end of their lives are found already dead to the world, having already detached themselves by their holy vows from the world and all its goods?

[1] "Beati mortui, qui in Domino moriuntur."—*Apoc.* xiv. 13.

Consider, my brother, how content you will feel if, following your vocation, it will be your good fortune to die in the house of God. The devil will certainly represent to you that if you retire into the house of God, you may perhaps afterwards repent of having left your own house and your own country, and deprived your parents of that succor which they might have expected from you. But say to yourself: shall I, at the point of death, repent of having put my resolution in execution, or shall I be content? I beseech you, therefore, to imagine yourself now already at the point of death, about to appear before the tribunal of Jesus Christ. Reflect what then, reduced to that state, you would wish to have done. Perhaps to have contented your parents, to have worked for your own family and your country, and then to die surrounded by brothers, and nephews, and relatives, after having lived in your own house with the title of pastor, of canon, of bishop, of a member of the cabinet, and after having done your own will? or rather, to die in the house of God, assisted by your good brethren in religion, who encourage you on the great passage to eternity, after having lived many years in religion, humbled, mortified, poor, far from parents, deprived of your own will, and under obedience, and detached from everything in the world,—all these things render death sweet and agreeable? " He who has been accustomed to deprive himself of the delights of the world," says St. Bernard, " will not regret having done so when he has to leave it." [1] Pope Honorius II., when dying, wished that he had remained in his monastery, occupied in washing the plates, and had not been Pope. Philip II. wished at his death that he had been a lay-brother in some religious order, intent on serving God, and had not been a king. Philip III., also King of Spain, said when he was

[1] " Qui consuevit se delectationibus mundi privare, mundum deserere non sentiet."

dying, "Oh that I had been in a desert, there to serve God, and that I had never been a monarch! for had such been the case, I should now appear with more confidence before the tribunal of Jesus Christ."

When, then, hell tempts you about your vocation, think of the hour of death, and set before your eyes that all-important moment "upon which eternity depends."[1] Thus you will overcome all temptations; you will be faithful to God; and certainly you will not repent of it at the point of death, but will give thanks to the Lord, and die contented. Gerard, brother of St. Bernard, died singing, at the very thought of dying in the house of God.

Father Suarez, of the Company of Jesus, felt at his death so great consolation and sweetness at dying in religion that he said, "I never thought it was so sweet to die."[2]

Another good religious, of the same society, when at the point of death, laughed; and being asked why he laughed, answered: "And why should I not laugh? Has not Jesus Christ himself promised paradise to him who leaves everything for his sake? Was it not he who said, *Every one that has left house, or brethren, or father, etc., shall receive a hundred-fold, and shall possess life everlasting?*[3] I have left all for God; God is faithful, he cannot fail to fulfil his promises; and so," he said, "why should I not rejoice and laugh, seeing myself assured of paradise?"

A certain lay-brother, who died some years ago, was asked, at his death, in which house he would rather be. He answered, "I desire nothing but to die and to be united with God."

Father Januarius Sarnelli, a short time before his

[1] "A quo pendet æternitas."
[2] "Non putabam tam dulce esse mori."
[3] "Qui reliquerit domum vel fratres, aut patrem, etc., centuplum accipiet, et vitam æternam possidebit."—*Matt.* xix. 29.

death, when conversing with God, uttered the following words: "O Lord, Thou knowest that all I have done, all I have thought, has been for Thy glory; now I wish to go to see Thee face to face, if it please Thee so;" then he said, "Come, I will begin a sweet agony;" and began to converse affectionately with God, and shortly after placidly expired, preserving the smile on his lips, and the body began to give forth a sweet odor, which, as they attested, was perceived for several days in the room in which he had died.

St. Bernard, then, speaking of the happy state of religious, had good reason to exclaim: "O secure life, in which death is expected without fear,—ay, sweetly desired and devoutly accepted !" [1]

Prayer.

O my Lord Jesus Christ! who, in order to obtain a happy death for me, hast chosen so bitter a death for Thyself; since Thou hast loved me to such an extent as to have chosen me to follow more closely Thy holy life, to have me thus more intimately united with Thy loving heart, bind me, I beseech Thee, wholly to Thee with the sweet cords of Thy love, that I may no more separate myself from Thee. O my beloved Redeemer! I wish to be grateful to Thee, and to correspond with Thy grace, but I fear my weakness may render me unfaithful; O my Jesus! do not permit this. Let me die rather than abandon Thee, or forget the peculiar affection Thou hast shown me.

I love Thee, O my dear Saviour! Thou art and shalt always be the only Lord of my heart and of my soul. I leave all and choose Thee alone for my treasure, O most pure Lamb of God, O my most ardent lover! *My beloved is white and ruddy, chosen out of thousands.* [2] Be gone, ye creatures, my only good is my God, he is my love, my all. I love Thee, O my Jesus! and in

[1] "O vita secura, ubi absque formidine mors expectatur, immo et exoptatur cum dulcedine, et excipitur cum devotione!"—*Ad Mil. T.* c. 1.

[2] "Dilectus meus candidus et rubicundus, electus ex millibus."— *Cant.* v. 10.

loving Thee I will spend the remainder of my life, be it short, or be it long. I embrace Thee, I press Thee to my heart, and I wish to die united with Thee. I wish nothing else. Make me live always burning with Thy love, and when I shall have arrived at the end of my life, make me to expire in an ardent act of love towards Thee.

Immaculate Virgin Mary, obtain thou this grace for me, I hope it from thee.

CONSIDERATION III.

The Account which he will have to render to Jesus Christ, on the Day of Judgment, who does not follow his Vocation.

The grace of vocation to the religious state is not an ordinary grace; it is a very rare one, which God grants only to a few. *He hath not done so to every nation.*[1] Oh, how much greater is this grace, to be called to a perfect life and to become one of the household of God, than if one were called to be the king of any kingdom on this earth! for what comparison can there be between a temporal kingdom of this earth and the eternal kingdom of heaven?

But the greater the grace is, the greater will be the indignation of the Lord against him who has not corresponded with it, and the more rigorous will be his judgment at the day of account. If a king were to call a poor shepherd to his royal palace, to serve him among the noblemen of his court, what would not be the indignation of this king were he to refuse such a favor, through unwillingness to leave his miserable stable and his little flock? God knows well the value of his graces, and therefore he chastises with severity those who despise them. He is the Lord; when he calls, he wishes to be obeyed, and obeyed promptly. When, therefore, by his inspiration, he calls a soul to a perfect life, if it does

[1] " Non fecit taliter omni nationi."—*Ps*. cxlvii. 20.

not correspond, he deprives it of his light, and abandons it to its own darkness. Oh, how many poor souls shall we see among the reprobate on the day of judgment for this very reason, that they were called and would not correspond !

Give thanks, then, to the Lord, who has invited you to follow him; but if you do not correspond, fear. Since God calls you to serve him nearer to his person, it is a sign that he wishes to save you. But he will have you to be saved in that path only which he indicates to you and has chosen for you. If you wish to save yourself on a road of your own choosing, there is great danger that you will not be saved at all; for if you remain in the world, when God wishes you to be a religious, he will not give you those efficacious helps prepared for you had you lived in his house, and without these you will not save yourself. *My sheep hear my voice.*[1] He who will not obey the voice of God shows that he is not, and will not be, one of his sheep, but in the valley of Josaphat he will be condemned with the goats.

PRAYER.

O Lord, Thou hast shown me such an excess of bounty as to choose me from among so many others, to serve Thee in Thy own house with Thy most beloved servants. I know how great is that grace, and how unworthy of it I have been. Behold, I am willing to correspond to so great a love. I will obey Thee. Since Thou hast been towards me so liberal as to call me when I did not seek Thee, and when I was so ungrateful, permit it not that I should offer to Thee that greater excess of ingratitude, to embrace again my enemy, the world, in which heretofore I have so oftentimes forfeited Thy grace and my eternal salvation, and thus to forsake Thee, who hast shed Thy blood and given Thy life for my sake. Since Thou hast called me, give me also the strength to correspond to the call. Already have I promised to obey Thee. I promise it again, but without the grace

---

[1] " Oves meæ vocem meam audiunt."—*John*, x. 27.

of perseverance I cannot be faithful to Thee. This perseverance I ask from Thee, and through Thy own merits it is that I
wish it and hope to obtain it. Give me the courage to vanquish
the passions of the flesh, through which the devil seeks to induce me to betray Thee. I love Thee, O my Jesus! to Thee I
consecrate myself entirely. I am already Thine, I will be always Thine. O Mary, my mother and my hope, thou art the
mother of perseverance. This grace is only dispensed through
thy hands; do thou obtain it for me. In thee do I confide.

CONSIDERATION IV.

The Torment which in Hell will be the Lot of him who is damned for having lost his Vocation.

The pain of having through one's own fault lost some
great good, or of having brought upon one's self voluntarily some great evil, is a pain so great that even in
this life it causes an insupportable torment. But what
torment will that youth, called by the singular favor of
God to the religious state, feel in hell when he then
perceives that if he had obeyed God he would have
attained a high place in paradise, and sees himself nevertheless confined in that prison of torments, without hope
of remedy for this his eternal ruin! *Their worm dieth not.*[1]

This will be that worm, which, living always, will
always gnaw his heart by a continual remorse. He will
say then, What a fool I was! I might have become a
great saint. And if I had obeyed, I would certainly
have become so; and now I am damned without remedy.

Miserable being! Then for his greater torment, on
the day of judgment he will see and recognize at the
right hand, and crowned as saints, those who have followed their vocation, and, leaving the world, have retired to the house of God, to which he also had been
once called. And then will he see himself separated
from the company of the blessed, and placed in the

---

[1] " Vermis eorum non moritur."—*Mark*, ix. 43.

midst of that innumerable and miserable crew of the damned, for his disobedience to the voice of God.

We know well, as we have considered above, that to this most unhappy lot he exposes himself, who, in order to follow his own caprice, turns a deaf ear to the call of God. Therefore, my brother, you who have already been called to become a saint in the house of God, consider that you will expose yourself to a great danger should you lose your vocation through your own fault. Consider that this very vocation which God in his sovereign bounty has given you, in order, as it were, to take you out from among the populace and place you among the chosen princes of his paradise, will, through your own fault, should you be unfaithful to it, become an especial hell for you. Make your choice then, for God leaves it in your own hands, either to be a great king in paradise, or a reprobate in hell, more despairing than the rest.

Prayer.

No, my God, permit me not to disobey Thee and to be unfaithful. I see Thy goodness, and thank Thee for that instead of casting me away from Thy face, and banishing me into hell, as I have so often deserved, Thou callest me to become a saint, and preparest for me a high place in paradise. I see that I should deserve a double torment, should I not correspond with this grace, which is not given to all. I will obey Thee. Behold, I am Thine, and always will be Thine. I embrace with joy all the pains and discomforts of the religious life, to which Thou invitest me. And what are these pains in comparison with the eternal pains, which I have deserved? I was entirely lost through my sins; now I give myself entirely to Thee. Dispose of me and my life as Thou pleasest. Accept, O Lord! of one already condemned to hell, as I have been, to serve Thee and love Thee in this life and in the next. I will love Thee as much as I have deserved to be doomed to hate Thee in hell, O God, worthy of an infinite love! O my Jesus! Thou hast broken those chains by which the world held me bound; Thou hast delivered me from the servitude of my enemies. I will love Thee much, then, O my love! and for the love I bear Thee, I will always love Thee and obey Thee. Always will I thank Thee, O Mary, my advocate, who hast obtained this mercy for me. Help me, and suffer me not to be ungrateful to that God who has loved me so much. Obtain for me that I may die rather than be unfaithful to so great a grace. Thus I hope.

CONSIDERATION V.

The Immense Glory which Religious enjoy in Heaven.

Consider, in the first place, that which St. Bernard says, that it is difficult for religious who die in the religious state to be damned. "From the cell to heaven the way is easy; one scarcely ever descends from his cell into hell." And the reason which the saint adduces is, "because one scarcely ever perseveres in it until death, unless he be predestinated." [1] For a religious with difficulty perseveres until his death, if he be not of the number of the elect of paradise. Therefore, St. Laurence Justinian called the religious state the gate of paradise. "Of that heavenly city this is the gate." [2] And he said that "therefore the religious have a great sign of their predestination." [3]

Consider, moreover, that the reward of heaven, as the Apostle says, is "a crown of justice;" [4] wherefore God, though he rewards us for our works more abundantly than we deserve, rewards us nevertheless in proportion to the works we have done. *He will render to every one according to his works.* [5] From this consider how exceed-

[1] "Facilis via de cella ad coelum. . . . Vix unquam aliquis a cella in infernum descendit: quia vix unquam, nisi coelo praedestinatus, in ea usque ad mortem persistit."—*De Vit. Sol.* c. 4.

[2] "Illius coelestis civitatis, iste est introitus."

[3] "Magnum quippe praedestinationis indicium est."—*De Disc. mon.* c. 7.

[4] "Corona justitiae."—2 *Tim.* iv. 8.

[5] "Reddet unicuique secundum opera ejus."—*Matt.* xvi. 27.

ingly great will be the reward which God will give in heaven to good religious, in consideration of the great merits they daily acquire.

The religious gives to God all his goods of this earth, and is content to be entirely poor, without possessing anything. The religious renounces all attachment to his parents, friends, and country, in order to unite himself more closely to God. The religious continually mortifies himself in many things which he would enjoy in the world. The religious, finally, gives to God his whole self, by giving him his will through the vow of obedience.

But the dearest thing that we have is our own will, and what God, of all other things, requires of us most is our heart; that is to say, our will. *My son, give Me thy heart.*[1] He who serves God in the world will give him his possessions, but not himself; he will give him a part and not the whole, for he will give him indeed his goods by alms-deeds, his food by fasting, his blood by disciplines, etc.; but he will always reserve for himself his own will, fasting when he pleases, praying when he likes. But the religious, giving him his own will, gives himself and gives all, gives not only the fruits of the tree, but the whole tree itself. Whence he may then truly say to him, O Lord! having given Thee my will, I have nothing more to give to Thee.

And, therefore, in all that he does through obedience he is sure to do the will of God perfectly, and merits by all, not only when he prays, when he hears confessions, when he preaches, or fasts, or practises other mortifications, but also when he takes his food, when he sweeps his room, when he makes his bed, when he takes his rest, when he recreates himself; for, doing all this through obedience, in all he does the will of God. St. Mary Magdalene de Pazzi said that all that is done through

---

[1] "Præbe, fili mi, cor tuum mihi."—*Prov.* xxiii. 26.

obedience is a prayer. Hence, St. Anselm, speaking of those who love obedience, asserted that all that religious do is meritorious for them. St. Aloysius Gonzaga said that in religion one sails, as it were, in a vessel, in which he even advances who does not row.

Oh, how much more will a religious gain in one month by observing his Rule than a secular, with all his penance and prayers, in a year! Of that disciple of Dorotheus called Dositheus, it was revealed that for the five years he had lived under obedience, there was given to him in heaven the glory of St. Paul the Hermit and of St. Anthony the Abbot, both of whom had, for so many years, lived in the desert. Religious, it is true, have to suffer the inconveniences of regular observance: *Going, they went and wept.* But when are they called to the other life, they will go to heaven, but, *coming, they shall come with joyfulness, carrying their sheaves.*[1] Whence they shall then sing, *The lines are fallen unto me in goodly places, for my inheritance is goodly to me.*[2] These bonds which have bound me to the Lord have become for me exceedingly precious, and the glory they have acquired for me is exceedingly great.

Prayer.

Is it possible, O my God and my true lover! that Thou desirest so much my good, and to be loved by me, and that I, miserable that I am, desire so little to love and to please Thee? For what end hast Thou favored me with so many graces, and taken me out of the world? O my Jesus! I understand Thee. Thou lovest me much, Thou wilt have me love Thee much also, and be all Thine, in this life and in the next. Thou wishest that my love should not be divided with creatures, but wilt have it be wholly for Thyself, the only good, the only lovely

---

[1] " Euntes ibant et flebant. . . . Venientes autem venient cum exultatione, portantes manipulos suos."—*Ps.* cxxv. 6.

[2] " Funes ceciderunt mihi in præclaris, etenim hereditas mea præclara est mihi."—*Ps.* xv. 6

one, and worthy of infinite love. Ah! my Lord, my treasure, my love, my all, yet I pant and truly desire to love Thee, and to love no other but Thee. I thank Thee for this desire Thou hast given me; preserve it in me, always increase it in me, and grant that I may please Thee, and love Thee on this earth as Thou desirest, so that I may come hereafter to love Thee face to face, with all my strength in paradise. Behold, this is all that I ask from Thee. Thee will I love, O my God! I will love Thee, and for Thy love I offer myself to suffer every pain. I will become a saint, not that I may enjoy great delight in heaven, but to please Thee much, O my beloved Lord! and to love Thee much forever. Graciously hear me, O eternal Father! for the love of Jesus Christ.

My Mother Mary, for the love of this thy Son, help thou me. Thou art my hope; from thee I hope every good.

CONSIDERATION VI.

The Interior Peace that God gives Good Religious to Enjoy.

The promises of God cannot fail. God has said, *Every one that has left house, or brethren, or sisters, or father, or mother, . . . or lands for My name's sake, shall receive an hundredfold, and shall possess life everlasting.*[1] That is, the hundredfold on this earth, and life everlasting in heaven.

The peace of the soul is a good which is of greater value than all the kingdoms of the world. And what avails it to have the dominions of the whole world without interior peace? Better is it to be the poorest villager, and to be content, than to be the lord of the whole world, and to live a discontented life. But who can give this peace? The unquiet world? Oh no, peace is a good that is obtained only from God. "O God!" prays the Church, "give to Thy servants that peace which the world cannot give."[2] Therefore he is called the God of

---

[1] "Omnis qui reliquerit domum, vel fratres aut sorores, aut patrem aut matrem, . . . aut agros, propter nomen meum, centuplum accipiet et vitam æternam possidebit."—*Matt.* xix. 29.

[2] "Deus, . . . da servis tuis illam, quam mundus dare non potest, pacem."

all consolation. But if God be the sole giver of peace, to whom shall we suppose will he give that peace but to those who leave all, and detach themselves from all creatures, in order to give themselves entirely to their Creator? And therefore is it seen that good religious shut up in their cells, though mortified, despised, and poor, live a more contented life than the great ones of the world, with all the riches, the pomps, and diversions they enjoy.

St. Scholastica said that if men knew the peace that good religious enjoy, the whole world would become a monastery; and St. Mary Magdalene of Pazzi said that all, if they knew it, would scale the walls of the monasteries, in order to get into them. The human heart having been created for an infinite good, all creatures cannot content it, they being finite, imperfect, and few; God alone, who is an infinite good, can render it content. *Delight in the Lord and He will give thee the request of thy heart.*[1] Oh no; a good religious united with God envies none of the princes of the world who possess kingdoms, riches, and honors. "Let the rich," he will say with St. Paulinus, "have their riches, the kings have their kingdoms, to me Christ is my kingdom and my glory."[2] He will see those of the world foolishly glory in their displays and vanities; but he, seeking always to detach himself more from earthly things, always to unite himself more closely to his God, will live contented in this life, and will say, *Some trust in chariots, and some in horses, but we will call upon the name of the Lord, our God.*[3]

St. Teresa said that one drop of heavenly consolation

[1] "Delectare in Domino, et dabit tibi petitiones cordis tui."—*Ps.* xxxvi. 4.

[2] "Sibi divitias suas habeant divites, sibi regna sua reges; nobis Christus regnum et gloria est."—*Ep. ad Aprum.*

[3] "Hi in curribus, et hi in equis; nos autem in nomine Domini Dei nostri invocabimus."—*Ps.* xix. 8.

is of greater value than all the pleasures of the world. Father Charles of Lorraine, having become a religious, said that God, by one moment of the happiness that he gave him to feel in religion, superabundantly paid him for all he had left for God. Hence his joyfulness was sometimes so great that, when alone in his cell, he could not help beginning to leap. The Blessed Seraphino of Ascoli, a Capuchin lay-brother, said that he would not exchange a foot length of his cord for all the kingdoms of the world.

Oh, what contentment does he find who, having left all for God, is able to say with St. Francis, "My God and my all!" [1] and with that to see himself freed from the servitude of the world, from the thraldom of worldly fashion, and from all earthly affections. This is the liberty that is enjoyed by the children of God, such as good religious are. It is true that in the beginning, the deprivation of the conversations and pastimes of the world, the observances of the Community, and the rules, seem to be thorns; but these thorns, as our Lord said to St. Bridget, will all become flowers and delights to him who courageously bears their first sting, and he will taste on this earth that peace which, as St. Paul says, surpasseth all the gratifications of the senses, and all the enjoyments of feasts, of banquets, and of the pleasures of the world: *The peace of God which surpasseth all understanding.* [2] And what greater peace can there be than to know that one pleases God ?

Prayer.

O My Lord and my God, my all! I know that Thou alone canst make me contented in this and in the next life. But I will not love Thee for my own contentment, I will love Thee only to content Thy heart. I wish this to be my peace, my only

---

[1] " Deus meus et omnia."

[2] " Pax Dei, quæ exsuperat omnem sensum."—*Phil.* iv. 7.

28

satisfaction during my whole life, to unite my will to Thy holy will, even should I have to suffer every pain in order to do this. Thou art my God, I am Thy creature. And what can I hope for greater than to please Thee, my Lord, my God, who hast been so partial in Thy love towards me? Thou, O my Jesus! hast left heaven to live for the love of me—a poor and mortified life. I leave all to live only for the love of Thee, my most blessed Redeemer. I love Thee with my whole heart; if only Thou wilt give me the grace to love Thee, treat me as Thou pleasest.

O Mary, Mother of my God! protect me and render me like to thee, not in thy glory, which I do not deserve, as thou dost, but in pleasing God, and obeying his holy will, as thou didst.

CONSIDERATION VII.

The Damage done to Religious by Tepidity.

Consider the misery of that religious who, after having left his home, his parents, and the world with all its pleasures, and after having given himself to Jesus Christ, consecrating to him his will and his liberty, exposes himself at last to the danger of being damned, by falling into a lukewarm and negligent life, and continuing in it. Oh, no; not far from perdition is a lukewarm religious, who has been called into the house of God to become a saint. God threatens to reject such, and to abandon them if they do not amend. *But because thou art lukewarm, I will begin to vomit thee out of My mouth.*[1]

St. Ignatius of Loyola, seeing a lay-brother of his Order become lukewarm in the service of God, called him one day and said to him, Tell me, my brother, what did you come in religion to do? He answered, To serve God. O my brother! replied the saint, what have you said? If you had answered that you came to serve a cardinal, or a prince of this earth, you would be more

[1] " Sed quia tepidus es, . . . incipiam te evomere ex ore meo."— *Apoc.* iii. 16.

excusable; but you say that you came to serve God, and do you serve him thus?

Father Nieremberg says that some are called by God to be saved only as saints, so that if they should not take care to live as saints, thinking to be saved as imperfect Christians, they will not be saved at all. And St. Augustine says that such are in most cases abandoned by God: "Negligent souls God is accustomed to abandon."[1] And how does he abandon them? By permitting them from lighter faults, which they see and do not mind, to fall into grievous ones, and to lose divine grace and their vocation. St. Teresa of Jesus saw the place prepared for her in hell, had she not detached herself from an earthly, though not a grievously culpable, affection. *He that contemneth small things, shall fall by little and little.*[2]

Many wish to follow Jesus Christ, but from afar, as St. Peter did, who, when his Master was arrested in the garden, says St. Matthew, *followed Him afar off.*[3] But by doing so that will easily happen to them which happened to St. Peter; namely, that, when the occasion came, he denied Jesus Christ. A lukewarm religious will be contented with what little he does for God; but God, who called him to a perfect life, will not be contented, and, in punishment for his ingratitude, will not only deprive him of his special favors, but will sometimes permit his fall. "When you said, It is enough, then you perished,"[4] says St. Augustine. The fig-tree of the Gospel was cast into the fire, only because it brought forth no fruit.

Father Louis de Ponte said, "I have committed many faults, but I have never made peace with them." Miserable is that religious who, being called to perfection,

---

[1] "Deus negligentes deserere consuevit."—*In. Ps.* 118, s. 10.

[2] "Qui spernit modica, paulatim decidet."—*Ecclus.* xix. 1.

[3] "Sequebatur eum a longe."—*Matt.* xxvi. 58.

[4] "Si dixeris: Sufficit; periisti."—*Serm.* 169, *E. B.*

makes peace with his defects. As long as we detest our imperfections, there is hope that we may still become saints; but when we commit faults and make little of them, then, says St. Bernard, the hope of becoming saints is lost. *He who soweth sparingly shall also reap sparingly.*[1] Common graces do not suffice to make one a saint; extraordinary ones are necessary. But how shall God be liberal with his favors towards that one who acts sparingly and with reserve in his love towards him?

Moreover, to become a saint, one must have courage and strength to overcome all repugnances; and let no one ever believe, says St. Bernard, that he will be able to attain to perfection if he does not render himself singular among others in the practice of virtue. "What is perfect cannot but be singular."[2] Reflect, my brother, for what have you left the world and all? To become a saint. But that lukewarm and imperfect life which you lead, is that the way of becoming a saint? St. Teresa animated her daughters by saying to them, "My sisters, you have done the principal thing necessary to become saints; the least remains yet to be done." The same I say to you; you have, perhaps, done the chief part already; you have left your country, your home, your parents, your goods, and your amusements; the least remains yet to be done, to become a saint; do it.

Prayer.

O my God! reject me not, as I deserve, for I will amend. I know well that so negligent a life as mine cannot satisfy Thee. I know that I have myself, by my lukewarmness, shut the door against the graces which Thou didst desire to bestow upon me. O Lord! do not yet abandon me, continue to be merciful towards me; I will rise from this miserable state. I will for the future be more careful to overcome my passions, to follow Thy inspirations, and never will I through slothfulness omit my

[1] "Qui parce seminat, parce et metet."—2 *Cor.* ix. 6.
[2] "Perfectum non potest esse, nisi singulare."

duties, but I will fulfil them with greater diligence. In short, I will, from this time forward, do all I can to please Thee, and I will neglect nothing which I may know to be pleasing to Thee. Since thou, O my Jesus! hast been so liberal with Thy graces towards me, and hast deigned to give Thy blood and Thy life for me, there is no reason I should act with such reserve towards Thee. Thou art worthy of all honor, all love, and to please Thee one ought gladly to undergo every labor, every pain. But, O my Redeemer! Thou knowest my weakness, help me with Thy powerful grace; in Thee I confide. O immaculate Virgin Mary! thou who hast helped me to leave the world, help me to overcome myself and to become a saint.

CONSIDERATION VIII.

How Dear to God is a Soul that gives itself entirely to Him.

God loves all those who love him: *I love them that love Me.*[1] Many, however, give themselves to God, but preserve still in their hearts some attachment to creatures, which prevents them from belonging entirely to God. How, then, shall God give himself entirely to that one who, besides his God, loves creatures still? It is just that he should act with reserve towards those who act with reserve towards him. On the contrary, he gives himself entirely to those souls, who, driving from their hearts everything that is not God, and does not lead them to his love, and giving themselves to him without reserve, truly say to him, *My God and my all.*[2] St. Teresa, as long as she entertained an inordinate affection, though not an impure one, could not hear from Jesus Christ what afterwards she heard, when, freeing herself from every attachment, she gave herself entirely to the divine love; namely, the Lord saying to her, "Now, because thou art all mine, I am all thine."

Consider that the Son of God has already given him-

---

[1] "Ego diligentes me diligo."—*Prov.* viii. 17.
[2] "Deus meus, et omnia."

self entirely to us: *A child is born to us, and a son is given to us.*[1] He has given himself to us through the love he bears to us." *He hath loved us, and hath delivered Himself for us.*[2] It is, then, just, says St. John Chrysostom, that when a God has given himself to you, without reserve,—"he has given thee all, nothing has he left to himself,"[3]—you also should give yourself to God, without reserve; and that always henceforth, burning with divine love, you should sing to him:

> Thine wholly always will I be;
> Thou hast bestowed Thyself on me,
> Wholly I give myself to Thee.

St. Teresa revealed to one of her nuns, appearing to her after her death, that God loves a soul that, as a spouse, gives itself entirely to him, more than a thousand tepid and imperfect ones. From these generous souls, given entirely to God, is the choir of Seraphim completed. The Lord himself says that he loves a soul that attends to its perfection, so much that he seems not to love any other. *One is my dove, my perfect one is but one.*[4] Hence Blessed Giles exhorts us, "One for one,"[5] by which he wishes to say that this one soul we have we ought to give wholly, not divided, to that One who alone deserves all love, on whom depends all our good, and who loves us more than *all.* "Leave all and you shall find all,"[6] says Thomas à Kempis. Leave all for God, and in God you will find all. "O soul!" concludes St. Bernard, "be alone, that you may keep yourself for him alone."[7] Keep yourself alone, give no

---

[1] " Parvulus natus est nobis, filius datus est nobis."—*Isa.* ix. 6.

[2] " Dilexit nos, et tradidit semetipsum pro nobis."—*Eph.* v. 2.

[3] "Totum tibi dedit, nihil sibi reliquit."

[4] "Una est columba mea, perfecta mea."—*Cant.* vi. 8.

[5] " Una uni."

[6] " Dimitte omnia, et invenies omnia."—*Imit.* book 3, c. 32.

[7] "O anima! sola esto, ut soli te serves."—*In Cant.* s. 40.

part of your affections to creatures, that you may belong alone to Him who alone deserves an infinite love, and whom alone you ought to love.

Prayer.

My beloved to me and I to him.[1] As then, O my God! Thou hast given Thyself entirely to me, I should be too ungrateful if I should not give myself entirely to Thee; since Thou wouldst have me belong wholly to Thee, behold, O my Lord! I give myself entirely to Thee. Accept me through Thy mercy, disdain me not. Grant that this my heart, which once loved creatures, may turn now wholly to Thy infinite goodness. "Let me henceforth die," said St. Teresa, "let another than myself live in me. Let God live in me, and give me life. Let him reign, and let me be his slave, for my soul wishes no other liberty." This my heart is too small, O God most worthy of love, and it is too little able to love Thee, who art deserving of an infinite love. I should then commit against Thee too great an injustice, should I still divide it by loving anything besides Thee. I love Thee, my God, above everything. I love only Thee; I renounce all creatures, and give myself entirely to Thee, my Jesus, my Saviour, my love, my all. I say, and always will say, *What have I in heaven, and besides Thee, what do I desire on earth? . . . Thou art the God of my heart, and the God that is my portion forever.*[2] I desire nothing, either in this life or in the next, but to possess the treasure of Thy love. I am unwilling that creatures should have any more a place in my heart; Thou alone must be its master. To Thee only shall it belong for the future. Thou only shalt be my God, my repose, my desire, all my love, "Give me only Thy love and Thy grace, and I am rich enough."[3] O most holy Virgin Mary! obtain for me this, that I may be faithful to God, and never recall the donation which I have made of myself to him.

[1] "Dilectus meus mihi et ego illi."—*Cant.* ii. 16.

[2] "Quid mihi est in cœlo? et a te quid volui super terram? Deus cordis mei, et pars mea Deus in æternum."—*Ps.* lxxii. 25.

[3] "Amorem tui solum cum gratia tua mihi dones, et dives sum satis."

CONSIDERATION IX.

How Necessary it is, in order to become a Saint, to have a Great Desire for such a Thing.

No saint has ever attained to sanctity without a great desire. As wings are necessary to birds in order to fly, so holy desires are necessary to the soul in order to advance in the road of perfection. To become a saint, we must detach ourselves from creatures, conquer our passions, overcome ourselves, and love crosses. But to do all this, much strength is required, and we must suffer much. But what is the effect of holy desire? St. Laurence Justinian answers us: "It supplies strength, and makes the pain easier to be borne."[1] Hence the same saint adds that he has already vanquished who has a great desire of vanquishing. "A great part of the victory is the desire of vanquishing."[2] He who wishes to reach the top of a high mountain will never reach it if he has not a great desire to do so. This will give him courage and strength to undergo the fatigue of ascending, otherwise he will stop at the foot, wearied and discouraged.

St. Bernard asserts that we acquire perfection in proportion to the desire for it which we preserve in our heart. St. Teresa said that God loves generous souls that have great desires; for which reason the saint exhorted all in this way, "Let our thoughts be high. . . . for thence will come our good. We must not have low and little desires, but have that confidence in God that, if we make the proper efforts, we shall by little and little attain to that perfection which, with his grace, the saints have reached." In this way, the saints attained, in a

---

[1] "Vires subministrat, pœnam exhibet leviorem."—*De Disc. mon.* c. 6.

[2] "Magna victoriæ pars est vincendi desiderium."—*De Casto Conn.* c. 3.

short time, a great degree of perfection, and were able to do great things for God. *Being made perfect in a short time, he fulfilled a long time.*[1] Thus St. Aloysius Gonzaga attained in a few years (he lived not over twenty-three years) such a degree of sanctity that St. Mary Magdalene of Pazzi, in an ecstasy, seeing him in heaven, said it seemed to her, in a certain way, that there was no saint in heaven who enjoyed a greater glory than Aloysius. She understood at the same time that he had arrived at so high a degree by the great desire he had cherished of being able to love God as much as he deserved, and that, seeing this beyond his reach, the holy youth had suffered on earth a martyrdom of love.

St. Bernard, being in religion, in order to excite his fervor, used to say to himself, "Bernard, for what did you come here?"[2] I say the same to you: what have you come to do in the house of God? To become a saint? And what are you doing? Why do you lose the time? Tell me, do you desire to become a saint? If you do not, it is sure that you will never become one. If, then, you have not this desire, ask Jesus Christ for it; ask Mary for it; and if you have it, take courage, says St. Bernard, for many do not become saints, because they do not take courage. And so I repeat, let us take courage, and great courage. What do we fear? What inspires this diffidence in us? That Lord, who has given us strength to leave the world, will give us also the grace to embrace the life of a saint. Everything comes to an end. Our life, be it a contented or a discontented one, will also come to an end, but eternity will never terminate. Only that little we have done for God will console us in death and throughout eternity. The fatigue will be short, eternal shall be the crown, which is already, so to speak, before our eyes. How satisfied are the saints now with all they

[1] " Consummatus in brevi, explevit tempora multa."—*Wis.* iv. 13.
[2] " Bernarde, ad quid venisti?"

have suffered for God! If a sorrow could enter paradise, the Blessed would be sorry only for this, that they have neglected to do for God what they might have done more, but which now they are unable to do. Take courage, then, and be prompt, for there is no time to lose; what can be done to-day we may not be able to do to-morrow. St. Bernardine of Sienna said that one moment of time is of as great a value as God himself, for at every moment we may gain God, his divine grace, and higher degrees of merits.

Prayer.

Behold, O my God! here I am. *My heart is ready, O my God! my heart is ready.*[1] See, I am prepared to do all that Thou shalt require from me. *O Lord, what wilt Thou have me to do?*[2] Tell me, O Lord, what Thou desirest of me. I will obey Thee in all. I am sorry for having lost so much time in which I might have pleased Thee, and yet have not done so. I thank Thee that still Thou givest me time to do it. Oh, no, I will not lose any more time. I will and desire to become a saint, not to obtain from Thee a greater glory and more delights. I will become a saint, that I may love Thee more, and to please Thee in this life and in the next. Make me, O Lord! to love and please Thee as much as Thou desirest. Behold, this is all I ask from Thee, O my God! I will love Thee. I will love Thee; and, in order to love Thee, I offer myself to undergo every fatigue, and to suffer every pain. O my Lord! increase in me always this desire, and give me the grace to execute it. Of myself I can do nothing, but assisted by Thee I can do all. Eternal Father, for the love of Jesus Christ, graciously hear me. My Jesus, though the merits of Thy Passion, come to my succor. Or Mary, my hope! for the love of Jesus Christ, protect me.

[1] " Paratum cor meum, Deus, paratum cor meum."—*Ps.* lvi. 8.
[2] " Domine, quid me vis facere ?"—*Acts,* ix. 6.

CONSIDERATION X.

The Love we owe to Jesus Christ in consideration of the Love he has shown to us.

In order to understand the love which the Son of God has borne to us, it is enough to consider what St. Paul says of Jesus Christ: *He emptied Himself, taking the form of a servant. . . . He humbled Himself, becoming obedient even to the death of the cross.*[1] "He emptied himself." O God! what admiration has it caused, and will it, through all eternity, cause to the angels to see a God who became man for the love of man, and submitted himself to all the weaknesses and sufferings of man! *And the Word was made flesh.*[2] What a cause of astonishment would it not be to see a king become a worm for the sake of worms! But an infinitely greater wonder it is to see a God made man, and after this to see him humbled unto the painful and infamous death of the cross, on which he finished his most holy life.

Moses and Elias, on Mount Thabor, speaking of his death, as it is related in the Gospel, called it an excess: *They spoke of His decease* (the Latin word is "excessus," which also means "excess") *that He should accomplish in Jerusalem.*[3] Yea, says Bonaventure, it is with reason the death of Jesus Christ was called an excess, for it was an excess of suffering and of love, so much so that it would be impossible to believe it, if it had not already happened.[4] It was truly an excess of love, adds St. Augustine, for to this end the Son of God wished to come on

---

[1] "Exinanivit semetipsum, formam servi accipiens. . . . Humiliavit semetipsum, factus obediens usque ad mortem, mortem autem crucis."—*Phil.* ii. 7.

[2] "Et Verbum caro factum est."—*John*, i. 14.

[3] "Dicebant excessum, quem completurus erat in Jerusalem.'"—*Luke*, ix. 31.

[4] "Excessus doloris, excessus amoris."

earth, to live a life so laborious and to die a death so bitter, namely, that he might make known to man how much he loved him. "Therefore Christ came, that man should know how much God loved him."[1]

The Lord revealed to his servant Armella Nicolas that the love he bore to man was the cause of all his sufferings and of his death. If Jesus Christ had not been God, but only man and our friend, what greater love could he have shown us than to die for us? *Greater love hath no man than this, that a man lay down his life for his friends.*[2] Ah, how, at the thought of the love shown us by Jesus Christ, the saints esteemed it little to give their life and their all for so loving a God! How many youths, how many noblemen, are there not, who have left their house, their country, their riches, their parents, and all, to retire into cloisters, to live only for the love of Jesus Christ! How many young virgins, renouncing their nuptials with princes and the great ones of the world, have gone with joyfulness to death, to render thus some compensation for the love of a God who had been executed on an infamous gibbet, and died for their sake!

This appeared to St. Mary Magdalene of Pazzi to be foolishness; hence she called her Jesus a fool of love. In exactly the same manner the Gentiles, as St. Paul attests, hearing the death of Jesus Christ preached to them, thought it foolishness not possible to be believed. *We preach Christ crucified, unto the Jews indeed a stumbling-block, and unto the Gentiles foolishness.*[3] How is it possible, they said, that a God, most happy in himself, who is in want of nothing, should die for the sake of man, his

---

[1] "Propterea Christus advenit, ut cognosceret homo quantum eum diligat Deus."—*De catech. rud.* c. 4.

[2] "Majorem hac dilectionem nemo habet, ut animam suam ponat quis pro amicis suis."—*John*, xv. 13.

[3] "Prædicamus Christum crucifixum, Judæis quidem scandalum, Gentibus autem stultitiam."—1 *Cor.* i. 23.

servant? This would be as much as to believe that God became a fool for the love of men. Nevertheless, it is of faith that Jesus Christ, the true Son of God, did, for love of us, deliver himself up to death. *He hath loved us, and hath delivered Himself for us.*[1] The same Mary Magdalene had reason then to exclaim, lamenting the ingratitude of men towards so loving a God, "O love not known! O love not loved!" Indeed, Jesus Christ is not loved by men, because they live in forgetfulness of his love.

And, in fact, a soul that considers a God who died for its sake, cannot live without loving him. *The charity of Christ presseth us.*[2] The soul will feel itself inflamed, and as if constrained to love a God who has loved it so much. Jesus Christ could have saved us, says F. Nieremberg, with only one drop of his blood; but it was his will to shed all his blood, and to give his divine life, that at the sight of so many sufferings and of his death we might not content ourselves with an ordinary love, but be sweetly constrained to love with all our strength a God so full of love towards us. *That they also who live may not live any more for themselves, but unto Him who died for them.*[3]

Prayer.

Indeed, O my Jesus, my Lord, and my Redeemer! only too much hast Thou obliged me to love Thee; too much my love has cost Thee. I should be too ungrateful if I should content myself to love with reserve a God who has given me his blood, his life, and his entire self. Oh, Thou hast died for me, Thy poor servant; it is but just that I should die for Thee, my God, and my all. Yes, O my Jesus! I detach myself from all, to give myself to Thee. I put away from me the love of all creatures, in order to consecrate myself entirely to Thy love. *My*

---

[1] "Dilexit nos, et tradidit semetipsum pro nobis."—*Eph.* v. 2.

[2] "Charitas enim Christi urget nos."—2 *Cor.* v. 14.

[3] "Ut et qui vivunt, jam non sibi vivant, sed ei qui pro ipsis mortuus est."—*Ibid.* v. 15.

beloved is chosen from among thousands.[1] I choose Thee alone out of all things for my good, my treasure, and my only love. I love Thee, O my love! I love Thee. Thou art not satisfied that I should love Thee a little only. Thou art not willing to have me love anything besides Thee. Thee I will please in all things, Thee will I love much; and Thou shalt be my only love. My God, my God, help me, that I may fully please Thee.

Mary, my queen, do thou also help me to love my God much. Amen. So I hope; so may it be.

CONSIDERATION XI.

The Great Happiness which Religious enjoy in dwelling in the same House with Jesus Christ in the Blessed Sacrament.

The Venerable Mother Mary of Jesus, foundress of a convent in Toulouse, said that she esteemed very much her lot as a religious, for two principal reasons. The first was, that religious, through the vow of obedience, belong entirely to God; and the second, that they have the privilege of dwelling always with Jesus Christ in the Blessed Sacrament. And in truth, if people of the world deem it so great a favor to be invited by kings, to dwell in their palaces; how much more favored should we esteem ourselves, who are admitted to dwell continually with the King of Heaven in his own house?

In houses of the religious, Jesus Christ dwells for their sake in the church, so that they can find him at all hours. Persons of the world can scarcely go to visit him during the day, and in many places only in the morning. But the religious finds him in the tabernacle, as often as he wishes, in the morning, in the afternoon, and during the night. There he may continually entertain himself with his Lord, and there Jesus Christ rejoices to converse familiarly with his beloved servants, whom, for this end, he has called out of Egypt, that he may be their companion during this life, hidden under the veil

---

[1] " Dilectus meus . . . electus ex millibus."—*Cant.* v. 10.

of the Most Holy Sacrament, and in the next unveiled in paradise. "O solitude," it may be said of every religious house, "in which God familiarly speaks and converses with his friends!" [1] The souls that love Jesus Christ much do not know how to wish for any other paradise on this earth than to be in the presence of their Lord, who dwells in this sacrament for the love of those who seek and visit him.

His conversation hath no bitterness, nor His company any tediousness. [2] He finds tediousness in the company of Jesus Christ, who does not love him. But those who on this earth have given all their love to Jesus Christ, find in the sacrament all their pleasure, their rest, their paradise, and therefore they keep their hearts always mindful to visit, as often as they can, their God in the sacrament, to pay their court to him, giving vent to their affections at the foot of the altar, offering him their afflictions, their desires of loving him, of seeing him face to face, and, in the mean time, of pleasing him in all things.

Prayer.

Behold me in Thy presence, O my Jesus! hidden in the sacrament, Thou art the self-same Jesus who for me didst sacrifice Thyself on the cross. Thou art he who lovest me so much, and who hast therefore confined Thyself in this prison of love. Amongst so many, who have offended Thee less than I, and who have loved Thee better than I, Thou hast chosen me, in Thy goodness, to keep Thee company in this house, where, having drawn me from the midst of the world, Thou hast destined me always to live united with Thee, and afterwards to have me nigh Thee to praise and to love Thee in Thy eternal kingdom. O Lord! I thank Thee. How have I deserved this happy lot? *I have chosen to be an abject in the house of my God, rather than*

---

[1] "O solitudo, in qua Deus cum suis familiariter loquitur et conversatur!"

[2] "Non habet amaritudinem conversatio ejus; nec tædium convictus illius, sed lætitiam et gaudium."—*Sap.* viii. 16.

dwell in the tabernacles of sinners.[1] Happy indeed am I, O my Jesus! to have left the world; and it is my great desire to perform the vilest office in Thy house rather than dwell in the proudest royal palaces of men. Receive me, then, O Lord! to stay with Thee all my life long; do not chase me away, as I deserve. Be pleased to allow that, among the many good brothers who serve Thee in this house, I, though I am a miserable sinner, may serve Thee also. Many years already have I lived far from Thee. But now that Thou hast enlightened me to know the vanity of the world, and my own foolishness, I will not depart any more from Thy feet, O my Jesus! Thy presence shall animate me to fight when I am tempted. The nearness of Thy abode shall remind me of the obligation I am under to love Thee, and always to have recourse to Thee in my combats against hell. I will always keep near to Thee, that I may unite myself to Thee, and attach myself closer to Thee. I love Thee, O my God! hidden in this sacrament. Thou, for the love of me, remainest always on this altar. I, for the love of Thee, will always remain in Thy presence as much as I shall be able. There enclosed Thou always lovest me, and here enclosed I will always love Thee. Always, then, O my Jesus, my love, my all! shall we remain together,—in time in this house, and during eternity, in paradise. This is my hope, so may it be. Most holy Mary, obtain for me a greater love for the Most Holy Sacrament.

CONSIDERATION XII.

The Life of Religious resembles mostly the Life of Jesus Christ.

The Apostle says that the eternal Father predestines to the kingdom of heaven those only who live conformably to the life of the incarnate Word. *Whom He foreknew, He also predestinated to be made conformable to the image of His Son.*[2] How happy, then, and secure of paradise

---

[1] "Elegi abjectus esse in domo Dei mei, magis quam habitare in tabernaculis peccatorum."—*Ps.* lxxxiii. 11.

[2] "Quos præscivit, et prædestinavit conformes fieri imaginis Filii sui."—*Rom.* viii. 29.

should not religious be, seeing that God has called them to a state of life which of all other states is the most conformed to the life of Jesus Christ.

Jesus, on this earth, wished to live poor as the son and helpmate of a mechanic, in a poor dwelling, with poor clothing and poor food : *Being rich, He became poor for your sake, that through His poverty you might become rich.*[1] Moreover, he chose a life the most entirely mortified, far from the delights of the world, and always full of pain and sorrow, from his birth to his death ; hence by the prophet he was called *The man of sorrows.*[2] By this he wished to give his servants to understand what ought to be the life of those who wish to follow him: *If any man will come after Me, let him deny himself, take up his cross, and follow Me.*[3] According to this example, and to this invitation of Jesus Christ, the saints have endeavored to dispossess themselves of all earthly goods, and to load themselves with pains and crosses, in order thus to follow Christ, their beloved Lord.

Thus acted St. Benedict, who, being the son of the lord of Norcia, and a relative of the Emperor Justinian, and born amidst the riches and the pleasures of the world, while yet a youth of only fourteen years, went to live in a cavern on Mount Sublaco, where he received no other sustenance but a piece of bread brought him every day as an alms by the hermit Romanus.

So acted St. Francis of Assisi, who renounced in favor of his father the whole lawful portion of his inheritance, even to the shirt he had on his back, and, thus poor and mortified, consecrated himself to Jesus Christ. Thus St. Francis Borgia, St. Aloysius Gonzaga, the one

---

[1] " Propter vos egenus factus est, cum esset dives, ut illius inopia vos divites essetis."—2 *Cor.* viii. 9.

[2] " Vir dolorum."—*Isa.* liii. 3.

[3] " Si quis vult post me venire, abneget semetipsum, et tollat crucem suam, et sequatur me."—*Matt.* xvi. 24.

29

being Duke of Candia, the other of Castiglione, left all their riches, their estates, their vassals, their country, their house, their parents, and went to live a poor life in religion.

So have done so many other noblemen and princes even of royal blood. Blessed Zedmerra, daughter of the King of Ethiopia, renounced the kingdom to become a Dominican nun. Blessed Johanna of Portugal renounced the kingdom of France and England, to become a nun. In the Benedictine Order alone, there are found twenty-five emperors, and seventy-five kings and queens, who left the world to live poor, mortified, and forgotten by the world, in a poor cloister. Ah! indeed, these and not the grandees of the world, are the truly fortunate ones.

At present, worldlings think these to be fools, but in the valley of Josaphat they shall know that they themselves have been the fools ; and when they see the saints on their thrones crowned by God, they shall say, lamenting and in despair, *These are they whom we had sometime in derision, . . . we fools esteemed their life madness, but now they are numbered among the children of God, as their lot is among the saints.*[1]

Prayer.

Ah! my Master, and my Redeemer, Jesus, I am then of the number of those fortunate ones whom Thou hast called to follow Thee. O my Lord! I thank Thee for this. I leave all ; would that I had more to leave, that I might draw near to Thee, my king and my God, who for the love of me, and to give me courage by Thy example, hast chosen for Thyself a life so poor and so painful. Walk on, O Lord, I will follow Thee. Choose Thou for me what cross Thou wilt, and help me. I will always carry it with constancy and love. I regret that for the past I have abandoned Thee, to follow my lusts and the vanities of the

---

[1] " Hi sunt quos habuimus aliquando in derisum. . . . Nos insensati vitam illorum æstimabamus insaniam. Ecce quomodo inter filios Dei computati sunt, et inter Sanctos sors illorum est."—*Wisd.* v. 3 et seq.

world ; but now I will leave Thee no more. Bind me to Thy cross, and if through weakness I sometimes resist, draw me by the sweet bonds of Thy love. Suffer it not that I should ever leave Thee again. Yes, my Jesus, I renounce all the satisfactions of the world ; my only satisfaction shall be to continue to love Thee, and to suffer all that pleases Thee. I hope thus to come myself one day in Thy kingdom, to be united with Thee by that bond of eternal love, where, loving Thee in Thy revealed glory, I need no more fear to be loosed and separated from Thee. I love Thee, O my God, my all ! and will always love Thee. Behold my hope, O Most Holy Mary ! thou who, because the most conformed to Jesus, art now the most powerful to obtain this grace. Be thou my protectress !

CONSIDERATION XIII.

The Zeal which Religious ought to have for the Salvation of Souls.*

He who is called to the Congregation of the Most Holy Redeemer will never be a true follower of Jesus Christ, and will never become a saint, if he fulfils not the end of his vocation, and has not the spirit of the Institute, which is the salvation of souls, and of those souls that are the most destitute of spiritual succor, such as the poor people in the country.

This was truly the end for which our Redeemer came down from heaven, who protests, *The spirit of the Lord*

---

* Although in this consideration, and in some other passages, St. Alphonsus may have had specially in view the Congregation of missionaries which he founded, yet the subject refers to all religious of both sexes, and to all persons who serve God. All are called to exercise directly or indirectly this charitable apostolate; every one according to his talent or his means, whether by a generous co-operation in the works that have for their object the defence of faith or the conversion of sinners, or by prayer and the other practices of piety. (See page 67.) All can share in the magnificent reward that the Lord reserves for his evangelical laborers (*Matt.* x. 40 et seq.; *James* v. 20). ED.

. . . hath anointed me to preach the Gospel to the poor.[1] He sought no other proof of Peter's love for him but this, that he should procure the salvation of souls: *Simon, son of John, lovest thou me? . . . Feed my sheep.*[2] He did not impose upon him, says St. John Chrysostom, penance, prayers, or other things, but only that he should endeavor to save his sheep: " Christ said not to him, throw your money away, practise fasting, fatigue your body with hard work, but he said, Feed my sheep."[3] And he declares that he would look upon every benefit conferred on the least of our neighbors as conferred on himself. *Amen, I say to you, since you have done it unto one of these my least brethren, you have done it unto me.*[4]

Every religious ought, therefore, with the utmost care, to entertain within himself this zeal, and this spirit of helping souls. To this end every one ought to direct his studies, and when he shall afterwards have been assigned to his work by his Superiors, he ought to give to it all his thoughts, and his whole attention. He could not call himself a true brother of this Congregation, who, through the desire of attending only to himself and of leading a retired and solitary life, would not accept with all affection such an employment, when imposed on him by obedience.

What greater glory can a man have than to be, as St. Paul says, a co-operator with God in this great work of the salvation of souls? He who loves the Lord ardently is not content to be alone in loving him, he would draw all to his love, saying with David, *O magnify the Lord with*

[1] " Spiritus Domini . . . unxit me, evangelizare pauperibus."— *Luke,* iv. 18.

[2] " Simon Joannis, diligis me? . . . Pasce oves meas."— *John,* xxi. 17.

[3] " Non dixit Christus: Abjice pecunias, jejunium exerce. macera te laboribus; sed dixit: Pasce oves meas."

[4] " Amen dico vobis : quamdiu fecistis uni ex his fratribus meis minimis, mihi fecistis."—*Matt.* xxv. 40.

me, and let us extol his name together.[1]   Hence St. Augustine exhorts all those who love God, "If you love God, draw all men to his love."[2]

A good ground to hope for his own salvation has he who with true zeal labors for the salvation of souls. "Have you saved a soul," says St. Augustine, "then you have predestinated your own."[3]   The Holy Ghost promises us, *When thou shalt have labored for the welfare of a poor man, and by thy labor shalt have filled him* (with divine grace), *the Lord will fill thee with light and peace.*[4]   In this—namely, in procuring the salvation of others—St. Paul placed his hope of eternal salvation, when he said to his disciples of Thessalonica, *For what is our hope, or joy, or crown of glory? Are not you, in the presence of our Lord Jesus Christ at his coming?*[5]

Prayer.

O my Lord Jesus Christ! how can I thank Thee enough, since Thou hast called me to the same work that Thou didst Thyself on earth ; namely, to go with my poor exertions and help souls to their salvation ?   How have I deserved this honor and this reward, after having offended Thee so grievously, and been the cause to others also of offending Thee ?   Yes, O my Lord! Thou callest me to help Thee in this great undertaking.   I will serve Thee with all my strength.   Behold, I offer Thee all my labor, and even my blood, in order to obey Thee.   Nor do I by this aspire to satisfy my own inclination, or to gain applause and

[1] "Magnificate Dominum mecum, et exaltemus nomen ejus."—*Ps.* xxxiii. 4.

[2] "Si Deum amatis, omnes ad ejus amorem rapite."—*In Ps.* xxxiii. *en.* 2.

[3] "Animam salvasti, animam tuam prædestinasti."

[4] "Cum effuderis esurienti animam tuam, et animam afflictam repleveris, requiem tibi dabit Dominus, et implebit splendoribus animam tuam."—*Isa.* lviii. 10–11.

[5] "Quæ est enim nostra spes, aut gaudium, et corona gloriæ ? Nonne vos ante Dominum Jesum Christum estis in adventu ejus ?"— 1 *Thess.* ii. 19.

esteem from men; I desire nothing but to see Thee loved by all as Thou deservest. I prize my happy lot, and call myself fortunate, that Thou hast chosen me for this great work, in which I protest that I will renounce all praises of men and all self-satisfaction, and will only seek Thy glory. To Thee be all the honor and satisfaction, and to me only the discomforts, the blame, and the reproaches. Accept, O. Lord! this offering, which I, a miserable sinner, who wish to love Thee and to see Thee loved by others, make of myself to thee, and give me strength to execute it.

Most Holy Mary, my advocate, who lovest souls so much, help me.

CONSIDERATION XIV.

How Necessary to Religious are the Virtues of Meekness and Humility.

Our most lovely Redeemer Jesus willed to be called a lamb, for the very reason that he might show us how meek and humble he was himself. These were the virtues which he principally wished his followers should learn from him: *Learn from me, because I am meek and humble of heart.*[1] And these virtues he principally requires of religious who profess to imitate his most holy life.

He who lives as a solitary in a desert has not so much need of these virtues; but for him who lives in a Community, it is impossible not to meet, now and then, with a reprimand from his Superiors, or something disagreeable from his companions. In such cases, a religious who loves not meekness will commit a thousand faults every day, and live an unquiet life. He must be all sweetness with everybody,—with strangers, with companions, and also with inferiors if he should ever become Superior; and if he be an inferior, he must consider that one act of meekness in bearing contempt and reproach is of greater value to him than a thousand fasts and a thousand disciplines.

[1] "Discite a me quia mitis sum et humilis corde."—*Matt.* xi. 29.

St. Francis said that many make their perfection consist in exterior mortifications, and, after all, are not able to bear one injurious word. " Not understanding," he added, "how much greater gain is made by patiently bearing injuries."[1] How many persons, as St. Bernard remarks, are all sweetness when nothing is said or done contrary to their inclination, but show their want of meekness when anything crosses them! And if any one should ever be Superior, let him believe that one reprimand made with meekness will profit his subjects more than a thousand made with severity. *The meek are useful to themselves and to others,*[2] as St. John Chrysostom teaches. In short, as the same saint said, the greatest sign of a virtuous soul is to see it meek on occasions of contradiction. A meek heart is the pleasure of the heart of God. *That which is agreeable to him is faith and meekness.*[3] It would be well for a religious to represent to himself, in his meditations, all the contrarieties that may happen to him, and thus arm himself against them; and then, when the occasion happens, he ought to do violence to himself, that he may not be excited and break out in impatience. Therefore, he should refrain from speaking when his mind is disturbed, till he is certain that he has become calm again.

But to bear injuries quietly, it is above all necessary to have a great fund of humility. He who is truly humble is not only unmoved when he sees himself despised, but is even pleased, and rejoices at it in his spirit, however the flesh may resent it ; for he sees himself treated as he deserves, and made conformable to Jesus Christ, who, worthy as he was of every honor, chose, for the love of us, to be satiated with contempt and injuries.

---

[1] " Non intelligentes quanto majus sit lucrum in tolerantia injuriarum."

[2] " Mansuetus utilis sibi et aliis."—*In Act. hom.* 6.

[3] " Beneplacitum est illi fides et mansuetudo."—*Ecclus.* i. 34.

Brother Juniper, a disciple of St. Francis, when an injury was done to him, held up his cowl, as if he expected to receive pearls falling from heaven. The saints have been more desirous of injuries than worldlings are covetous of applause and honor. And of what use is a religious who does not know how to bear contempt for God's sake? He is always proud, and only humble in name and a hypocrite, whom divine grace will repulse, as the Holy Ghost says: *God resisteth the proud, but to the humble he giveth grace.*[1]

Prayer.

O my most humble Jesus, who, for the love of me, didst humble Thyself, and become obedient unto the death of the cross, how have I the courage to appear before Thee, and call myself Thy follower? for I see myself to be such a sinner and so proud that I cannot bear a single injury without resenting it. Whence can come such pride in me, who for my sins have so many times deserved to be cast forever into hell with the devils? Ah, my despised Jesus, help me and make me conformable to Thee. I will change my life. Thou, for love of me, hast borne so much contempt; I, for love of Thee, will bear every injury. Thou, O my Redeemer! hast rendered contempt too honorable and desirable, since Thou hast embraced it with so much love, during Thy own life. *Far be it from me to glory but in the cross of our Lord Jesus Christ.*[2] O my most humble mistress Mary, mother of God! thou who wast in all, and especially in suffering, the most conformed to thy Son, obtain for me the grace to bear in peace all injuries which henceforward shall be offered to me. Amen.

[1] " Deus superbis resistit, humilibus autem dat gratiam."—I *Peter,* v. 5.

[2] " Mihi absit gloriari, nisi in cruce Domini nostri Jesu Christi."— *Gal.* vi. 14.

CONSIDERATION XV.

How much Religious ought to confide in the Patronage of Mary.

If it is true, and most true it is, that, according to the saying of St. Peter Damian, the divine mother, the most holy Mary, loves all men with such an affection that after God there is not, nor can there be, any one who surpasses or equals her in her love,—"She loves us with an invincible love," [1]—how much must we think this great queen loves religious, who have consecrated their liberty, their life, and their all to the love of Jesus Christ ? She sees well enough that the life of such as these is more conformable to her own life, and to that of her divine Son; she sees them often occupied in praising her, and continually attentive to honor her by their novenas, visits, rosaries, fasts, etc. She beholds them often at her feet, intent on invoking her aid, asking graces of her, and graces all conformed to her holy desires; that is, the grace of perseverance in the divine service, of strength in their temptations, of detachment from this world, and of love towards God. Ah, how can we doubt that she employs all her power and her mercy for the benefit of religious, and especially of those who belong to this holy Congregation of the Most Holy Redeemer in which, as it is well known, we make special profession of honoring the Virgin Mother by visits, by fasting on Saturdays, by special mortifications during her novenas, etc., and by everywhere promoting devotion to her by sermons and novenas in her honor !

She, the great mistress, is grateful. *I love those who love Me.* [2] Yes, she is so grateful that, as St. Andrew of Crete says, "To him who does her the least service she

---

[1] "Amat nos amore invincibili."—*In Nat. B. V.* s. 1.

[2] "Ego diligentes me diligo."—*Prov.* viii. 17.

is accustomed to return great favors."[1] She promises
liberally those who love her, and who promote her honor
among others, to deliver them from sin: "Those that
work by me shall not sin."[2] She also promises to them
paradise: "Those that explain me shall have life everlasting."[3]

For which reason we especially ought to thank God
for having called us to this Congregation, where by the
usages of the Community and the example of our companions, we are often reminded, and in some way constrained, to have recourse to Mary, and continually to
honor this our most loving mother, who is called, and is,
the joy, the hope, the life, and the salvation of those
who invoke and honor her.

Prayer.

My most beloved, most lovely, and most loving queen, I always thank my Lord and thee, who hast not only drawn me,
out of the world, but also called me to live in this Congregation,
where a special devotion is practised to thee. Accept of me
then, my mother, to serve thee. Among so many of thy beloved
sons, do not scorn to let me serve thee also, miserable though I
am. Thou after God shalt always be my hope and my love.
In all my wants, in all my tribulations and temptations, I will
always have recourse to thee ; thou shalt be my refuge, my consolation. I am unwilling that any one except God and thee
should comfort me in my combats, in the sadness and the tediousness of this life. For thy service I renounce all the kingdoms of the whole world. My kingdom on this earth shall be
to serve, bless, and love thee, O my most lovely mistress !
"whom to serve is to reign,"[4] as St. Anselm says. Thou art
the mother of perseverance ; obtain for me to be faithful to thee
until death. By so doing I hope, and firmly hope, one day to
come where thou reignest, to praise and bless thee forever, to

---

[1] "Solet maxima pro minimis reddere."—*In Dorm. B. V.* s. 3.

[2] "Qui operantur in me, non peccabunt."--*Off. of the Blessed Virg.*

[3] "Qui elucidant me, vitam æternam habebunt."—*Ib.*

[4] "Cui servire regnare est."

depart no more from thy holy feet. Jesus and Mary, I protest, with your loving servant Alphonsus Rodriguez, "my most sweet loves, let me suffer for you, let me die for you, let me be all yours, and not at all my own."[1]

Prayer.

(*Taken from St. Thomas of Aquinas.*)

Grant me, O my God! to know Thy will, and to accomplish it perfectly to Thy glory. Give me the strength not to fail in prosperity, so as to exalt myself presumptuously; not to fail in adversity, so as to be cast down by it. Let me feel joy or sorrow at nothing else, but what leads me to Thee, or separates me from Thee. Let me desire to please none, let me fear to displease none, but Thee. Let all the goods of the world be vile to me, and all Thy gifts dear to me, for the love of Thee, and be Thou dear to me above everything. Let all joy without Thee be tediousness to me, and let every fatigue which is for Thee be pleasing to me, so that outside of Thee I may wish for nothing. Grant that to Thee I may always direct all my thoughts and all my affections. Make me, O Lord, obedient without reply, poor without desire, chaste without defilement, patient without murmur, humble without simulation, joyous without dissipation, fearful without diffidence, diligent without solicitude, prudent without duplicity. Grant me the ability to do good without presumption, to reprove without becoming haughty, to edify my neighbor by my example without dissimulation. Give me a watchful heart, that vain thoughts may not carry me away from Thee; a noble heart, that is not bowed down by unworthy affections; a right heart, that is not moved by perverse intentions; a heart strong in tribulations; a heart free from earthly attachment. Give me to be enlightened in knowing Thee, diligent in seeking Thee, wise in finding Thee, persevering in pleasing Thee, grateful in thanking Thee. Finally, give me strength in this life to embrace every punishment due to my sins, and then, in the next, the grace forever to see Thee, possess Thee, and love Thee, face to face. Amen.

O Mary, my queen, my hope, and my mother! I love thee,

[1] "Jesu et Maria, amores mei dulcissimi! pro vobis patiar, pro vobis moriar; sim totus vester, sim nihil meus."

I confide in thee. I beseech thee by the love of Jesus, by the joy thou didst feel in becoming his mother, and by the sorrow thou didst feel at his death, obtain of God for me a great sorrow for my sins and the pardon of them, perseverance in a good life, a pure love towards God with a perfect conformity to his holy will. Thou art the refuge of sinners, thou art then my refuge. To thee I recommend my soul and my eternal salvation. Receive me as thy servant, and as such protect me always, and especially at the time of my death. Thou with thy powerful intercession must save me; this is my hope, thus may it be!

ANSWER TO A YOUNG MAN WHO ASKS COUNSEL ON THE CHOICE OF A STATE OF LIFE.

I read in your letter that some time ago you felt inspired by God to become a religious, and that afterwards many doubts arose in your mind, and especially this one, that, without becoming a religious, you might sanctify yourself also in the world.

I will answer your letter briefly, for, should you wish to read something more complete, you can read a little work of mine, which has already been printed, under the title "Counsels concerning Religious Vocation," in which I have treated this matter more fully. Here I will only say, briefly, that this point of the choice of a state of life is of the greatest importance, as upon it depends our eternal salvation. He who chooses the state to which God calls him will save himself with facility, and for him who does not obey the divine call it will be difficult—yes, morally impossible—to save himself. The greatest number of those who are damned, are damned for not having corresponded to the call of God.

In order, therefore, that you may be able to choose that state, which will be the surest for attaining eternal salvation, consider that your soul is immortal, and that the only end for which God has placed you in this world was, not certainly that you may acquire money and honors on this earth, and thus live a comfortable and delightful life, but that by holy virtues you may merit eternal life.[1] In the day of judgment it will avail you nothing to have advanced your family, and to have made

---

[1] "Finem vero, vitam æternam."—*Rom.* vi. 22.

a figure in the world; it will only avail you to have served and loved Jesus Christ, who is to be your judge.

You have a thought which tells you that you will also be able to sanctify yourself by remaining in the world. Yes, my dear sir, you will be able, but it is difficult, and if you are truly called by God to the religious state, and yet remain in the world, it is, as I have said above, morally impossible, because those helps will be denied you which God had prepared for you in religion, and without them you will not save yourself. To sanctify yourself it is necessary for you to employ the means,— such as, to avoid evil occasions, to remain detached from earthly goods, to live a life recollected in God; and to maintain this, it is necessary to receive the sacraments frequently, to make your meditation, your spiritual reading, and to perform other devout exercises, every day, otherwise it is impossible to preserve the spirit of fervor. Now, it is difficult, not to say impossible, to practise all this in the midst of the noise and the disturbances of the world; for family affairs, the necessities of the house, the complaints of parents, the quarrels and persecutions with which the world is so full, will keep your mind so occupied by cares and fears that you will barely be able in the evening to recommend yourself to God, and even this will be done with many distractions. You would wish to make your meditation, to read spiritual books, to receive Holy Communion often, to visit every day the Sacrament of the altar; but from all this you will be prevented by the affairs of the world, and the little you do will be imperfect, because it is done in the midst of a thousand distractions, and with coldness of heart. Your life will thus be always unquiet, and your death more unquiet still.

On one side, worldly friends will not fail to inspire you with a fear of embracing the religious life, as being a hard life and full of troubles. On the other, the world offers you amusements, money, and a contented life. Reflect well, and do not allow yourself to be led into error. Be persuaded that the world is a traitor that makes promises and does not care about the fulfilment of them. It offers you indeed all these earthly things, but suppose it should give them to you, could it also give you peace of soul? No, God only can give true peace. The soul is created only for God, to love him in this life and to enjoy him in the next, and therefore God only can content it. All the pleasures and riches of the earth cannot give true peace; nay, those who in this life abound the most with such goods are the most troubled and afflicted, as Solomon confesses who had them in abundance. *All,* says he, *is vanity and affliction of spirit.*[1] If the world, with its goods, could make us happy, the rich, the great, the monarchs, who are in no want of wealth, honors, and amusements, would be fully contented. But experience shows how it is with these mighty ones of the earth; the greater they are, the greater are the vexations, fears, and afflictions they have to suffer. A poor Capuchin lay-brother, who goes about girded with a cord over a sackcloth, who lives on beans, and sleeps in a small cell on a little straw, is more contented than a prince with all his gilded trappings and riches, who has every day a sumptuous table, and who goes half sick to bed under a rich canopy, unable to sleep on account of the anguish which drives sleep away. He is a fool who loves the world and not God, said St. Philip Neri; and if these worldlings live such an unquiet life, much more unquiet still will be their death, when the priest, at their side, will intimate to them that they are about to be chased away from this world, saying: "Depart hence, Christian soul, from this world. Embrace the crucifix, for this world is at an end for you."[2]

[1] "Universa vanitas et afflictio spiritus."—*Eccles.* i. 14.
[2] "Proficiscere, anima christiana, de hoc mundo."

The misery is, that in the world they think little of God, and just as little of the next life, where they must remain forever. All, or almost all, their thoughts are given to the things of this earth, and this is the cause that their life is so unhappy, and their death still more.

Nevertheless, that you may ascertain what state you ought to embrace, imagine yourself at the point of death, and choose that one which you would then wish to have chosen. Should you have erred, by neglecting the divine call, in order to follow your own inclinations, and to live with more liberty, there will then be no longer time to remedy the error. Consider that everything here below will come to an end. *The fashion of this world passeth away.*[1] The scenes of this world must finish for each one of us. Everything passes, and death draws near, and at every step we take we approach nearer to it, and, through death, nearer to eternity. For this we are born. *Man shall go into the house of his eternity.*[2] Death will be upon us when we least think of it. Alas! when death draws near, what will then appear all the goods of this world, but the unreal pageantry of a theatre,—vanities, lies, and foolishness? And what profit will it then be, as Jesus Christ warns us, *if we should have gained the whole world and lost our souls?*[3] It will help us only to die an unhappy death.

On the contrary, a young man who has left the world to give himself entirely to Jesus Christ, how contented will he feel, as he passes his days in the solitude of his cell, far from the tumult of the world and the dangers of losing God, which are in the world! In the monastery he will not have the entertainments of music, theatres, and balls, but he will have God to console him and to

[1] "Præterit enim figura hujus mundi."—1 *Cor.* vii. 31.
[2] "Quoniam ibit homo in domum æternitatis suæ."—*Eccles.* xii. 5.
[3] "Quid prodest homini, si mundum universum lucretur, animæ vero suæ detrimentum patiatur?—*Matt.* xvi. 26."

make him enjoy peace. I mean all that peace which is possible in this valley of tears, into which every one is sent to suffer, and to merit by his patience that full peace which is prepared for him in heaven. But in this life even, far from the pastimes of the world, one loving look cast from time to time on the crucifix, one " Deus meus, et omnia," pronounced with affection, one " my God " said with a sigh of love, will console him more than all the pastimes and feasts of the world, which leave only bitterness behind them.

And if he lives content in such a life, more content will he be still at his death at having chosen the religious state. How much will it then console him to have spent his life in prayer, in spiritual reading, in mortification, and in other exercises of devotion, especially if he has been in an Order employed in saving souls by preaching and hearing confessions,—things which at his death will all increase his confidence in Jesus Christ, who is truly grateful and liberal in rewarding those who have labored for his glory!

But let us come to a conclusion with regard to your vocation. Since the Lord has called you to leave the world, and to be entirely his in religion, I tell you: Rejoice and tremble at the same time. Rejoice, on one hand, and always thank the Lord, because to be called by God to a perfect life is a grace which he does not give to all.[1] On the other hand, tremble, because if you do not follow the divine call, you will put your eternal salvation in great danger. It is not my intention here to relate to you the many examples of young men who, because they made no account of their vocation, have lived a miserable life and died a horrible death. Hold for certain that, as God has called you, you will never have peace, if you remain in the world; and at your death you will be very unquiet, on account of the re-

[1] " Non fecit taliter omni nationi."—*Ps.* cxlvii. 20.

morse that then will torment you, for having neglected to obey God, who had called you to the religious state.

At the end of your letter you express a wish to learn from me whether, in case you should not have the courage to enter religion, it would be better to marry, as your parents wish, or to become a secular priest. I answer: The married state I cannot recommend to you, because St. Paul does not counsel it to any one, except there be a necessity for it, arising out of habitual incontinence, which necessity, I hold for certain, does not exist in your case.

With regard, then, to the state of a secular priest,* take notice that a secular priest has on him all the obligations of a priest, and all the distractions and dangers of a layman; for, living in the midst of the world, he cannot avoid the troubles which arise from his own household and from his parents, and cannot be free from the dangers to which his soul is exposed. He will have temptations in his own house, being unable to exclude women from it, whether relatives or servants, nor prevent other strangers from coming to see them. You should then stay there altogether retired in a separate room, and attend only to divine things. Now, this it is very difficult to practise; and therefore small, and very small, is the number of those priests who attend to their perfection in their own houses.

On the contrary, entering a monastery of strict observance, you will be freed from the disagreeable duty of thinking about your food and clothing, because there the Order provides you with all, there you will not have your parents to come and continually trouble you with all the disturbances that happen in their house; there no women enter to disturb your mind; and thus, far from

---

* In Italy we often see priests who live with their parents or relatives.—ED.

the tumult of the world, you will have no one to hinder you in your prayers and your recollection.

I have said *a monastery of strict observance;* because if you want to enter another, where they live more freely, it is better for you to stay at home and attend there to the salvation of your soul as well as you can; for entering an Order where the spirit is relaxed, you expose yourself to the danger of being lost. Though you should enter with the resolution to attend to prayer and to the things of God only, yet, carried along by the bad example of your companions, and seeing yourself derided and even persecuted, if you do not live as they do, you will leave off all your devotions, and do as the others do, as experience shows it to be commonly the case. But should God give you the grace of vocation, be careful to preserve it, by recommending yourself often to Jesus and Mary in holy prayer. I know that if you resolve to give yourself entirely to God, the devil from that moment will increase his efforts to tempt you to fall into sin, and especially to make you entirely his, and to remain his.

I conclude by offering you the assurance of my respectful consideration; I pray the Lord to make you belong entirely to himself, and remain, etc.

ADVICE TO A YOUNG PERSON IN DOUBT ABOUT THE STATE OF LIFE WHICH SHE OUGHT TO EMBRACE.

My dear Sister in Jesus Christ:

You are deliberating about the choice of a state of life. I see that you are agitated because the world wishes you to belong to itself, and to enter the married state; and, on the other hand, Jesus Christ wishes you to give yourself to him by becoming a nun in some convent of exact observance.

Remember that on the choice which you make your eternal salvation will depend. Hence, I recommend you, as soon as you read this advice, to implore the Lord, every day, to give you light and strength to embrace that state which will be most conducive to your salvation; that thus you may not afterwards, when your error is irreparable, have to repent of the choice you have made for your whole life, and for all eternity.

Examine whether you will be more happy in having for your spouse a man of the world, or Jesus Christ, the Son of God and the King of heaven; see which of them appears to you the better spouse, and then make your choice. At the age of thirteen, the holy virgin St. Agnes was, on account of her extraordinary beauty, sought after by many. Among the rest, the son of the Roman Prefect asked her for his spouse; but looking at Jesus Christ, who wished her to belong to him, she said, I have found

---

* The holy author supposes in this case, as well as in the preceding answer, that the person to whom this advice is addressed is called to be a religious, or has at least the beginning of a vocation to the religious state, but the world keeps her back, and she hesitates. This supposition does not, however, hold good as regards the foregoing letter that treats of the spiritual exercises.—ED.

a spouse better than you and all the monarchs of this world; therefore I cannot exchange him for any other. And rather than exchange him she was content to lose her life, and cheerfully suffered martyrdom for Jesus Christ. The holy virgin Domitilla gave a similar answer to the Count Aurelian; she, too, died a martyr, and was burned alive, because she would not forsake Jesus Christ. Oh, how happy do these holy virgins now feel in heaven, how happy will they feel for all eternity, at having made so good a choice ! The same happy lot awaits you, and will await all young persons who renounce the world in order to give themselves to Jesus Christ.

In the next place, examine the consequences of the state of the person who chooses the world, and of the person who makes choice of Jesus Christ. The world offers earthly goods, riches, honors, amusements, and pleasures. On the other hand, Jesus Christ presents to you scourges, thorns, opprobrium, and crosses; for these were the goods which he chose for himself all the days of his mortal life. But then he offers you two immense advantages which the world cannot give—peace of soul in this life, and paradise in the next.

Moreover, before you decide on embracing any state, you must reflect that your soul is immortal; that is, that after the present life which will soon end, you must pass into eternity, in which you will receive that place of punishment or of reward which you will have merited by your works during life. Thus, you must remain for all eternity in the house either of eternal life or of eternal death, in which, after your departure from this world, it will be your lot first to dwell: you will be either forever saved and happy amid the joys of paradise, or forever lost and in despair in the torments of hell. In the mean time, consider that everything in this world must soon end. Happy all that are saved; miserable the soul that is damned. Keep always in mind that great maxim of Jesus Christ: "What will it profit a man to gain the whole world if he lose his own soul?" This maxim has sent so many from the world to shut themselves up in the cloister, or to live in the deserts; it has inspired so many young persons with courage to forsake the world in order to give themselves to God and to die a holy death.

On the other hand, consider the unhappy lot of so many ladies of fortune, so many princesses and queens, who in the world have been attended, praised, honored, and almost adored; but if they are damned, what do they now find in hell of so much riches, of so many pleasures, of so many honors enjoyed in this life, but pains and remorse of conscience, which will torment them forever, as long as God shall be God, without any hope of remedy for their eternal ruin.

But let us now cast a glance at the goods which the world gives in this life to its followers, and to the goods which God gives to her who loves him and forsakes the world for his sake. The world makes great promises; but do we not all see that the world is a traitor that promises what it never performs? But though it should fulfil all its promises, what does it give? It gives earthly goods, but does it give the peace and the life of happiness which it promises? All its goods delight the senses and the flesh, but do not content the heart and the soul. Our souls have been created by God for the sole purpose of loving him in this life, and of enjoying him in the next. Hence, all the goods of the earth, all its delights, and all its grandeurs, are outside the heart; they enter not into the soul, which God only can content. Solomon has even called all worldly goods vanities and lies, which do not content but rather afflict the soul. *Vanity of vanities and affliction of spirit.*[1] This we know also from ex-

---

[1] "Vanitas vanitatum et afflictio spiritus."—*Eccles*. i. 14.

perience, for we see that the more a person abounds in these goods, the greater her anguish and misery of mind. If by its good the world gave content to the soul, great indeed should be the happiness of princesses and queens, who want neither amusements, nor comedies, nor festivities, nor banquets, nor splendid palaces, nor beautiful carriages, nor costly dresses, nor precious jewels, nor servants, nor ladies of honor to attend and pay homage to them. But no; they who imagine them to be happy are deceived. Ask them whether they enjoy perfect peace, if they are perfectly content, and they will answer: What peace? what content? They will tell you that they lead a life of misery, and that they know not what peace is. The maltreatment which they receive from their husbands, the displeasure caused by their children, the wants of the house, the jealousies and fears to which they are subject, make them live in the midst of continual anguish and bitterness. Married women may be called martyrs of patience, if they bear all with resignation; but unless they are patient and resigned, they will suffer a martyrdom in this world, and a more painful martyrdom in the next.

The remorse of conscience, though they had nothing else to suffer, keeps married persons in continual torment. Being attached to earthly goods, they reflect but little on spiritual things; they seldom approach the sacraments, and seldom recommend themselves to God; and, being deprived of these helps to a good life, they will scarcely be able to live without sin, and without continual remorse of conscience. Behold, then, how all the joys promised by the world become to married persons sources of bitterness, of fears, and of damnation. How many of them will say, Unhappy me, what will become of me after so many sins, after the life which I led, at a distance from God, always going from bad to worse? I would wish for retirement in order to spend a little time in mental prayer, but the affairs of the family and of the house, which is always in confusion, do not permit this. I would wish to hear sermons, to go to confession, to communicate often; I would wish to go often to the church, but my husband does not wish it. My unceasing occupations, the care of children, the frequent visits of friends, keep me confined to the house; and thus it is not without some difficulty that I can hear Mass at a late hour on festivals. How great was my folly in entering the married state, when I could become a saint in a convent! But all these lamentations only serve to increase their pain; because they see that it is no longer in their power to change the unhappy choice they have made of living in the world. And if their life is unhappy, their death will be much more miserable. At that awful hour they will be surrounded by servants, by their husbands, and children, bathed in tears; but instead of giving them relief, all these will be to them an occasion of greater affliction. And thus afflicted, poor in merits, and full of fears for their eternal salvation, they must go to present themselves to Jesus Christ to be judged by him. But, on the other hand, how great will be the happiness which a nun who has left the world for Jesus Christ will enjoy, living among so many spouses of God, and in a solitary cell, at a distance from the turmoils of the world, and from the continual and proximate danger of losing God, to which seculars are exposed. How much greater will be her consolation at death, after having spent her years in meditations, mortifications, and in so many spiritual exercises; in visits to the Holy Sacrament, in confessions, Communions, acts of humility, of hope, and love of Jesus Christ! And though the devil should endeavor to terrify her by the faults committed in her younger days, her Spouse, for whom she has left the world, will console her, and thus, full of confidence, she will die in the embraces of her crucified Redeemer, who will conduct her to heaven, that there she may enjoy eternal happiness.

Thus, my dear sister, since you must make choice of a state of life, make the choice now which you shall wish at death to have made. At death, every one who sees that for her the world is about to end says, Oh that I had led the life of a saint! Oh that I had left the world and given myself to God! But what is then done, is done, and nothing remains for her but to breathe forth her soul, and to go to hear from Jesus Christ the words, Come, blessed soul, and rejoice with me for eternity; or, Begone forever to hell at a distance from me. You, then, must choose the world or Jesus Christ. If you choose the world, you will probably sooner or later repent of the choice; hence, you ought to reflect well upon it. In the world the number of persons who are lost is very great; in religion, the number of those who are damned is very small. Recommend yourself to Jesus crucified, and to most holy Mary, that they may make you choose the state which is most conducive to your eternal salvation. If you wish to become a nun, resolve to become a saint; if you intend to lead a loose and imperfect life, like some religious, it is useless for you to enter a convent; you should then only lead an unhappy life and die an unhappy death. But if you resolve not to become a religious, I cannot advise you to enter the married state, for St. Paul does not counsel that state to any one, except in case of necessity, which I hope does not exist for you. At least remain in your own house and endeavor to become a saint. I entreat you to say the following prayer for nine days:

My Lord Jesus Christ, who hast died for my salvation, I implore Thee, through the merits of Thy passion, to give me light and strength to choose that state which is best for my salvation. And do thou, O my Mother, Mary, obtain this grace for me by thy powerful intercession.

DISCOURSE TO PIOUS MAIDENS.[*]

My dear Sisters in Jesus Christ :

I do not intend to explain the privileges and blessings acquired by those maidens who consecrate their virginity to Jesus Christ ; I shall only glance at them.

Excellence of Virginity.

First, they become in the eyes of God as beautiful as the angels of heaven.[1] Baronius[2] relates that upon the death of a holy virgin named Georgia, an immense multitude of doves was seen flying around her ; and when the body was carried to the church, they ranged themselves along that part of the roof which corresponded to the situation of the corpse, and did not leave until she was buried. Those doves were thought to be angels who accompanied that virginal body.

Moreover, a maiden who leaves the world, and dedicates herself to Jesus Christ, becomes his spouse. In the Gospel, our Redeemer is called Father, or Master, or Shepherd of our souls ; but, with regard to those virgins, he calls himself their spouse ; they *went out to meet the bridegroom.*[3]

When a young woman wishes to establish herself in the world, she will examine, if she be prudent, which of all her suitors is the most noble and the richest. Let us then learn from the Spouse in the sacred Canticles, who

[1] " Erunt sicut Angeli Dei in cœlo."—*Matt.* xxii. 30.
[2] *Ann.* 480.
[3] " Exierunt obviam Sponso."—*Matt.* xxv. 1.

[*] Missions, ch. 8, § 3.

well knows—let us learn from her what manner of spouse is he whom consecrated virgins aspire to. Tell me, O sacred Spouse, what manner of spouse is he who makes you the most fortunate of women ? *My beloved is white,* she says, *and ruddy, chosen among thousands.*[1] He is all white, by reason of his purity; and ruddy, by reason of the love with which he burns. He is, in fine, so noble and so kind as to be the most amiable of spouses.

With reason, then, did the glorious virgin St. Agnes, as we learn from St. Ambrose, when it was proposed to her to marry the son of the Prefect of Rome, reply that she had a much more advantageous match in view.[2] When some ladies were endeavoring to persuade St. Domitilla to marry Count Aurelian, nephew of the Emperor Domitian, saying there was no obstacle, as he was willing that she should remain a Christian, the saint replied, Tell me, if a monarch and a clown both pretended to a maiden, which would she choose ? Now I, should I marry Aurelian, would have to leave the King of Heaven; it would be folly—I will not do so. And thus, in order to remain faithful to Jesus Christ, to whom she had already consecrated her virginity, she was willing to be burned alive, a death which her barbarous suitor caused her to suffer.[3]

Those spouses of Jesus Christ who leave the world for his sake, become his beloved; they are called the first fruits of the lamb: *The first fruits to God and to the Lamb.*[4] Why the first fruits ? Because, says Cardinal Ugone, as the first fruits are more grateful than any other to man, so virgins are dearer to God than any others. The divine spouse feeds amongst the lilies: *Who feeds amongst*

---

[1] " Dilectus meus candidus, et rubicundus, electus ex millibus."— *Cant.* v. 10.

[2] " Sponsum offertis ? meliorem reperi."—*De Virg.* l. 1.

[3] Croiset, Exerc. May 12.

[4] " Primitiæ Deo et Agno."—*Apoc.* xiv. 4.

the lilies.[1] And what is meant by lilies, if not those devout maidens who consecrate their virginity to Jesus Christ? The Venerable Bede writes that the song of the virgins—that is, the glory which they give to God by preserving untouched the lily of their purity—is far more pleasing to him than the song of all the other saints. Wherefore the Holy Ghost says that there is nothing comparable to virginity.[2] And hence, Cardinal Ugone remarks that dispensations are often granted from other vows, but never from the vow of chastity; and the reason is, because no other treasure can compensate for the loss of that. And it is for the same reason that theologians say, the Blessed Mother would have consented to forego the dignity of Mother of God, could it have been had only at the expense of her virginity.

Who on this earth can conceive the glory which God has prepared for his virgin spouses in paradise? Theologians say that virgins have in heaven their own "aureola," or special crown of glory, which is refused to the other saints who are not virgins.

But let us come at once to the most important point in our discourse.

This young woman will say, Cannot I become holy in the married state? I do not wish to give you the reply in my own words; hear those of St. Paul, and you will see the difference between the married woman and the virgin: *And the unmarried woman, and the virgin, thinketh on the things of the Lord, that she may be holy, both in body and in spirit; but she that is married, thinketh on the things of the world, how she may please her husband.*[3] And the

---

[1] "Qui pascitur inter lilia."—*Cant.* ii. 16.

[2] "Omnis ponderatio non est digna continentis animæ."—*Ecclus.* xxvi. 20.

[3] "Mulier innupta et virgo cogitat quæ Domini sunt, ut sit sancta corpore et spiritu; quæ autem nupta est, cogitat quæ sunt mundi, quomodo placeat viro."—1 *Cor.* vii. 34.

Apostle adds: *And I speak this for your profit, not for a snare, but for that which is decent, and which may give you power to attend upon the Lord without impediment.*[1]

In the first place, I say that married persons can be holy in the spirit, but not in the flesh; on the contrary, virgins who have consecrated their virginity to Jesus Christ are holy both in soul and body. *Holy both in body and in spirit;* and mark those other words, *to attend upon the Lord without impediment.* Oh, how many obstacles have not married women to encounter in serving the Lord! And the more noble they are, the greater the obstacles. A woman, to become holy, must adopt the necessary means, which are, much mental prayer, constant use of the sacraments, and continual thought of God. But what time has a married woman for thinking upon God? *She that is married thinketh on the things of the world,*[2] says St. Paul. The married woman has to think of providing her family with food and raiment. She has to think of rearing her children, of pleasing her husband and her husband's relatives; whence, as the Apostle says, her heart is divided between God, her husband, and her children. Her husband must be attended to; the children cry and scream, and are continually asking for a thousand things. What time can she have to attend to mental prayer, who can scarce attend to all the business of the house? How can she pray amid so many distracting thoughts and disturbances? Scarcely can she go to church, to recollect herself, and communicate upon the Sunday. She may have the good desire, but it will be difficult for her to attend to the things of God as she ought. It is true that in this want of opportunities she may gain merit, by resignation to the will of God, who

---

[1] " Porro hoc ad utilitatem vestram dico . . . , ad id quod honestum est, et quod facultatem præbeat sine impedimento Dominum obsecrandi."—*Ibid.* 35.

[2] "Quæ nupta est, cogitat quæ sunt mundi, quomodo placeat viro."

requires of her, in that state, chiefly patience and resignation; but in the midst of so many distractions and annoyances, without prayer, without meditation, without frequenting the sacraments, it will be morally impossible for her to have that holy patience and resignation.

But would to God that married women had no other evil to contend with besides that of not always being able to attend to their sanctification as much as they should! The greater evil is the danger to which they are continually exposed of losing the grace of God, by reason of the intercourse which they must continually have with the relatives and friends of their husband, as well in their own houses as in the houses of others. Unmarried women do not understand this, but married women and those who have to hear their confessions know it well. Let us, however, now have done with the unhappy life which is led by married women, the ill-treatment that they receive from their husbands, the disobedience of children, the wants of a family, the annoyance of mothers-in-law and relatives, the throes of childbirth, always accompanied by danger of death, not to mention the afflictions of jealousy, and scruples of conscience with regard to the rearing-up of their children,—all of this breeds a tempest under which poor married women have continually to groan ; and God grant that in this tempest they may not lose themselves, so as to meet with hell in the other world, after having suffered a hell in this! Such is the unenviable lot of those maidens who choose the world!

But what! such a maiden replies, are there no married women holy? Yes, I answer, there are; but who are they? Such only as become holy through their sufferings, by suffering all from God without finding fault, and with continual patience. And how many married women are to be found in such a state of perfection? They are very rare; and if you find any, they are always in sorrow,

that when they could have done so they did not consecrate themselves to Jesus Christ. Amongst all the devout married women I have known, I never knew one to
be satisfied with her condition.

The greatest happiness, then, falls to the lot of those
maidens who consecrate themselves to Jesus Christ.
Those have to encounter none of the dangers which married women must necessarily be placed in. They are not
bound to earth by love of children, or men, or dress, or
gallantry, whilst married women are obliged to dress
with pomp and ornaments, in order to appear with their
equals and please their husbands. A maiden who has
given herself to Jesus Christ requires only what dress
will cover her; nay, she should give scandal if she were
to wear any other, or make use of any ornaments. Moreover, virgins have no anxiety about house or children or
relatives; their whole care is centred in pleasing Jesus
Christ, to whom they have consecrated their soul, their
body, and all their love; whence it is that tney have more
time, and a mind more disengaged for frequent prayer
and Communion.

But let us now come to the excuses sometimes brought
forward by those who are cold in the love of Jesus
Christ.

Such a one will say, I should leave the world if I had
some convent to go to, or, at least, if I could always
spend my time in devotion at the church when I should
please; but I could not remain at home, where I have
bad brothers who illtreat me; and, on the other hand,
my parents are unwilling to have me frequent the church.
But, I ask you, is it in order to save yourself, or lead an
easy life you leave the world? Is it to do your own will
or the will of Jesus Christ? If you wish to become holy
and serve Jesus Christ, I ask you another question: in
what does holiness consist? Holiness does not consist
in living in a convent, or spending the entire day in a

church, but in being at confession and Communion as often as you can, in obedience, in doing everything assigned you at home, in being retired, in bearing labor and contempt. And if you were to be in a convent, how should you be employed? Do you imagine you should always be either in church or in your cell, or in the refectory, or at recreation? In the convent, although the Sisters have a time marked out for prayer, for Mass, and for Communion, they have also their hours appointed for the business of the house, and more especially the lay-sisters, who, as they do not attend in the choir, have nearly all the labor of the house, and consequently least time for prayer. All exclaim, Let us be in a convent, let us have a convent. How much more easy is it for devout girls to become holy in their own houses than in a convent! How many such have I known to regret having entered a convent, especially when the Community was large, the poor lay-sister in certain offices having scarcely time to say the rosary!

But, Father, such a girl will answer, I have at home a peevish father and mother; I have bad brothers; all of them use me ill; I cannot stand this. Well I say, and if you marry, will you not have to deal with mothers and sisters-in-law, and perhaps undutiful children, and perhaps a harsh husband? Oh, how many cruel husbands are there not, who when first married promised great things, but shortly afterwards ceased to be husbands, and became the tyrants of their wives, treating them not as companions but as slaves? Inquire of many married women whether this be not the fact. But, without going beyond your own home, you all know how your mothers fared. One thing, at least, is certain, that all you should have to suffer at home, after having given yourself to God, you should suffer for the love of Jesus Christ, and he knows how to make your cross sweet and light to you. But how dreadful is it not to suffer for the world's sake !—to suffer without merit ! Courage, then ! if Jesus Christ has called you to his love, and wishes to have you for his spouse, go on joyfully; it will be his care to afford you consolation even in the midst of sufferings. This, of course, will be only in case you truly love him, and live as his spouse.

Means to preserve Virginal Purity.

Hear, then, for the last time, the means that you are to adopt in order to become holy, and live a true spouse of Jesus Christ; and these are, to practise the virtues becoming his spouse. We read in the Gospel[1] that the kingdom of heaven is likened unto virgins. But to what virgins ? Not to the foolish, but to the wise. The wise were admitted to the nuptials, but the door was shut in the face of the foolish; to whom the spouse said, I know you not[2]—you are indeed virgins, but I do not acknowledge you for my spouses. The true spouses of Jesus Christ follow the spouse whithersoever he goeth. *These follow the Lamb whithersoever he goeth.*[3] What is the meaning of following the Lamb ? St. Augustine[4] says that it means the imitation of the Lamb both in body and mind. After you have consecrated your body to him, you must consecrate to him your whole heart, so that your heart may be entirely devoted to his love; and, therefore, you must adopt all the means that are necessary for making you belong entirely to Jesus Christ.

1. The first of those means is mental prayer, to which you must be most attentive. But do not imagine that, in order to pray thus, it is necessary for you to be in a convent, or remain all day in the church. It is true

---

[1] *Matt.* xxv. 1.
[2] " Nescio vos."
[3] " Sequuntur Agnum quocumque ie..."—*Apoc.* xiv. 4.
[4] *De S. Virginit.* c. 27.

31

that at home there is much disturbance created by the persons there; nevertheless, those who wish can find time and place for prayer: this is in the morning before the others rise, and at night after the others have gone to bed. In order to pray, it is not necessary to be always on bended knees; you can pray whilst laboring, and even when walking out on business (should you have no other opportunity), by raising your soul to God, and thinking on the Passion of Jesus Christ, or any other pious subject.

2. The second means is, the frequentation of the sacraments of confession and Communion. With regard to confession, each one has to make choice of a confessor, whom she is to obey in everything, otherwise she will never walk steadily in the way of perfection. As to Communion, she must not depend solely upon obedience; she must desire it, and ask for it. This divine food must be hungered after; Jesus Christ must be desired. It is frequent Communion that renders his spouses faithful to Jesus Christ, especially in the preservation of holy purity. The Most Holy Sacrament preserves the soul in every virtue; and it appears that its most special effect is to preserve untouched the chastity of virgins, according to that of the prophet, who calls this sacrament *the corn of the elect, and wine springing forth virgins.*[1]

3. The third means is, retirement and caution: *As the lily amongst the thorns, so is my beloved amongst the daughters.*[2] For a virgin to think of remaining faithful to Jesus Christ amid the conversations, the jests, and other amusements of the world, is useless; it is necessary that she preserve herself amid the thorns of absti-

---

[1] "Frumentum electorum et vinum germinans virgines."—*Zach.* ix. 17.

[2] "Sicut lilium inter spinas. sic amica mea inter filias."—*Cant.* ii. 2.

nence and mortification, by using not only the greatest modesty and reserve in speaking with men, but even all austerity and penitential exercises when necessary. Such are the thorns which preserve the lilies; I mean young maidens, who otherwise should soon be lost. The Lord calls the cheeks of his spouse as beautiful as those of the turtle: *Thy cheeks are beautiful as the turtle dove's.*[1] And why so? Because the turtle, by instinct, avoids the company of other birds, and always remains alone. That virgin, then, appears beautiful in the eyes of Jesus Christ who does all that she can to hide herself from the eyes of others. St. Jerome says that Jesus is a jealous spouse.[2] Hence he is much displeased when he sees a virgin dedicated to him endeavoring to appear before men to please them. Pious maidens endeavor to appear repulsive, that they may not attract men. The Venerable Sister Catharine of Jesus, afterwards a Teresian nun, washed her face with the filthy water of tar, and then designedly exposed her face to the sun, that she might lose her complexion. St. Andregesina having, as we are told by Bollandus, been promised in marriage, prayed the Lord to deform her, and was heard, for she was immediately covered with a leprosy which caused every one to avoid her; and as soon as her suitor had ceased his offers, her former beauty was restored. It is related by James di Viatrico that there was a certain virgin in a convent whose eyes had inflamed a prince. The latter threatened to set fire to the monastery if she would not yield to him; but she plucked out her eyes and sent them to him in a basin, the bearer of which was instructed to say, "Here are the darts which have wounded your heart—take them, and leave me my soul untouched."[3] The same author tells of St. Euphemia,

[1] " Pulchræ sunt genæ tuæ sicut turturis."—*Cant.* i. 9.
[2] "Zelotypus est Jesus."—*Ep. ad Eust.*
[3] *Vita S. Ansb.* 9 Febr.

that, having been promised by her father to a certain count, who left no means untried to obtain her, she, in order to free herself from his addresses, cut off her nose and lips, saying to herself, "Vain beauty, you shall never be to me an occasion of sin!" St. Antoninus tells something similar (and his account is confirmed by Baronius) of the Abbess Ebba, who, fearing an invasion of the barbarians, cut off her nose and upper lip to the teeth; and that all the other nuns, to the number of thirty, following her example, did the same. The barbarians came, and seeing them so deformed, set fire to the monastery through rage and burned them alive; and hence the Church, as Baronius tells us, has enrolled them among her martyrs. This is not allowable for others to do; those saints did so by the especial impulse of the Holy Ghost. But it sufficiently well answers the purpose of showing you what virgins who loved Jesus Christ have done to prevent men from seeking them. Devout virgins at present should at least move as modestly, and be seen as little as possible by men. Should it happen that a virgin should, by chance, and without any fault of hers, receive by violence any insult from men, be it known to you that after it she will remain as pure as before. St. Lucia made an answer of this kind to the tyrant who threatened to dishonor her. "If you do," she said, "and I be so treated against my will, my crown shall be double." It is the consent only that is hurtful; and know, moreover, that if a virgin be modest and reserved, men will have no inclination to interfere with her.

4. The fourth means of preserving purity is the mortification of the senses. St. Basil says, "A virgin should not be immodest in any respect,—in tongue, ears, eyes, touch, and still less in mind."[1] A virgin, in order to

[1] " Nulla in parte mœchari convenit virginem, non lingua, non aure, non oculo, non tactu, multoque minus animo."—*De vera Virg.*

keep herself pure, must be modest in her speech, conversing seldom with men, and that only through necessity, and in few words. Her ears must be pure, by not listening to worldly conversations. Her eyes must be pure, by being either closed, or fixed upon the earth in the presence of men. She must be pure in touch, using therein all possible caution, both as regards herself and others. She must be pure in spirit, by resisting all immodest thoughts, through the help of Jesus and Mary. And to this end, she must mortify herself with fasting, abstinence, and other penitential exercises; which things she must not practise without the consent of her confessor, otherwise they should injure her soul by making her proud. Those acts of penance must not be made without the confessor's permission, but they must be desired and sought for; for the confessor, if he does not see the penitent wishing for them, will not give them. Jesus is a spouse of blood, who espoused our souls upon the cross, whereon he shed all his blood for us. *A bloody spouse art thou to me.*[1] Therefore those spouses who love him, love tribulation, infirmity, sorrows, ill-treatment, and injuries; and receive them not only with patience, but with joy. Thus may we understand that passage which says that *virgins follow the Lamb whithersoever He goeth.*[2] They follow their spouse Jesus with joy and gladness whithersoever he goeth, even through sorrow and disgrace, as has been done by so many holy virgins, who have followed him to torments and to death, smiling and rejoicing.

5. Finally, Sisters, in order that you may obtain perseverance in this holy life, you must recommend yourselves often and much to Most Holy Mary, the Queen of Virgins. She is the mediatrix who negotiates those espousals, and brings virgins to espouse her Son. *After*

---

[1] " Sponsus sanguinum tu mihi es."—*Exod*. iv. 25.

[2] " Sequuntur Agnum quocumque ierit."—*Apoc.* xiv. 4.

her shall virgins be brought to the King.[1]　It is she, in fine, who obtains fidelity for those chosen spouses; for, without her assistance, they should be all unfaithful.

CONCLUSION.

Come on, then, you who intend to live no longer for the world, but for Jesus Christ alone. (I address myself to those who feel themselves called by that divine Spouse to consecrate themselves to his love.) I do not wish that you should make any vow this morning, or oblige yourselves at once to perpetual chastity. You should do that when God inspires you, and your confessor is willing. I only desire you by a simple act, and without any obligation, to thank Jesus Christ for having called you to his love; and to offer yourselves to him henceforward for your entire lives. Say then to him:

O my Jesus, my God, and my Redeemer! who hast died for me, compassionate me who burn to call myself Thy spouse. I burn, because I see that Thou hast called me to that honor; nor do I know how to thank Thee for that grace. I should now have been in hell; and Thou, instead of chastising me, hast called me to be Thy spouse. Yes, my spouse, I leave the world, I leave all through love of Thee, and give myself entirely to Thee. What world?—what world do I speak of? My Jesus, henceforward Thou art to be my only good—my only love. I see that Thou wishest to have my entire heart, and I wish to resign it entirely to Thee. Receive me in Thy mercy, and do not reject me as I have deserved that Thou shouldst. Forget all the offences that I have given Thee, of which I repent with my whole soul; would that I had died before offending Thee! Pardon me; inflame me with Thy holy love, and give me Thy aid, in order that I may be faithful to Thee, and never leave

---

[1] "Adducentur Regi virgines post eam."—*Ps.* xliv. 15.

Thee more. Thou, my spouse, hast given Thyself all to me. Behold! I give myself entirely to Thee. Mary, my Queen and my Mother, chain my heart to that of Jesus Christ; and fasten both hearts so that they be never sundered more.

I leave you now my blessing, in order that you may be so bound to Jesus Christ as never again to depart from him. Give your hearts now to Jesus Christ; say, Jesus, my spouse, henceforward I wish to love only Thee, and nothing else.

THE VOCATION TO THE PRIESTHOOD.*

I.

Necessity of a Divine Vocation to take Holy Orders.

To enter any state of life, a divine vocation is necessary; for without such a vocation it is, if not impossible, at least most difficult to fulfil the obligations of our state, and obtain salvation. But if for all states a vocation is necessary, it is necessary in a particular manner for the ecclesiastical state. *He that entereth not by the door into the sheepfold, but climbeth up another way, the same is a thief and a robber.*[1] Hence he who takes holy orders without a call from God is convicted of theft, in taking by force a dignity which God does not wish to bestow upon him.[2] And before him St. Paul said the same thing: *Neither doth any man take the honor to himself, but he that is called by God, as Aaron was. So Christ also did not glorify Himself that He might be made a high priest; but he that said unto Him: Thou art My Son, this day I have begotten Thee.*[3]

No one, then, however learned, prudent, and holy he may be, can thrust himself into the sanctuary unless he is first called and introduced by God. Jesus Christ him-

---

[1] "Qui non intrat per ostium in ovile ovium, sed ascendit aliunde, ille fur est et latro."—*John,* x. 1.

[2] "Latrones et fures appellat eos qui se ultro, ad non sibi datam desuper gratiam, obtrudunt."—*In Jo.* x. 10.

[3] "Nec quisquam sumit sibi honorem, sed qui vocatur a Deo tamquam Aaron. Sic et Christus non semetipsum clarificavit ut pontifex fieret; sed qui locutus est ad eum: Filius meus es tu."—*Heb.* v. 4, 5.

---

* *Selva,* ch. 10.

self, who among all men was certainly the most learned and the most holy, *full of grace and truth,*[1] *in whom are hid all the treasures of wisdom and knowledge,*[2]—Jesus Christ, I say, required a divine call in order to assume the dignity of the priesthood.

In entering the sanctuary, even after God himself had called them to it, the saints trembled. When his bishop ordered St. Augustine to receive ordination, the saint through humility regarded the command as a chastisement of his sins.[3] To escape the priesthood St. Ephrem of Syria feigned madness; and St. Ambrose pretended to be a man of a cruel disposition.

To avoid the priesthood, St. Ammonius the Monk cut off his ears, and threatened to pluck out his tongue, if the persons who pressed him to take holy orders should continue to molest him. In a word, St. Cyril of Alexandria says, "The saints have dreaded the dignity of the priesthood as a burden of enormous weight."[4] Can any one, then, says St. Cyprian, be so daring as to attempt of himself, and without a divine call, to assume the priesthood?[5]

As a vassal who would of himself take the office of minister should violate the authority of his sovereign, so he who intrudes himself into the sanctuary without a vocation violates the authority of God. How great should be the temerity of the subject who, without the appointment, and even in opposition to the will of the monarch, should attempt to administer the royal patrimony, to decide lawsuits, to command the army, and to

---

[1] "Plenum gratiæ et veritatis."—*John*, i. 14.

[2] "In quo sunt omnes thesauri sapientiæ et scientiæ absconditi."—*Col.* ii. 3

[3] "Vis mihi facta est merito peccatorum meorum."—*Epist.* 21, *E. B.*

[4] "Omnes sanctos reperio divini ministerii ingentem veluti molem formidantes."—*De Fest. pasch. hom.* 1.

[5] "Ita est aliquis sacrilegæ temeritatis, ac perditæ mentis, ut putet sine Dei judicio fieri sacerdotem?"—*Epist.* 55.

assume the viceregal authority? "Among you," asks St. Bernard in speaking to clerics, "is there any one so insolent as, without orders and contrary to the will of the pettiest monarch, to assume the direction of his affairs?"[1] And are not priests, as St. Prosper says, the administrators of the royal house?[2] Are they not, according to St. Ambrose, the "leaders and rectors of the flock of Christ?"[3] according to St. Chrysostom, the "interpreters of the divine judgments,"[4] and according to St. Denis, the "vicars of Christ?"[5] Will any one who knows all this dare to become the minister of God without a divine call?

To think of exercising royal authority is, according to St. Peter Chrysologus, criminal in a subject.[6] To intrude into the house of a private individual, in order to dispose of his goods and to manage his business, would be considered temerity; for even a private individual has the right of appointing the administrators of his affairs. And will you, says St. Bernard, without being called or introduced by God, intrude into his house to take charge of his interests and to dispose of his goods?"[7]

The Council of Trent has declared that the Church regards not as her minister, but as a robber, the man who audaciously assumes the priesthood without a vocation.[8] Such priests may labor and toil, but their labors

[1] "Auderetne aliquis vestrum terreni cujuslibet reguli, non præcipiente aut etiam prohibente eo, occupare ministeria, negotia dispensare?"—*De Conv. ad cler.* c. 19.

[2] "Dispensatores regiæ domus."—*De Vita cont.* l. 2, c. 2.

[3] "Duces et rectores gregis Christi."—*De Dign. sac.* c. 2.

[4] "Interpretes divinorum judiciorum."

[5] "Vicarii Christi."—*Hom.* 17.

[6] "Regnum velle servum, crimen est."—*Serm.* 23.

[7] "Quid istud temeritatis, imo quid insaniæ est? tu irreverenter irruis, nec vocatus, nec introductus."—*De Vita cler.* c. 5.

[8] "Decernit sancta Synodus eos qui ea (ministeria) propria temeritate sibi sumunt, omnes, non Ecclesiæ ministros, sed fures et latrones per ostium non ingressos habendos esse."—*Sess.* 23, *cap.* 4.

shall profit them little before God. On the contrary, the works which are meritorious in others shall deserve chastisement for them. Should a servant who is commanded by his master to take care of the house, through his own caprice labor in cultivating the vineyard, he may toil and sweat, but instead of being rewarded he shall be chastised by his master. Thus, in the first place, because they are not conformable to the divine will, the Lord shall not accept the toils of the man who, without a vocation, intrudes himself into the priesthood. *I have no pleasure in you, saith the Lord of Hosts, and I will not receive a gift of your hand.*[1] In the end God will not reward, but will punish the works of the priest who has entered the sanctuary without a vocation. *What stranger soever cometh to it* (the tabernacle), *shall be slain.*[2]

Whosoever, then, aspires to holy orders must, in the first place, carefully examine if his vocation is from God. "For," says St. John Chrysostom, "the more sublime the dignity, the more should one assure one's self of a divine vocation."[3] Now to know whether his call is from God, he should examine the marks of a divine vocation. He, says St. Luke, who wishes to build a tower, first computes the necessary expenses, in order to know if he has the means of completing the edifice.[4]

II.

Marks of a Divine Vocation to the Sacerdotal State.

Let us now see what are the marks of a divine vocation to the sacerdotal state.

[1] "Non est mihi voluntas in vobis, dicit Dominus exercituum, et munus non suscipiam de manu vestra."—*Mal.* i. 10.

[2] "Quisquis externorum accesserit (ad tabernaculum), occidetur."—*Num.* i. 51.

[3] "Quoniam dignitas magna est, et revera divina sententia comprobanda."—*In* 1 *Tim. hom.* 5.

[4] "Quis enim ex vobis, volens turrim ædificare, non prius sedens computat sumptus qui necessarii sunt, si habeat ad perficiendum?"—*Luke,* xi. 28.

Nobility is not a mark of a divine vocation. To know, says St. Jerome, whether a person should become the guide of the people in what regards their eternal salvation, we must consider not nobility of blood, but sanctity of life.[1] "When God wishes to raise any one to a dignity, he regulates his choice according to the sanctity of life, and not according to the titles of nobility."[2]

Nor is the will of parents a mark of a divine vocation. In inducing a child to take priesthood, they seek not his spiritual welfare, but their own interest, and the advancement of the family. "How many mothers," says St. John Chrysostom, or the author of *The Imperfect Work*, have eyes only for the bodies of their children and disdain their souls! To see them happy here below is all that they desire : as for the punishments that perhaps their children are to endure in the next life, they do not even think of them."[3] Oh, how many priests shall we see condemned on the day of judgment for having taken holy orders to please their relatives !

Neither nobility of birth, nor the will of parents, is a mark of a vocation to the priesthood; nor is talent or fitness for the offices of a priest a sign of vocation; for along with talent, a holy life and a divine call are necessary. What, then, are the marks of a divine vocation to the ecclesiastical state ?

I. PURITY OF INTENTION.

The first is a good intention. It is necessary to enter the sanctuary by the door; but there is no other door

[1] "Principatum in populos, non sanguini deferendum, sed vitæ."— *In Tit.* I.

[2] "Quos dignos divina probet electio secundum vitæ, non generis, meritum."

[3] "Matres corpora natorum amant, animas contemnunt; desiderant illos valere in sæculo isto, et non curant quid sint passuri in alio."—*Hom.* 35.

than Jesus Christ: *I am the door of the sheep. . . . By me, if any man enter in, he shall be saved.*[1] To enter, then, by the door, is to become a priest not to please relatives, nor to advance the family, nor for the sake of self-interest or self-esteem, but to serve God, to propagate his glory, and to save souls. "If any one," says a wise theologian, the learned continuator of Tournely, "presents himself for Holy Orders without any vicious affection and with the sole desire to be employed in the service of God and in the salvation of his neighbor, he, we may believe, is called by God."[2] Another author asserts that he who is impelled by ambition, interest, or a motive of his own glory, is called not by God, but by the devil.[3] "But," adds St. Anselm, "he who enters the priesthood through so unworthy motives shall receive not a blessing, but a malediction, from God."[4]

2. SCIENCE AND TALENTS.

The second mark is the talent and learning necessary for the fulfilment of the duties of a priest. Priests must be masters to teach the people the law of God. *For the lips of the priest shall keep knowledge, and they shall seek the law at his mouth.*[5] Sidonius Apollinarius used to say, "Ignorant physicians are the cause of many deaths."[6]

[1] "Ego sum ostium ovium. . . . Per me si quis introierit, salvabitur."—*John*, x. 7.

[2] "Si enim aliquis, liber ab omni vitioso affectu, ad clerum, Deo deserviendi causa et salutis populi gratia solum, se conferat, vocari a Deo præsumitur."—*De Ord.* q. 4, a. 4.

[3] "Ambitione duceris, vel avaritia? inhias honori? Non te vocat Deus, sed diabolus tentat."—*Hall.* p. 1, s. 3, c. 2, § 4.

[4] "Qui enim se ingerit, et propriam gloriam quærit, gratiæ Dei rapinam facit; et ideo non accipit benedictionem sed maledictionem."—*In Heb.* 5.

[5] "Labia enim sacerdotis custodient scientiam, et legem requirent ex ore ejus."—*Mal.* ii. 7.

[6] "Medici parum docti multos occidunt."—*Lib.* 2, *ep.* 12.

An ignorant priest, particularly a confessor, who teaches false doctrines and gives bad counsels, will be the ruin of many souls; because, in consequence of being a priest, his errors are easily believed. Hence, Ivone Carnotensis has written: "No one should be admitted to Holy Orders unless he has given sufficient proofs of good conduct and learning." [1]

A priest must not only have a competent knowledge of all the rubrics necessary for the celebration of Mass, but must be also acquainted with the principal things which regard the sacrament of penance. It is true, every priest is not obliged to hear confessions, unless there is great necessity for his assistance in the district in which he lives; however, every priest is bound to be acquainted with what a priest must ordinarily know in order to be able to hear the confessions of dying persons; that is, he is bound to know when he has faculties to absolve, when and how he ought to give absolution to the sick, whether conditionally or absolutely; what obligation he ought to impose on them if they are under any censure. He should also know at least the general principles of moral theology.

3. POSITIVE GOODNESS OF CHARACTER.

The third mark of an ecclesiastical vocation is positive virtue.

Hence, in the first place, the person who is to be ordained should be a man of innocent life, and should not be contaminated by sins. The Apostle requires that they who are to be ordained priests should be free from every crime. [2] In ancient times, a person who had com-

---

[1] " Nulli ad sacros Ordines sunt promovendi nisi quos vita et doctrina idoneos probat."

[2] "Et constituas per civitates presbyteros, sicut et ego disposui tibi: si quis sine crimine est, etc."—*Tit.* i. 5.

mitted a single mortal sin could never be ordained, as we learn from the First Council of Nice.[1] And St. Jerome says that it was not enough for a person to be free from sin at the time of his ordination, but that it was, moreover, necessary that he should not have fallen into mortal sin since the time of his baptism.[2] It is true that this rigorous discipline has ceased in the Church, but it has been always at least required that he who had fallen into grievous sins should purify his conscience for a considerable time before his ordination. This we may infer from a letter to the Archbishop of Rheims, in which Alexander III. commanded that a deacon who had wounded another deacon, if he sincerely repented of his sin, might, after being absolved, and after performing the penance enjoined, be permitted again to exercise his order; and that if he afterwards led a perfect life, he might be promoted to priesthood.[3] He, then, who finds himself bound by a habit of any vice cannot take any Holy Order without incurring the guilt of mortal sin. "I am horrified," says St. Bernard,[4] "when I think whence thou comest, whither thou goest, and what a short penance thou hast put between thy sins and thy ordination. However, it is indispensable that thou do not undertake to purify the conscience of others before thou purifiest thy own." Of those daring sinners who, though full of bad habits, take priesthood, an ancient author, Gildas, says, "It is not to the priesthood that

[1] "Qui confessi sunt peccata, canon (ecclesiasticus ordo) non admittit."—*Can.* 9.

[2] "Ex eo tempore quo in Christo renatus est, nulla peccati conscientia remordeatur."—*In Tit.* 1.

[3] "Et si perfectæ vitæ et conversationis fuerit, eum in presbyterum (poteris) ordinare."—*Cap.* 1 *De diacono. Qui cler.*

[4] "Horreo considerans unde, quo vocaris, præsertim cum nullum intercurrerit pœnitentiæ tempus. Et quidem rectus ordo requirit ut prius propriam, deinde alienas curare studeas conscientias."—*Epist.* 8.

they should be admitted, but to the pillory."[1] They, then, says St. Isidore, who are still subject to the habit of any sin should not be promoted to Holy Orders.[2]

But he who intends to ascend the altar must not only be free from sin, but must have also begun to walk in the path of perfection, and have acquired a habit of virtue. In our *Moral Theology*,[3] we have shown in a distinct dissertation (and this is the common opinion) that if a person in the habit of any vice wish to be ordained, it is not enough for him to have the dispositions necessary for the sacrament of penance, but that he must also have the dispositions required for receiving the sacrament of Holy Orders; otherwise he is unfit for both: and should he receive absolution with the intention of taking Orders without the necessary dispositions, he, and the confessor who absolves him, will be guilty of a grievous sin. For it is not enough for those who wish to take Holy Orders to have got out of the state of sin; they must also, according to the words of Alexander III.[4]—cited in the preceding paragraph—have the true positive virtue necessary for the ecclesiastical state. From the words of the pontiff we learn that a person who has done penance may exercise an order already received, but he who has only done penance cannot take a higher order. The Angelic Doctor teaches the same doctrine: "Sanctity is required for the reception of Holy Orders, and we must place the sublime burden of the priesthood only upon walls already dried by sanctity; that is, freed from the malignant humor of sin."[5] This

---

[1] "Multo digniores erant ad catastam pœnalem, quam ad sacerdotium trahi."—*Cast. in Eccl. ord.*

[2] "Non sunt promovendi ad regimen Ecclesiæ, qui adhuc vitiis subjacent."—*Sent.* l. 3, c. 34.

[3] L. 6, n. 63 et s.

[4] "Si perfectæ vitæ est et conversationis fuerit."

[5] "Ordines sacri præexigunt sanctitatem; unde pondus Ordinum imponendum est parietibus jam per sanctitatem desiccatis, id est ab humore vitiorum."—2. 2. q. 189, a. 1.

is conformable to what St. Denis wrote long before:
" Let no one be so bold as to propose himself to others
as their guide in the things of God, if he has not first,
with all his power, transformed himself into God to the
point of perfect resemblance to him." [1] For this St.
Thomas adduces two reasons: the first is, that as he who
takes orders is raised above seculars in dignity, so he
should be superior to them in sanctity. [2] The second
reason is, that by his ordination a priest is appointed to
exercise the most sublime ministry on the altar, for which
greater sanctity is required than for the religious state. [3]

Hence the Apostle forbade Timothy to ordain neophytes; that is, according to St. Thomas, neophytes in
perfection as well as neophytes in age. [4] Hence the
Council of Trent, in reference to the words of Scripture,
And a spotless life in old age, [5] prescribes to the bishops to
admit to ordination only those who show themselves
worthy by a conduct full of wise maturity. [6] And of this
positive virtue, it is necessary, according to St. Thomas,
to have not a doubtful but a certain knowledge. [7] This,

---

[1] " In divino omni non audendum aliis ducem fieri, nisi secundum
omnem habitum suum factus sit deiformissimus et Deo simillimus."
—*De Eccl. Hier.* c 3.

[2] " Ad idoneam executionem Ordinum, non sufficit bonitas qua-
liscumque, sed requiritur bonitas excellens, ut, sicut illi, qui Ordinem
suscipiunt, super plebem constituuntur gradu Ordinis, ita et superiores sint merito sanctitatis; et ideo praeexigitur gratia quae sufficiat
ad hoc quod digne connumerentur in plebe Christi."—*Suppl.* q. 35, a. 1.

[3] " Quia per sacrum Ordinem aliquis deputatur ad dignissima
ministeria, quibus ipsi Christo servitur in Sacramento altaris; ad
quod requiritur major sanctitas interior, quam requirat etiam religionis status."—2. 2. q. 184, a. 8.

[4] " Qui non solum aetate neophyti, sed et qui neophyti sunt perfec-
tione."

[5] " Aetas senectutis, vita immaculata."—*Wisd.* iv. 9.

[6] " Sciant episcopi debere ad hos (sacros) Ordines assumi dignos
duntaxat, et quorum probata vita senectus sit."—*Sess.* 23, *cap.* 12.

[7] " Sed etiam habeatur certitudo de qualitate promovendorum."—
Suppl. q. 36, a. 4.

32

according to St. Gregory, is particularly necessary with regard to the virtue of chastity.[1] With regard to chastity the Holy Pontiff required a proof of many years.[2]

III.

To what Dangers one exposes one's self by entering Holy Orders without a Vocation.

From what has been said, it follows that he who takes Holy Orders without the marks of a vocation cannot be excused from the guilt of grievous sin. This is the doctrine of many theologians,—of Habert, of Natalis Alexander, and of the continuator of Tournely. And before them St. Augustine taught the same. Speaking of the chastisement inflicted on Core, Dathan, and Abiron, who, without being called, attempted to exercise the sacerdotal functions, the holy Doctor said: "God struck them that they might serve as an example, and thus to warn off him who would dare to assume a sacred charge. Indeed, this is the chastisement reserved for those who would thrust themselves into the office of bishop, priest, or deacon." [3] And the reason is, first, because he who thrusts himself into the sanctuary without a divine call cannot be excused from grievous presumption; secondly, because he will be deprived of the congruous and abundant helps without which, as Habert writes, he will be absolutely unable to comply with the obligations of his state,[4] but will fulfil them only with very great difficulty.

[1] "Nullus debet ad ministerium altaris accedere, nisi cujus castitas ante susceptum ministerium fuerit approbata."—*Lib.* 1, *ep.* 42.

[2] "Ne unquam ii qui ordinati sunt, pereant, prius aspiciatur si vita eorum continens ab annis plurimis fuit."—*Lib.* 3, *ep.* 26.

[3] "Condemnati sunt ut daretur exemplum, ne quis non sibi a Deo datum munus pontificatus invaderet. . . . Hoc patientur quicumque se in episcopatus, aut presbyteratus, aut diaconatus, officium conantur ingerere."—*Serm.* 30, *E. B. app.*

[4] "Non sine magnis difficultatibus poterit saluti suæ consulere."

He will be like a dislocated member, which can be used only with difficulty, and which causes deformity.[1]

Hence Bishop Abelly writes: "He who of himself, without inquiring whether he has a vocation or not, thrusts himself into the priesthood will no doubt expose himself to the great danger of losing his soul; for he commits against the Holy Spirit that sin for which, as the Gospel says, there is hardly or very rarely any pardon."[2]

The Lord has declared that his wrath is provoked against those who wish to rule in his Church without being called by him. On this passage St. Gregory says, "It is by themselves and not by the will of the Supreme Head that they reign."[3] Divine vocation is entirely wanting to them, and they have followed only the ardor of vile cupidity, not certainly to accept, but to usurp this sublime dignity.[4] How many intrigues, adulations, entreaties, and other means, do certain persons employ in order to procure ordination, not in obedience to the call of God, but through earthly motives? But woe to such men, says the Lord by the prophet Isaias: *Woe to you, apostate children, . . . that you would take counsel, and not of me.*[5] On the day of judgment they shall claim a reward,

---

[1] "Manebitque in corpore Ecclesiæ velut membrum in corpore humano suis sedibus motum, quod servire potest, sed ægre admodum et cum deformitate."—*De Ord* p. 3, c. 1, § 2.

[2] "Qui sciens et volens, nulla divinæ vocationis habita ratione, sese in sacerdotium intruderet, haud dubie seipsum in apertissimum salutis discrimen injiceret, peccando scilicet in Spiritum Sanctum, quod quidem peccatum vix aut rarissime dimitti ex Evangelio discimus."—*Sac. chr.* p. 1, c. 4.

[3] "Ipsi regnaverunt, et non ex me . . . , iratus est furor meus in eos."—*Os.* viii. 4.

[4] "Ex se, et non ex arbitrio summi Rectoris, regnant: nequaquam divinitus vocati, sed sua cupidine accensi, culmen regiminis rapiunt potius quam assequuntur."—*Past.* p. 1, c. 1.

[5] "Væ filii desertores, dicit Dominus, ut faceretis consilium, et non ex me !"—*Isa.* xxx. 1.

but Jesus Christ shall cast them off. *Many will say to Me in that day, have we not prophesied in Thy name* (by preaching and teaching), *and cast out devils in Thy name* (by absolving penitent sinners), *and done many miracles in Thy name* (by correcting the wicked, by settling disputes, by converting sinners). *And then will I profess unto them: I never knew you; depart from me, you that work iniquity.*[1] Priests who have not been called are indeed workmen and ministers of God, because they have received the sacerdotal character; but they are ministers of iniquity and rapine, because they have of their own will, and without vocation, intruded themselves into the sheepfold. They have not, as St. Bernard says,[2] received the keys, but have taken them by force. They toil, but God will not accept; he will, on the contrary, punish their works and labors, because they have not entered the sanctuary by the straight path. The labor of fools shall afflict them that know not how to go to the city.[3] The Church, says St. Leo, receives only those whom the Lord chooses, and by his election makes fit to be his ministers.[4] But, on the other hand, the Church rejects those whom, as St. Peter Damian has written, God has not called; for instead of promoting her welfare, they commit havoc among her members; and instead of edifying, they contaminate and destroy her children.[5]

[1] "Multi dicent mihi in illa die. Domine, Domine, nonne in nomine tuo prophetavimus (prædicando, docendo), et in nomine tuo dæmonia ejecimus (absolvendo pœnitentes), et in nomine tuo virtutes multas fecimus (corrigendo, lites componendo, errantes reducendo)?—Et tunc confitebor illis: Quia nunquam novi vos: discedite a me, qui operamini iniquitatem."—*Matt.* vii. 22.

[2] "Tollitis, non accipitis claves; de quibus Dominus queritur: 'Ipsi regnaverunt, et non ex me.'"—*De Conv. ad cler.* c. 19.

[3] "Labor stultorum affliget eos, qui nesciunt in urbem pergere."—*Eccles.* x. 15.

[4] "Eos Ecclesia accipit, quos Spiritus Sanctus præparavit, . . . et dignatio cœlestis gratiæ gignit."—*In die ass. suæ,* s. 2.

[5] "Nemo deterius Ecclesiam lædit."—*Cont. cler. aul.* c. 3.

Whom He (the Lord) *shall choose, they shall approach to Him.*[1] God will gladly admit into his presence all whom he has called to the priesthood, and will cast off the priest whom he has not chosen.[2] St. Ephrem regards as lost the man who is so daring as to take the order of priesthood without a vocation. And Peter de Blois has written: "What ruin does not prepare for himself the bold man who of the sacrifice makes a sacrilege, and of life an instrument of death."[3] He who errs in his vocation exposes himself to greater danger than if he transgressed particular precepts; for if he violates a particular command, he may rise from his fault, and begin again to walk in the right path; but he who errs in his vocation mistakes the way itself. Hence the longer he travels in it, the more distant he is from his home. To him we may justly apply the words of St. Augustine: "You run well, but the wrong road."[4]

It is necessary to be persuaded of the truth of what St. Gregory says, that our eternal salvation depends principally on embracing the state to which God has called us.[5] The reason is evident; for it is God that destines, according to the order of his providence, his state of life for each individual, and, according to the state to which he calls him, prepares for him abundant graces and suitable helps. "In the distribution of his graces," says St. Cyprian, "the Holy Spirit takes into consideration his own plan and not our caprices."[6] And

[1] "Quos elegerit (Dominus), appropinquabunt ei."—*Num.* xvi. 5.

[2] "Obstupesco ad ea quæ soliti sunt quidam insipientium audere, qui temere se conantur ingerere ad munus sacerdotii assumendum; licet non adsciti a gratia Christi; ignorantes, miseri, quod ignem et mortem sibi accumulant."—*Or. de sacerd.*

[3] "Quam perditus est, qui sacrificium in sacrilegium, qui vitam convertit in mortem !"—*Epist.* 123.

[4] "Bene curris, sed extra viam."

[5] "A vocatione pendet æternitas."

[6] "Ordine suo, non nostro arbitrio, Sancti Spiritus virtus ministratur."—*De Sing. cler.*

according to the Apostle: *And whom He predestinated; them He also called. And whom He called, them He also justified.*[1] Thus to vocation succeeds justification, and to justification, glory; that is, the attainment of eternal life. He, then, who does not obey the call of God, shall neither be justified nor glorified. Father Granada justly said that vocation is the main wheel of our entire life. As in a clock, if the main wheel be spoiled, the entire clock is injured, so, says St. Gregory Nazianzen, if a person err in his vocation, his whole life will be full of errors; for in the state to which God has not called him, he will be deprived of the helps by which he can with facility lead a good life.

Every one, says St. Paul, *hath his proper gift from God; one after this manner, and another after that.*[2] The meaning of this passage, according to St. Thomas and other commentators, is, that the Lord gives to each one graces to fulfil with ease the obligations of the state to which he calls him. "God," says the Angelic Doctor, "gives to every man not only certain aptitudes, but also all that is necessary to exercise them."[3] And in another place he writes: "God does not destine men to such or such a vocation without favoring them with gifts at the same time, and preparing them in such a way as to render them capable of fulfilling the duties of their vocation; for says St. Paul: *Our sufficiency is from God, who also hath made us fit ministers of the New Testament.*[4] As each person, then, will be able to discharge with fa-

---

[1] "Quos prædestinavit, hos et vocavit; et quos vocavit, hos et justificavit; quos autem justificavit, illos et glorificavit."—*Rom.* viii. 30.

[2] "Unusquisque proprium donum habet ex Deo: alius quidem sic, alius vero sic."—1 *Cor.* vii. 7.

[3] "Cuicumque datur potentia aliqua divinitus, dantur etiam per quæ executio illius potentiæ possit congrue fieri."—*Suppl.* q. 35. a. 1.

[4] "Illos quos Deus ad aliquid eligit, ita præparat et disponit, ut ad id ad quod eliguntur, inveniantur idonei, secundum illud: 'Idoneos nos fecit ministros Novi Testamenti'" (2 *Cor.* iii. 5).—P. 3, q. 27, a. 4.

cility the office to which God elects him, so he will be unfit for the fulfilment of the office to which God does not call him. The foot which is given to enable us to walk cannot see; the eye, which is given to see is incapable of hearing; and how shall he who is not chosen by God to the priesthood be able to discharge its obligations?

It belongs to the Lord to choose the workmen who are to cultivate his vineyard: *I have chosen you . . . and have appointed you that you should go, and should bring forth fruit.*[1] Hence the Redeemer did not say, Beg of men to go and gather the harvest; but he tells us to ask the master of the crop to send workmen to collect it.[2] Hence he also said, *As the Father hath sent Me, I also send you.*[3] When God calls, he himself, says St. Leo, gives the necessary helps.[4] This is what Jesus Christ has said: *I am the door. By Me if any man enter in he shall be saved, and he shall go in, and go out, and shall find pastures.*[5] "He shall go in:"[6] what the priest called by God undertakes, he shall easily accomplish without sin, and with merit. *And shall go out:*[7] he shall be in the midst of perils and occasions of sin, but with the divine aid he shall readily escape injury. *And shall find pastures:*[8] finally, in consequence of being in the state in which God has placed him, he will be assisted in all the duties of his ministry

[1] "Ego elegi vos, et posui vos, ut eatis et fructum afferatis."—*John*, xv. 16.

[2] "Rogate ergo dominum messis, ut mittat operarios in messem suam."—*Luke*, x. 2.

[3] "Sicut misit me Pater, et ego mitto vos."—*John*, xx. 21.

[4] "Qui mihi honoris est auctor, ipse mihi fiet administrationum adjutor; dabit virtutem, qui contulit dignitatem."—*In die ass. suæ*, s. 1.

[5] "Ego sum ostium. Per me si quis introierit, salvabitur; et ingredietur, et egredietur, et pascua inveniet."—*John*, x. 9.

[6] "Ingredietur."

[7] "Et egredietur."

[8] "Et pascua inveniet."

by special graces, which will make him advance in perfection. Hence he will be able to say with confidence, *The Lord ruleth me: and I shall want nothing. He hath set me in a place of pasture.*[1]

But priests whom God has not sent to work in his Church, he shall abandon to eternal ignominy and destruction. *I did not send prophets,* says the Lord by the prophet Jeremiah, *yet they ran.* He afterwards adds: *Therefore I will take you away, carrying you, and will forsake you . . . and I will bring an everlasting reproach upon you, and a perpetual shame which shall never be forgotten.*[2]

In order to be raised to the sublimity of the priesthood, it is necessary, as St. Thomas says, for a man " to be exalted and elevated by divine power above the natural order of things,"[3] because he is appointed the sanctifier of the people, and the vicar of Jesus Christ. But in him who raises himself to so great a dignity shall be verified the words of the Wise Man: *There is that hath appeared a fool after he was lifted up on high.*[4] Had he remained in the world, he should perhaps have been a virtuous layman; but having become a priest without a vocation, he will be a bad priest, and instead of promoting the interest of religion, he will do great injury to the Church. Of such priests the Roman Catechism says: " Such ministers are for the Church of God the gravest embarrassment and the most terrible scourge."[5] And

---

[1] " Dominus regit me, et nihil mihi deerit; in loco pascuæ ibi me collocavit."—*Ps.* xxii. 1.

[2] " Non mittebam prophetas, et ipsi currebant.—Propterea ecce ego tollam vos portans, et derelinquam vos . . . ; et dabo vos in opprobrium sempiternum, et in ignominiam æternam, quæ nunquam oblivione delebitur."—*Jer.* xxiii. 21–39.

[3] " Ut divina virtute evehatur, et transmittatur supra naturalem rerum ordinem."—*Apud Hab. de Ord.* p. 3, c. 1, § 2.

[4] " Stultus apparuit, postquam elevatus est in sublime."—*Prov.* xxx. 32.

[5] " Hujusmodi hominum genere nihil infelicius, nihil Ecclesiæ Dei calamitosius esse potest."—P. 2, c. 7, q. 3.

what good can be expected from the priest who has entered the sanctuary without a vocation? "It is impossible," says St. Leo, "that a work so badly begun should finish well."[1] St. Laurence Justinian has written: "What fruit, I ask, can come from a corrupted root?"[2] Our Saviour has said, *Every plant which my heavenly Father hath not planted, shall be rooted up.*[3] Hence Peter de Blois writes that when God permits a person to be ordained without a vocation, the permission is not a grace but a chastisement. For a tree which has not taken deep root, when exposed to the tempest, shall soon fall and be cast into the fire.[4] And St. Bernard says that he who has not lawfully entered the sanctuary shall continue to be unfaithful; and instead of procuring the salvation of souls, he shall be the cause of their death and perdition.[5] This is conformable to the doctrine of Jesus Christ: *He that entereth not by the door into the sheepfold, . . . the same is a thief and a robber.*[6]

Some may say, if they only were admitted to orders who have the marks of vocation which have been laid down as indispensable, there should be but few priests in the Church, and the people should be left without the necessary helps. But to this the Fourth Council of Lateran has answered: "It is much better to confer the

[1] "Difficile est ut bono peragantur exitu, quæ malo sunt inchoata principio."—*Epist.* 87.

[2] "Qualem, oro, potest fructum producere corrupta radix?"—*De Compunct.*

[3] "Omnis plantatio, quam non plantavit Pater meus cœlestis, eradicabitur."—*Matt.* xv. 13.

[4] "Ira est, non gratia, cum quis ponitur super ventum, nullas habens radices in soliditate virtutum."—*De inst. ep.* c. 3.

[5] "Qui non fideliter introivit, quidni infideliter agat et contra Christum? faciet ad quod venit, ut mactet utique et disperdat."—*De Vita cler.* c. 7.

[6] "Qui non intrat per ostium . . . , ille fur est et latro.—Fur non venit nisi ut furetur, et mactet, et perdat."—*John*, x. 1-10.

priesthood on a small number of virtuous clerics than to
have a large number of bad priests." [1] And St. Thomas
says that God never abandons his Church so as to leave
her in want of fit ministers to provide for the necessity
of the people. [2] St. Leo justly says that to provide for
the wants of the people by bad priests would be not to
save but to destroy them. [3]

[1] "Satius est maxime in ordinatione sacerdotum paucos bonos
quam multos malos habere."—*Cap.* 27.

[2] "Deus nunquam ita deserit Ecclesiam suam, quin inveniantur
idonei ministri sufficientes ad necessitatem plebis."—*Suppl.* q. 36, a. 4.

[3] "Non est hoc consulere populis, sed nocere."—*Epist.* 87.

APPENDIX.

MEANS TO BE ADOPTED IN ORDER TO KNOW ONE'S VOCATION.

We collect and briefly indicate in this Appendix the principal means by which one may easily arrive at the knowledge of God's designs relatively to the state of life that one should embrace.

I.

It is, above all, of the highest importance that the heart be free from sin; the Lord loves to communicate himself to those who have a pure heart: *Blessed are the clean of heart; for they shall see God.*[1]

II.

Let your conduct be well regulated. For this purpose, see the Rule of Life which St. Alphonsus offers you,[2] and try to follow it faithfully.

III.

Look upon the affair of choosing a state of life, in accordance with the will of God, as a matter of your greatest concern, since on the choice that you make depends your eternal salvation.

IV.

Have a good intention and a sincere desire to know and to do the will of God, whatever it may be. It is, therefore, necessary that you hold yourself entirely detached and in a pious indifference in regard to all the states of life, in order not to put any obstacle in the way of the movements of grace, as you have seen above, page 299, n. 1, 2, and 3.

[1] Matt. v. 8. [2] Vol. i., at the end.

V.

Carefully avoid dissipation ; at least, retire into the solitude of your heart, after the example of St. Catharine of Sienna, always remembering that God is near you, and that he wishes to speak to your heart. You will understand his voice the more quickly and the more distinctly, the less you communicate with the world.

VI.

St. Alphonsus explains to you at length, in the letter quoted above (see page 285), the utility of a retreat. If it is not in your power to make it, either at home or in some religious house, where you may find all that you require for this purpose, try to supply its place by leading a retired life, and by frequently meditating on the Last Things. Nothing is more apt to enlighten you and to keep you in a good disposition.

VII.

In your doubts consult a wise director, who, as the representative of God, may instruct you and guide you in a safe manner.

VIII.

Let the grace of knowing your vocation and of faithfully corresponding to it be the only, or at least the principal, object that you have in view in all your exercises of piety,—in your meditations, Communions, prayer, mortifications, and all your good works.

IX.

Ordinarily, the Lord does not delay to enlighten those who have recourse to him, especially in behalf of a cause so holy and so agreeable to his heart. If, however, he would leave you in uncertainty for a time more or less long, to try your fidelity, to purify you more, or to strengthen you and raise you to a very high perfection, take care not to relax in anything ; humbly resign yourself, and wait with confidence and in peace for the break of day ; for your Heavenly Father will surely hear you and your perseverance will not fail to be crowned with success.

X.

While waiting for the Lord to enlighten you, do not be less faithful in fulfilling all your duties in the condition of life in which his divine Providence has placed you. It would be a great fault to neglect your actual duties in the expectation of a change ; God would withdraw his hand, instead of stretching it forth to aid you.

XI.

In general, the following are the principal signs of a true vocation :

1. A GOOD INTENTION ; that is, the intention to embrace such a state only to please God and to arrive more surely at the haven of salvation.

2. THE INCLINATION and THE APTITUDE to exercise the duties proper to this state.

3. THE KNOWLEDGE of the duties that this state imposes, and the FIRM WILL to fulfil them till the end.

4. THAT THERE IS NO GRAVE IMPEDIMENT, such as the great poverty in which one might leave one's father or one's mother.

5. THE FAVORABLE ADVICE of a wise director.   ED.

HYMN

Sighs of Love to Jesus Christ.

THE SOUL THAT GIVES ITSELF ALL TO JESUS.

World, thou art no more for me ;
World, I am no more for thee ;—
All affections, dear or sweet,
All are laid at Jesus' feet.

He has so enamoured me
Of his heavenly charity,
That no earthly goods inspire
Aught of love or vain desire.

Jesus. Love, be Thou my own ;
Thee I long for,—Thee alone ;
All myself I give to Thee,
Do whate'er Thou wilt with me.

Life without Thy love would be
Death. O Sovereign Good ! to me.
Bound and held by Thy dear chains,
Captive now my heart remains.

O my Life ! my soul from Thee
Can henceforth no longer flee ;
By Thy loving arrows slain,
Now Thy prey it must remain.

If ungrateful worms like me
Merit not the love of Thee,
Thou, sweet Lord, hast well deserved
To be ever loved and served.

Then, O God, my heart inflame ;
Give that love which Thou dost claim ;
Payment I will ask for none,
Love demands but love alone.

God of Beauty, Lord of Light !
Thy good will is my delight ;
Now henceforth Thy will divine
Ever shall in all be mine.

Come, O Jesus, I implore.
Pierce Thy heart, 'tis mine no more ;
Kindle in my breast Thy fire,
That of love I may expire.

Ah ! my Spouse, I love but Thee ;
Thou my Love shalt ever be.
Thee I love ; I love and sigh
For Thy love one day to die.

INDEX.

33